Linguistic Theory and Psychological Reality

MIT Bicentennial Studies

Linguistic Theory and Psychological Reality

Edited by
MORRIS HALLE
JOAN BRESNAN
GEORGE A. MILLER

Contributors
JOAN BRESNAN, GEORGE A. MILLER, ERIC WANNER,
MICHAEL MARATSOS, KEITH STENNING, RAY JACKENDOFF,
EDGAR B. ZURIF, SHEILA E. BLUMSTEIN, SUSAN CAREY,
AND MORRIS HALLE

The MIT Press
Cambridge, Massachusetts, and London, England

First MIT Press paperback edition, 1981
Third printing, 1979
Second printing, 1978
Copyright © 1978 by The Massachusetts Institute of Technology

This book was set in VIP Times Roman
by Photo Graphics Inc.
and printed and bound
by Halliday Lithograph Corporation
in the United States of America

Library of Congress Cataloging in Publication Data

Main entry under title:
Linguistic theory and psychological reality.
   (MIT Bicentennial studies ; 4)
   Bibliography: p.
   Includes index.
   1. Psycholinguistics. 2. Generative   grammar. 3. Children—Language. I.
Halle, Morris. II. Bresnan, Joan. III. Miller, George Armitage, 1920–
P37.L48   401′ .9   77–29054
ISBN 0-262-08095-8 (hard)
ISBN 0-262-58043-8 (paper)

Contents

1 A Realistic Transformational Grammar

JOAN BRESNAN

2 Semantic Relations among Words

GEORGE A. MILLER

3 An ATN Approach to Comprehension

ERIC WANNER AND MICHAEL MARATSOS

4 Anaphora as an Approach to Pragmatics

KEITH STENNING

5 Grammar as Evidence for Conceptual Structure

RAY JACKENDOFF

6 Language and the Brain

EDGAR B. ZURIF AND SHEILA E. BLUMSTEIN

7 New Models in Linguistics and Language Acquisition
MICHAEL MARATSOS

8 The Child as Word Learner
SUSAN CAREY

9 Knowledge Unlearned and Untaught: What Speakers Know about the Sounds of Their Language
MORRIS HALLE

Series Foreword

As part of its contribution to the celebration of the U.S. Bicentennial, MIT has carried out studies of several social and intellectual aspects of the world we inhabit at the beginning of our third century. Our objective has been to inquire how human beings might deal more intelligently and humanely with these factors, most of which are closely linked to developments in science and technology.

The papers prepared for these inquiries are being published in a Bicentennial Studies Series of which this volume is a part. Other studies in the series deal with the future of computing and information processing, the social impact of the telephone, the economics of the new international economic order, administrative and economic factors in air pollution, and world change and world security.

It is our hope that these volumes will be of interest and value to those concerned now with these questions and, additionally, will provide useful historical perspective to those concerned with the same or similar questions on the occasion of the U.S. Tricentennial.

Jerome B. Wiesner

Symposium:
New Approaches to a Realistic Model of Language

at the
Convocation on Communications
March 9–10, 1976
Massachusetts Institute of Technology

Morning session,
March 9. Chairman: Morris Halle, MIT
Introductory Remarks
George A. Miller, The Rockefeller University
Toward a Realistic Model of Transformational Grammar
Joan Bresnan, MIT

Afternoon session,
March 9. Chairman: Osamu Fujimura, Bell Telephone Laboratories
Psychological Aspects of Syntactic Processing
The Autonomy of Syntactic Processing
Kenneth Forster, Monash University, Australia, and MIT
Models of Comprehension Based on Augmented Transition Networks
Ronald M. Kaplan, Xerox Corporation
Garden Paths in Relative Clauses
Eric Wanner, Harvard University
The Organization of Sentence Processors
Merrill F. Garrett, MIT
Language and the Brain: Evidence from Aphasia
Sheila Blumstein, Brown University and Aphasia Unit, Boston
V. A. Hospital
Edgar Zurif, Aphasia Unit, Boston V. A. Hospital

Morning Session,
March 10. Chairman: Benson R. Snyder, MIT
Semantic Relations among Words
George A. Miller, The Rockefeller University
Ray Jackendoff, Brandeis University
Language Acquisition: The Role of the Lexicon
Susan Carey, MIT
Michael Maratsos, University of Minnesota

Preface

This volume grew out of a series of workshops and meetings that were organized at the Massachusetts Institute of Technology with a grant from the American Telephone and Telegraph Company as one of several activities leading up to the Convocation on Communication that was held in Cambridge, Massachusetts, on March 9–10, 1976, to mark the centennial of the invention of the telephone. It was appropriate to focus on questions of language on that occasion, for not only is the transmission of the spoken language the primary function of the telephone, but Alexander Graham Bell, the telephone's inventor, had throughout his life a deep scientific interest in problems of language. Although his contributions to our understanding of speech and language have been overshadowed by his technological contribution, Bell is certainly one of the intellectual ancestors of the modern student of language.

Each of the workshops on language and cognition that met at MIT at irregular intervals during 1975 and the beginning of 1976 brought together between twenty and thirty researchers affiliated with different groups in this country and abroad. Our thinking, like that of most students of language in this generation, had been influenced by the work of our MIT colleague, Noam Chomsky. Chomsky has sometimes startled students of language with the observation that linguistics is a branch of psychology, specifically, that branch of psychology devoted to understanding the particular organ we call human language, and there can be little doubt that any adequate psychology of man must provide some way to understand the human capacity for language. It was a belief shared by quite a few among us that developments in linguistics and psychology were leading to similar conclusions by separate routes and that this was an appropriate time to explore the implications of these apparently parallel developments for future, perhaps joint, work. This volume represents a few initial steps in the direction of that goal.

The most striking results of the last decade's work in linguistics, especially of the work carried out at MIT by Chomsky and others, was a fundamental reevaluation of the respective roles assigned to the transformational component and to the lexicon in accounting for the facts. During the past twenty years, since transformations were first introduced into the armamentarium of syntacticians, these computa-

This work was supported in part by the National Institute of Mental Health, Grant No. MH 13390–10.

tional devices have been the subject of searching investigations because it was widely held that they played a particularly significant role in the functioning of language. More recently it has become evident that transformations are not altogether optimal for some of the tasks assigned to them. This discovery, as noted in Bresnan's chapter, elicited different responses from different researchers: some proposed to overcome the difficulties by increasing the power of transformations, whereas others—among them Bresnan in her contribution—have explored the consequences of limiting the power and role of transformations.

One consequence of the move to limit the power of transformations is the need to account in another way for the facts that previously were explained with the help of transformations. An obvious candidate for this role is the lexical component—that is, the repository of the information that speakers have about each of the many thousands of words that every normal person understands and uses. Since, as Bloomfield has remarked, the lexicon is "a list of basic irregularities," it was widely felt that little of interest was to be discovered by studying it closely. This estimate proved quite wrong—as should, no doubt, have been expected—once the lexicon was subjected to serious scrutiny. One part of Bresnan's chapter is a further contribution to this topic.

By a fortunate coincidence, interest in the lexicon developed at about the same time among psychologists. As our workshops were getting under way, George A. Miller and Philip Johnson-Laird had just completed their monumental *Language and Perception* (1976), a large portion of which is devoted to an inquiry into the form and function of lexical entries. Miller's chapter in this volume reflects a further development of the views represented in *Language and Perception* as modified by reflections subsequent to the book's publication. Much of what is new in his chapter stems from the discussions of this topic in our workshop.

A person who has command of a language possesses a certain kind of knowledge, which allows him to produce and understand an unlimited number of sentences. All of us know from direct experience that occasionally this knowledge becomes inaccessible to us, as when we fail to recall a particular word (that is just "on the tip of the tongue"), or when we are guilty of a solecism ("You must renew your subscription by the fifth of the month in which you expire") or when we misunderstand a perfectly well-formed sentence ("The horse raced past the barn fell down"). There is thus a distinction to be made between the knowledge that makes it possible for us to speak and understand a language and the way in which we employ this knowledge in producing and comprehending actual utterances.

The production and understanding of sentences has been a topic of great interest to psychologists; much of their interest in developments in linguistics during the past twenty years has been directly related to their hope that these developments would help us to a deeper understanding of what it means to understand sentences in a given language. The results of many of these inquiries have not been altogether unambiguous; good evidence was found for the psychological reality of constituent structure, but early studies of transformational relations between sentences produced inconclusive and often inconsistent results. In reaction, attempts were made to explain syntactic processing in terms of concepts developed in automatic parsing systems rather than in terms of specific transformations postulated by linguists. Such a nontransformational model underlies the work by Wanner and Maratsos reported in Chapter 3. In discussions of this work in our workshops it was suggested that the parsers described by these workers are not incompatible with a transformational model of language, especially one in which the role of transformations is sharply limited (see Bresnan's remarks in Chapter 1).

It is a common experience for us to see objects in random arrangements of shapes, lines, and colors. We see a man in the moon, and landscapes, castles, and fantastic beasts in the cloudy sky. There is also a linguistic analogue of this effect that is no doubt well known to anyone who has experimented with concocting grammatically deviant utterances: utterances that appear clearly deviant to the experimenter will often be judged well-formed by his subject, who will point out certain—albeit highly implausible—contexts in which the concocted utterance might be normal, rather than deviant. Such reactions are evidence of a familiar fact: a sentence can express different meanings in different contexts—which is the central problem of pragmatics. In his chapter on anaphora Keith Stenning proposes to recognize explicitly the role that our ability to invent plausible contexts for utterances plays in our understanding of the relation between an anaphoric expression and its antecedent. He points out that in many instances an expression will be understood as the anaphor of an antecedent that receives no overt linguistic expression in the discourse. He concludes that a successful account of the antecedent–anaphor relation will have to recognize explicitly the fact that it is a relation between a linguistic entity (the anaphoric phrase) and a feature of a—real or imagined—context, situation, or state of affairs. A sketch of such an account makes up the heart of Stenning's chapter.

Ray Jackendoff's contribution is an attempt to use the information about semantic structure that is provided by the interpretation of various syntactic configurations in order to gain insights into basic attributes of human cognition. It stands to reason that at some level of representation—which Jackendoff proposes to call conceptual structure—the information conveyed by language must be compatible with that conveyed by other perceptual systems, for example, vision. It has turned out that in dealing with the minimal predicates required by the semantic component, constant recourse must be had to nonlinguistic (conceptual) knowledge; moreover, the mechanisms independently needed to deal with nonlinguistic conceptual knowledge provide an almost trivial account of the required predicates. A semantic theory must, therefore, be a subpart of the general theory of conceptual structure. Under the further assumption that semantic projection rules are of a simple character, grammatical structure and grammatical parallelism can be used as direct evidence about semantic structure, from which conceptual structure may be inferred fairly directly. Jackendoff analyzes three different kinds of semantic entities to illustrate this approach.

The remaining chapters are concerned with the way the knowledge of a language is acquired and lost. The chapter by Edgar Zurif and Sheila Blumstein surveys some recent work on aphasia in the light of different theoretical models of language. Michael Maratsos inquires into the implications that a model of language with a restricted transformational component has for our understanding of the way children acquire the syntax of their mother tongue. The chapters by Susan Carey and by Morris Halle, which conclude this volume, deal with the learning of words and sounds, rather than with the learning of phrases and sentences. Carey observes that many six-year-olds have a vocabulary of 14,000 words or more. Since the average child has a vocabulary of only about fifty words by the time he is eighteen months old, the implication is that during the ensuing four and a half years children acquire words at a rate of more than eight per day, or close to one per hour for every waking hour of their lives. This rapid rate obviously does not allow for much trial-and-error, nor for extensive reinforcement schedules. It therefore raises serious questions that learning theorists will have to come to grips with. Halle cites examples from the acquisition of the sound structure of English, which, like the word acquisition facts discussed by Carey, cannot be plausibly accounted for in terms of standard learning-theory concepts. In addition, Halle discusses certain other facts that normal speakers of English must be credited with having knowledge of, yet for which it is very difficult even to imagine a plausible sequence of steps that might lead to acquisition. In Halle's view, these facts are instances of innate knowledge, knowledge that is not learned but that is, rather, genetically programmed into each normal member of our species.

The editors of this volume want to express thanks to the American Telephone and Telegraph Company for the generous support that made these workshops possible and to Dr. Norman Dahl for his help and advice with innumerable practical matters. We are also indebted to Katherine Miller, without whose editorial assistance this book would never have materialized. Above all, we wish to express gratitude to all the participants in the workshops, whose influence informs every sentence in this volume, and especially to Kenneth Forster, Merrill Garrett, and Ronald Kaplan for leading discussions in the workshops and for their contributions to the Convocation on Communication.

Morris Halle

Participants: Workshop on Language and Cognition

Alan Bell, Ned Block, Sheila E. Blumstein, Gordon T. Bowden,
Diane Bradley, Joan Bresnan, Susan Carey, Paul Chapin, Noam
Chomsky, Anne Cutler, Norman C. Dahl, Robert Fiengo, J. A.
Fodor, Kenneth I. Forster, Osamu Fujimura, Howard Gardner,
Merrill F. Garrett, Morris Halle, Reid Hastie, Ray Jackendoff,
Ronald M. Kaplan, Martin Kay, Mary-Louise Kean, Paul Kiparsky,
Dennis Klatt, Barbara Klein, James Lackner, Mark Liberman, John
Limber, Michael Maratsos, Edward Martin, Max Matthews, Lise
Menn, George A. Miller, Katherine Miller, David Pisoni, Mary C.
Potter, Alan Prince, David Rosenfield, Elizabeth Selkirk, Beau Shiel,
Hermina Sinclair-DeZwaart, Benson R. Snyder, Keith Stenning,
Virginia Valian, Eric Wanner, and Edgar B. Zurif.

Notes on Contributors

Sheila E. Blumstein is Associate Professor of Linguistics at Brown University and Research Associate at the Aphasia Research Center, Boston University School of Medicine.

Joan Bresnan is Associate Professor of Linguistics at the Massachusetts Institute of Technology.

Susan Carey is Assistant Professor of Psychology at the Massachusetts Institute of Technology.

Morris Halle is Ferrari P. Ward Professor of Modern Languages and Linguistics at the Massachusetts Institute of Technology.

Ray Jackendoff is Associate Professor of Linguistics at Brandeis University.

Michael Maratsos is Associate Professor of Child Psychology at the Institute of Child Development at the University of Minnesota.

George A. Miller is Professor at The Rockefeller University.

Keith Stenning is Lecturer in Psychology at the University of Liverpool, England.

Eric Wanner is Adjunct Associate Professor of Psychology at The Rockefeller University and Editor for the Behavioral Sciences at Harvard University Press.

Edgar B. Zurif is Associate Professor in Neurology (Neuropsychology) at the Aphasia Research Center, Boston University School of Medicine, and Research Staff member at the Boston Veterans' Administration Hospital.

Linguistic Theory and Psychological Reality

1 A Realistic Transformational Grammar

JOAN BRESNAN

The Realization Problem

More than ten years ago Noam Chomsky expressed a fundamental assumption of transformational grammar: "A reasonable model of language use will incorporate, as a basic component, the generative grammar that expresses the speaker-hearer's knowledge of the language." This assumption is fundamental in that it defines basic research objectives for transformational grammar: to characterize the grammar that is to represent the language user's knowledge of language, and to specify the relation between the grammar and the model of language use into which the grammar is to be incorporated as a basic component. We may call these two research objectives the grammatical characterization problem and the grammatical realization problem. In the past ten years linguistic research has been devoted almost exclusively to the characterization problem; the crucial question posed by the realization problem has been neglected—How *would* a reasonable model of language use incorporate a transformational grammar?

If we go back to the context in which Chomsky expressed this assumption about the relation of grammar to language use, we find that it is couched within an admonition: "A generative grammar is not a model for a speaker or a hearer. . . . No doubt, a reasonable model of language use will incorporate, as a basic component, the generative grammar that expresses speaker-hearer's knowledge of the language; but this generative grammar does not, in itself, prescribe the character or functioning of a perceptual model or a model of speech-production" (1965, p. 9). In retrospect, this caution appears to have been justified by the rather pessimistic conclusions that have since been drawn in

This chapter discusses research in progress by the author, which is likely to be modified and refined. Some matters have been simplified to make exposition easier. A fuller account is planned in Bresnan (in preparation). The ideas presented here owe much to my association with members of the MIT Workshop on Language and Cognition during the past two years. I would like particularly to thank Morris Halle for his constant encouragement and George Miller for his unfailing interest in new ideas. I am also grateful to the John Simon Guggenheim Memorial Foundation for the Fellowship that enabled me to work on these ideas from August 1975 to August 1976 under the freest possible conditions. To my friend Mary MacDonald, who provided those conditions—as well as the realistic point of view of the language teacher—I also give many thanks.

literature. In their review of this literature, Fodor, Bever, and Garrett (1974) conclude that the experimental evidence tends to support the psychological reality of grammatical *structures,* but that the evidence does not consistently support the reality of grammatical *transformations* as analogues of mental operations in speech perception and production. In particular, the derivational theory of complexity—the theory that the number of transformations operating in the grammatical derivation of a sentence provides a measure of the psychological complexity in comprehending or producing the sentence—cannot be sustained.

These conclusions have invited the inference that it is a mistake to attempt to "realize" a transformational grammar within a model of language use. This view seems to be shared by a good number of linguists and psychologists, perhaps for different reasons. Some linguists may believe that the realization problem is uninteresting at this point because—to put it bluntly—psychology has not yet provided anything like a reasonable model of language use, with or without grammar. And a number of psychologists may have concluded that no model of language use that incorporates a transformational grammar, or indeed any kind of grammar, is reasonable.

However, it is possible to take a different view of the matter. If a given model of grammar cannot be successfully realized within a model of language use, it may be because it is psychologically unrealistic in significant respects and therefore inadequate in those respects as an empirical theory of the human faculty of language. From this point of view, previous attempts to realize transformational grammars as models for a speaker or hearer are valuable and informative. By showing us in what respects grammars may be psychologically unrealistic, they can guide us in our efforts to construct better theories of grammar. To take this position is to take seriously Chomsky's "realist interpretation" of transformational grammar.

Accordingly, the proper conclusion to draw about the familiar model of transformational grammar presented in Chomsky's *Aspects of the Theory of Syntax* (1965) may simply be that it is psychologically unrealistic. Linguistic research by Chomsky and many others on the characterization problem has shown the *Aspects* model to be inadequate in significant ways as a theory of language, and the model has undergone important changes. I will argue that these new developments in transformational linguistics, together with independent developments in computational linguistics and the psychology of language, make it feasible to begin to construct realistic grammars.

Let me explain briefly what I consider a realistic grammar to be. First, such a grammar must be psychologically real in the broad sense. This sense of "the psychological reality of linguistic concepts" has been very well expressed by Levelt (1974):

A linguistic concept is psychologically real to the extent that it contributes to the explanation of behavior relative to linguistic judgments, and nothing more is necessary for this. Although the term [psychological reality of linguistic concepts] is misleading, it does indeed have content in that it refers to the question as to whether constructions which are suited to the description of one form of verbal behavior (intuitive judgments) are equally suited to the description of other verbal processes (the comprehension and retention of sentences, etc.). (vol. 3, p. 70)

A realistic grammar must be not only psychologically real in this broad sense, but also realizable. That is, we should be able to define for it explicit realization mappings to psychological models of language use. These realizations should map distinct grammatical rules and units into distinct processing operations and informational units in such a way that different rule types of the grammar are associated with different processing functions. If distinct grammatical rules were not distinguished in a psychological model under some realization mapping, the grammatical distinctions would not be "realized" in any form psychologically, and the grammar could not be said to represent the knowledge of the language user in any psychologically interesting sense.

Clearly, these are strong conditions to impose on a linguistic grammar. But their value is correspondingly great. Theoretical linguistics has greatly advanced our understanding of the abstract structure of human languages. Under the conditions imposed, these advances could be brought directly to bear on the experimental investigation of human cognition.

Toward a More Realistic Transformational Grammar

The familiar *Aspects* model of transformational grammar is depicted schematically in Figure 1.1. This model has three essential characteristics. First, the meaning, or semantic interpretation, of a sentence is

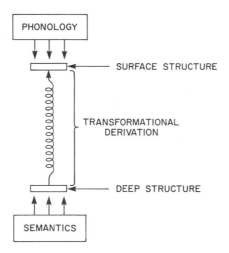

Figure 1.1 *Aspects* model of transformational grammar

determined from its deep structure. Second, the pronunciation, or
phonetic interpretation, of a sentence is determined from its surface
structure. And third, the role of transformations is seen as converting
the semantically relevant level of linguistic description into the
phonetically relevant level. As Figure 1.1 suggests, transformations
bear the central and primary descriptive burden of the grammar. The
helical line connecting deep structure to surface structure represents
the transformational cycle introduced in Chomsky (1965).

Although subsequent research has shown that each of these properties of the model is incorrect, this is still the picture that many
linguists and psychologists have of a transformational grammar, a fact
that attests both to the intuitive appeal of the model and to its
enormous fruitfulness in guiding linguistic research. In fact, in one
successor to the *Aspects* model these essential features were carried
over intact; I am referring to the generative semantics model of
grammar, in which deep structure is identified with semantic representation. In the generative semantics model many lexical, semantic,
and even pragmatic relations were treated as transformational relations.

I will be concerned, however, with a different line of linguistic
research, known as the lexical-interpretive theory of transformational
grammar. Within this line of research, the inadequacies of the *Aspects*
model have been seen as calling for a basic reorganization and
restructuring of the grammar. It is perhaps easiest to see the overall

effect of the changes by comparing Figure 1.1 with Figure 1.2. To visualize the changes from the *Aspects* model to the lexical-interpretative model, imagine that the transformational derivation has been contracted and rotated 90 degrees clockwise. Shortening the transformational derivation is compensated for by greatly enlarging the lexicon (which was invisible in Figure 1.1) and the semantic component. Rotating the transformational component expresses new relations among the semantic, syntactic, and phonological components. I will not be concerned here with the new phonological relations; for discussions of these I refer you to Halle (1973), Selkirk (forthcoming), and Bresnan (in preparation).

As the name "lexical-interpretive model of transformational grammar" indicates, nontransformational rules—lexical and interpretive rules—play a large role. Lexical, semantic, and pragmatic relations are distinguished from transformational relations and factored out of the transformational derivation. The rules of each subcomponent have distinguishing properties that have been the subject of much recent research. Here I can only briefly illustrate the division of labor among the components, focusing on the lexical rules and the surface interpretive rules of Figure 1.2. (For a fuller account, see Bresnan, in preparation.)

Lexical rules   The existence of a class of lexical rules of word formation, differing from syntactic transformations, was postulated by Chomsky (1970a) and constitutes what is called the lexicalist

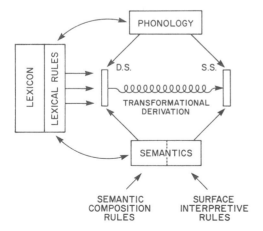

Figure 1.2 Lexical-Interpretative model of transformational grammar

the psycholinguistic hypothesis. A word-formation rule, plainly, is a regularity governing the formation of words. Examples of two word-formation rules studied by Dorothy Siegel (1974) are given in (1) and (2). (Rule (1) is an oversimplified representation of what are probably two distinct rules. In particular, the deverbal adjective formation involves not -*d*, but -EN (the past participle marker): compare *broken hearts* vs. **breaked hearts*.)

(1) Noun or Verb + -*d* = Adjective
    Examples: [N salary] + -*d* = [A[N salari] ed]
                                                    "a salaried employee"
                [V hurry] + -*d* = [A[V hurri] ed]
                                                    "too hurried a manner"
(2) *un*- + Adjective = Adjective
    Example: *un*- + [A happy] = [A un [A happy]]   "unhappy"

Rule (1) forms adjectives from nouns or verbs by suffixing -*d*. Rule (2) forms adjectives from adjectives by prefixing *un*-. (The negative *un*-, meaning "not," must be distinguished from the verbal prefix *un*-, which indicates reversal of an activity, as in *to unbutton*; on this distinction, see Siegel 1973). Rule (2) applies only to adjectives: *un*- cannot be prefixed to a simple noun (**unsalary*) or to a simple verb (**unhurry*),[1] but it can be prefixed to adjectives that are themselves formed from nouns or verbs, as by rule (1): *unsalaried, unhurried*. These words therefore have the morphological analyses shown in (3):

(3) [A un [A[N salari] ed]]
     [A un [A[V hurri] ed]]

Similarly, the adjectives formed by rule (2) can undergo further word-formation rules, such as the noun formations that yield the words in (4):

(4) [N[A un [A true]] th]   "untruth"
     [N[A un [A happy]] ness]   "unhappiness"

The theoretical interest of these rules, pointed out by Siegel (1973), is that they express generalizations that are not adequately explained by transformations. Consider, for example, the conse-

---

[1] Osvaldo Jaeggli (personal communication) has observed that negative *un*- also appears with a few simple nouns in English, including *unconcern* and *unrest* (cf. example (4)).

quences of attempting to derive sentence (5) transformationally from a source like (6).

(5) Antarctica is uninhabited.
(6) Not [something inhabits Antarctica]

Two things must be done to (6): it must be passivized, and *not* (in the form of *un-*) must be prefixed to *inhabit*. Suppose that *not* is prefixed first, yielding (7)—

(7) [something un-inhabits Antarctica]

—and that passivization then applies to (7) to yield (5). In this case we have given up the generalization expressed by rule (2) that *un-* is prefixed only to *adjectives*; by prefixing it to the verb *inhabit*, we have produced an active verb *uninhabit,* which is not only morphologically aberrant, but nonexistent. On the other hand, if we suppose that passivization is applied first, (8) results:

(8) Not [Antarctica is inhabited (by something)]

Now *not*-prefixing is to apply to the passivized verb *inhabited,* but the result will still be morphologically aberrant, because in English a passive verb is itself a verb, not an adjective.

That passive verbs are indeed verbs can be demonstrated in a number of ways, but I will mention just one. English verbs are distinguished from adjectives (and from nouns) by their ability to take direct noun phrase complements. Compare:

(9) a.   Jeff *suspected Mary.*   V NP
     b.   *Jeff was *suspicious Mary.* *Adj NP
     c.   Jeff was *suspicious of Mary.* Adj PP

In (9a) the verb *suspected* has the direct noun phrase complement, *Mary,* and the sentence is well-formed. But as (9b,c) show, the "object," *Mary,* of the adjective *suspicious* must be mediated by a preposition. Now, unlike an adjective, a passive verb too may take a direct noun phrase complement:

(10) a.   Mary was *taught French.*   V NP
      b.   *Mary was *untaught French.* *Adj NP

Example (10a) shows us that, like a verb, passive *taught* can take a noun phrase complement; (10b) shows us that, like an adjective, *untaught* cannot.[2] (It must be remembered that the syntactic differences between verb and adjective are manifested in different ways in other languages.) Thus it is clear that *untaught* is an adjective, a product of rules (1) and (2).

Now look again at (5), *Antarctica is uninhabited.* By employing rules (1) and (2), we can analyze the sentence directly as NP *be* Adj, parallel in structure to a sentence like *Jeff was suspicious.* By rule (1), [$_V$ inhabit] + *-d* = [$_A$[$_V$ inhabit] ed]]: *Antarctica is* [$_A$ *inhabited*]. By rule (2), *un-* + [$_A$[$_V$ inhabit] ed] = [$_A$ un [$_A$[$_V$ inhabit] ed]]: *Antarctica is* [$_A$ *uninhabited*].

We see, therefore, that if we try to derive sentence (5), *Antarctica is uninhabited,* by using the passive transformation, we are forced to give up independently motivated morphological generalizations—the generalization expressed by rule (2), that *un-* is a prefix that derives adjectives from adjectives, and the generalization that passive verbs are verbs.

I will add only one final observation in support of this conclusion. (For further evidence see Wasow 1977 and Hust 1977.) The transformational analysis of a sentence like (5) employs a passive transformation, which presupposes an active source: the surface subject (*Antarctica*) must be the underlying object of an active verb (*inhabit*) as in (6). Since only verbs that can be followed by objects may be passivized, the transformational analysis therefore makes the prediction shown in (11), pointed out by Siegel (1973):

(11)   Prediction of transformational analysis:
       Verbal root V in the form un-V-ed will be a transitive verb.

By contrast, the lexical analysis, which employs rules (1) and (2), does not make this prediction; the suffix *-d* of rule (1) can be attached to some intransitive verbs.

(12)   Some un-V-ed forms having intransitive verbal roots:
       undescended, unhurried, untraveled, unsettled, unpracticed, unarmed

An *undescended* testicle, for example, is a testicle that has not descended (into the scrotum); *descend* is an intransitive verbal root

---

[2] N. Ostler (personal communication) has observed three English adjectives that can have direct nominal complements: *worth, like,* and *near,* as in *It's worth a lot of money, He looks like her, This is nearer the truth.* But *like* and *near* are also used as prepositions, and *worth* is never used attributively: **a worth book.*

here. The other examples in (12) all have usages in which they cannot be plausibly derived from transitive verbs—for example, *We are still unsettled, A provincial person is untraveled, To the unpracticed eye,* . . . The evidence of these intransitive *un-* forms thus favors the lexical analysis over the transformational analysis.

The case of the so-called unpassive construction illustrates very well how research into nontransformational components of the grammar has provided new insights into the functioning of syntactic transformations. As a result of such research it appears that syntactic transformations do not play a role in word formation, and that we can therefore exclude from the class of possible transformations all those that involve the relabeling of syntactic categories, as by transforming verbs into adjectives, adjectives into nouns, and so on. (For further discussion of word-formation rules, see Chapter 2.)

At the same time, this research shows that other components of the grammar must take over some of the functions of transformations in the *Aspects* model. For example, one function of transformations has been to account for distributional regularities in selectional restrictions. A verb like *frighten* takes an animate object in the active:

(13) a.   ?John frightens sincerity.
      b.   Sincerity frightens John.

But it takes an animate *subject* in the passive:

(14) a.   ?Sincerity is frightened by John.
      b.   John is frightened by sincerity.

The passive transformation is intended to account for this relation by transforming (13a) into (14a) (Chomsky 1965). Notice, however, that an adjective like *undaunted* takes an animate subject, reflecting the selectional restrictions that hold for the object of the verbal root *daunt*:

(15) a.   ?John daunts nothing.
      b.   Nothing daunts John.
(16) a.   ?Nothing is undaunted.
      b.   John is undaunted.

Yet we can no longer invoke the passive transformation to account for this relation.

Another function of transformations in the *Aspects* model has been to associate underlying grammatical functions, such as logical subject and logical object, with surface configurations of grammatical categories. In *The boy may be frightened by sincerity, the boy* is understood as the logical object of *frighten,* and *sincerity* is understood as the logical subject; these are the functional relations that obtain in the deep structure, before passivization applies. However, similar functional relations can be found in sentences like those in (17) and (18).

(17) a. The boy was undaunted by defeat.
      b. His creative writing style is unfettered by the rules of composition.
      c. Her candor is unimpaired by tact.
(18) a. This problem is not solvable by ordinary methods.
      b. This function is computable by a right-moving Turing machine with two states.

And these sentences, according to the lexicalist hypothesis, are not transformationally derived from active deep structure sources, because that would bring transformations into word formation. Their deep structures are quite similar to their surface structures.

We can now see why lexical rules must play a large role in the lexical-interpretive theory of transformational grammar. Morphological and semantic relations between words like *daunt* and *undaunted* must be expressed by means of these nontransformational rules. (See Aronoff 1976 and Anderson 1977.)

Surface interpretive rules The surface interpretive rules shown in Figure 1.2 include rules governing the possible relations between anaphoric elements, such as pronouns, and their antecedents. It has been known for some time that these anaphoric rules seem to apply to transformationally derived structures, as in (19).

(19) a. Peter hates the woman who rejected him.
      b. The woman who rejected Peter is hated by him.
      c. The woman who rejected him is hated by Peter.
      d. He hates the woman who rejected Peter.

In the first three examples of (19) it seems possible to interpret *him* as referring to Peter, but this is not possible in the last example. To explain these facts, Langacker (1969) and Ross (1967a) independently proposed conditions under which a pronominalization transformation could apply to both active and passive sentences, substituting a pronoun for a noun phrase identical to another, coreferential noun phrase. (For a fuller discussion of transformational approaches to pronominalization, see Bresnan, in preparation, and Wasow 1976.)

Recently, however, a new interpretive approach has been advanced by Lasnik (1976) and further developed in Reinhart (1976). The basic idea is to assume that pronouns are simply pronouns in deep structure: they are generated as noun phrases like other noun phrases. Then it is assumed that coreference between noun phrases is always possible, except under the following condition:

(20) The Noncoreference Rule:
Given two noun phrases NP_1, NP_2 in a sentence, if NP_1 precedes and commands NP_2 and NP_2 is not a pronoun, then NP_1 and NP_2 are noncoreferential.

NP_1 "precedes and commands" NP_2 when NP_1 is to the left of NP_2 and is not in a subordinate clause from which NP_2 is excluded. This notion will be illustrated below. (See Lasnik 1976 and Reinhart 1976 for the more precise formulations.)

The Noncoreference Rule (20) is an interpretive rule in that it explicitly limits the possible interpretations of a transformationally derived sentence. Here is how it applies to the examples of (19). In (19a): *Peter* is NP_1 and *Peter* precedes and commands *him*, NP_2; but since *him* is a pronoun, rule (20) is inapplicable; therefore it is possible for *Peter* and *him* to be coreferential. In (19b): *Peter* is again NP_1; in this sentence *Peter* precedes but does not command *him*, NP_2, because *Peter* is in a subordinate clause (*who rejected Peter*) that excludes *him*; so again rule (20) is not applicable and *him* can be coreferential with *Peter*. In (19c): Now *him* is NP_1; *him* precedes but does not command *Peter*, NP_2, because *him* is contained in a subordinate clause (*who rejected him*) that excludes *Peter*; once again rule (20) does not apply and coreference is possible. Finally, (19d): *He* is NP_1; *he* precedes and commands *Peter*, NP_2; but since *Peter* is not a pronoun, rule (20) does apply here, thus stipulating that *he* (NP_1) and *Peter* (NP_2) cannot be coreferential.

A very important difference between the Noncoreference Rule and the previous transformational account is that when NP_1 and NP_2 do not meet the conditions for applying the rule, their coreference possibilities are free. This is illustrated in (21).

(21) a. People who know Kennedy love Kennedy.
      b. People who know Kennedy love him.
      c. People who know him love Kennedy.

In all three sentences of (21) the first NP (*Kennedy* or *him*) precedes but does not command the second NP (*Kennedy* or *him*). Given the pronominalization transformation, we would have to say that its application in (21a) was optional. But now compare (22), where the situation is changed; in (22a) the second *Kennedy* does not seem to be coreferential with the first.

(22) a. Kennedy said that Kennedy was happy.
      b. Kennedy said that he was happy.

The pronominalization transformation does not explain this subtle contrast, but the Noncoreference Rule does: the first *Kennedy* in (22a) precedes and commands the second *Kennedy*, NP_2, and NP_2 is not a pronoun; therefore rule (20) applies and the two *Kennedy*'s are noncoreferential.

The contrast between (21a) and (22a) reappears in examples like (23a,b):

(23) a. People who know Kennedy well are saying that the senator
          is happy.
      b. Kennedy is saying that the senator is happy.

The fact that *the senator* can be coreferential with *Kennedy* in (23a), though not in (23b), follows from the Noncoreference Rule (20) and the fact that *the senator* is not a pronoun. If the pronoun *he* is substituted for *the senator* in (23b), the coreferential interpretation becomes possible, as predicted by (20).

These new results suggest that the interpretive account is descriptively superior to previous transformational accounts of pronominalization. But there is an even more important advantage of the new approach. Previous transformational theories have described coreference relations grammatically, assuming that the anaphoric relation between a pronoun and its antecedent should be specified by rules of the grammar, such as a pronominalization transformation. The new interpretive account drops this assumption. Consequently, since coreference relations are not the result of rules of sentence grammar, we are free to treat sentence-internal and inter-sentence coreference in the same way. The transformational theory of pronominalization cannot do this, because pronominalization is a rule of sentence grammar and hence sentence-bound.

Thus, as Lasnik (1976) points out, the Noncoreference Rule (20) not only accounts for the absence of coreference between noun phrases within a sentence—

(24) *He* finally realized that *Oscar* is unpopular.

—but in exactly the same way it also accounts for the failure of coreference within a discourse: within the second sentence of (25), as in (24), *he* and *Oscar* cannot corefer.

(25) I spoke to *Oscar* yesterday. You know, *he* finally realized that *Oscar* is unpopular.

No pragmatic explanation for this persistent failure of coreference is apparent, for the second *Oscar* can be coreferential with *Oscar* in a preceding sentence:

(26) I spoke to *Oscar* yesterday. You know, I finally realized that *Oscar* is unpopular.

And *he* can also be coreferential with *Oscar* in a preceding sentence:

(27) I spoke to *Oscar* yesterday. You know, *he* finally realized that I am unpopular.

But if we assume, with Lasnik (1976), that coreference is a transitive relation, then the failure of coreference within the second sentence of (25) follows from the Noncoreference Rule (20).

This result—the unification of sentence anaphora with discourse anaphora—is a major advantage of the new interpretive approach over previous accounts. It accords with the view expressed by Stenning in Chapter 4:

Before trying to explain what are perceived as parts of sentence structure in a theory of sentence types, it is important that the same regularities be searched for at levels above the sentence. If they are found there, their explanation must be assigned there. From the present point of view, the sentence grammar should be seen as placing limitations on certain very general principles for the construction of quantificational and referential structures in texts and contexts.

In summary, just as the *Aspects* model of transformational grammar suggested to many that virtually the entire computational burden of relating meaning to surface form is borne by transformations, so the lexical-interpretive model should suggest the cooperating interaction of separate information-processing systems. Schematic as this overview has been, it allows a basic idea to be expressed very simply: As nontransformational relations are factored out of the transformational component, the transformational complexity of sentences is reduced, deep structures more closely resemble surface structures, and the grammar becomes more easily realized within an adequate model of language use.

The next section will show how this idea suggested by the lexical-interpretive model can be radically extended to yield a more realistic model of transformational grammar. But let us first anticipate a possible objection.

"Clearly," the objection runs, "if you eliminate a lot of transformations, you may get a more efficient syntactic processing system, but this greater efficiency of one component is purchased by a greater inefficiency of the other components. So it is hard to see why the model as a whole will be more realistic."

In answer to this objection, I must make explicit several assumptions. First, I assume that the syntactic and semantic components of the grammar should correspond psychologically to an active, automatic processing system that makes use of a very limited short-term memory. This accords with the assumptions of Chapter 3. Second, I assume that the pragmatic procedures for producing and understanding language in context belong to an inferential system that makes use of long-term memory and general knowledge. The extreme rapidity of language comprehension then suggests that we should minimize the information that requires grammatical processing and maximize the information that permits inferential interpretation. Finally, I assume that it is easier for us to look something up than it is to compute it. It does in fact appear that our lexical capacity—the long-term capability to remember lexical information—is very large.

The Active–Passive Relation

The minimal semantic information about verbs that must be represented in the lexicon is their logical argument structure: the intransitive verb *sleep* is represented by a one-place relation and the transitive verb *hit* by a two-place relation, as in (28) and (29).

(28) x SLEEP
(29) x HIT y

Naturally, other semantic information will be represented as well: for example, concepts like agent, patient, or theme may be associated with the argument positions. (See Chapters 2 and 5, and Anderson 1977.)

Information about the syntactic contexts in which verbs can appear is not sufficient to represent their argument structure, for two verbs may have different types of argument structure in the same syntactic contexts. *Eat* and *sleep* provide an example. Both verbs can be used intransitively, as in *John ate* and *John slept*. Yet *John ate* implies that John ate something; the verb *eat* has a logical object even when it lacks a grammatical object. In this respect, the argument structure of *eat* differs from that of *sleep*. This simple observation raises the major question to be explored here: How are the logical argument structures of verbs related to their syntactic contexts?

A familiar answer to this question is the transformational one. In the case of verbs like *eat*, Chomsky (1964a) proposed a transformation of unspecified-object deletion that applies as in (30):

(30)   a.   John ate something $\Rightarrow$
       b.   John ate.

Given this transformation, the different argument structures of *eat* and *sleep* correspond to different deep structure contexts into which the verbs can be inserted: in deep structure, *eat* has a grammatical object, which corresponds to its logical object, but *sleep* does not. Generative semantics can be seen as an attempt to carry out consistently the program of identifying logical functions (for example, logical subject and logical object) with grammatical functions at a single level of deep syntactic structure.

But there is another way to establish a correspondence between the argument structure of a verb and its syntactic contexts. Instead of transforming the syntactic structure, it is possible to operate on the argument structure. For example, the argument structure of *eat* can be converted from a two-place relation into a one-place relation. A logical operation that has precisely this effect is the variable-binding operation of quantification. The relation in (31a) is a two-place relation, whereas that in (31b) is a one-place relation.

(31)   a. x EAT y
       b. $(\exists y)\, x$ EAT y

If (31b) is taken as the lexical argument structure for the intransitive verb *eat*, it is easy to explain both how *John ate* differs from *John slept* and how *John ate* is related to *John ate something*.

It is natural to provide (31b) as *lexical* information, because the intransitive use of otherwise transitive verbs is a property of individual verbs. It is a property of *eat*, but not of *hit*, for example:

(32)   *John hit.

Entering (31b) in the lexicon, moreover, avoids the counterintuitive conclusion that *John ate* should require more grammatical processing than *John ate something* or *John ate it*. This follows from the assumptions stated earlier about the realization of the grammar.

In order to make the lexical association between argument structure and syntactic structure explicit, it is necessary to define a set of grammatical functions: subject, object, and so on. Otherwise there is no way to distinguish *John hit something* from *Something hit John*: in both sentences *hit* has the argument structure x HIT y. A notation for referring to these grammatical functions is given in Table 1.1. The list is provisional and incomplete; other grammatical functions will be considered later.

As indicated in the table, NP_1 will refer to the NP immediately dominated by S; NP_2 will refer to the NP immediately dominated by VP and to the right of its V; NP_p will refer to the NP immediately dominated by PP, a prepositional phrase; and LOC will refer to a PP immediately dominated by VP. Although the set of possible grammatical functions for natural languages—subject, object, locative, and so forth—can be considered universal, the way in which they are mapped into particular languages will vary. In a language like English, having highly rigid word order and little inflection, the grammatical functions can be defined configurationally; in a language having free word order and richer inflection, the grammatical functions can be defined, at least partly, in terms of case. (The universality of grammatical functions is proposed by Perlmutter and Postal 1977; the configurational definition of grammatical functions in English is

Table 1.1 Grammatical functions

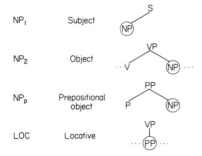

NP₁	Subject	
NP₂	Object	
NPₚ	Prepositional object	
LOC	Locative	

proposed by Chomsky 1965; a definition of grammatical functions of Walbiri by means of case is given in Hale, Jeanne, and Platero 1977.)

With this notation, partial lexical representations can now be provided for the verbs *sleep, hit, eat, lie,* and *rely on*:

(33) *sleep:* V, [———],   NP₁ SLEEP
(34) *hit:*   V, [——— NP],   NP₁ HIT NP₂
(35) *eat:*   V, [——— NP],   NP₁ EAT NP₂
                   [———],   (∃y) NP₁ EAT y
(36) *lie:*   V, [——— PP],   NP₁ LIE LOC
(37) *rely:*   V, [——— [PP *on* NP]],   NP₁ RELY-ON NPₒₙ

The material in square brackets will be referred to as the *syntactic contexts*; they represent the immediate syntactic context for lexical insertion of the verbs. The formulas to the right will be called the *functional structures*; they combine the grammatical functions with the logical argument structures.

Observe that the syntactic contexts in (33)–(37) diverge from the functional structures in several respects. First, the syntactic context ignores material outside of the verb phrase, but the functional structure makes reference to NP₁, the subject. Next, the verb *eat* has two syntactic contexts; one is like that for *sleep,* but even with that context *eat* still has a logical object, unlike *sleep.* Finally, both *lie* and *rely* are inserted into their syntactic contexts before PPs, but their functional structures are different: *lie* is represented by a relation between an individual designated by the subject and a location designated by the locative; *rely on* is represented as a relation between individuals designated by the subject and the prepositional object of *on*.

Because *rely* is inserted before a PP rather than a NP, it is syntactically intransitive; nevertheless, it is logically transitive in its functional representation. Let us briefly consider the evidence for this discrepancy.

The *on*-phrase following *rely* behaves syntactically like a PP: it can be preposed as a unit in the relative clause in (38).

(38)   [He is someone you can rely [$_{PP}$ on whom]] $\Rightarrow$
        [He is someone [$_{PP}$ on whom] you can rely]

This behavior is shared by the PP following *lie*:

(39)   [Here is something you can lie [$_{PP}$ on which]] $\Rightarrow$
        [Here is something [$_{PP}$ on which] you can lie]

The *on*-phrase following *rely* can undergo emphatic preposing:

(40)   On that, you can rely!

The same is true for *lie*:

(41)   On that, you can lie!

Of course, the PP following *lie*, being locative in the functional structure, differs in some ways from the PP associated with *rely*: for example, it can be used to answer a *where* question:

(42)   Where does the cat lie for comfort? — On the mat.

But this is not true of *rely*:

(43)   *Where does John rely for support? — On Mary.

Instead of (43), however, we can have (44):

(44)   On whom does John rely for support? — On Mary.

It is a pervasive generalization of transformational grammar that transformations do not move nonconstituent sequences of categories. For example, the sequence *on his clothes* is not a constituent sequence (that is, a phrase) in (45):

(45)   John put on his clothes.

And it cannot undergo movement as a unit:

(46)   *On which clothes did John put?
        Which clothes did John put on?

From these facts, therefore, it can be concluded that the sequence *on NP* following *rely* is indeed a prepositional phrase, as it is represented in (37).

At the same time, *rely on* has a functional representation that is logically transitive. Note that its prepositional object can be passivized:

(47)   All of us are relying on her for support.
       She is being relied on for support by all of us.

In contrast, the object of *on* is not passivizable with *lie* (but compare footnote 3):

(48)   All of the cats are lying on the mat.
       *The mat is being lain on by all the cats.

It should be noted that some verbs have two uses, one like *lie* in (36) and another like *rely* in (37). One example is *arrive*:

(49)   *arrive*:   V,   [___ PP], NP_1 ARRIVE LOC
(50)   *arrive*:   V,   [___ [PP *at* NP]], NP_1 ARRIVE-AT NP_{at}

Corresponding to the distinct functional structures are the following contrasts (noted by Quirk et al. 1972):

(51)   They arrived at the new Stadium.
       *The new Stadium was arrived at.
(52)   They arrived at the expected result.
       The expected result was arrived at.

The two representations of *arrive* accord with other differences:

(53)   Where will they arrive? —   At the new Stadium.
                              — *At the expected result.

But both *at*-phrases behave as syntactic units:

(54)   Here is the Stadium [PP at which] they arrived.
       Here is the result [PP at which] we have just arrived.

Thus, the prepositions *on* and *at* in (37) and (50) function as transitivizers of their verbs. This is a well-developed semantic process in English.

If it should seem odd to associate a semantic unit (the logically transitive relation) with elements that do not form a structural unit,

notice that we do this anyway for discontinuous verbs like
bring . . . to, put . . . to shame, take . . . to task. For example, to
bring someone to means to "revive someone."

However, in some cases the transitivizing process may result in the
structural incorporation of the preposition into the verbal category V.
An example might be *care for* in the sense of "tend" or "minister
to": *Mary is caring for the sick snakes.* Here *for* is apparently not
separable from the verb: **For what is she caring? — For the sick
snakes; *For the snakes she is caring!* This verb *care for* appears to
be the root of the deverbal adjective in *The snakes looked cared-for
and complacent.* Negative *un-* may be prefixed: *the uncared-for
snakes.*

Now observe that the notation developed for expressing the functional structures of active verbs can also be used to express functional
structures for passive verbs. Consider (55) and (56):

(55)   The cat was eating.
(56)   The cat was eaten.

The passive verb (*be*) *eaten* is syntactically an intransitive verb, just
as (*be*) *eating* is. The difference in the logical argument structures of
(*be*) *eating* and (*be*) *eaten* is that in the former the logical object has
been eliminated, but in the latter the logical subject has been
eliminated:

(57) $(\exists y)\ x$ EAT y
(58) $(\exists x)\ x$ EAT y

Further, the grammatical subject, *the cat,* plays the role of the logical
subject, x, in (57), but it plays the role of the logical object, y, in (58).
This information is expressed in the functional structures:

(59) $(\exists y)\ NP_1$ EAT y
(60) $(\exists x)\ x$ EAT NP_1

Accordingly, it is possible to provide lexical entries for the passive
verbs (*be*) *eaten*, (*be*) *hit*, and (*be*) *relied on*, as in (61)–(63):

(61)   *eat+en*:   V,   [*be* ____], $(\exists x)\ x$ EAT NP_1
(62)   *hit+$\emptyset$*:   V,   [*be* ____], $(\exists x)\ x$ HIT NP_1
(63)   *reli+ed*:   V,   [*be* ____ [*on*]], $(\exists x)\ x$ RELY-ON NP_1

As for the agentive *by*-phrase that optionally appears with passives, it
can be analyzed simply as an optional prepositional phrase that

functions semantically to identify the logical subject of the passive verb. This is illustrated in (64).

(64) $eat+en$: V, $[be$ ____ $[_{PP} \, by \, NP] \,]$,

$(\exists x) \, (x \text{ EAT } NP_1 \, \& \, x = NP_{by})$

Let us now compare the passive lexical entries (61)–(63) with those for the corresponding active verbs in (34)–(37). We see that the syntactic contexts are related by the simple rule: $[$ ____ (P) NP . . .$]$ → $[be$ ____ (P) . . . $]$. And the passive functional structures are related to the active functional structures by the operations: "Eliminate NP_1" and either "Replace NP_2 by NP_1" or "Replace NP_p by NP_1." These operations will be referred to collectively as the active–passive relation. Since the syntactic contexts appear to be redundant—that is, predictable from the functional structures—there may be no need to state the contextual rule separately. (In a more detailed analysis we would take *be* to be a verb subcategorized for passives, as *get* is: compare Hasegawa 1968, Bresnan 1972, and Emonds 1976.)

The active–passive relation does not apply to the functional structures of the nonpassivizing verbs that have been discussed—which is as it should be. But given the lexical entry to *put* shown in (65), the active–passive relation will produce (66).

(65) *put*: V, $[$ ____ NP PP$]$, NP_1 PUT NP_2 LOC
(Someone put your clothes into the closet.)
(66) $put+\emptyset$: V, $[be$ ____ PP$]$, $(\exists x) \, x$ PUT NP_1 LOC
(Your clothes were put into the closet.)

It will not create *The closet was put your clothes into,* because there is no lexical relation between *the closet* and *put.* (There is, of course, nothing wrong with the phrase *put your clothes into* when the verb is not passivized: *The closet to put your clothes into is the one on the left.*) If there were a lexical relation in English for *put your clothes into,* the active–passive relation might apply to it, as it does for *make use of* in *The closet was made use of.* The set of lexical relations is not fixed: it can change to embody those concepts that become important for communication.[3]

---

[3] For example, on encountering passives like *The mat is being lain on by the cats,* we find it relatively easy to imagine the mat as an object of some special activity of the cats; when we do this, we seem to be hypothesizing a new, logically transitive, relation of *lying on.*

We can see, then, that it is the lexical relation between the noun phrase and its verb that governs passivization, not the syntactic relation between them. A noun phrase that follows *lie on, rely on, arrive at,* bears the same syntactic relation to each verb, namely, V [$_{PP}$ P NP]; but the ability of the NP to passivize depends upon its lexical relation to the verb, as expressed in the functional structure. Similarly, *make* is followed by a noun phrase in both (67a) and (67b).

(67)   a.   The boys made good cakes.
         b.   The boys made good cooks.

Yet the lexical relation of this noun phrase to the verb is different in the two examples. In (67b) *good cooks* does not function as an object of the verb (as NP$_2$), but as what has been called a predicate nominative or a subjective complement (on which see Quirk et al. 1972). Unlike the object, the subjective complement plays a role in determining concord; in English a subjective complement NP agrees in number with the subject. Further, the syntactic NP that functions as a subjective complement never passivizes:

(68)   a.   Good cakes were made by the boys.
         b.   *Good cooks were made by the boys.

An active–passive relation exists in many languages of the world, having highly different syntactic forms. The syntactic form of the relation seems to vary chaotically from language to language. But an examination of functional structures reveals a general organizing principle. Perlmutter and Postal (1977) have proposed that the active–passive relation can be universally identified as a set of operations on grammatical functions: "Eliminate the subject," "Make the object the subject."

A basic assumption is that human languages must be organized for communication, which requires both efficiency of expression and semantic stability. The functional structures outlined here for passive verbs are designed to provide a direct mapping between their logical argument structures and the syntactic contexts in which they can occur. As we will see, with these functional structures in the lexicon of our grammar, we can achieve efficiency in grammatical processing, immediately extracting the logical relation for a word we know from the syntactic form in which it appears (or vice versa). At the same time, the various syntactic forms in which a verb appears are semantically stable: they are associated with the same underlying logical relation by operations like the active–passive relation.

Previous theories of transformational grammar have provided for semantic stability at the cost of grammatical efficiency: complex sentences can be related to semantically interpretable structures only through long chains of transformational operations on syntactic structures. In contrast, the lexical operations in the theory proposed here need not be involved in grammatical processing at all, although they may be involved in organizing the lexicon for communication (as in learning). Perhaps the active–passive relation belongs to a universal "logic of relations" by which the lexicon of a human language—the repository of meanings—can be organized.[4]

The Interpretation of Passives in Complex Sentences

The preceding section began with the question, How is the logical argument structure of a verb related to the various syntactic contexts in which it appears?

The familiar transformational response to this question is to hypothesize a syntactic deep structure in which logical subjects and objects of verbs correspond directly to their grammatical subjects and objects. Syntactic transformations then map this deep structure into the various surface structures in which the verb appears.

I have proposed an alternative solution, constructed by defining a set of lexical functional structures that provide a direct mapping from the logical argument structure of a verb into its various syntactic contexts. The relations between the functional structures of a given verb in different syntactic contexts can be expressed as operations on its logical argument structure. In this way, as we have seen, the active–passive relation can be expressed as a (universal) relation on lexical functional structures rather than as a transformational operation on syntactic structures.

I will now show how these lexical functional structures permit us to extract, directly from the surface structure of a sentence, information equivalent to that provided by the syntactic deep structures of previous transformational theory. This information will be referred to

---

[4] The idea that lexical rules defined on grammatical functions may be universal was suggested to me by Moira Yip. See Yip (1977) for an illuminating study of such a rule in Chinese.

as "the interpretation," or "the functional interpretation." In the use of this term I am deliberately excluding the semantic interpretation of pronouns, articles, quantifiers, and other logical elements, which I assume to be provided by a separate inferential system.

In order to interpret a simple sentence it is necessary to find the functional structure of its verb, identify the grammatical functions of its phrases, and assign the phrases their functional interpretation with respect to the verb. These tasks might be performed by any of a number of different procedures, but the tasks themselves are logically separable.

The lexicon provides us with the functional structure of the verb in its immediate syntactic context, as illustrated in (69).

(69)   Mary was annoyed by John.
     annoy+ed: V,   [*be* ____ [$_{PP}$ *by* NP]],
              ($\exists x$) (x ANNOY NP$_1$ & x = NP$_{by}$)

To identify the grammatical functions of *Mary* and *John* in sentence (69), we apply the grammatical functions defined in Table 1 to the syntactic structure in which the phrases appear. This is shown in Figure 1.3. We now have the information given in (70).

(70)   ($\exists x$) (x ANNOY NP$_1$ & x = NP$_{by}$)
     NP$_1$: *Mary*
     NP$_{by}$: *John*

To complete the interpretation of the sentence, it is necessary to assign the phrases their functional interpretation with respect to the verb. This is done by (i) assigning indices to the subject *Mary* and the prepositional object *John*, and (ii) substituting these indices into the

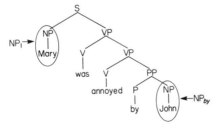

Figure 1.3 Identification of grammatical functions for interpretation of *Mary was annoyed by John*

appropriate argument positions in the lexical functional structure, as shown in (71).

(71) (i) $(\exists x)\, (x \text{ ANNOY } NP_1 \,\&\, x = NP_{by})$
            $NP_1\colon Mary = i$
            $\underline{NP_{by}\colon John = j}$

      (ii) $Mary = i,\ John = j$
            $(\exists x)\, (x \text{ ANNOY } i \,\&\, x = j)$

From (71 ii) it is possible to infer "John annoyed Mary" or, rather, "Someone named *John* annoyed someone named *Mary.*" (The notation harmlessly suppresses several logical niceties.)

Now let us turn to the interpretation of passives in complex sentences. In the sentences to be considered here, the main verb has, not an object (or noun phrase complement), but a verbal complement. As an illustration, Figure 1.4 shows the syntactic structure for the complex sentence *John tends to annoy Mary.*

In Figure 1.4 the verb *tend* is immediately followed by an infinitival verb phrase, denoted by $\overline{VP}$. In English the syntactic category $\overline{VP}$ can have the grammatical function of verbal complement. Just as the syntactic category NP can be distinguished from its grammatical functions as subject (NP_1), object (NP_2), and so on, so must the syntactic verb phrase be distinguished from its grammatical function as verbal complement. The notation ( )VP is introduced for this purpose and is defined (for English) as a $\overline{VP}$ immediately dominated by VP. Not all infinitival verb phrases function as complements: in particular, those that are immediately dominated by NP do not; for example, in the sentence *To annoy Mary seems to be John's purpose in life,* diagrammed in Figure 1.5, *to annoy Mary* functions as the subject (NP_1) of *seems.* The different grammatical functions of

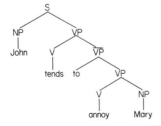

Figure 1.4 Syntactic structure of *John tends to annoy Mary*

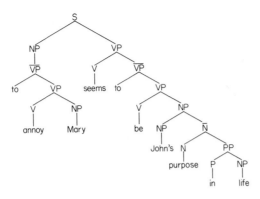

Figure 1.5 Syntactic structure of *To annoy Mary seems to be John's purpose in life*

infinitival verb phrases play an important role in interpreting their understood subjects, but we will be concerned only with verbal complements. (For a full discussion, see Bresnan, in preparation.)

The notation for the verbal complement function, ( )VP, is designed to indicate that a verbal complement is functionally incomplete, in a sense to be explained directly. Any verb can be lexically inserted into a $\overline{VP}$, as *annoy* has been inserted in *John tends to annoy Mary* (Figure 1.4). The syntactic context for *annoy* is satisfied whether or not a subject NP precedes it:

(72) *annoy*:   V,   [_____ NP],   NP$_1$ ANNOY NP$_2$

But the functional structure for *annoy* cannot be completely satisfied within the $\overline{VP}$, because verb phrases do not contain grammatical subjects, by definition. In this sense, a verbal complement is functionally incomplete: the lexical functional structure of its main verb should contain an unsatisfied NP$_1$.

To interpret such a complex sentence, it is necessary to complete its verbal complement, which means that the unfilled subject NP$_1$ within the verbal complement must be assigned the index of some phrase in the syntactic structure. The lexical functional structure of a complement-taking verb like *tend* will tell us which phrase provides the index we need:

(73) *tend*:   V,   [_____ $\overline{VP}$],   TEND ((NP$_1$)VP)

In (73) the functional structure for *tend* indicates that its verbal complement, ( )VP, is to be completed by the index of the grammatical subject of *tend*, NP$_1$. Notice that this grammatical subject of *tend* does not function as a logical subject of *tend*. *Tend* has no logical subject; it functions semantically as an operator on its functionally closed complement. In this respect, *tend* resembles a modal verb.

Figure 1.6 shows the syntactic structure for *Mary tends to be annoyed by John*. An explicit procedure for providing this structure with its functional interpretation can easily be devised. (There are, of course, many other possible procedures.)

To interpret the structure of Figure 1.6, we use the lexical functional structure for *tend* in the context [_____ $\overline{VP}$], which is given in (73). Then we identify the grammatical functions of the phrases in the sentence, applying the definitions of NP$_1$ and ( )VP, as shown in Figure 1.7. We now have the information given in (74).

(74)   TEND ((NP$_1$)VP)
       NP$_1$: *Mary*
       ( )VP: *to be annoyed by John*

The next step in interpreting the sentence is to assign the phrases their functional interpretation with respect to the verb. To do this, we (i) assign indices to the subject *Mary* and to the verbal complement *to be annoyed by John*, and (ii) substitute these indices into the appropriate argument positions in the lexical functional structure. Step (i) is shown in (75).

(75)   TEND ((NP$_1$)VP)
       NP$_1$: *Mary* $= i$
       ( )VP: *to be annoyed by John* $= f$

Notice that the verbal complement phrase is indexed by f, which

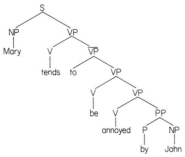

Figure 1.6 Syntactic structure of *Mary tends to be annoyed by John*

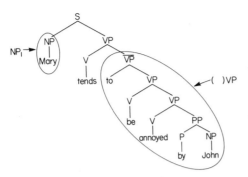

Figure 1.7 Identification of grammatical functions for interpretation of *Mary tends to be annoyed by John*

denotes a function. The index f is a function of subject and object indices; when f is applied to the index i, it tells us that the verbal complement that it indexes aplies to i—to *Mary*, in this case. Making the appropriate substitutions, step (ii), we arrive at (76).

(76)   *Mary* $= i$, *to be annoyed by John* $= f$
            TEND $(f(i))$

Since *to be annoyed by John* has not yet been interpreted, all that (76) really tells us is that Mary tends to . . . . To complete the interpretation of the sentence, we must now interpret *(to) be annoyed by John*. From (76), we already know one thing about the interpretation of this phrase: it "applies to" i. What that means, in turn, is that in the functional interpretation of f, $NP_1 = i$. Thus, we start anew with the information in (77).

(77) $f =$ *to be annoyed by John*
            $NP_1 = i$

Now, just as we did in the case of the simple sentence, we find the lexical functional structure of *annoyed* in the context [*be* ___ [PP *by* NP]] and identify the grammatical functions of the phrases in the syntactic structure, which is the $\overline{VP}$ in Figure 1.7. We now have the information in (78).

(78) $f =$ *to be annoyed by John*
            $NP_1 = i$
            $(\exists x) (x \text{ ANNOY } NP_1 \text{ \& } x = NP_{by})$
            NP_{by}: *John*

To complete the interpretation of f, we must (i) assign the prepositional object *John* an index, and (ii) substitute indices into their appropriate positions in the lexical functional structure. The result is called $f(i)$:

(79) $f(i)$: John $= j$, $(\exists x)$ $(x$ ANNOY i & $x = j)$

Taking (76) and (79) together, we have (80):

(80) *Mary* $= i$, TEND $(John = j$, $(\exists x)$ $(x$ ANNOY i & $x = j)$ $)$

Notice that in (80) a comma loosely connects each of the formulas *Mary* $= i$ and *John* $= j$ to the formula following it. This comma connective can be construed to mean that the person designated by the index has the property described by the formula. Then from (80) we can infer that Mary has a complex tendency, which consists of being in an annoying relation with John, where Mary is the one annoyed (the logical object of *annoy*) and John is the annoyer (*Mary tends to be annoyed by John*).

If we apply the interpretive procedure outlined above to the sentence *John tends to annoy Mary,* we arrive at (81).

(81) *John* $= i$, TEND $(Mary = j$, $(i$ ANNOY $j)$ $)$

From (81) we infer that John has a complex tendency, which consists of annoying Mary; again, John is the annoyer and Mary the annoyed.

The point to be emphasized is that all of the functional information that is relevant to the interpretation of these sentences — the fact that Mary is the logical object of *annoy,* and so on — has been extracted from the surface structure and the lexicon. There is no need to compute the grammatical relations of *John* and *Mary* in some deep structure tree in order to find their functional relations in the sentence. In fact, there is no need to compute the surface syntactic structure prior to determining the grammatical functions of its parts: the structural and functional relations can be determined by procedures operating simultaneously, in parallel.

The same interpretive procedure can be applied to sentence (82).

(82) John tries to annoy Mary.

The syntactic form of (82) is identical to that for *John tends to annoy Mary,* shown in Figure 1.4. But the lexical functional structure of *try* differs in one important respect from that of *tend*: the grammatical subject of *try* is also the logical subject of *try*, as shown in (83).

(83)   *try*:   V,   [____ $\overline{VP}$],   NP$_1$ TRY ((NP$_1$)VP)

By following the interpretive procedure just outlined, we can derive the following interpretation of (82):

(84)   *John* = *i, i* TRY (*Mary* = *j, i* ANNOY *j*)

Similarly, sentence (85) has the same syntactic structure as that shown in Figure 1.6 for *Mary tends to be annoyed by John*, but its interpretation will be as in (86).

(85)   Mary tries to be annoyed by John.
(86)   *Mary* = *i, i* TRY (*John* = *j*, ($\exists x$) (*x* ANNOY *i* & *x* = *j*))

Observe that in both (84) and (86) *Mary* is the logical object of *annoy*; the interpretations differ in that *John* is the logical subject of *try* in (84) and *Mary* is the logical subject of *try* in (86).

Before proceeding further, it should be noted that some noun phrases are meaningless in themselves but derive an interpretation from restricted contexts. One example is the expletive *there*:

(87)   There's a knack to it.

There has an existential meaning in contexts of the form: [____ be NP . . .]. This special interpretation can be represented in the lexical entry for *be*, as indicated in part in (88). (See Jenkins 1975 for a study of the syntactic contexts of *be* in existentials; he gives evidence that the syntactic contexts must be base-generated.)

(88)   *be*:   V,   [____ NP],   NP$_1$ BE NP$_2$,
          THERE BE NP$_2$ $\equiv$ NP$_2$ EXISTS

The entry provided for *there* itself is shown in (89).

(89)   *there*:   [$_{NP}$ ____],   THERE

Although (89) permits *there* to be inserted into a NP position, *there* will find an interpretation only in the appropriate contexts of *be*. To derive this interpretation, *there* will simply be treated as its own index (THERE) and substituted into an appropriate position in a lexical functional structure. It will follow that sentence (90) will have no

interpretation, but sentence (87) will be correctly interpreted, as in
(91).

(90) *There sang.
(91) There is a knack to it.
 THERE BE i $\equiv$ i EXISTS
 $i = a$ knack to it

For the complex sentence *There tends to be a knack to it, there* is
lexically inserted in its position as grammatical subject of *tend*. The
interpretive procedure automatically provides us with (92); then we
obtain (93) from (88).

(92) TEND (THERE BE i, $i = a$ knack to it)
(93) TEND (i EXISTS, $i = a$ knack to it)

In other words, sentences like *There tends to be a knack to it* can
simply be base-generated; if the meaningless index THERE cannot be
eliminated by the rules of interpretation, the sentence is functionally
ill-formed.

It is possible to use the same approach in dealing with fragments of
idioms, like *the cat* in (94).

(94) The cat tends to get his tongue.

The meaning of the idiom is simply listed in the lexicon and its
meaningless parts are treated as their own indices and passed through
the functional structures until they find their interpretation. The
interesting aspect of this approach is that it requires that idioms —
despite their abnormal meanings — have normal syntactic structure in
order to be interpreted. This property of idioms is in fact general and
well known.[5]

Just as some meaningless noun phrases — expletives and idiom
fragments — must serve as their own indices, so certain noun phrases
must derive their index from other phrases. An example is the
reflexive pronoun:

(95) John likes himself.

Reflexives have a very simple analysis in the present framework. The

[5] This consequence was pointed out to me by Jane Grimshaw. See Katz (1973) for a
recent discussion of the structural properties of English idioms.

general rule for their functional interpretation is given in (96). (For a more complete analysis, see Bresnan, in preparation.)

(96)   A reflexive pronoun is coindexed with the subject, NP_1.

This rule applies automatically in the course of the functional interpretation of the sentence. That is, as soon as we arrive at the information "NP_2: reflexive pronoun," we can assign NP_2 the index of the current NP_1. In this way sentence (97) is automatically assigned the indicated interpretation.

(97)   John tries to like himself.
       John $= i$, i TRY (i LIKE i)

One of the consequences of rule (96) is that the reflexive pronoun cannot function as subject: in that situation there would be no NP_1 to derive its index from. Thus both (98) and (99) must be ill-formed:

(98)   *Himself likes John.
(99)   *Himself is liked by John.

It is also possible to reformulate the Noncoreference Rule (20) as a condition on this indexing procedure: informally, a nonpronominal noun phrase cannot be coindexed with a noun phrase that precedes and commands it.

Let us now return to the question of the active–passive relation. In previous theories of transformational grammar, passive sentences are derived by syntactic transformations. The relation between active and passive sentences in English is expressed by assigning passive sentences activelike deep structures, then transformationally displacing the syntactic subject (the first NP to the left of the verb) into a *by*-phrase and moving the syntactic object (the first NP to the right of the verb) into the original position of the subject. These theories do not explain the dependence of the transformational relation on grammatical functions; indeed, the dependence is not even recognized, since transformations are defined as structure-dependent operations, and functional information is not expressed in the syntactic structures to which transformations apply. Additional principles have to be invoked to make sure that "the first NP to the right of the verb" is the correct one, namely, the grammatical object. For example, in a sentence like (100) the first NP to the right of the verb, *disapprove of,* can be *children*:

(100)   Doctors may disapprove of children smoking.

Yet *children* is the wrong NP for passivization:

(101)   *Children may be disapproved of smoking by doctors.

The correct NP is the one that functions as the object of *disapprove of*:

(102)   Children smoking may be disapproved of by doctors.

It has required some ingenuity to explain this fact in the transformational theory of passivization, yet it and many other facts equally difficult to explain are simple and obvious consequences of the alternative theory proposed here. (For one transformational account of (100)–(102), see Bresnan 1976a.)

Likewise, "the first NP to the left of the verb," required by the passive transformation, has to be the grammatical subject of the verb. Yet passive verbs appear in constructions where there is no subject, such as the verbal complement constructions already discussed. For example, to account for sentences like (103) —

(103)   Mary tends to be annoyed by John.

— it was proposed (in Bresnan 1972) that the verb *tend* takes a sentential complement in deep structure, as shown in (104).

(104) $[_S[_{NP}\Delta]$ $[_{VP}$ tend $[_S$ John annoy Mary]]]

The dummy subject, Δ, was designed to account for the fact that *tend* is logically subjectless. The passive transformation could apply to the sentential complement of *tend*, and then a raising transformation would move the passivized subject into the subject position for *tend*, replacing Δ. The raising transformation had to be made obligatory in some way, because the fact is that *tend* never appears with sentential complements:

(105)   *It tends that John annoys Mary.
        *It tends for John to annoy Mary.

In English there are quite a few verbs like *tend*, which simply take infinitival complements. (See Kajita 1968 for a study of these verbs in a transformational framework.)

In the case of verbs like *try,* the transformational analysis requires even more ingenuity. Perlmutter (1968) showed that such verbs are subject to a "like-subject constraint" that requires their deep structure complement subjects to be identical to the main verb subjects:

(106)   *John tried for a doctor to examine him.
(107)   John tried to see a doctor.

Janet Fodor (1974) demonstrated that this constraint has to be applied, not in deep structure, but after the passive transformation has applied in the complement:

(108)   John tried to be examined by a doctor.
(109)   *John tried for a doctor to be seen by him.

She showed, moreover, that the constraint itself is not enough to get the correct results; the subject in the complement, however it arrived in subject position, has to be deleted, obligatorily:

(110)   *John tried for him(self) to see a doctor.
(111)   *John tried for him(self) to be examined by a doctor.

And in some cases the correct complement subject might never "arrive." For example, unless both passive and raising transformations apply to the deep structure (112), it is impossible to derive (113).

(112)   [$_S$ Mary tried [$_S$ it not to seem [$_S$ John annoy her(self)]]]
(113)   Mary tried not to seem to be annoyed by John.

Recently, Chomsky and Lasnik (1977) have proposed that a special "rule of control," a lexical property of *try,* applies to the surface structures of sentences containing *try,* and rules out all of the bad sentences that are derived from (112):

(114)   *Mary tried for it not to seem that John annoys her.
         *Mary tried for it not to seem that she is annoyed by John.
         *Mary tried for John not to seem to annoy her.
         *Mary tried for her not to seem to be annoyed by John.

They go on to suggest that lexical insertion might apply, not to deep structures, but to structures that have undergone all the requisite transformations. These "surface structures" would contain a record of all the movements in their transformational derivations.

    The simple and obvious solution to all these problems was proposed by Brame (1976): the verb *try* does not take a sentential complement at all; it is simply subcategorized to take an infinitival verb phrase complement — or $\overline{\text{VP}}$, in the terms used here; the fact that passivized verbs appear in the complement to *try* simply indicates that there is no passive transformation. This, of course, is the solution adopted in the present theory.[6]

A question that must be asked is why the passive transformation has been perceived as a structure-dependent operation. The answer seems to be that certain noun phrases can be passivized (that is, they can be preposed by the passive transformation) even though they bear no logical relation to the passivizing verb. An example:

(115)   The hot dog is believed to be dangerous to our health.

In (115) *the hot dog* is not the logical object of *believe* but the logical subject of *to be dangerous to our health*. In other words, we can't "believe the hot dog." The logical object of *believe* is the proposition that the hot dog is dangerous to our health. From this it has been concluded that the passive transformation is blind to grammatical functions — that it is purely structure-dependent. (This reasoning appears in Bresnan 1972, Wasow 1977, Anderson 1977, and elsewhere.)

As can now be seen, this reasoning confuses grammatical functions with logical functions: it is based on the assumption that if *the hot dog* is not a logical object of *believe*, it cannot have been a grammatical object of *believe*. But the assumption is not necessary.

Once grammatical functions are distinguished from logical functions, it is easy to account for sentences like (115). The active verb *believe* is assigned the lexical representation in (116).

(116)   *believe*:   V,   [___ NP $\overline{\text{VP}}$], NP_1 BELIEVE ((NP_2)VP)

The active–passive relation provides the representation in (117).

(117)   *believe+d*:   V,   [*be* ___ $\overline{\text{VP}}$], $(\exists x)$ (*x* BELIEVE ((NP_1)VP))

Observe that the lexical functional structure in (117) is almost identical to that for *tend*, repeated here:

(73)   *tend*:   V,   [___ $\overline{\text{VP}}$],   TEND ((NP_1)VP)

---

[6] Brame (1976) argues on independent grounds for base-generation of structures that have previously been derived through passive, equi-NP deletion, and other transformations.

Therefore, the interpretive procedure already outlined will automatically provide the desired interpretation for sentence (115).

In short, we simply analyze *believe* as having a grammatical object that serves as the logical subject of its verbal complement. However, for other verbs, such as *compel,* the lexical representation (and therefore the functional interpretation) is different: their grammatical objects serve also as their logical objects:

(118)   We must compel John to see a doctor.
          compel: V,   [____ NP $\overline{\text{VP}}$],   NP$_1$ COMPEL NP$_2$ ((NP$_2$)VP)

But — as expected — the grammatical objects of both types of verbs can be reflexive pronouns:

(119)   We compel ourselves to be honest.
(120)   We believe ourselves to be honest.

Thus the difference between *compel* and *believe* parallels the difference between *try* and *tend*.

The Need for Transformations

The analysis of the active–passive relation that has been described in the preceding sections permits a great simplification of the syntactic component of grammar; all of the sentences discussed there have "deep structures" that are identical to their surface structures. This immediately raises the question: Is there any need at all for a level of deep structure distinct from surface structure? Or — to put it slightly differently — is there any need for syntactic transformations that map syntactic structures into syntactic structures?

In answer to this question, let me first point out that the active–passive relation is *function-dependent,* in the sense that it relates (lexical) functional structures. And the active–passive relation is not unique; it can be shown that the transformations that interact with the passive can themselves be expressed as function-dependent relations (see Bresnan, in preparation). Moreover, the interpretive procedure that has been constructed is also function-dependent, in that it combines lexical functional structures. Syntactic transformations, on the other hand, are *structure-dependent*: they are assumed to map syntactic structures into syntactic structures. Therefore, let me reformulate the question. Is there any need for structure-dependent rules of grammar?

Recall that some of the earliest work in transformational grammar was devoted to demonstrating the empirical inadequacies of phrase structure grammars for natural languages. (See Levelt 1974, vol. 2, for a recent survey.) Although phrase structure grammars can naturally represent the fact that words are grouped hierarchically into phrases, many cross-phrasal regularities in natural languages cannot be adequately described within these grammars. To give just one illustration, a verb in English normally shows number agreement with its subject noun phrase, immediately to its left:

(121) a. The problem *was*/**were* unsolvable.
     b. The problems *were*/**was* unsolvable.

Here the choice of plural *were* or singular *was* must depend on agreement with the number of *the problem(s)*. This type of local regularity could be described within a phrase structure grammar by means of context-sensitive rules, as could the inverted forms in (122), although there would be a certain redundancy of description.

(122) a. *Was*/**were* the problem unsolvable?
     b. *Were*/**was* the problems unsolvable?

However, in many cases the number of a verb agrees with that of a noun phrase at some distance from it:

(123) a. **Which problem* did your professor say she thought *were* unsolvable?
     b. *Which problem* did your professor say she thought *was* unsolvable?
(124) a. *Which problems* did your professor say she thought *were* unsolvable?
     b. **Which problems* did your professor say she thought *was* unsolvable?

In (123) and (124) the number of *was/were* agrees with *which problem(s)*. Furthermore, this type of syntactic dependency can extend as far as memory or patience permits:

(125) a. Can you tell me which problem your professor is likely to have said she thought was unsolvable?
     b. Can you tell me which problem your professor is likely to have said she thought everyone knew was unsolvable?

In contrast to the local type of number agreement in (121) and (122), the distant type of agreement in (123)–(125) cannot be adequately described even by context-sensitive phrase structure rules, for the possible context is not correctly describable as a finite string of phrases.

The transformational solution to this problem is to state number agreement as a local regularity and to formulate a transformation of Question Movement, which can displace a phrase to an interrogative position. To illustrate, (123b) would be formed from the structure shown in Figure 1.8.

The Question Movement transformation provides a solution to many other syntactic problems unrelated to number agreement. For example, some verbs of English, like *put, dart, glance,* require a prepositional phrase complement in simple sentences. *Put* requires both a direct object noun phrase and a locative prepositional phrase:

(126) a. You put the diamonds into a sack.   V NP PP
       b. *You put the diamonds.   *V NP
       c. *You put into a sack.   *V PP
       d. *You put the diamonds a sack.   *V NP NP
       e. *You put the diamonds stealthily.   *V NP Adv

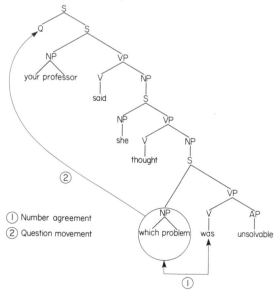

Figure 1.8 Transformational derivation of example (123b), *Which problem did your professor say she thought was unsolvable?*

(We distinguish this *put* from the athletic *put* in *put the shot.*) Yet in certain complex interrogative constructions, (126b,c,e) can occur as subsentences. For example, (126b) so occurs in (127).

(127)   Into which sack do you think *you put the diamonds*?

Question Movement transforms the structure shown in Figure 1.9 into that for (127) by displacing the prepositional phrase to the interrogative position. Note that in the structure of Figure 1.9 *put* has a prepositional phrase complement.

   Now observe that, as in Figure 1.8, the noun phrase *which sack* can itself be displaced to interrogative position, leaving the preposition *into* behind:

(128)   Which sack do you think you put the diamonds into?

The subsentence *you put the diamonds into* is not well-formed as an independent sentence, but its occurrence in (128) follows from the application of Question Movement. Conversely, the subsentence *you put the diamonds into the box,* which *is* well-formed, creates ungrammaticality when it occurs in (129):

(129)   *Which sack do you think you put the diamonds into the box?

The reason is that (129) is not a well-formed source for Question Movement:

(130)   *[Q you think [you put the diamonds into the box which sack]]

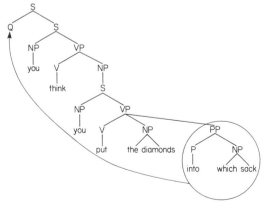

Figure 1.9 Transformational derivation of example (127), *Into which sack do you think you put the diamonds?*

Once again, Question Movement permits a simple and natural statement of a local regularity that cannot be adequately described by
means of phrase structure rules alone.

Now let us view Question Movement in reverse. When a sentence
begins as *What* . . . , it is not clear exactly where *what* will fit into the
functional interpretation. This can be true even over extended fragments of the sentence, as examples like (128) showed. Viewed in
reverse, Question Movement relates a phrase that is in a displaced
position, outside of its clause, to some position within the clause
where a grammatical function can be assigned. Since the interrogative
phrase has no assigned grammatical function in its displaced position,
(inverse) Question Movement is not a function-dependent rule of
English.

Consequences

Let us now consider some of the consequences of reorganizing
transformational grammar by eliminating from the syntactic component all rules that are function-dependent, in the sense explained in
the preceding section. The grammar will contain a set of phrase
structure rules, which define the basic, or canonical, sentence patterns of the language. The lexicon will contain a set of lexical
functional structures, which provide a direct mapping between the
logical argument structures of words and the syntactic patterns in
which they appear. Rules of functional interpretation will combine
functional structures to associate composite meanings with complex
sentences. A restricted class of structure-dependent transformations
will deform or (if they apply inversely) restore the basic sentence
patterns, associating displaced phrases with their functional positions.

As outlined, this theory of grammar has interesting consequences
for linguistics and psychology. A major consequence — the emergence of the English active–passive relation as an instance of a
linguistic universal — has already been discussed (pp. 20–23). In what
follows we can only glance at other consequences.

Rule ordering In the discussion of the interpretation of passives, a
simple procedure was defined for combining functional structures — a
procedure that is recursive, or iterative. This recursiveness is necessary simply because one functional structure can be embedded in

another, and each is interpreted by the same procedure. The choice of lexical items is quite free, up to their ability to receive a combined interpretation, and this depends only on their intrinsic structure. As a result, sentences like (131) are directly generated and automatically provided with the correct functional interpretations:

(131) a. John wants to appear to be loved by Mary.
       b. John appears to want to be loved by Mary.
       c. Mary is expected to be elected.

By contrast, in the transformational analysis of these sentences, passive, raising, and equi-NP deletion transformations are assumed to apply cyclically to each other's outputs, resulting in different orders of application in two derivations (131a,b) or in multiple applications in the same derivation (131c). It has often been noted that such transformations do not appear to be extrinsically ordered with respect to each other (see Koutsoudas 1972, 1973, and the references cited there; also Chomsky and Lasnik 1977). This property is explained by the theory proposed here: there is no extrinsic ordering among lexical representations.[7]

In previous transformational theory, the passive transformation has another unexplained ordering property: it never applies to a noun phrase that has already been moved by Question Movement (QM):

(132) a. The boys asked Q they should talk to *which girls* ⇒ (by QM)
       b. The boys asked *which girls* they should talk to. ⇒ (by passive)
       c. *Which girls* were asked they should talk to by the boys.

If there were a structure-dependent passive transformation, there would be no reason why it should not apply to *which girls* in (132b), for that is the first NP to the right of the verb. As a function-dependent rule, however, passivization can affect only the grammatical object of the passivizing verb, and in (132b) the displaced interrogative NP (*which girls*) is not the grammatical object of *ask*. This explanation is confirmed by the observation that passivization *can* apply to an interrogative NP that has *not* been moved by

---

[7] This consequence is pointed out by Schmerling (1977). She proposes a new analysis of English imperatives that provides some evidence for a nontransformational approach to passivization like the one advanced here.

Question Movement, so long as that NP is the object of the verb:

(133)   a.   Q the boys asked *which girls* question ⇒ (by passive)
        b.   Q *which girls* were asked questions by the boys ⇒ (by QM)
        c.   *Which girls* were asked questions by the boys?

One attempt to explain such observations in previous transformational theory was to propose that Question Movement belongs to a class of so-called postcyclic transformations that apply after the cyclic transformations like the passive. But the fact that Question Movement applies to structures that are already passive — as in (134b) — is an immediate consequence of the present theory.

(134)   a.   Q which boys asked the girls questions
                                               (active form) ⇒ (by QM)
             Which boys asked the girls questions?
        b.   Q the girls were asked questions by *which boys*
                                               (passive form) ⇒ (by QM)
             Which boys were the girls asked questions by?

Phonological effects of transformations   It has been recognized for some time that transformations that move or delete material can produce phonological perturbations in sentences. A very well known type of example was pointed out by L. Horn, who observed that a sentence like (135), pronounced without contracting *want to* to *wanna,* is ambiguous between (a) and (b), whereas (136) is not.

(135)   Teddy is the man I want to succeed.
        a.   Teddy is the man (whom) I want ⌐ to succeed.

             "I want Teddy to succeed"

        b.   Teddy is the man (whom) I want to succeed⌐.

             "I want to succeed Teddy"

(136)   Teddy is the man I wanna succeed.
        =   Teddy is the man (whom) I want to succeed⌐.

             "I want to succeed Teddy"

When the relative pronoun derives from an underlying position between *want* and *to*, contraction to *wanna* is blocked, as in (135a). Question Movement can be shown to produce the same effects.

Yet certain transformations that have been assumed to move or delete material do not behave as expected: they produce no phonological perturbations at all; their structural effects are "invisible" to the contraction rules. For example, the equi-NP deletion transformation, though it is supposed to delete a pronoun from between *want* and *to*, fails to block contraction, as we see in (137).

(137) a. I wanna succeed Teddy.
       b. I want [pro (= I) to succeed Teddy]

(This fact and its implications were observed by Baker and Brame 1972 and Brame 1976.)

Similarly, the subject raising transformation does not affect the contraction of *going to* to *gonna* in (138).

(138) a. There's gonna be a movie made about us.
       b. There is going [___to be a movie made about us]

In the transformational theory, *there* would first be inserted into the complement of *be going* on a lower transformational cycle as the subject of *to be . . . made*; it would then be moved into position as subject of *be going* on a higher transformational cycle — that is, it would be moved from a position between *going* and *to be . . . made*, in which case contraction of *going to* should be blocked. If *there* were inserted directly as subject of the higher cycle, (139) would be produced.

(139) There's a movie gonna be made about us.

The unexpected behavior of these transformations is an immediate consequence of the present theory. Infinitival complements are not derived by equi-NP deletion and subject raising transformations; they are generated directly by the phrase structure rules. The verbs *want* and *be going* simply have infinitival verb phrase complements. In this respect they are very much like modal verbs. Unlike modals, however, they do not invert:

(140) a. Will you see him?
       b. *Wanna you see him? vs. Do you wanna see him?
       c. *Are gonna you see him? vs. Are you gonna see him?

(On the verbal nature of the English modals, see Pullum and Wilson 1977.)

Language acquisition In his major study of the early stages of language acquisition, Brown (1973) has observed that the use of *wanna* in sentences like *I wanna go* is acquired by children before the use of *want* with a full sentential complement, as in *I want John to go*. This order of acquisition can be considered something of a puzzle, given a transformational analysis of such sentences, in which the infinitive is derived by deletion from an underlying full sentential complement containing a pronominal subject. How can the derived structure be mastered before the basic structure? But in the present theory, the verb + infinitive construction is a basic structure, like the modal + infinitive construction. (See Chapter 7 for further discussion of the acquisition of VP complements.)

Again, in the usual transformational analysis of passivization (for example, that of Chomsky 1965), a short passive, *John was killed,* is transformationally derived from a long passive, similar to *John was killed by someone,* by deletion of the *by*-phrase. In contrast, in the theory proposed here both short and long passives are basic structures; the long passive, however, requires semantic interpretation of the *by*-phrase, because the agent is present in this prepositional phrase from the beginning. As Maratsos reports in Chapter 7, there is no known evidence that long passives are acquired by children *before* short passives; in fact, short passives are spontaneously produced before long ones (Brown 1973).

Although the present theory does not predict that short passives must be acquired before long passives, it does suggest that what is crucial to the acquisition of long passives is the ability to integrate the postverbal prepositional phrase semantically. And Maratsos and Abramovitch (1975) do in fact present evidence that the comprehension of long passives by children crucially involves the semantic integration of an appropriate prepositional phrase. They report that nonsentences like **The cat is licked the dog* and **The cat is licked po the dog* (*po* being a nonsense syllable) are neither imitated nor interpreted as passive sentences by children, whereas *The cat is licked by the dog* and **The cat is licked of the dog* are interpreted as passives; furthermore, *from* is sometimes substituted for both *of* and *by* in imitations. They remark: "Apparently *of* was able to mediate the passive schema because of the common membership of *of* and *by* in the class of prepositions; the fact that in imitations *from*, another preposition, was the only other morpheme commonly substituted (once even for *po*) where *by* should appear further indicates that children code the *by* of passives not as a unique morpheme but as one belonging to the general class of prepositions.''

Derivational complexity   The theory proposed here will yield a very different assessment of derivational complexity from those associated with previous theories of transformational grammar. Although further research is required in this area, I will make two suggestions that may be of interest.

The first suggestion arises from the proposed treatment of the verbal complement system. Recall that infinitival complements to verbs like *tend* and *try* are generated directly in the base, by means of a phrase structure rule VP → V $\overline{\text{VP}}$. Lexical functional structures have been constructed for the verbs *tend* and *try* in these syntactic contexts, and an explicit procedure has been designed for interpreting the construction by indexing the grammatical subject and the verbal complement. The verbal complement is indexed by a function f, which is then itself interpreted by reapplying the procedure. As a result, *Mary tends to* . . . can be partially interpreted before proceeding to the interpretation of the complement (*to*) *be annoyed by John*.

A point that is of interest here is that fragments of sentences, like *Mary tends to* or *Mary tries to*, frequently occur in discourses:

(141)   A: Does Sally still get silly at staff parties?
         B: She tends to.

It is natural to suppose that in comprehending A's question, B has already interpreted $f = get\ silly\ at\ staff\ parties$; so in replying, B can simply retrieve the index, apply it to the current subject, and insert both into the lexical functional structure for *tends*. Thus, this theory suggests that sentences involving ellipsis (141B) are derivationally *less* complex than sentences without ellipsis (141A).

Fodor, Bever, and Garrett (1974) refer to psychological research that bears on this suggestion:

In an unpublished experiment by Jenkins, Fodor, and Saporta (1965), similar kinds of structural differences were evaluated for their effects on complexity: for example, such variants of the comparative construction as "John swims faster than Bob swims," "John swims faster than Bob," "John swims faster than Bob does." If DTC [the derivational theory of complexity] is true, relative complexity should increase from the first to the third sentence, since the first sentence is fewer transformational steps from its base structure than either of the others, and the third sentence requires one step more than the second for its derivation. . . . When tachistoscopic thresholds were measured for such sentences, however, the first type turned out to be most difficult, whereas the other two types were indistinguishable. (p. 324)

Verb phrase ellipsis has proved to be a very recalcitrant problem in previous transformational theories, because ellipsis can occur in what have been considered transformed structures. For example, in (142) both *there*-insertion and raising would have to have applied in the syntactic formation of B's answer.

(142)   A: Is there a chance that she will succeed?
        B: There seems to be.

Recall that in the theory proposed here, the expletive *there* is base-generated as the subject of verbs like *seem* and *tend*, and is interpreted by normal procedures (see pp. 30–31). Thus, the existence of such fragments as (142B) poses no problem in this theory; no complication of the theory is required to explain it along the lines proposed here.

In the transformational theory, however, *there*-insertion structurally displaces an underlying subject NP, which is shifted to the right of *be*. Thus (142B) would have to be derived from a structural source containing the displaced NP. The NP would then have to be either deleted under identity to part of the preceding discourse (Sag 1976) or interpreted as identical to part of the preceding discourse (Wasow 1976, Williams 1977). Only in that way would it be possible to account for the contrast between (142) and (143).

(143)   A: Do you like succotash?
        B: *There seems to be.

In the present theory this contrast follows from the fact that $f = like$ *succotash* is uninterpretable when applied to *there*.

What is unexplained in the transformational theory is why verb phrase ellipsis is subject to the same conditions as pronominalization:

(144) a. John will want to go if Mary wants to.
       b. John will want to if Mary wants to go.

In (144a) *Mary wants to* can be interpreted as "Mary wants to go."
But in (144b) *John will want to* is interpreted as meaning something
other than "John will want to go." Note that in (144b) *John will want
to* precedes and commands *Mary wants to go.* (Recall the discussion
of this notion of precedes and commands in connection with Rule
(20).) When this structural relation is changed, cointerpretation is
possible:

(145) If John wants to, Mary will (also) want to go.

In (145) *John wants to* precedes but does not command *Mary will
(also) want to go,* because the former is contained in a subordinate
clause that excludes the latter. It should also be noted that the
insertion of a heavy pause before *if* in (144b) may "break" the
subordination of the *if*-clause, making cointerpretation possible.

These facts have an explanation in the present theory. Verbal
complement anaphors can be generated in the base by means of
phrase structure rules such as $\overline{VP} \rightarrow to$ (VP). Since the Noncoreference Rule (20) has been reformulated as a condition on the indexing
procedure (p. 32), it can be applied to verbal complement indexing as
well as to noun phrase indexing. This will mean that an anaphor —
pronoun or elliptical VP (*to* $\emptyset$) — cannot be coindexed with a full,
nonanaphoric phrase that the anaphor precedes and commands.
Consequently, (146) will be parallel to (147).

(146) *She$_i$* will try to go if *Mary$_j$* wants to go. $i \neq j$
(147) John will want *to$_f$* if Mary wants *to go$_g$*. $f \neq g$

In both of these examples the anaphors (*she* and *to*) precede and
command the full, nonanaphoric phrases (*Mary* and *to go*). But when
the anaphors precede and command other *anaphors,* nothing prevents
their coindexing.

(148) *She* will try to go if *she* wants to go.
(149) John will want *to* if Mary wants *to.*

As predicted by the hypothesis that such anaphors are freely cointer-
preted except where prohibited by rules of the sentence grammar,

both types of anaphors can be understood as referring to the same things in these examples.

The unification of pronominal and elliptical anaphora achieved in this theory is itself a major consequence, having many interesting implications for linguistics. (See Bresnan, in preparation.)

The second suggestion regarding derivational complexity concerns the relative complexity of passives and actives. If the comprehension of a sentence involves the extraction of its functional interpretation from its surface form, the present theory suggests that the main task in the comprehension of simple sentences is to associate nouns with the functional structures of verbs. Thus in this theory the same task is involved in comprehending an active sentence like (150) as in comprehending a passive sentence like (151).

(150)   The girl hit the boy.
(151)   The boy was hit by the girl.

Specifically, the noun phrases must be assigned their functional interpretation with respect to the verb. In the procedure outlined for the interpretation of passives, indices are assigned to the noun phrases and then substituted into the lexical functional structure in their appropriate positions. In this procedure, we begin with the information displayed in (152) for the active and (153) for the passive.

(152) NP_1 HIT NP_2
        NP_1: *the girl*
        NP_2: *the boy*
(153) $(\exists x)$ $(x$ HIT NP_1 & $x = NP_{by})$
        NP_1: *the boy*
        NP_{by}: *the girl*

Note that the lexical functional structure for the passive (153) is not identical to that for the active (152). In (153) *the girl* is indirectly associated with the logical subject of *hit*. Therefore, recognizing that *the girl* indeed is the logical subject of *hit* might take longer in (151) than in (150).

However, it is plausible to suppose that this recognition could be facilitated by additional information about the logical subject of a verb (the x argument) or the logical object (the y argument). For example, if we know that the logical subject of *eat* must be animate, that hot dogs are inanimate, and that girls are animate, we might more rapidly recognize that *the girl* is the logical subject of *eat* in (154); consider (155):

(154)   The hot dog was eaten by the girl.
(155) $(\exists x)\ (x\ \text{EAT NP}_1\ \&\ x = \text{NP}_{by})$

ANIMATE
NP$_1$: *the hot dog*
NP$_{by}$: *the girl*

These remarks may contribute to an understanding of experimental results like those of Slobin (1966b). Using a picture-verification test with six- to seven-year-old children, Slobin found a complexity difference between passives and actives, but only when the passives were "reversible." A reversible passive is one whose noun phrases can be sensibly interchanged (*The girl was hit by the boy, The boy was hit by the girl*); an example of a nonreversible passive would be *The kite was flown by the girl*. Nonreversible passives were found *not* to be more complex than their corresponding actives.

But more recently, Forster and Olbrei (1973) have found significant differences between responses to actives and passives by measuring decision latencies (how quickly subjects decided whether the example was "an intelligible grammatical sentence") and by measuring the mean number of lexical items correctly identified during their "rapid serial visual presentation" procedure. The actives were faster or less difficult than the passives. Moreover, Forster and Olbrei found only weak or insignificant reversibility effects in their experiments, and the reversibility effect was independent of the syntactic effect (passive vs. active). Forster (1976) comments on Slobin (1966b) as follows: "From my point of view, the problem with this experiment is that it used a picture verification technique. That is, after seeing the sentence, the subject is shown a picture, and must say whether the sentence is a true description of the picture. Apparently there are some grounds for doubting that this procedure taps on-line sentence processing."

If Forster's experimental procedures do tap "on-line sentence processing," then they show that the automatic grammatical processing of passives must be more complex than that of actives. It is this automatic grammatical processing that provides us with the information in (152) and (153): this includes finding the lexical functional structure of the verb in its syntactic context and identifying the grammatical functions of the phrases in the sentence. For a simple active transitive sentence of the form NP V NP, the first NP will be NP_1 and the second NP will be NP_2. For a passive sentence of the form NP *be* V-*ed by* NP, the first NP will be NP_1 and the second NP may or may not be NP_{by}: *The boy was hit by the fence, The books were put by the magazines.* The identification of the grammatical function of the *by*-phrase in passives is inherently complicated by the fact that the *by*-phrase is a prepositional phrase. But once this automatic grammatical processing has done its work, knowledge can enter into the process of comprehension, in the way suggested here.

Forster's work thus supports the assumption that there is a psychological analogue to the rules of grammar that provide the structural and functional information needed for semantic interpretation. The same is shown by the experiments reported in Chapter 3. It must be assumed that this "mental parser" operates extremely rapidly, providing the minimal information that is needed in the larger tasks of understanding and using language.

The realization problem The theory of grammar outlined in this chapter can be explicitly realized in various psychologically interesting models of language production and comprehension. I will informally illustrate here just one possible realization mapping, to make good my claim to have a realizable transformational grammar. The general psychological model I will use is one like that described in Chapter 3.

The phrase structure rules of the grammar, which define the basic structural patterns of a language, can be realized in a syntactic pattern-recognition system known as a transition network system, illustrated in Figure 1.10. As described in Chapter 3, a transition network system accepts a sentence by scanning the words in the sentence one by one and making appropriate transitions which define a path through the network. Such systems employ a memory (a pushdown store) which keeps track of the states left and returned to. Any sentence that can be generated by the phrase structure rules can be recognized by a transition network system.

Corresponding to each phrase structure rule in Figure 1.10 is an equivalent transition network diagram, consisting of a set of states connected by arcs. Four types of arc are shown. The CAT arcs permit a transition to be made if the word scanned belongs to the

PHRASE STRUCTURE RULES   TRANSITION NETWORKS

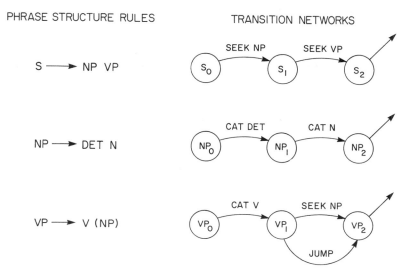

Figure 1.10

lexical category specified on the arc; if it does, the input string is advanced one word. The JUMP arcs permit a transition to be made without advancing the input string; they allow partially similar networks to be merged, just as partially similar phrase structure rules can be collapsed with the parenthesis notation. The unlabeled arcs leaving one state but not entering another designate the "accepting states." The SEEK arcs permit a transition to be made if a phrase of the type sought has been accepted; if one has, the input string is advanced to the next word after that phrase. In effect, a SEEK arc calls for a subcomputation involving another network.

The sentence *The girl hit the boy* can be accepted by the transition network system represented in Figure 1.10 by starting in state S_0, switching to state NP_0, and testing the first word *the* to see whether it belongs to the category Det(erminer). Next, since *the* is a Det, a transition is made to state NP_1, and the second word *girl* is scanned and tested. Then, since *girl* is a N(oun), a transition is made to state NP_2, which is an accepting state for a noun phrase. Since a noun phrase *the girl* has been found, the transition can be made from state S_0 to state S_1, the scanner advances to the next word in the sentence, and the process continues in the obvious way.

The sequence of transitions made in accepting a sentence determines a well-formed labeled bracketing of the sentence. The initial states of each network — state S_0, state NP_0, state VP_0 — correspond to left brackets [s, [np, [vp, and the accepting states — state S_2, state NP_2, state VP_2 — correspond to right brackets s], np], vp]. A CAT transition corresponds to the labeling of lexical categories; for example, when *girl* satisfies CAT N, it can be bracketed [n *girl* n]. Since each well-formed labeled bracketing is equivalent to a surface structure (or surface phrase-marker (Peters and Ritchie 1973)), we can speak of the transition network system as "accepting surface structures." This means that a sentence that has a certain labeled bracketing is accepted by a sequence of transitions that corresponds to that bracketing.

The transition network system just described can be augmented with a set of operations that assign grammatical functions to the phrases being parsed. This is illustrated (partially) in Figure 1.11. The ASSIGN and ASSEMBLE operations of Figure 1.11 identify and combine the functional structure of a verb with its subjects, objects, and complements in the sentence. The function assignments and operations make use of a working memory for functional information.

In recognizing the sentence *The girl hit the boy,* as the transition is made from state S_0 to state S_1 the information that *the girl* is the grammatical subject, NP_1: *the girl,* is placed in the working memory. Next, as the transition is made from state VP_0 to state VP_1 in

AUGMENTED TRANSITION NETWORKS

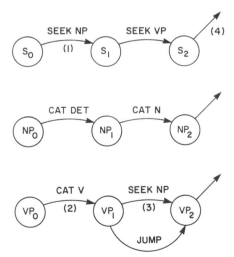

FUNCTION ASSIGNMENTS
and OPERATIONS

1. ASSIGN NP_1 (Subject) to current phrase

2. ASSIGN Functional Structure (Relation) to current word

3. ASSIGN NP_2 (Object) to current phrase

4. ASSEMBLE Clause

Figure 1.11

recognizing *hit,* the information NP_1 HIT NP_2 is added to the working memory. (This information is derived from the lexicon.) Then, when the transition is made from state VP_1 to state VP_2 in recognizing *the boy,* the information that *the boy* is the grammatical object, NP_2: *the boy,* comes in. When the entire sentence is accepted in state S_2, the stored functional information can be assembled, or combined. Thus, as the transitions are made through the networks, a functional analysis is built up in the working memory. The functional analysis need not resemble the surface structure accepted, even in the order of constituents.

The augmented transition network (ATN) just described is easily extendible to complex sentences with verbal complements. Figure 1.12 shows the additions that correspond to the phrase structure rules, VP → V (NP) ($\overline{VP}$) and $\overline{VP}$ → *to* VP. The new arc-label, WORD *to,* connecting state $\overline{VP}_0$ to state $\overline{VP}_1$ recognizes the infinitival marker *to.* The ATN shown in Figure 1.12 recognizes sentences like *The girl tried to hit the boy,* automatically extracting the structural and functional information needed for their interpretation, as represented in (156).

(156) $[_S[_{NP}[_{Det}$ the $_{Det}][_N$ girl $_N]_{NP}][_{VP}[_V$ tried $_V][_{\overline{VP}}$ to
        $[_{VP}[_V$ hit $_V][_{NP}[_{Det}$ the $_{Det}][_N$ boy $_N]_{NP}]_{VP}]_{\overline{VP}}]_{VP}]_S]$

$$
\text{Clause:} \begin{bmatrix} NP_1\text{: }\textit{the girl} \\ \text{Relation: } NP_1 \text{ TRY } ((NP_1)VP) \\ (\ )VP\text{: } \begin{bmatrix} \text{Relation: } NP_1 \text{ HIT } NP_2 \\ NP_2\text{: }\textit{the boy} \end{bmatrix} \end{bmatrix}
$$

In these simplified illustrations, I have not applied the indexing procedure given on pages 24–30, but have merely shown how an ATN can extract the minimal functional information needed for the interpretation of the sentence.

Having seen how the phrase-structural, lexical, and functional components of the grammar can correspond to separate components of an ATN system, let us now consider the transformational component of the grammar, represented by Question Movement. Since the grammar is being realized within a model of sentence comprehension, the assumption is that Question Movement applies in reverse to surface structures in which the interrogative phrase occurs in its displaced position outside of the clause, as in (157).

(157)   *Which boy* did the girl try to hit____?

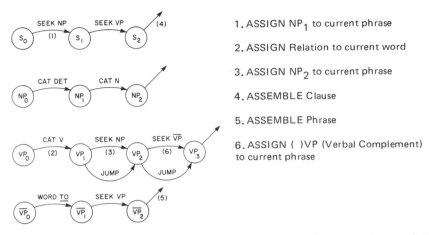

1. ASSIGN NP_1 to current phrase

2. ASSIGN Relation to current word

3. ASSIGN NP_2 to current phrase

4. ASSEMBLE Clause

5. ASSEMBLE Phrase

6. ASSIGN ( )VP (Verbal Complement) to current phrase

Figure 1.12 Augmented Transition Network system incorporating verbal complement networks

In order to generate surface structures like (157), phrase structure rules must be provided for the displaced phrase and for the empty position in the clause from which it is displaced. One set of rules for doing this is (158). (*Aux*, here and in Figure 1.13, stands for any inverted auxiliary. A detailed analysis of the English auxiliary verbs is not required for the purposes of this illustration.)

(158) $\bar{S} \rightarrow$ (NP Aux) S   (phase structure rule for the displaced noun phrase)

$NP \rightarrow \emptyset$ (phrase structure rule for the empty noun phrase position)

The rule $NP \rightarrow \emptyset$ indicates that the nonterminal symbol, NP, may be left dominating no terminal string. (Alternatively, the rule could be formulated with a designated terminal symbol such as Δ: $NP \rightarrow \Delta$.)

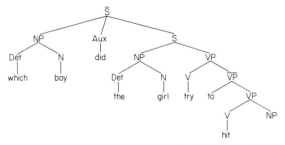

Figure 1.13 Surface structure of *Which boy did the girl try to hit?*

By adding the rules in (158) to the other phrase structure rules, the surface structures shown in Figures 1.13 and 1.14 can be generated.

By themselves, these phrase structure rules will overgenerate, producing many ill-formed strings in which too many or too few empty positions occur. If there are too few empty positions, as in (159) —

(159)   *Which boy did the girl try to hit the table?

— the inverse Question Movement transformation will not be able to apply, and the displaced interrogative phrase *which boy* will not receive a functional interpretation. If there are too many empty positions, as in (160) —

(160)   *Which girl hit [∅]

— the transitive verb *hit* will not receive the necessary functional interpretation. Such cases can be accounted for simply by assuming that every sentence must have a complete and coherent functional interpretation assigned by the rules of the grammar.

As already observed (p. 40), the inverse rule of Question Movement is a structure-dependent operation, for in the displaced position the interrogative phrase has no grammatical function assigned to it. This suggests that in comprehending a sentence we need to remember the displaced phrase so that we can refer to it when we come to the empty position in the sentence from which it is displaced. ATN parsing systems, as described in Woods (1973) and in Chapter 3, have a special HOLD facility which does just this. A displaced phrase is held, without an assigned grammatical function, in a temporary memory cell until an empty position is encountered and the phrase

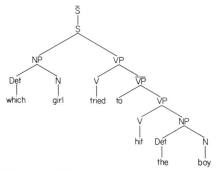

Figure 1.14 Surface structure of *Which girl tried to hit the boy?*

can be retrieved, permitting a transition to be made. Thus, corresponding to the phrase structure rules (158) are the transition networks diagrammed in Figure 1.15. The HOLD and RETRIEVE HOLD operations correspond to the Question Movement transformation. Like Question Movement, they are structure-dependent operations which make no reference to functional information. Apart from the surface structure and the functional interpretation, an ATN system does not distinguish a level of deep syntactic structure in the usual sense — but it does make use of a level of "remembered" syntactic structure in the HOLD facility. The fundamental structure-dependent property of transformations corresponds to this capability to remember syntactic structure.

With these additions, an ATN will accept the sentence *Which boy did the girl try to hit?* assigning to it the structural and functional information shown in (161), as the reader can easily verify.

(161) $[_{\bar{S}}[_{NP}[_{Det}$ which $_{Det}][_{N}$ boy $_{N}]_{NP}][_{Aux}$ did $_{Aux}][_{S}[_{NP}[_{Det}$ the $_{Det}]$
       $[_{N}$ girl $_{N}]_{NP}][_{VP}[_{V}$ try $_{V}][_{\overline{VP}}$to $[_{VP}[_{V}$ hit $_{V}][_{NP}$ $_{NP}]_{VP}]$ $_{\overline{VP}}]$ $_{VP}]$ $_{S}]_{\bar{S}}]$

$$\text{Clause:} \begin{bmatrix} \text{NP}_1\text{: } \textit{the girl} \\ \text{Relation: NP}_1 \text{ TRY } (\,(\text{NP}_1)\text{VP}) \\ (\,)\text{VP:} \begin{bmatrix} \text{Relation: NP}_1 \text{ HIT NP}_2 \\ \text{NP}_2\text{: } \textit{which boy} \end{bmatrix} \end{bmatrix}$$

Notice that after the verb *hit* is recognized, an NP is sought. There is no NP following *hit* in the sentence *Which boy did the girl try to hit?* Nevertheless, a transition through the NP network diagrammed in Figure 1.15 can be made by retrieving the stored NP *which boy* from the HOLD cell; the transition goes directly from state NP_0 to state

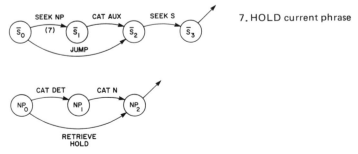

7. HOLD current phrase

Figure 1.15 Augmented Transition Networks corresponding to phrase structure rule (158) and illustrating HOLD facility

NP$_2$. This is why the accepted surface structure in (161) contains the labeled brackets [$_{NP}$ $_{NP}$] after *hit*.

Labeled brackets that surround no terminal string correspond to what Chomsky (1977) calls a "trace" and Bresnan (1976b, p. 389) calls a "structural residue." (Chomsky's conception of traces is far broader than that adopted here because he assumes that syntactic transformations that leave traces are involved in the derivation of passives and other constructions that are derived nontransformationally in the present theory.) The same labeled brackets provide precisely the structural information needed to explain the phonological perturbations produced by Question Movement and similar transformations (Selkirk, forthcoming). The same labeled brackets correspond to what Wanner and Maratsos refer to as "the gap" in Chapter 3. Thus the computational, syntactic, phonological, and psychological analyses converge at this point.

The experiments reported by Wanner and Maratsos indicate an increase in memory load or processing load during the comprehension of sentences containing gaps. The increase is quite specifically located in what they call the "critical region" of a sentence, the region lying between a "displaced" relative pronoun and the gap. When clauses interrupted by a memory task in the critical region are compared with clauses interrupted outside of the critical region, a significant difference in error scores emerges. The development of more refined measures of processing load will surely contribute to a more exact understanding of how grammatical information is employed in sentence processing.

In closing this discussion, I wish to reemphasize that the correspondences I have informally outlined are intended to be only illustrative of the possibilities for research on the grammatical realization problem. The conception of transformational grammar presented in this chapter is realizable in many different models of language use. In itself, it is intended to be neutral with respect to "top–down" or "bottom–up" parsing systems, and to production or perception models. Indeed, the realization outlined here suggests one respect in which ATN systems may model linguistic comprehension inadequately: in recognizing sentences, transition network systems appear to make insufficient use of lexical information.[8]

---

[8] This possible inadequacy of ATN systems as psychological models of language processing was pointed out by George Miller in discussions of the MIT Workshop on Language and Cognition.

Referring to Figure 1.12, we can see that the path that will be taken through the verb networks is completely independent of the lexical information about verbs that is extracted along the way. Thus, the verb categorized between state VP_0 and state VP_1 could be *sleep, hit, tend,* or *compel.* Each verb can appear in specific syntactic contexts of which the language user surely has knowledge; yet the syntactic parser continues, blind to this information, making transitions that are determined only by the state it is in and the category of the word it is scanning. The result is that in recognizing complex sentences many unnecessary blind alleys can be taken, requiring extensive backing up, as described in Chapter 3. Conceivably this could be the way we actually recognize sentences: but perhaps it is not.

One way to reduce syntactic nondeterminacy within an ATN system would be to build the relevant lexical information directly into the syntax. For example, a separate verb network diagram could be provided for each possible type of syntactic context. This technique is employed in Chapter 3, Figure 3.4, where separate states have been provided for intransitive verbs (V_I), simple verbs (V_S), and transitive verbs taking infinitival complements (V_T). The approach is equivalent grammatically to the use of phrase structure rules to describe verbal subcategorization, as in Chomsky (1957); in *Aspects* (1965, pp. 79–127) Chomsky criticized and abandoned this use of phrase structure rules in transformational grammar. A different solution to this problem has been developed by Ronald Kaplan (Kaplan 1977), and of course other solutions are possible outside of the ATN framework (for example, that of Marcus 1976).

I will leave the discussion of the realization problem at this point. It is clearly a problem on which joint research in theoretical linguistics, artificial intelligence, and experimental psychology should be very fruitful.

Conclusion

A realistic grammar should be psychologically real in the broad sense: it should contribute to the explanation of linguistic behavior and to our larger understanding of the human faculty of language. These broadly psychological and philosophical aims have inspired all work in transformational grammar since Chomsky first articulated his "realist" conception of linguistic theory. Yet the field of transformational grammar has undergone many changes and divisions, proliferating in divergent theories of grammar. How can we choose among these various theories? From a broad philosophical perspective, it is not necessary to do so, any more than it is necessary to choose among various theories of geometry, all of which contribute to our understanding of space and form and perhaps, in some way, even to the explanation of human behavior. But from a scientific perspective — if our goal is to explain human spatial perception, for example — we must find or construct the best theory.

The difficulty in linguistics is that we can characterize our knowledge of language in too many ways. What has been called the grammatical characterization problem — the problem of representing the language user's knowledge of language — is not very well defined. Therefore, it does not seem reasonable to argue that the grammatical characterization problem should be solved in advance of what has been called the grammatical realization problem: it is not clear that we will ever come to a solution to the grammatical characterization problem as it has been defined in the past.

But the grammatical realization problem can clarify and delimit the grammatical characterization problem. We can narrow the class of possible theoretical solutions by subjecting them to experimental psychological investigation as well as to linguistic investigation. Within the program of research proposed here, joint work by linguists, computer scientists, and psychologists could lead to a deeper scientific understanding of the role of language in cognition.

2 Semantic Relations among Words

GEORGE A. MILLER

Knowing a vocabulary is a precondition for speaking and understanding a language; the general concern of this chapter is what a person learns when he learns a vocabulary. By "vocabulary" is meant a collection of lexical units in some natural language. What "lexical units" are is one of the questions that must be considered here, but for expository convenience they can be called "words," if it is recognized that the term is not well defined.

The Mental Lexicon

Someone who has learned a vocabulary has access to whatever he has learned about any given word, and that knowledge is available to support both speaking and listening to speech. The rapidity of access during ordinary speech is not well understood, but for a person who knows a language well the *sound* of a word is sufficient for immediate retrieval (or reconstruction) of information associated with that phonological shape.

Phonological access enables a listener to understand what he hears spoken. But how is a speaker able to gain access to a word he may want to utter, a word whose phonological shape remains as yet unrealized? It is generally assumed that the process is reversible: it is possible to go from other knowledge to the sound as well as from the sound to other knowledge. That is to say, there must be some second mode of access, by way of the *meaning* of a word, that enables a speaker to find words to express his ideas and intentions and so to realize them acoustically. Although hypotheses about alternative mechanisms for conceptual access have been debated extensively, the need for something more than phonological access seems beyond dispute. A central concern of this chapter is the conceptual organization a person develops as he learns a vocabulary; a characterization of this conceptual organization adequate for the purposes of cognitive psychology should also be an adequate linguistic characterization of the lexical component of language.

Preparation of this manuscript was supported in part by Grant No. GM21796 from the Public Health Services to The Rockefeller University. Special acknowledgment is gratefully made for the contributions of Ray Jackendoff, who collaborated in writing the section on Sentential Concepts, and of Philip N. Johnson-Laird, with whom many of the ideas here presented were jointly conceived.

The traditional method of organizing a linguistic account of a lexicon is exhaustive and alphabetical; theoretical considerations are predominantly diachronic, supplemented by practical wisdom about criteria for separate entries and ways to phrase definitions. Although the extensive experience and rigorous scholarship of lexicographers have provided an invaluable collection of linguistic facts, serious formulations of general theories based on those facts have only recently been undertaken—they might be dated from the work of Lyons (1963) and Katz and Fodor (1963). (The state of the art prior to that time is summarized in Ullmann 1962.) Theories of the synchronic organization of lexical knowledge were undoubtedly inhibited by the inevitable exceptions to almost every generalization; lexical information is characteristically information that a person must learn by rote. Psychologists know, however, that even rote learning is subject to lawful principles and that cognitive economy depends on the intelligible organization of what is learned.

Conventional dictionaries indicate some of the kinds of information associated with a word: spelling, pronunciation, etymology, syntactic category, and inflected forms; phrases suggesting different senses, sentences illustrating use, comments on usage of nearly synonymous words, and pictures or tables where appropriate. From definitional phrases it is often possible to trace extended conceptual relations to other words (as in a thesaurus) and to infer the need for general information of a type more appropriate to an encyclopedia than to a dictionary. A person who masters a vocabulary in some language has to learn much of this information about every word. It will be convenient to speak of this word knowledge as his "mental lexicon."

In order to explore how such diverse information might be integrated and represented in the memories of language users, it is necessary to consider what use is made of it. The mental lexicon is needed most immediately to produce and understand sentences, so lexical information must be represented in a manner compatible with what people know about the syntax and semantics of sentences in their language. Sometimes even this larger sentential context is insufficient; for a broader view of how lexical information is used it would be necessary to consider the texts and discourses into which sentences can enter. At this level one begins to glimpse processes of real psychological interest—thoughts, memories, percepts, desires, feelings, intentions—as these are expressed in everyday speech.

It is clear, therefore, that a person's word knowledge must be organized in a manner compatible with a wide variety of linguistic and psychological demands. The organization of lexical memory must be sufficiently flexible to enable it to contribute to phonological, syntactic, inferential, metaphoric, and pragmatic processes.

It is generally assumed that much—perhaps the most important part—of the mental lexicon is a passive store available for use by the more active components of the information processing systems involved in language use. Although new words can be acquired and seldom-used words forgotten, for most purposes the mental lexicon is thought of as a fixed data base. It cannot be totally passive, however. Consider, for example, the names of the integers; if these are regarded as words stored in the mental lexicon, the lexicon would be infinitely large and therefore take infinitely long to acquire. It seems more reasonable to regard the names of integers as words that are not stored passively in the mental lexicon, but that can be generated by rule as needed. Moreover, there are constructions like *the Boston-to-Chicago flight,* where *Boston-to-Chicago* has all the integrity of any other word (Keyser and Postal 1976). Since the number of such pairs that a person can form is limited only by the number of place names he knows, there are obviously too many to be learned individually.

Once the possibility of generative processes in the mental lexicon is admitted, it becomes unclear how much theoretical use to make of them. As far as possible, therefore, the present discussion will adopt what seems to be the conservative strategy; consideration will be limited to that part of the lexicon that can most plausibly be regarded as innocent of active operations that can construe new interpretations, decompose complex words, combine words into phrases, or deduce consequences. Insofar as such mental operations do occur, it will be assumed that they are the result of active information processing controlled by systems outside the lexicon proper.

In order to achieve the necessary complexity and flexibility in a passive memory, it would be necessary to store many kinds of information with each word. A summary of all the kinds of information a person must have about a word in order to produce and understand it appropriately would be formidable. Even a minimal list must include at least the following kinds:

A.   Pronunciation (and spelling for written languages)
    (i)   Phonology (including stress features)
    (ii) Morphology (including inflected and derivative forms)

B. Syntactic categorization
    (i)   Major category (noun, verb, adverb, preposition, . . .)
    (ii) Subcategorization (syntactic contexts)
C. Meaning
    (i)   Definition (concept expressed; relation to other concepts)
    (ii) Selectional restrictions (semantic contexts)
D. Pragmatic constraints
    (i)   Situation (relation to general knowledge)
    (ii) Rhetoric (relation to discourse contexts)

The central concern of this chapter is with C, the characterization of the meanings or concepts that words can express and their relations to the meanings expressed by other words. It will prove impossible to ignore other types of information, however, because decisions about how to characterize a word's meaning must take into account its use in grammatical sentences (B), and its use in expressing certain sentential concepts in particular situations (D). And since some of the strongest evidence for semantic relations between words is given by their phonological and morphological similarities, even A cannot be ignored.

At the present time it is D, the types of discourse in which a word is normally used, that is least well understood. Ignorance on this score is unfortunate, not merely because this kind of information is of the most direct psychological interest, but also because an adequate characterization of it would reflect the nature of the cognitive processes that control and exploit linguistic communication—processes that provide the most general context in which to analyze uses and meanings of words. Pragmatic questions can be answered only on the basis of information about the speaker and hearer, about their shared information, about the situation in which they are acting, about the normal course of events in such situations, and about plausible alternative states of affairs—information that runs well beyond what anyone would propose to include in a grammar or dictionary. The density and complexity of these pragmatic problems are impressive and of great psychological importance.

The richness of these boundary conditions for language use can go far to explain the difficulties psychologists encounter in subjecting this kind of cognitive activity to experimental test. An experiment is ordinarily designed to explore some limited aspect of language use—usually by the experimenter's choice of particular words or syntactic constructions—and, ceteris paribus, none of the rest of this complex system is assumed to affect the performance under investigation. One hopes that this assumption is justified, at least in the laboratory, but when apparently similar experiments yield contradictory results one suspects it is not.

The need for pragmatic theories is obvious. Nevertheless this chapter does not try to meet that need. Although it is necessary to keep constantly in mind that a sentence can be used for different purposes and with different meanings in different situations, it is a legitimate psychological question to ask how people form and interpret the concepts that are literally expressed by the sentences they utter. The answer cannot provide a complete account of all that a psychologist would like to know about language use and acquisition, but it seems a necessary step toward such an account.

The discussion will begin, therefore, with a more detailed consideration of the psychology of sentences; for that, the first requirement is a notation in which to express hypotheses about the literal meanings of sentences.

Sentential Concepts

The psychological entities of immediate concern will be called sentential concepts. Presumably the semantic component of a grammar can relate a sentential concept to a sentence (or set of sentences) that expresses it, although the concept need not be expressed as a sentence. It would be desirable if, to a certain extent, semantic relations could parallel the syntactic relations among sentence constituents. The concern of this section, however, is to introduce a notation to represent the results of psychological analyses of sentential concepts; representing the results of syntactic analysis in this notation will for the moment be a secondary concern. The notation will be as general as possible—a mere outline of a more serious notation that might grow from further studies of sentential concepts.

Some notational conventions   Assume a set A of assignable pointers, $x, y, z, \ldots$ An assigned pointer will have the logical status of a constant or a bound variable, although logical quantification will be deliberately omitted from the notation. It will be assumed that in the use of natural language, values are assigned to pointers by the pragmatic component of the theory (often on the basis of information not expressed in the immediate phrase or sentence). How people construct and use a list of assigned pointers to define the context of discourse is one of several critically important questions for pragmatic theory.

Little of a general nature will be said about what assignable pointers can point to. The pointers are available as required for assignment to various mental contents—percepts, concepts, images, feelings, dispositions to respond, and so forth. Among their values are sentential concepts and various other kinds of concepts that form constituents of sentential concepts. A theory of assignable pointers would, of course, specify such important matters as which mental contents count as which kinds of concepts, how to distinguish a pointer to a particular entity from a pointer to all (or some) entities of that type, when to assign a new pointer and when to stay with a pointer already assigned, and so on. In fact, it is difficult to develop a notation that expresses such matters unambiguously. The hope is that the notation adopted here is neutral to the eventual choice of a psychologically adequate theory of assignable pointers.

Call the set of sentential concepts Σ, and let s, s', s'', . . . be individual members of this set. Critical features of the notation are based on two assumptions. First, sentential concepts remain psychologically invariant under combination; this corresponds more or less to the logician's criterion of compositionality of senses. Second, sentential concepts can be analyzed into concepts resembling functions and their arguments. Therefore, if x, y, z, . . . are assignable pointers and if P, Q, R, . . . are members of the set of predicative concepts Π, then, given parentheses to indicate the domains of functions, sentential concepts can be represented by such expressions as P (x), Q (x, y), NOT (R (z)), and so on.

A number of important types of values for assignable pointers can appear as the arguments of predicative concepts. One type might be called nominal concepts, the kind typically represented by such noun phrases as *the table, Fred, you, fifty million Frenchmen, some sand,* and so forth. It is not necessary that there actually be objects in the world for a nominal concept to identify; *the present king of France* and *many unicorns* express perfectly legitimate nominal concepts that happen not to designate real objects.

A second kind of argument to a predicative concept is a locational concept, which is a concept of a place as distinct from an object. Such concepts are expressed by phrases like *here, there, downstairs, over the hill, along the road.* An important subclass of locational concepts are directions, expressed by such phrases as *upward, away, toward Henry, into the dungeon.*

Third, sentential concepts themselves can serve as arguments to predicative concepts, as reflected in the embedding of sentences in examples like *That the earth is round never bothered Galileo* and *Martha believes that peanut butter is good for you.*

A great variety of predicative concepts is required. To start with, they can be classified in terms of the number of arguments they take. A predicate taking one argument is thought of as a property (or attribute) of that argument; a predicate taking two or more arguments can be thought of as a relation among those arguments. If the set of properties Π_p and the set of two-place relations Π_r are partitioned out of Π, rules of concept formation can be written as

If $x \in A$ and $P \in \Pi_p$, then $P(x) \in \Sigma$.
If $x, y \in A$ and $P \in \Pi_r$, then $P(x, y) \in \Sigma$.

(Similar rules can be formulated for relations with more than two arguments.) $P(x)$ is the form of the sentential concept expressed by such sentences as *This cheese stinks, Thirty dogs died, My foot hurts*; $P(x, y)$ is the form of the sentential concept expressed by such sentences as *Sylvia ate your apple, Some railroads go through Siberia, Sincerity impresses Sam.* If no pointer is assigned to one of the arguments of a relational predicate, as in such short passives as *Your apple was eaten,* the assumed existence of the unassigned argument can be represented by the existential logical quantifier, $(\exists x) P(x, A)$, where A is assigned and x is not. (See also discussion of the active–passive relation in Chapter 1.)

Many predicate concepts—which might be called predicative operators—take sentential concepts as their arguments; they can operate on a sentential concept to yield another sentential concept. An obvious example is negation: NOT (s) is a sentential concept formed by applying the operator NOT to the sentential concept s; if s is true, then NOT (s) is false. A more complex example might be some kind of tense operator that can be applied to a temporally indefinite sentential concept to yield another sentential concept that characterizes a state of affairs at some moment or throughout some period of time. So if Π_o is the set of predicative operators, such rules can be added as

If $s \in \Sigma$ and $P \in \Pi_o$, then $P(s) \in \Sigma$.

There are other kinds of operators as well. If Ω is the set of nominal concepts, there is a class of nominal operators N_o that maps members of Ω into other members of Ω. Phrases such as *the father of, a part of, a member of,* and *three groups of* express nominal operators. Parallel to the rule for Π_o, then, would be the rule:

If $O \in \Omega$ and $N \in N_o$, then $N(O) \in \Omega$.

For example, if John is Mary's father, then FATHER *(Mary)* = *John* maps one nominal concept onto another.

Similarly, many prepositions of English express locational operators, mapping nominal concepts into locational concepts, as in *beside the house, across the street, up the chimney.* If Λ is the set of locational concepts and Λ_o is the set of locational operators, the rule would be

If $O \in \Omega$ and $L \in \Lambda_o$, then $L(O) \in \Lambda$.

Compound predicates Operators provide various ways to combine predicates. For example, if $P \in \Pi_o$ and $Q \in \Pi_p$, then $P(Q(x))$ can be a sentential concept built from a combination of these two predicates. Procedurally, this notation seems to represent a routine to compute the sentential concept $s = Q(x)$ first, then to use the result to compute $P(s)$. It will be convenient to introduce a different kind of predicative operator, which maps predicative concepts into predicative concepts. For example, if $P, Q \in \Pi$, and P is an operator of this new sort, then $(P(Q))$ may be a new predicative concept. Procedurally, $(P(Q))(x)$ is a sentential concept that represents a routine to compute a new predicate first and then to apply that new predicate to an argument x. (Important conventions for representing the arguments of Q as arguments of the compound predicate $(P(Q))$ will not be introduced here, in order to avoid a detour from the central concern.)

The difference between sentential concepts of the forms $P(Q(x))$ and $(P(Q))(x)$ can be illustrated in terms of adverbs:

$P(T(x))$:   John probably travels.
$(R(T))(x)$:   John travels rapidly.

The predicative concepts P, T, and R represent the senses of *probably, travels,* and *rapidly,* respectively, and x points to John. "It is probable that John travels" and "It is probably the case that John travels'' are satisfactory paraphrases of the first sentence (that is, *probably* is a sentence modifier), but ''It is rapid (or it is rapidly the case) that John travels'' is not a satisfactory paraphrase of the second sentence (*rapidly* is a predicate modifier). Because it should be possible to express such distinctions in any satisfactory notation, both ways to combine predicates must be provided.

Certain prepositional phrases—as in *John hit the nail with a hammer*; *John came with his mother*; *John traveled by boat*—are also predicate modifiers. Since the prepositional phrase is decomposable into a preposition and a noun phrase and the noun phrase expresses a nominal concept, it could be claimed that the preposition expresses an operator that maps a nominal concept plus a predicative concept into a new predicative concept, which could be represented with a notation like

(W (z, H)) (x, y):   John hit the nail with a hammer.

Here the operator W represents the sense of the preposition *with*, z is the sense of its syntactic object, and H (x, y) represents the sense of x *hit* y.

Some theoretical issues   To illustrate issues that the notation does *not* prejudge, consider the concepts represented by the sentence *The book is on the table*. One way to formulate this is as a relation, ON, that holds between two objects B (the book) and T (the table): ON (B, T). Alternatively, it might be argued that ON is a locational operator, and that there is a general predicate, LOC, which asserts the relation of an object to the location it occupies: LOC $(B, ON (T))$. A third possibility is that *is on the table* should correspond to a predicative concept taking *the book* as its argument, in which case LOC must be treated as an operator mapping locational concepts into predicative concepts: (LOC $(ON (T))$) (B), which can be related to the second representation by the abstraction operator: (LOC $(ON (y))$) $=$ λx (LOC $(x, ON (y))$).

The third, most complex, formulation has the virtue of a closer resemblance to the conventional syntactic organization into a subject and a predicate, the latter decomposing into a verb and a prepositional phrase. If this approach is adopted, however, the sentential concept underlying *John fed the cat* should be treated not as FEED (J, C) but as (FEED (C)) (J), where the verb *feed* expresses, not a relation, but an operator mapping nominal concepts into predicative concepts: (FEED (y)) $= \lambda x$ (FEED (x, y)). Since the notation admits any of the above possibilities, deciding among them is a theoretical, not a notational issue. (The decision would, of course, be related to the syntactic question of whether the Verb Phrase is a valid grammatical constituent.)

Another example of a theoretical issue is the question of how to decompose nominal concepts into their deictic and their descriptive parts. For example, the expressions *the yellow cat* and *a yellow cat* differ in their deictic parts, in what claims they make about the existence and uniqueness of some individual; *the yellow cat* and *the red house* make similar claims of existence and uniqueness but differ in the description of the individual so picked out. As logical calculi are normally used to represent the results of semantic analysis, the descriptive parts are treated as predicative concepts; for example, *A yellow cat is mewing* might be taken to express a sentential concept of the logical form, $(\exists x)$ [M (x) & Y(x) & C (x)], where M, Y, and C are the predicative concepts expressed by the verb phrases *is mewing, is yellow,* and *is a cat,* respectively, and x is an assignable pointer. The deictic part of the phrase *a yellow cat* (the indefinite article) is represented by an existential quantifier, which is then followed by three occurrences of the variable x. The descriptive parts of the phrase, namely *yellow* and *cat,* have been exported from the argument of the predicate M and are represented as separate, independent sentential concepts conjoined to the main predication M (x).

The present notation tries to provide an alternative representation. Suppose that nouns express not predicative concepts but operators mapping pointers into nominal concepts—that is, they are nominal operators. Then the deictic part of a noun phrase can be treated as the argument of such an operator and the phrases *a cat* and *the cat* may be conceived of as expressing the nominal concept (not the sentential concept) C (x), where the assignment of x to *a* value or *the* value is a deictic problem to be resolved by the pragmatic component. On the basis of syntactic parallels between adjectives and adverbs, it might be proposed that adjectives are operators that map nominal operators into new nominal operators: *a yellow cat* expresses the nominal concept (Y (C)) (x). (Notice the structural similarity of this nominal concept to the sentential concept developed earlier for *John runs rapidly*.) Then *A yellow cat is mewing* will express some such sentential concept as M ((Y (C)) (x)), where the choice of the definite or indefinite article is determined by the discourse and situational context in which the deictic pointer x is to be assigned a value.

Again, the notation does not prejudge which of these representations is preferable. The issue must be decided on theoretical grounds: Which representation makes it possible to characterize the full range of meanings of English sentences? Which representation can be related to the syntax of English (and of other languages) in a general explanatory way? Which representation makes interesting claims about human linguistic and conceptual processing?

To illustrate the kinds of consideration that should influence a choice of one conceptual representation over another, note that in the preceding example it was necessary to draw a distinction contextually between a sentential and a nominal concept; C (x) could have been understood either way. And both interpretations are needed. If, say, the deictic part x has been assigned to *Tabby* (if x is a constant), C (x) could represent the sentential concept expressed by *Tabby is a cat*. Since one purpose of a conceptual notation would be to represent different interpretations of the same phrase or sentence, it is important that the conceptual notation be unambiguous. One possible solution in this case would be to assume that notations like C (x) are always sentential concepts and to introduce a nominalization operator, nom, that has the effect of converting sentential concepts into nominal concepts: the noun phrase *a cat* could then express the nominal concept nom C (x). The relation between nom C and C might be defined by means of a relation ISA expressing class membership or inclusion: C (x) = ISA (x, nom C).

On the other hand, advantage might be taken of the fact that a person's lexical information about *cat* includes the fact that it is a noun. If all nouns are understood to express nominal concepts, C would not have to be nominalized. In that case C (x) would be a nominal concept with a deictically assigned pointer as its argument, and it would be necessary to define the sentential concept as, say, ISA (x, C) or (ISA (C)) (x). Although this solution seems simpler in the present instance because it avoids the introduction of a nominalization operator nom, there are other places where nom seems unavoidable, for example, to account for the ambiguity of sentences like *John hates singing* (Wasow and Roeper 1972). The second solution, therefore, does not avoid nom, which will be needed in any case; its virtue is simply that nominalizing a concept expressed by a noun seems redundant. Following this line, the nominal concept C (x)—*a cat*—and the sentential concept M (x)—*It mews*—are to be distinguished by the syntactic categories of C and M, not by their conceptual notation. That is to say, if a theorist wishes to make the psychological claim that cathood and mewing are conceptually equivalent (that both are simply properties to be attributed to things), he would have to say that their difference is purely syntactic; marking one [+N] and the other [+V] would be an appropriate way to say it. Alternatively, if he wished to claim a psychological difference between nominal and predicative concepts, he should mark that difference explicitly in his conceptual notation; marking all nominal concepts with nom would be an appropriate way to do that.

Many of the problems that arise in formulating a conceptual theory of this type have to do with distinctions among sentential, predicative, and nominal concepts. One would hope to find psychological as well as syntactic evidence supporting possible representations; indeed, one would hope to find psychological and syntactic evidence supporting the *same* representations. But the notation itself imposes few syntactically or psychologically important distinctions on sentential concepts and their constituents.

Sentential Concepts and Words

A complete theory of sentential concepts would require much more careful discussion and would deal with many questions for which there are at present no satisfactory answers, but some way to represent sentential concepts is essential to any theory of word meanings for the simple reason that definitions of words always come round, one way or another, to sentences—sentences that paraphrase, sentences into which a definition can be substituted for the word defined, sentences illustrating use, sentences comparing or contrasting words. In the absence of any other approach, lexical concepts must be defined in terms of sentential concepts.

An example may be helpful. Suppose that someone asked about the verb *sprint* and was told that it means "move rapidly." The definition would not satisfy a lexicographer, but take it for what it is worth—after all, sentences like *John was sprinting* and *John was moving rapidly* do seem interchangeable in some contexts. This observation might suggest such equations between sentential concepts as SPRINT

(JOHN) = (RAPID (MOVE)) (JOHN). That equation in turn might lead to the proposal that (RAPID (MOVE)) is a conceptual analysis of the English verb *sprint*. Now, (RAPID (MOVE)) represents a predicative concept and, given an assignment for x, (RAPID (MOVE)) (x) represents a sentential concept; but anyone who analyzes *sprint* into a sentential concept is open to the complaint that he is analyzing words into sentences when every schoolboy knows that the truth is the other way. In order to avoid confusion, it is necessary to be explicit about the program that is being undertaken.

Entailment   First, equivalence or synonymy will not be claimed for the analyses proposed here. Since it is probably true that nothing can sprint without moving rapidly, but that something might be able to move rapidly without sprinting, the relation can be no stronger than an entailment: SPRINT (x) $\Vdash$ (RAPID (MOVE)) (x), where the (double) turnstile $\Vdash$ is used to indicate the relation of entailment between these sentential concepts. In addition to being a closer description of the facts, this weaker claim avoids what is sometimes called the paradox of analysis, namely, if the concept analyzed and the concept into which it is analyzed are literally the same, then a bare statement that the meaning is identical with itself is trivial, whereas if the two are not the same, the analysis is wrong.

Second, a procedural interpretation of what the entailment consists of might be something like:

Concept s (the concept analyzed) procedurally entails concept s' (the concept into which s is analyzed) if it is impossible to determine whether s truly represents a situation without doing all the mental computations that would be required to determine whether s' truly represents that situation.

This formulation raises difficult questions about how concepts truly represent situations, but it will be assumed that some plausible psychological account could be given of how such computations are performed. For the present, note particularly what is not said. The formulation does *not* say that it is impossible to determine that the concept analyzed truly represents a given situation without also determining that the concept into which it is analyzed truly represents that situation. Someone who has determined that SPRINT (x) truly represents a given situation will not necessarily have determined that

(RAPID (MOVE)) (x) also truly represents it, even though (if this analysis is correct) he will have performed all the mental computations that such a determination would require.

According to this formulation, the entailment relation is not stated explicitly in the definitional part of the information stored with *sprint*. Entailment is a relation between sentential concepts; recognizing that an entailment holds may be automatic and unconscious (as in determining anaphoric relations) or voluntary and conscious (as in paraphrase). In either case, however, to determine that sentential concept s entails sentential concept s', a person performs whatever information processing is required to establish, say, that s *and not* s' is a contradiction. On the assumption that lexical memory is a passive store, this processing is not performed by the lexical component—some external processing system is required. However, the external system would be unable to establish the entailment if lexical information did not support it. Since it would be inaccurate to call the lexical relation an entailment, a separate term is needed to denote the relation that must hold between lexical concepts if an entailment relation is to hold between sentential concepts that incorporate them. Following Katz and Fodor (1963), the lexical relation can be represented by a redundancy rule. Redundancy rules are not incorporated into lexical entries; they are theoretical statements abstracted by lexical analysis and applicable to many different pairs of words.

Third, the relation of entailment between sentential concepts is a hypothesis about how people who know English well are able to determine that the sentence *John was sprinting* entails the sentence *John was moving rapidly*. Procedurally, the two sentences would be separately translated into sentential concepts underlying them; then the computations required to determine whether both concepts can truly represent a situation would be examined in some way and it would be observed that one set of computations (properly) included the other. To say "*Sprints* means the same thing as *moves rapidly*" is a still stronger claim, however, for it asserts that the relation of entailment would hold between all pairs of sentences so related that one sentence uses *sprints* where the other uses *moves rapidly*. It is certainly possible to imagine that this entailment might hold for particular pairs of sentences but not for all.

Finally, what would it mean to say "*Sprint* can be analyzed (or decomposed) into (RAPID (MOVE))," where now the relation is be-

tween a word and a compound predicative concept, rather than
between two concepts? It will be assumed that (given an assignment
for x) this statement is shorthand for the following pattern of
relations:

x sprints x moves rapidly
   ↓   ↓
SPRINT (x) ⊩   (RAPID (MOVE)) (x)

According to this formulation, sentential concepts are critically involved in the analysis of lexical concepts, and paraphrase can be a
useful technique to discover and test lexical hypotheses. That is to
say, judgments of entailment relations between sentences can provide
empirical data to confirm or disconfirm hypotheses about entailment
relations between sentential concepts, and entailments between sentential concepts can provide constraints on the notations used to
represent the lexical concepts that they contain—on the information
processing required for correct use of a lexical concept and on the
redundancy rules relating lexical concepts. In order to make these
constraints as obvious as possible, the notation introduced for the
analysis of sentential concepts will be adapted with little change to
the analysis of word meanings.

Goals of Lexical Analysis

The problem now is to undertake—or at least illustrate—lexical
analysis of English words using the notations that have been introduced. First, however, a word is needed about goals. What should be
expected from such analyses?

The term "lexical analysis" will mean the conceptual analysis of
lexical units. For example, in the notation P (x, y) for relations,
different roles for the arguments x and y are to be inferred from their
order. Other information is assumed to be available: for example, if
the relation P is expressed by a verb, the word will be marked [+V]; it
may have some such subcategorization as [NP ____ NP]; the selectional restriction may require that x be assigned to an animate being;
and so on. But lexical analysis will be concerned only with a
characterization of the conceptual relation P.

One possible goal would be to sharpen the notations and make
them better suited to describe concepts. The notation P (x, y), which

treats a relation as a property of an ordered pair, is familiar in logical and programming languages and accords well with English grammar: in English there are relational predicates like *hits,* where HIT (x, y) is very different in meaning from HIT (y, x); this difference is expressed in the word order of the sentences *John hits Bill* and *Bill hits John.* However, English also has symmetric relational predicates like *marries,* where MARRY (x, y) and MARRY (y, x) are equivalent, yet since one order or the other must be chosen in this notation, the symmetry of the arguments is not revealed. Languages more highly inflected than English might well use affixes, rather than order, to indicate these differences; the analytic notation might capture it by the use of numerical suffixes to indicate the conceptual roles played by the indexes x and y—for example, HIT (x_1, y_2) versus MARRY (x_1, y_1). Then, in this notation, to commit murder might be MURDER (x_1, y_2), whereas to commit suicide might be MURDER (x_1, x_2). Thus, to affix subscripts in this manner would seem to lead to a more perspicuous notation for sentential concepts. Before adopting it, however, it would be well to consider how integer subscripts are to be assigned alternative roles, whether by special rule for each relational concept or by some general scheme with a fixed meaning for each integer (in the case of verbs, for example: "1" for the grammatical subject, "2" for the direct object, "3" for the indirect object; or "1" for the agent, "2" for the patient, "3" for the goal). A special rule for each relation might cost more in number of rules than it would be worth in notational simplification; on the other hand, a general rule could only be based on extensive analysis of the possible roles that arguments can play in different relational concepts. It is not important to settle such questions here; they are raised simply to illustrate one kind of goal that might motivate lexical analysis.

A goal of greater psychological interest would be to trace conceptual connections, if only to explain why certain ideas are so frequently associated in thought and memory. Indeed, some psychologists have claimed that word meanings are scientifically mysterious entities and may not exist at all; analysis might help to clarify such difficulties. In a sense, this goal amounts to determining what the notations can be applied to—whether, for example, ideas developed from analysis of sentence meanings can be applied to the analysis of word meanings; whether they can apply only to words or only to concepts or to both; whether similar notations can always be applied to concepts that seem intuitively similar; and so on. How, for example, can such notations represent the relations between the concepts expressed by pairs of words like *sprint* and *move,* or *father* and *son,* or *man* and *men,* or *table* and *furniture,* or *to* and *from*? The goal is to develop a consistent and principled account of such semantic relations among words; for that, it is necessary to take the words apart.

And last, probably the most obvious reason for doing lexical analysis would be to reduce the sprawling heterogeneity of sentential concepts to a relatively small number of primitive concepts from which all others can be derived. To the question, why a small number of irreducible concepts is preferable to a larger number, the answer seems to be that every such term adds some likelihood of error; if a term that might be misinterpreted in applying the theory can be reduced definitionally to another term, then the possibility of misapplication of the theory is to that extent reduced. Psychologically, the hope is to find that primitive concepts are cognitive universals, or that they reflect the structure of human intelligence, or that they have to be mastered before the great variety of more complex concepts can be learned, or that they might guide the development of a universal language. In any case, a great deal of detailed lexical analysis would be required in order to determine which concepts should be taken as cognitive atoms for building all the others.

Probably the best way to understand lexical analysis is to work through some examples. At various points we will encounter concepts that are difficult to analyze into anything simpler; these will be candidates for primitive concepts. Then, with some instances of such concepts in hand, it should be easier to see what is involved.

Nominal Concepts

A logical system consists of a vocabulary and axioms, along with rules of formation and inference. A formal language consists of a logical system along with an assignment of meanings to its expressions. A minimal assignment of meanings would be a set of rules determining the extensions of the constants, variables, and expressions in the logical system. If this mode of representation were applied to (fragments of) a natural language like English, then *table,* for example, might be considered as an element in the vocabulary and the set of all tables would be the extension of that term.

As a psychological theory of word knowledge in a natural language, this approach is severely limited (although some behaviorists have seemed to endorse it). Even if such an approach were adequate for descriptive purposes, it offers no explanation of how the correct extension of a term could be learned, remembered, or used. At the very least, a psychological theory should be concerned with the abstraction of patterns or criteria whereby particular instances in the extension of a term can be recognized. Since Frege, logicians have recognized a need to supplement extensional with intensional rules when discussing natural languages.

For psychological purposes the intension of a term can be thought of as a criterion or procedure whereby the extension of a term can be determined. The intension of *table* is whatever properties, images, formulas, processes, procedures, devices, methods, or criteria a person who knows *table* uses to determine whether some particular object can be referred to as a table. Logically, an intensional system need merely assume that such devices exist — it is not a logician's task to explain how they work. For the purposes of formal analysis a more general characterization of an intension would be that it is that part of what a person knows about a term that enables him to determine whether well-formed declarative sentences in which that term occurs are true or false. And that part is, of course, the knowledge that determines the word's extension.

Although a logical theory need not be concerned with how intensional knowledge should be characterized psychologically, this aspect of the problem has received detailed attention from psychologists. The traditional theory was that the word *table* is associated with a memory image of a table, and that the extension of the term is determined by matching that memory image with perceptual images of objects—when the match is close enough, the perceived object is accepted as an instance. The traditional criticisms of this theory are that many meaningful words do not have images associated with them, and that images are too particularistic to account for the variety of objects falling in the extension of a term.

Perceptual tests   A less iconic approach associates with the term a set of criterial (and characteristic though not criterial) features or attributes that can be used to test any perceptual image; recognition of instances is achieved according to rules relating the outcomes of perceptual tests to particular terms. The features that are available for testing are presumably those required by theories of perception and attention; they would be combined in various ways to provide an identification criterion for some class of objects. For example, perceptual tests for flat surfaces, connectedness, rigidity, and the like might be combined into a description of tables; if appropriate values are realized for the pattern of features, the word *table* is available to refer to that object.

Attempts to formulate such patterns of perceptual tests in detail, however, encounter a number of difficulties. For example, according to this characterization of an identification device, all instances that satisfy the several conjoined criteria should be equally acceptable. In fact, some objects are better instances than others. The boundaries of any perceptual category are vague; instances near the focus of the category are generally easiest to recognize and remember. Perhaps instances are not equivalent because, although all instances must satisfy criterial features, focal or paradigm instances also satisfy characteristic (but noncriterial) features. Or perhaps the nonequivalence of instances results from the availability of functional or dispositional information; in the case of tables, for example, shape is influenced by the purposes they are intended to serve, and rigidity is a dispositional property. Knowledge of such nonlinguistic facts as the uses to which objects can be put is not easily incorporated into an identification device formulated exclusively in terms of perceptual features. Some psychologists have suggested that such information is available in the form of sensorimotor schemata developed in the course of using or interacting with each class of objects; the possible uses of any particular object are recognized by inductive inferences.

The fact that psychologists are unable to say with any assurance whether the intension of *table* should be characterized as an image, rule, template, paradigm, sensorimotor schema, or something else not yet clearly formulated should not be overemphasized. At least the issue is clearly joined. There is general agreement that a person who speaks English must have some kind of internal representation whereby he is able to determine the extension of words like *table*. Ongoing research can be expected to clarify details. In the meanwhile, psycholinguists can adopt the approach of listing a number of attentional-judgmental features that can be tested for identification purposes, even though the exact mechanism is not yet known.

Hierarchical structures Certain relations between intensions follow directly from relations between the extensions that they determine.

For example, *article of furniture* is a superordinate term to *table* because all of the objects in the extension of *table* are also in the extension of *article of furniture*. This fact is sometimes proposed as an explanation for the hierarchic organization of nominal concepts. The extension of *thing* can be partitioned into animate things and inanimate things (objects); the extension of *object* can be partitioned into natural and artifactual objects; the extension of *artifact* can in turn be partitioned into structural and instrumental artifacts; the extension of *instrument,* into tools, weapons, clothing, documents, furnishings; the extension of *furniture,* into chairs, sofas, lamps, beds, tables; the extension of *table,* into dinner tables, card tables, operating tables, pool tables.

The relation between a word like *table* and a word like *furniture* is so common among words expressing nominal concepts that a technical term has been invented for it: hyponymy. According to Lyons (1968), word W_i is a hyponym of word W_j if, for any x, the sentence *x is a W_i* entails the sentence *x is a W_j*. This definition is not sufficient; in order to characterize this lexical taxonomy more fully, it is necessary to add, at the very least, that the direct hyponyms of a superordinate term form a contrastive set of terms whose extensions are mutually exclusive and whose combined extensions exhaust the extension of the superordinate term. The internal structure of such contrastive sets of terms has been the subject of many investigations—especially for kin terms, color terms, and plant and animal terms.

Of course, other hierarchic structures than hyponymy relate nominal concepts. The most familiar are those generated by part–whole relations (which might be called partonymy) and those generated by locative inclusion. A *venturi* is a part of a carburator, a *carburator* is a part of a gasoline engine, an *engine* is a part of a car. A *table* is in a *room* that is in a *house* that is in a *neighborhood* that is in a *town* that is in a *state*. These hierarchies can be characterized formally in terms of transitive, asymmetric relations like PART OF and INSIDE OF, but for various reasons hyponymy has received more theoretical attention.

Hyponymy lends itself to the theory of shared names. A single concrete object can be referred to as *dinner table, table, furniture, artifact, object,* and *thing,* but each of these terms is shared with a different range of other things. Hyponymy can be formalized in the notations of set theory. A theory of definition can be based on hyponymy: a hyponym can be defined by giving its direct superordinate plus a relative clause specifying how objects in its extension differ from other objects in the extension of the superordinate term. For example, a *dinner table* is a table that is used for dining; a *table* is an article of furniture that has a flat surface and is used to support smaller objects used in the course of eating, working, or playing games; an *article of furniture* is a human artifact that is used to make rooms and other areas suitable for human use; and so on. Hyponymy suggests an intuitively appealing way to characterize intensions. The intension of the hyponym includes everything that is included in the intension of the direct superordinate plus something more to distinguish the intension of the hyponym from the intensions of the other terms in the same contrastive set. The intension of *table*, for example, would include the intension of *article of furniture*. Obviously, hyponyms are more informative than are their superordinates.

Finally, hyponymy can be simply represented by semantic markers. For example, if the intensions of *table* and of *furniture* are characterized by lists of semantic markers, then the list of semantic markers associated with *table* should include the list associated with *furniture*; indeed, the total list of markers may not have to be included in the lexical entry for *table*, since it is possible to refer only to *furniture* and rely on a redundancy rule to the effect that anything marked either [+furniture] or [−furniture] will also carry the semantic markers [+artifact, +object, +thing]. (Note that these redundancy rules support entailments and can be combined like entailments: if anything marked [±furniture] is also marked [+artifact] and if anything marked [±artifact] is marked [+object], then anything marked [±furniture] must also be marked [+object].) For all these reasons, semantic analysis goes especially well for hyponymic relations between words.

Redundancy rules   Since redundancy rules have played an important role in attempts to characterize the lexical component of the base, they deserve further discussion. Note that no claim is made that a person cannot know what a table is unless he knows that it is furniture, or that he cannot know what furniture is unless he knows that anything marked for furniture must also be marked [+object]. The word *know* is treacherous in such contexts. In one sense, a person who knows English well knows that tables are furniture and that anything in a minimal contrastive set with *table* is furniture. In another sense, however, he does not know that he knows it. In fact, he may not even believe it. For example, an urban child might have some verbal understanding of what farmers are and do, and he might know the difference between friends and strangers, but he would not necessarily conclude that *farmer* is a hyponym of *stranger* just because all farmers are strangers to him. His evidence about *table* and *furniture* might be very similar. If it seems reasonable that this child would not believe that farmers must be strangers, why should it seem unreasonable if he did not believe that tables must be furniture? He can change a farmer from stranger to friend by getting to know him; maybe there is something comparable he could do to change a table from furniture to something else—break it up or burn it, for example.

It is no answer to find holes in the child's logic, because he isn't using logic—he is just learning what words mean, and doing it with surprising skill. Noticing that he is learning related ideas in different disguises may be a form of reflection that he can postpone until some teacher points it out to him. Redundancy rules are creatures of lexical theory, only dimly suspected even by those with considerable education. In order to account for a child's speed in learning new words once he learns a few related words, it suffices merely to suppose that there is a common part being learned over and over, and that learning that part gets faster with practice. When he learns *table* he also learns whatever *table* shares with *furniture*; when next he learns *chair* he learns whatever *chair* shares with *furniture,* but now it is slightly easier to learn that part; when he comes to learn *bed,* the part *bed* shares with *furniture* will be still easier to learn; and so on through a variety of hyponyms of *furniture*. But he doesn't have to recognize that there is a common part or know that it is called *furniture*. (Presumably the meaning of *stranger* is not a part of what he learns when he learns *farmer*; therefore a similar facilitation of subsequent learning would not occur in that case.) In this way a knowledge structure can be built up with an organization that conforms to what are called redundancy rules, but without any rule learning (in the usual sense) on the part of the child. All that need be assumed is that there is a common part. The simple assumption would be that this common part is intensional—that the intension of a superordinate word like *furniture* is a part of the intensions of all of its hyponyms.

If someone asks what that common part is in the case of furniture, however, an answer is not readily at hand. What do a framed picture, a double bed, and a carpet have in common except that all of them are called articles of furniture? (Wittgenstein made the point about games, which he said share nothing but a "family resemblance.") According to Rosch, Mervis, Gray, Johnson, and Boyes-Braem (1976), *table* would be a "basic object" in English: it is the most generic word in this hierarchy for which there are distinctive perceptual features and patterns of behavior. In general, basic terms are the first nouns learned and are the responses most spontaneously given in naming tasks. Nouns superordinate to basic terms have few, if any, criterial features; whatever the shared part of their meanings is, it is *not* to be found in the perceptual machinery needed to identify instances.

Some theorists have tried to identify nominal concepts with intensions. Certainly they would not want to claim that all lexical concepts are intensions. Words like *should* and *of* express some kind of meaning, yet they have no extensions and require no intensional identification procedures for their use. But for a basic nominal term it might be possible to equate the concept it expresses with whatever information a person must have in order to assign a pointer correctly to an instance of that concept. Much psychological research on concept learning has proceeded as if this equation were valid.

Equating nominal lexical concepts to intensions is a considerable improvement over equating them to their extensions, but it is still too limited for the purposes of psychological theory. The procedure that is used to identify an object as a table is not the same thing as the concept of tables. A venerable counterexample to this approach is *featherless biped*; it may indeed be true that *featherless biped* is an identification procedure that will correctly select all and only those organisms in the extension of the word *man,* but no one would care to argue that *featherless biped* is an adequate characterization of the concept expressed by the word *man.* If nominal concepts are regarded as intensions, and intensions as identification devices, then severe constraints must be placed on the acceptable kinds of identification devices. In general—taxonomists can provide many examples—given two or more identification devices (or "keys") for categorizing the same objects, it is extremely difficult, if not impossible, to decide which one is true. Indeed, if both keys give correct results, it is not even clear what is to be decided, and therefore it is equally unclear how any constraints on identification devices could lead to unique solutions.

General knowledge   The obvious conclusion is that the nominal concept expressed by a word like *table* is not the knowledge, whatever it may be, that enables people to determine the extension of the word. The intension of *table* may be part of the concept that *table* expresses, but it cannot be the whole of it. The purposes of psychology are better served by assuming that nominal concepts must be characterized by locating them in some body of organized knowledge, lay or technical, in which they are related to other concepts. In the case of *table,* a person who knows the meaning of the word has some organized knowledge and belief (the lay equivalent of a scientist's theory) about furniture—about where it is found and the uses to which articles of furniture are put, about the economics and esthetics of furniture, and so on and on—all of which is part of a more general body of organized knowledge and belief about concrete physical objects in general. *Table* gets its meaning from its place in this conceptual system. Lexical knowledge that conforms to redundancy rules is not isolated from this general conceptual system: the lexicon has a cognitive structure only because it is an integral part of everything a person knows and believes. This formulation may seem distressingly vague, but any attempt to reduce nominal concepts to something simpler seems doomed to failure.

No attempt will be made to draw a line between lexical information about a word and the general system of knowledge in which the concept that the word expresses is located. The most that might be claimed is that some information is involved in almost every use of the word, whereas other information is needed only occasionally and may not be available to everyone (a child, for example) who seems to know and use the word appropriately in most circumstances. Therefore, a nominal concept might be defined as this necessary conceptual core plus some kind of intensional procedures (based on the conceptual system) for determining the extension of the concept. This approach might at least make it possible to understand how someone who believes the earth is flat could converse satisfactorily about *up* and *down* with someone who believes the earth is round, even though in a larger context the meanings of those words would be very different for the two individuals. *Up* and *down* depend on core concepts about space so common and so general as to be compatible with very different theories about the shape of the earth.

Even so modest a commitment to intensions as a part of nominal concepts is not above challenge, however. A case can be made that knowing how to use a word has nothing to do with knowing its intension or its extension. Kripke (1972) and Putnam (1975) have illustrated the argument for the word *gold*. A person can know this word and use it correctly in a great variety of contexts without being able to determine its true extension—the fact that a person knows the word *gold* does not protect him against fraudulent merchandise. It is probably true that an adult who knows *table* will have an intensional basis (one or more) for determining membership in its extension, but if that ability is not a critical aspect of knowing and using *gold*, why should it be a critical aspect of knowing and using *table*?

Psychologically, this criticism seems to go too far. If it is taken to mean that people can learn to use any word without acquiring intensions whereby extensions are determined, it is simply false. At most it means that for some words a person can acquire superficial intensions that will support their use in social communication, though they are not sufficient to determine the real extensions of those words. But a superficial or incorrect intension is still an intension; it may not determine the true extension, but it determines some extension. It seems necessary, therefore, to distinguish among intensions, at least for certain technical terms. In addition to the socially shared extension determined by the intension based on the conceptual system that is learned by most users of the language, a technical term may also have a "real" extension that only experts can determine.

In the case of such technical terms there is, according to Putnam, a "division of linguistic labor." Presumably the average person has some rough intension for *gold*—a valuable, soft, yellow metal used in jewelry, dentistry, and as a basis for monetary exchange, perhaps—and then, appended as a sort of mental footnote, he knows that this intension is superficial: when correct identification is important, the footnote says, consult an expert. Thus, the average person may be in much the same position as a child with respect to the meanings of many technical terms. He knows some superficial and characteristic but noncriterial features, he knows some superordinate terms, and he knows (because experts have told him) that particular objects are true instances, but in general he is unable to verify that sentences in which such terms are used are really true or false. *Gold* is not a unique example, of course. The average person is dependent on experts for the real meanings of a great many words: *edible mushroom, cancer, antique, logarithm, sacred, petunia, surtax, tort, insect*; according to

Putnam, most people don't know the real intension of *water*. Every society seems to require experts who can settle such questions.

It is interesting that this division of linguistic labor introduces a social, pragmatic factor into even the study of such apparently simple matters as the correct application of a nominal term to the concrete objects it can refer to. That is to say, in order to evaluate sentences that include these words, it is necessary to know whether the speaker is an expert, or whether expert advice has been given—the sort of contextual information that is generally relegated to theories of the pragmatic rather than the semantic aspects of language.

That an average person knows and uses many words about which he is not an expert raises no serious problems for conceptual theories of meaning. It implies that the system of organized knowledge and belief relative to which his nominal concept is located and in terms of which his identification procedures are given is not complete—hardly a startling conclusion. And it implies that an average person will produce and understand many sentences that he would be unable to verify or falsify—a conclusion that would surprise only those (if there are any such) who assume that the sole purpose of language is the communication of truth.

Predicative Concepts

Relative to nominal concepts, the analysis of predicative concepts leads into less familiar territory and raises questions of greater linguistic and psychological interest. It is predication that turns nominal designations into sentences—that enables people to put language to use. Whereas hierarchical relations impose a semblance of order on nominal concepts, the uses of and conceptual relations among predicates seem like a jungle through which a theorist must carve his own paths.

Analysis of the verb *hand* Rather than discuss generalities about a topic so poorly understood, it seems advisable to begin with an example. For this purpose an analysis proposed by Miller and Johnson-Laird (1976) will be adapted to the analysis of the verb *hand* in such sentences as

(1) a. She handed her hat to him.
     b. She handed him her hat.

A paraphrase of (1) that captures all of the conceptual components to be discussed here is

(2)   She had her hat prior to some time t at which she used her hand to do something that caused her hat to travel to him, after which time he had her hat.

The difference between (1a) and (1b) is usually regarded as syntactic; (1b) might be derived from the structure underlying (1a) as a consequence of a dative-movement transformation that inverts the order of the direct and indirect objects and deletes *to*. Alternatively, the lexicon might include two strict subcategorizations for *hand*, [NP ___ NP PP] and [NP ___ NP NP], in which case a syntactic transformation would be unnecessary and the relation of synonymy between (1a) and (1b) would be explained lexically in terms of the same semantic analysis for both uses.

Some people report a difference in meaning for the two sentences. *She handed her hat to him*, they say, merely suggests that he took it, whereas *She handed him her hat* asserts that he took it—the sense expressed in (2). A person who respects this difference in meaning presumably distinguishes two different meanings of the verb *hand*— one resembling "offer" and another "offer and take." For a speaker who does not sense this difference, both (1a) and (1b) have the "offer and take" sense. In any case, it is the sense paraphrased in (2) that will be considered here.

Let the verb *hand* be represented as a predicative concept, HAND, taking three arguments: the pointer assigned to the grammatical subject will be x; to the indirect object, y; and to the direct object, z: HAND (x, y, z). Then (1) can be represented (to a first approximation) by HAND (SHE, HIM, HAT).

HAPPEN: Consider first the temporal shape of the handing episode in (1). It begins in the state: she-has-her-hat-and-he-does-not-have-it. Then an event occurs at some time t which results in a change of state. And the episode ends in the state: she-does-not-have-her-hat-and-he-does-have-it. This characterization raises two questions: how to represent changes of state, and how to reduce the redundancy of these state descriptions.

A predicative operator R (Rescher and Urquhart 1971) can be used to represent changes of state. R_t takes a temporally indefinite sentential concept s and forms a new sentential concept $R_t (s)$ to the general effect that *s is realized at time t*. In order to indicate a change of state at moment *t*, another predicative operator—call it HAPPEN—is needed to form a new statement to the effect that NOT (*s*) *is realized at t − 1 and s is realized at t*:

(3)   HAPPEN (*s*) $\Vdash$ ($\exists t$) [R_{t-1} (NOT (*s*)) & R_t (*s*)].

HAPPEN is a very general operator, characteristic of verbs that denote events. Note that the first conjunct of (3) will ordinarily be presupposed; that is to say, *s didn't happen* is not ordinarily the same concept as R_t (*s*) *for all t*. Note also that the operator AND (*s, s'*) is here replaced by the ampersand in the more readable notation *s* & *s'*.

GET: The two state descriptions—she-had-it-and-he-didn't and she-didn't-have-it-and-he-did—are clearly redundant. The fact that a hat cannot be in two places at the same time (which would surely be part of a language user's general knowledge) merely compounds the redundancy of such state descriptions for double-object verbs of motion. However, it is a general characteristic of double-object verbs, not limited to motion verbs like *hand,* that, in some sense of the ambiguous verb *have,* the event ends with the indirect object having the direct object (Green 1974). In the case of *hand,* either *x* or *y,* but not both, will have *z* at any moment *t*; since *y* has *z* after *t, x* cannot also have it. On the other hand, if *x tells y* some information *z, x* does *not* stop having *z* after *t*. What is common to both *tell* and *hand,* however, is that *y* does not have *z* before *t*. Thus, the simplest state description is *s* = HAVE (*y, z*), in which case the antecedent state would be NOT (*s*). Since NOT (*s*) seems to be presupposed by HAND, (3) would be satisfied. On this analysis, therefore, some part of the meaning of *hand* must be

(4)   GET (*y, z*) $\Vdash$ HAPPEN (HAVE (*y, z*)).

(Discussion of HAVE will be omitted here. See Bendix 1966; Miller and Johnson-Laird 1976.)

Actually, of course, two things happen in handing: the object changes its location as well as its possessor. Indeed, the former change seems to be causally related to the latter. So, in order to complete the analysis, it is necessary to consider also what happens at *t* that results in the transition from NOT (HAVE (*y, z*)) to HAVE (*y, z*). Roughly, *x uses x's* hand to *do* something, and what *x* does *causes z* to *travel* to *y*. This paraphrase introduces four new operators—USE, DO, CAUSE, and TRAVEL—which can combine as follows to provide additional parts of HAND:

(5)   USE $(x, hand, s_x)$ &   CAUSE $(s_x, (\text{TO (TRAVEL)})) (z, y))$.

Because the concepts associated with these operators—instrumentality, agency, causality, and motion—are required in the analysis of many English verbs, they will be discussed individually.

USE: The first conjunct of (5) corresponds to *x uses hand to s_x* or, more generally, USE (x, w, s_x) is *x uses w to s_x*, as in *Tom used a knife to open the box*. A fuller paraphrase would be: "*x* intentionally does something *s* that causes *w* to do something *s'* that allows s_x." *Use* contrasts with instrumental *with* in being intentional: *He broke the window with his elbow* is not synonymous with *He used his elbow to break the window*. If the operators ACT (to represent intentional acts) and ALLOW are introduced (for both of which accounts must be given) then USE can be defined:

(6)   USE (x, w, s_x) $\Vdash$ ACT (x, s) &   CAUSE $(s, \text{DO } (w, s'))$
            &   ALLOW (s', s_x).

ACT: Intention will be taken as an unanalyzed primitive and represented by INTEND (x, g), where *x* is understood to be animate and *g* is understood to be a goal that *x* intends to achieve. It is further assumed that intentions can stand in a causal relation to behavior, so:

(7)   ACT (x, s) $\Vdash$ CAUSE (INTEND (x, g), DO (x, s)).

ACT and DO are closely related; ACT is the intentional counterpart of unintentional DO.

DO: Let *s* denote a sentential concept whose argument is *x* and whose predicate concept is an event description (that is, whose predicate entails HAPPEN). Then the relation between *x* and the event will be DO (x, s). DO is essentially a place holder. That is to say, DO will be restricted to contexts in which *s* can be a dummy variable— see (6) for example, where DO (w, s') can be paraphrased as "*w* does something." For any context in which *s* cannot be a dummy variable—if what *x* does is relevant to the meaning—then DO is replaced by some operator that makes the action explicit.

CAUSE: Causation is too complex for brief explication. The following formulation is taken from Miller and Johnson-Laird:

(8)   CAUSE (s, s') $\Vdash$ BEFORE (HAPPEN (s), HAPPEN (s'))
            &   NOT (POSSIBLE $(s \, \& \, \text{NOT } (s'))$).

This formulation adds two more operators—BEFORE and POSSIBLE—for which accounts are needed. It is obvious that the plausibility of (8) depends heavily on POSSIBLE and on how a language user acquires general knowledge about which combinations of events are possible or impossible under given sets of circumstances. (A way to incorporate such knowledge into conceptual analyses will be proposed in the section on *Modals*.) For the present purposes POSSIBLE can be taken as an undefined term.

ALLOW: *Cause* and *allow* are closely related, as a comparison of (8) with the following formulation should show:

(9) ALLOW (s, s') $\Vdash$ BEFORE (HAPPEN (s), HAPPEN (s'))
              &   NOT (POSSIBLE (NOT (s) & s')).

Note that, although it is impossible for s' to occur unless s has occurred, the occurrence of s does not ensure the subsequent occurrence of s'; that is to say, (s and NOT (s')) may well be possible.

BEFORE: Sentential concepts of the form s *before* s' entail that there is some moment t such that s has been realized at t and s' has not yet been realized—that there is an interval between the first realization of s and the first realization of s'. In terms of the temporal operator R:

(10)   BEFORE (s, s') $\Vdash$ $(\exists t_0)$ [$(\exists t)$ [$t < t_0$ & $R_t (s)$]
               &   NOT ($(\exists t)$ [$t < t_0$ & $R_t (s')$])].

TRAVEL: Verbs of motion constitute a semantic field of English having *change of location* or, more briefly, *travel,* as the core concept. It is sufficient evidence that something has traveled if it appears where it wasn't before or if it is no longer where it was before. These conditions can be accommodated by

(11)   TRAVEL (z) $\Vdash$ $(\exists y)$ [HAPPEN (LOC $(z$, AT (y)))
               or   HAPPEN (NOT (LOC $(z$, AT (y))))]

for an appropriate choice of the location y as the origin or destination of motion; the first disjunct represents z *travels to* y and the second z *travels from* y. The notation

(12)   (TO (TRAVEL)) (z, y) $\Vdash$ HAPPEN (LOC $(z$, AT (y)))

reflects a judgment that *to* y is a predicate adverbial in z *traveled to* y. This analysis of TRAVEL introduces still another operator, AT.

AT: The sentence form z *is at* y seems to mean that z is included in the characteristic region of interaction with y:

(13)   LOC $(z,$ AT (y)) $\Vdash$ INCL $(z,$ REGION (y))
        & NOT (INCL $(y,$ REGION (z))).

The second conjunct in (13) is required to distinguish *at* from *with*; if z and y are commensurate, so that INCL is symmetrical between them, *with* is the preferred preposition.

The two operators used to define the locative concepts LOC and AT can both be taken as primitive concepts. The relation of spatial inclusion that is supposed to be captured by INCL probably derives rather directly from perception of spatial relations. REGION, an operator indicating the characteristic region of interaction with its argument, derives from general knowledge of objects and their uses.

HAND: Enough machinery has now been introduced to provide some rationalization for the following formulation:

(14)   HAND (x, y, z) $\Vdash$ USE $(x,$ *hand*, s_x)
        & CAUSE $(s_x,$ (TO (TRAVEL)) (z, y))
        & CAUSE (TRAVEL (z), GET (y, z)).

For those users of English who apparently have another meaning for *hand*, according to which x's action merely allows y to get z, rather than causes y to get z, the formulation would be

(15)   (HAND) (x, y, z) $\Vdash$ USE $(x,$ *hand*, s_x)
        & CAUSE $(s_x,$ (TO (TRAVEL)) (z, y))
        & ALLOW (TRAVEL (z), GET (y, z)).

This discussion has lifted the verb *hand* out of the English lexicon; Figure 2.1 summarizes diagrammatically the other concepts found dangling from it. HAND is analyzed directly into USE, CAUSE, GET, and TRAVEL; each of those operators is analyzed in turn, as indicated. The diagram does not reproduce the formal structure of the analyses, but it does make it easier to locate unreduced concepts.

As detailed as this analysis is, some omissions are obvious. For example, the noun *hand* introduced in (5) as the instrument x uses is not only undefined, but no explicit indication is given that the hand x uses is x's own hand. This relation of inalienable possession could be introduced by adding an appropriate HAVE relation between x and the hand in question, but this seems to go beyond the limits of

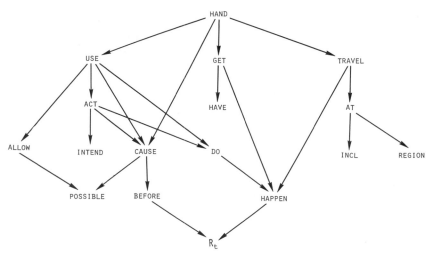

Figure 2.1 Simplified diagram of semantic decomposition of the English verb *hand*

lexicology—the fact that people have hands and enjoy a special user's privilege with respect to them is surely part of a person's general knowledge about people. Also omitted is any recognition of the intuition that when x hands z to y, not only does x use his hand to deliver z, but y also uses his hand to receive it. The characteristic region of interaction with the recipient is, in this case, his hand. Moreover, *hand* seems to implicate y's conscious acknowledgment that he has received z—one would not ordinarily say *She handed it to him* if what she had done was to slip it surreptitiously into his coat pocket. Some of these features of *hand* could be introduced by refining GET in the third conjunct of (15) to something like: USE $(y, hand, \text{ACCEPT} (y, z))$, with an appropriate formula for AC-CEPT. Also omitted are any explicit grounds for distinguishing handing from throwing — something more would have to be said about the temporal shape of the transfer. No doubt there are still other omissions. However, since this discussion of *hand* is merely an expository device to motivate the introduction of certain very general semantic operators, the definition offered in (14) will be left incomplete.

The general problem of completeness requires comment. How far to go in adding such features to a lexical analysis is an important question to which a principled answer could be most useful. After all general components of meaning have been specified as fully as possible, there may always be a residuum of meaning unique to each particular lexical item. Even the primitive concepts have a slippery way of introducing general knowledge into the supposedly lexical analysis.

If the preceding analysis is taken at face value, however, it leads to several candidates for the status of primitive concepts:

concepts of the propositional calculus
concepts of states and changes of state over time
the modal operators, POSSIBLE and R_t
the psychological operator, INTEND
the spatial predicates, INCL and REGION
the predicate HAVE

HAVE could be further analyzed, but since there are several ways of having something, the analysis becomes more complicated than instructive. In the case of the verb *hand,* the sense of HAVE is little more than locative coincidence, but that is only one of several senses. Briefly said, the notion that someone *has* something means that he can use it, and the notion that he *owns* something means that he can give permission to others to use it and can transfer that right to others. So a more primitive concept underlying the HAVE of ownership is PERMISSIBLE, a modal operator of deontic logic very similar to POSSIBLE.

Given these examples of possible primitive concepts, return now to the question of how best to characterize the relation between the concept analyzed and the concepts into which it is analyzed.

Reduction to Primitive Concepts

It is possible, by following the road map given in Figure 2.1, to expand the analysis of *hand* given in (14) until it is written entirely in undefined terms. The result looks something like this:

(16)   HAND (x, y, z) $\Vdash$ $(t_0, t_1, t_2, t_3, t_4, w)$ $[t_0 < t_1 < t_2 < t_3 < t_4$
          & R_{t_0-1} (NOT (INTEND (x, g)))
          & R_{t_0} (INTEND (x, g))
          & (t) $[t < t_0 \supset R_t$ (NOT (DO (x, s)))]
          & R_{t_1} (s) & (t) $[t < t_1 \supset R_t$ (NOT (DO $(hand, s')$)))]

$$\& \quad R_{t_2}(s') \,\&\, (t)\, [t < t_2 \supset R_t\, (\text{NOT}\, (s_x))\,]$$
$$\& \quad R_{t_3}(s_x) \,\&\, (t)\, [t < t_3 \supset R_t\, (\text{NOT}\, (\text{AT}\, (z, w)))\,]$$
$$\& \quad R_{t_4}(\text{AT}\, (z, w))\, \&\, (t)\, [t < t_4 \supset R_t\, (\text{NOT}\, (\text{HAVE}\, (y, z)))\,]$$
$$\& \quad \text{NOT}\, (\text{POSSIBLE}\, (\text{INTEND}\, (x, g)\, \&\, \text{NOT}\, (\text{DO}\, (x, s))))$$
$$\& \quad \text{NOT}\, (\text{POSSIBLE}\, (s\, \&\, \text{NOT}\, (\text{DO}\, (hand, s'))))$$
$$\& \quad \text{NOT}\, (\text{POSSIBLE}\, (\text{NOT}\, (s')\, \&\, s_x))$$
$$\& \quad \text{NOT}\, (\text{POSSIBLE}\, (\text{AT}\, (z, w)\, \&\, \text{NOT}\, (\text{HAVE}\, (y, z))))\,]$$

A cursory glance at (16) indicates that about half the conditions specify the temporal shape of handing and half require judgments about what is possible (based, presumably, on general knowledge and belief).

Since this expansion is even less intelligible than (14), however, it is difficult to avoid asking what it is needed for. In particular, a psychologist will ask such questions as: When a person who knows English well uses *hand* as a verb—either as a speaker or as a listener—must he be consciously aware of this fully expanded conceptual structure? Is the reduction of *hand* into its primitive concepts a necessary part of understanding the meaning of *hand*? Is the fully primitivized structure in (16) what a person retrieves when he retrieves *hand* from lexical memory?

The dilemma such questions pose is obvious: if someone answers them affirmatively, he seems to assume an implausible amount of mental computation per word, but if he answers negatively, he seems to deny the relevance of lexical analysis for psychological accounts of linguistic communication. Since neither answer is attractive, an intermediate position might be proposed: on some occasions a person may find it necessary to pursue such entailments, so he must have such information stored somewhere in memory, but it is not always necessary to retrieve everything known about a word in order to understand how it is being used in a particular context. That is, the meaning of *hand* would be thought of as a conceptual unit, a gestalt, that normally functions as a whole but that can, like any gestalt, be taken apart by special acts of attention when necessary. In order to make this intermediate position explicit, however, some additional theory should account for variability in depth of analysis: what determines when a lexical concept must be expanded or how far it must be expanded? There is little reason to expect such a theory to be simple.

The essential characteristic of this approach is that a lexical concept is expanded into a compound of (presumably) primitive concepts by rules like those illustrated in (1) through (13). What seems to be needed is a more general approach to the interdefinition of primitive concepts, an approach in terms of which such a system of rules could be seen as a special case. At the present time, however, no alternative to the decompositional approach is available.

Semantic Fields

The notion that languages are organized around semantic fields has been developed differently by different writers. It will be assumed here that a semantic field has two parts: a conceptual field and a lexical field. The meaning of any word depends on how it works together with other words in the same lexical field to cover or represent the conceptual field. If that statement sounds vague, then it accurately captures the flavor of most writing on this subject.

The notion might be made less vague if it were possible to decide whether two words (or two senses of words) are in the same semantic field. Consider two possible approaches toward making such decisions; in order to talk about them, they will be identified as the analytic hypothesis and the intuitive hypothesis. By the analytic hypothesis is meant the assumption that any two words that can be analyzed into common conceptual components are to that extent in the same semantic field, and that the more concepts two words have in common, the smaller is the smallest semantic field that contains them both. By the intuitive hypothesis is meant the assumption that people can make intuitive judgments of the similarity of meaning between any two words, and that the greater the judged similarity of meaning, the smaller is the smallest semantic field that contains them both.

One might hope to find that both hypotheses are correct; indeed, one might try to argue that the analytic hypothesis explains people's intuitive judgments of semantic similarity. It seems, however, that this approach is wrong. Consider some of the kinds of facts that must be accounted for.

First, some positive examples. One of the component operators in HAND is TRAVEL. It does seem to be possible to isolate a well-behaved semantic field of about two hundred verbs of motion, all of which have TRAVEL as a component operator: *move, come, go, bring, take, walk, run, rise, raise, drop, fall, . . .*—including *hand* and *travel,* of course. Another of the component operators in HAND is HAVE. The sense of *have* that involves rights of use and transfer is central to a reasonably well behaved semantic field of about a hundred verbs of possession, all of which have POSSESS as a component operator: *own, buy, sell, give, take, steal, lend, pay, . . .*— including the appropriate sense of *have,* of course. When attention is confined to examples like these—like verbs of motion or verbs of possession—there is a congruence of analysis and intuition. In these cases, it does seem possible to account for people's intuitive judgments of similarity of meaning in terms of a shared semantic component that can be identified by lexical analysis. The account is complicated by words like *take,* which can occur both as a verb of motion and as a verb of possession, thus indicating that it is not words, but their senses, that are the central concern of any analysis of lexical concepts. (See, however, the discussion of polysemy and disambiguation.)

Now consider some negative examples. One component operator in HAND is CAUSE. It does not seem possible to isolate a well-behaved semantic field of verbs of causation, all of which have CAUSE as a component operator. The lexical field of causative verbs would include *raise* and *give* and *kill* ("cause to rise" and "cause to have" and "cause to die"), which are not intuitively similar in meaning, and it would exclude *rise* and *receive* and *die,* which are intuitively similar in meaning to the causatives *raise, give,* and *kill.* It seems necessary to conclude, therefore, that this lexical field of causative verbs does not work together to cover an underlying conceptual field of causal relations and so does not qualify as a semantic field.

Another negative example can be found for temporal relations. In discussing HAND, a special operator HAPPEN was introduced to mean that there is some moment of time t prior to which a given state of affairs was not realized and subsequent to which it was realized. However, it does not seem possible to isolate a well-behaved semantic field of event verbs, all of which have HAPPEN as a component operator. The lexical field would include *go* and *get* and *die* and all other action verbs of English, and would exclude stative verbs like *be, have, contain, know, like.* Although two such lexical fields would share important syntactic characteristics, they would not have any intuitive conceptual coherence and so would not qualify as semantic fields. One way to describe what is going on here is to say that causation and time cannot be confined to any single semantic field; they must be expressed in every semantic field.

Are there other negative examples? Miller and Johnson-Laird (1976) propose the following candidates: causal relations, temporal relations, spatial relations, quantitative relations, and, above all, personal relations. Each of these concepts can be (and in some language is) marked syntactically.

From the point of view of lexical analysis, these concepts are used to elaborate the internal structure of a semantic field. Perhaps the clearest example of how they work is the relation of class inclusion (a quantitative relation) that underlies much of the hierarchical structure of nominal semantic fields. Note that no one would accept a semantic field of, say, superordinate nouns, including *furniture, tree,* and *music* (on the grounds that they include *chair, pine,* and *song,* respectively), because there is no intuitive coherence to the collection of concepts that results. The concept of hyponymy cannot be confined to a single semantic field.

It is not difficult to find more examples, but this should be enough, if not to prove the point, at least to illustrate what the point is. If primary psychological importance is assigned to a native speaker's intuitions about similarities of meaning, then (at least) two different kinds of lexical concepts must be distinguished: on the one hand are concepts that are central to semantic fields—concepts like color, kinship, living thing, motion, possession, perception, and communication; on the other hand are concepts that provide the internal structure of those fields—concepts like space, time, quantity, cause, and person.

Where does this argument leave the matter of linguistic primitives? If primitives are pursued ruthlessly down to the level suggested earlier, then neither of these types of concept is primitive. For example, TRAVEL can be analyzed into changes that HAPPEN AT a location and CAUSE can be analyzed into cooccurrences that are POSSIBLE or IMPOSSIBLE. Nevertheless, there is something special about changes that occur in the spatial domain, and there is something special about possible cooccurrences that are thought of as causally related. Both concepts have an intuitive salience that is difficult to defend on formal grounds because they are not the primitive concepts that emerge from formal analysis.

CAUSE and TRAVEL are patterns of primitive concepts that recur frequently and give an impression of underlying concepts into which words can be analyzed. These recurrent patterns would explain many regularities that are consistently reported in lexical analyses, but those regularities need not be interpreted to mean that all word meanings can be reduced to patterns of a relatively small set of primitive concepts. Even after the general location of a word in a semantic field is determined by these recurring semantic patterns, there are nearly always subtle shades of meaning difference that are not captured by the analysis.

Although little is known about the details, it is generally assumed that the meanings of some words are easier to learn if the meanings of other words are already familiar. If this plausible assumption is true, the facilitation in learning may be mediated by these recurrent patterns of primitive concepts. One might even speculate that while a word is being learned in terms of its relations to familiar patterns of primitive concepts—while it is in a person's listening but not his speaking vocabulary, perhaps—the time required to comprehend the word might be some function of the complexity of those relations, but that once the concept is a single cognitive chunk—once it is thoroughly overlearned and automatic—such differences in processing times would disappear.

In short, there are many reasons for a psychologist to want to know what these recurrent patterns of primitive concepts are. But the ambition to reduce lexical variety to some relatively small and manageable set of concepts should not be one of them.

Polysemy and Lexical Disambiguation

Exploration of semantic fields reveals how a single concept can be elaborated and expressed by a variety of words. The other side of this picture is polysemy—how a single word can express a variety of concepts. Polysemy was once thought to be the central problem for linguistic studies of semantics; certainly it is one of the most perplexing. Much recent work in semantics, however, has neglected polysemy, preferring instead to treat such matters as lexical decomposition, truth conditions, synonymy, and paraphrase, where progress seems more promising.

Psychologically, the remarkable fact about polysemy is how little trouble it causes. In any dictionary the words with the most and longest entries (those that are the most polysemous) are the words that occur most frequently in ordinary use, yet these common words are also the easiest to produce and understand. Because of its large stock of different words, English is relatively free of polysemy; French, for example, is more polysemous than English, and (spoken) Chinese is far more polysemous than either French or English. Yet people who use those languages experience no abnormal difficulty understanding one another. Selecting an appropriate concept out of the long list of concepts that a common word might express should demand special cognitive effort and be subject to frequent errors. Errors do occur, of course, probably more often than people realize, but they pose no important problems for casual communication. Indeed, polysemy can be exploited deliberately for special effects, as in puns and the *double entendre,* garden-path jokes, evasive replies, and the like.

The process to be explained, therefore, is lexical disambiguation. How are people able to recognize so quickly and accurately which one or two of a large number of alternative meanings a word expresses on any particular occasion? The answer must, of course, involve the use of context: the immediate linguistic context, the discourse context, and the situation in which the communication occurs. Disambiguation probably relies also on general knowledge of the topic under discussion. As a first pass, however, it is convenient to focus on the immediate linguistic context.

Linguistic context   It is not necessary, but it seems in fact to be the case, that most words can be accurately disambiguated on the basis of information in the sentences in which they occur; when the immediate sentence is inadequate, the preceding or succeeding sentence will generally settle any questions. The fact that disambiguation is almost always possible on the basis of local linguistic clues is convenient for a theorist, but it should be kept in mind that although this mode of disambiguation is theoretically available, people may not always use it. Disambiguation is possible on other grounds that may be simpler psychologically, and normally all the different sources of information available for the resolution of lexical ambiguity will be consistent in pointing to the same interpretations.

In order to establish a hypothesis that can be improved later, the problem can be divided into two parts. Assume, first, that a polysemous word is associated in the mental lexicon with information that can be characterized as a set of concepts the word can be used to express. The whole set is probably retrieved whenever the word is heard. Second, assume that there are cognitive processes that search the immediate linguistic context of the word for clues to which concept is intended on any particular occasion of its use. Note that on this view it does not matter greatly what the alternative concepts actually are. It is necessary merely to have associated with each concept a set of contextual features adequate to select it over all the others. Therefore, it is the parts of the lexical entry other than its definition that must be exploited for the purposes of disambiguation. A minimal list of such kinds of information was proposed in the introduction to this chapter (pp. 62–63).

First on the list is the pronunciation of the word. By definition, polysemy cannot be resolved on that basis. Next on the list is the syntactic category of the word. From experience with a sizable corpus, Kelly and Stone (1975) estimate that between 60 and 70 percent of the disambiguations involve determining the part of speech; they observe that, with a few exceptions (like words ending in -ed or -ing), these are the easiest ambiguities to resolve. The contextual information required to determine a word's syntactic category is given by its alternative subcategorizations, another kind of information on the list.

To take an example that has been considered by other workers (Macnamara 1971; Kelly and Stone 1975; Caramazza, Groeber, and Zurif 1976), the word *line* can be used as a noun or a verb. When it is marked [+N] its subcategorization as a common noun will be [Det ____] or [Det Adj ____]; the occurrence of a determiner or a determiner followed by an adjectival construction in the context immediately preceding *line* should suffice to indicate that only the nominal concepts that *line* can express need be considered. When *line* is marked [+V], it may be intransitive (*The men line up*) with the subcategorization [NP ____ up], or transitive with the subcategorizations [NP ____ up NP] (*The officers line up the men*) and [NP ____ NP] (*Trees line the streets*). To identify *line* as a verb, therefore, it is necessary that the immediate context satisfy one of these patterns. It is obvious that the necessary contextual information is precisely the kind that a good parsing system provides (see Chapter 3), so these problems will not be explored here.

There is left, therefore, the difficult 30 to 40 percent where the same part of speech can express different concepts and disambiguation must occur on some nonsyntactic basis. For example, in *Trees line their streets* the sense of *line* is that something is arranged in a row or a series, whereas in *Silks line their coats* the sense is that something covers the inside of something else. Perhaps the most robust semantic difference is that, in the second sense, the direct object of the verb must have an inside to be covered. In order to use this difference for disambiguation it would be necessary to retrieve the direct object of *line* and to determine whether it can refer to some kind of container. In uses like *Books line their walls,* however, both senses are acceptable; the books are presumably arranged in rows and the interior walls of the rooms (since rooms are containers) are covered with books. In order to distinguish these two concepts expressed by the verb *line,* the condition that *line* means "cover the inside of" when the direct object is a container must be formulated as a selectional restriction, another kind of information on the list. This fact implies that the lexical entries for words denoting containers must include that information.

To continue with this example, the worst ambiguities of *line* are found among its nominal uses. Consider the senses of *line* in the following phrases: *line of sight, line of rope, line of flight, line of march, line of trees, line of battle, line of kings, line of duty, line of work, line of merchandise, line of argument, line of thought, line of poetry, line of type.* As long as the prepositional phrase is present, there is no serious problem of disambiguation, but often it is omitted. How do people decide that *A line was missing* probably means "line of type"; that *He follows the party line* probably means "line of argument" or "line of thought"; that *He hit it on a line to the shortstop* probably means "line of flight"; that *He was behind the enemy line* probably means "line of battle"; that *They threw a line to the swimmer* probably means a "line of rope"; that *Everyone in his office has to toe the line* probably means "line of duty"?

This diversity (and this is only a sample) poses a formidable problem. Presumably it would be necessary to appeal to still another kind of information on the list, the person's situational expectations given the circumstances set by the general discourse. But that is the most poorly understood information of all—there is danger of exchanging one area of ignorance for another.

Two approaches seem open. The first is to assume that *line* really does have all these different meanings, plus whatever others can be extracted from good dictionaries. This is the lexicographic approach;

the bigger the dictionary, the more senses of a word it will distinguish. This strategy calls for making as many conceptual distinctions as possible, associating with each concept a set of appropriate selectional restrictions and clues to the appropriate discourse contexts, and providing the disambiguator with a correspondingly elaborate set of search procedures and decision rules for following all these subtle conceptual distinctions. Obviously, the more compulsive the lexicography, the more problems of disambiguation there will be. Moreover, the number of distinctions that could be drawn is limited only by the size of the corpus (by the number of different discourse contexts in which *line* can occur)—and that, given the possibility of metaphor, is no limit at all. Sooner or later it will become necessary to stop drawing distinctions and to start grouping minimally different senses together.

The second strategy is just the opposite: to stop drawing distinctions sooner rather than later. A new sense is introduced only when it is clear that to combine it with some other would result in a meaning so general as to be useless. Ullmann (1962) has observed that most polysemy comes from relatively modest extensions of existing meanings, not from historical convergences of words with different etymologies (homonyms). What is wanted are meanings that can be extended, plus rules characterizing what extensions are likely to seem intelligible to a native speaker.

Core senses   To continue with *line* as an example, the noun might have a central meaning: "something one-dimensional connecting two points." The problem is to characterize the relations between this core sense and all the particular senses of *line* listed in the dictionary. Those relations should not be specific to *line,* but should apply to other semantic extensions elsewhere in the lexicon, in which case they might be formulated as rules that people learn when they master their English vocabulary. For example, a row of objects (trees, points, people, chairs, or whatever) can be called a line, even though there is nothing one-dimensional that extends continuously from one end to the other. But the objects are *in line.* The acceptability (in American English) of the phrases *in line* and *out of line* suggests that lines can be regarded as containers—something that objects can be in or out of. This relation between the core sense and the extended sense is not unique to *line*; there are many things that are not containers that things can be *in* or *out of* in much the same way:

trouble, love, tune, view, action. Thus, it might be possible to find a general rule that would characterize semantic extensions of all these words—including, of course, *line.*

Yet even if such a rule could be found, it would still be necessary to know when it was appropriate to apply it. Selecting from a list of rules the right one to generate the extended sense seems almost as great a problem as selecting the right sense from a list of alternative senses. The general theory of disambiguation would be simpler with such rules, but the problem of disambiguating a particular polysemous word would be little eased. Therefore, whichever strategy is adopted, contextual information must play an important role in disambiguation.

It does seem counterintuitive, however, to suppose that a hearer waits until encountering a polysemous word before noting its context. If people rely on general knowledge of what follows in the normal course of events under the circumstances set by the discourse context, they must really rely on it. That is to say, in the midst of a conversation about somebody on a ship saving a drowning swimmer, it would be distinctly odd to have to execute a disambiguation routine to discover whether the context is the nautical kind in which *line* might be understood as *rope.* Any nautical knowledge the hearer has will already have been brought to bear. If there is some central or core sense of *line* as "something one-dimensional connecting two points," only the most rudimentary nautical knowledge—for example, that ships carry rope—would be required to infer that a rope would fit that description in the situation under discussion. But even if some landlubber could not draw that inference, he could probably understand the gist of the account if he knew only this core sense. Suppose, therefore, that the mental lexicon contains only one or two nominal concepts that *line* can express; given an occurrence of *line,* the problem is not to choose among fifty or more prestored concepts or rules, but to sharpen a core concept in a manner appropriate to the discourse and the sentence in which the word occurs. In other words, perhaps *line* looks so polysemous because lexicographers have dragged in a lot of contextual information that is really not part of its meaning.

This approach requires two assumptions: (a) it is possible to identify central or core senses of polysemous words, and (b) it is possible to formulate construal rules governing the ways a core sense can be extended to provide other senses.

With respect to the claim that there are core senses, no general methods for identifying them can be offered at the present time. The hope that such methods may be found, however, is nourished by some of Ross's (1976) observations about active verbs. In English it is possible to create derived verbs by attaching such prefixes as *re-* or *mis-* to other verbs: *rewind* and *misspell* are familiar examples. Moreover, the process is productive, as Ross illustrates with such examples as *re-toilet-train* and *misfondle,* which are unfamiliar but perfectly comprehensible. The relevance to assumption (a) is that the sense of the verb that is incorporated in such constructions is almost always the core sense. For example, *lift* has one sense ("pick up") as a verb of motion and another sense ("steal") as a verb of possession. In order to decide which is the core sense and which is derived, ask people to paraphrase the sentence *They relifted my table.* Since this sentence is easily understood to mean that the table was picked up again, but is an odd way to say that the table was stolen again, most paraphrases will involve the motional sense, thus indicating that motion, not possession, provides the core sense of *lift.* Or, again, *hit the bottle* has an extended sense of "drank liquor excessively," but in *The drunk mis-hit the bottle,* the verb *mis-hit* is understood to incorporate the core sense of *hit* as a contact verb, not the extended sense of drinking. Some exceptions can be found (for example, *The platoon retook hill 29* is understood to incorporate the derived sense of *take* as "capture"), and the test is limited to active verbs, but Ross's observation suffices to illustrate what a method for identifying core senses might look like.

Construal rules   With respect to (b), the need for construal rules, attention can be called to syncategorematicity. A word (*of, the, some, right,* for example) is syncategorematic if its meaning depends on the other words it is used with. A notorious example is the adjective *good* (Katz 1964), which can mean "sharp" when used with *knife,* "comfortable" when used with *chair,* "focal" when used with *red,* "skillful" when used with *violinist,* and so on. It would be absurd to suggest that all these various meanings should be entered into lexical memory for *good.* The problem is less dramatic for other adjectives, but it still exists. A big insect is not as big as a small horse; the size expressed by *big* or *small* depends on the average size of whatever is denoted by the noun it modifies. Even *red,* which seems relatively self-sufficient, takes different values when used to modify *paint, hair, brick,* or *light.* It is apparent that construal rules will be needed in any case; they are simply one type of redundancy rule and serve to simplify the statement of hypotheses about lexical concepts. If construal rules are necessary for syncategorematic terms, they may as well be introduced for other words as well.

Some examples of construal rules may be helpful. Katz proposes that functional information stored with the head noun determines the sense of *good*. In the absence of contextual information to the contrary, the normal use for knives is cutting and a good knife is one that cuts well; the normal use for chairs is sitting, and a good chair is one that seats well; and so on. A construal rule would be:

(17)   Given a noun phrase in which a positive (negative) evaluative adjective modifies the noun, the combination is to be construed as meaning that the entity denoted by the noun has in greater (lesser) than average degree those properties required for the expected activity, use, or appearance of such objects.

Evaluative adjectives could then be defined as all those whose definitions include, say, the concepts POSITIVE VALUE or NEGATIVE VALUE: senses of *good, great, swell, fine, nice, excellent* on the one hand, or of *bad, lousy, rotten, stinking, terrible, awful* on the other. Since no long list of meanings for *good* is required, no serious problems of disambiguation arise. However, sometimes the normal basis for evaluation may be replaced by a basis given or implied in the context.

A second construal rule applies to a set of English nouns that can be used as verbs, where the verbal sense is related to the nominal sense in a regular way. *Paint* is an example: it is a mass noun, but when used as a verb, *x paints y,* it means that "*x* covers the surface of *y* with paint." The same relation holds between the nominal and verbal senses of other mass nouns such as *butter, color, dye, enamel, grease, oil, plaster, salt, sand, shellac, soap, tar, varnish, water.* (It even holds for some count nouns, like *blanket, carpet, paper*; oddly, *dust* can be construed as both "to cover" and "to uncover.") Since there are many such noun/verb pairs in English, a rule can be formulated for construing the sense of the verb given the sense of the noun:

(18)   When nouns of type M are used as verbs, the meaning of x Ms y is to be construed as "x covers the surface of y with M."

Without an independent criterion to determine which nouns are of type M, the rule is relatively weak. Yet it accounts for some of the polysemy of *line*.

When *line* is used as a verb, it has this covering sense: *Wrinkles lined his face* can be construed as "Wrinkles covered (the surface of) his face with lines," or *Mary lined her paper for writing* can be construed as "Mary covered (the surface of) her paper with lines for writing." (The covering sense is dominant, to the exclusion of the core meaning of *line,* when the verb is used to mean "x covered the inside surface of y," as in *Silk lined her coat, Bookcases lined the room,* or, perhaps, *The money lined his own pockets.*)

Rule (18) represents common information that must be learned for every type M word. Presumably the learning gets easier with repeated instances; a person who knows the meaning of the noun *sand* and has already encountered several examples of this construal rule should have little trouble understanding what is meant the first time he hears *sand* as a verb in a sentence like *The Highway Department is expected to sand all icy roads.* With this much preparation, it is not difficult to interpret such sentences as *When he jarred my elbow he coffeed my shirt,* even though the use of *coffee* as a verb may never have been heard before.

Both rules (17) and (18) involve knowledge of conventional use; it is difficult to characterize most type M nouns without describing their use for covering things. For example, paint is paint if it can cover, adhere to, and protect surfaces—regardless of its base or color or even whether it is wet or dry. Once again it is seen that functional knowledge must be included in entries in the mental lexicon. Since this functional knowledge is different for different type M words, however, each application of the construal rule can be modulated appropriately—the "covering" that is construed for *He salted his steak* is not the same "covering" required for *He buttered his bread.*

Some construal rules are quite simple. For example, if *un-* can be prefixed to an adjective, the result is an antonymous adjective: *happy/ unhappy, profitable/unprofitable, afraid/unafraid,* and so on (see Rule (2) in Chapter 1).

(19)   An adjective prefixed by *un-* is to be construed as the negation of the sense of that adjective.

Rules creating causative verbs from nouns or adjectives by affixing *en-, dis-, -ify, -ize,* or *-en* are only slightly more complicated.

Another example is a construal rule for double-purpose causative verbs — verbs (like *line up*) that are causative when used transitively and noncausative when used intransitively. *Turn* in *Mary turned the wheel* is causative: DO (*Mary, s*) & CAUSE (*s*, (ROUND (TRAVEL)) (WHEEL)). In *The wheel turned,* however, the agent is omitted and the causative sense has vanished: (ROUND (TRAVEL)) (WHEEL). Miller and Johnson-Laird (1976) propose that the former analysis can serve for both the transitive and intransitive uses if it is supplemented by a construal rule:

(20)   Given a sentence in which a causative verb of type DP is used intransitively without an agent, the verb is construed as if all operators involving the agent or the agent's actions are deleted.

A causative verb of type DP is, of course, a double-purpose verb; its conceptual analysis will either have to be marked specifically as DP or else written in some special format different from that used for other transitive causative verbs. In the example above, *turn* is a verb of type DP and *The wheel turned* omits the agent, so the rule applies. Since there is no agent to serve as the first argument of DO (*x, s*), that part of the transitive analysis must be deleted; since there is no action of the agent to serve as the first argument of CAUSE (*s, s'*), that operator must also be deleted; all that is left is (ROUND (TRAVEL)) (*y*), which is the correct noncausative interpretation of the intransitive verb. Since intransitivity is a syntactic property, no serious problems of disambiguation arise.

A final example can be based on what Miller and Johnson-Laird call the principle of implication, which they illustrate for verbs. The verb *tie* has a meaning that is equivalent to "fasten"; *move* has a meaning equivalent to "sell"; *see* has a meaning equivalent to "visit"; and so on. The idea is that fastening something implies tying it, selling something implies moving it to the customer, visiting something implies seeing it. These implications are relative to particular circumstances, but a qualified construal rule can be formulated:

(21)   Where a simple implication of the form *If s, then s'* is usually true in the normal course of events, given certain circumstances, then under those circumstances it is frequently possible to construe the verb in *s'* as equivalent in meaning to the verb in *s*.

So qualified, (21) can be little more than a rule of thumb; in the form given it relates different senses, but does little to reduce the problem of disambiguation. Sharpening the rule would necessitate surveying a variety of cases where this kind of construal works and contrasting them with cases in which it fails.

This small sample of construal rules gives some idea of the variety that can be expected. (Other examples can be found in Carroll and Tanenhaus 1975; their "rule-schemes" for word formation include rules for construing the meanings of compound words.) Although much work will be required, core senses supplemented by construal rules probably offer the best hope of progress in understanding disambiguation processes. The approach is superior, on the one hand, to an assumption that every common word is indefinitely polysemous or, on the other, to an assumption that no general principles relate superficially different meanings to one another.

It may be objected that several psychological studies suggest that words with multiple meanings have multiple entries in semantic memory (see, for example, Rubenstein, Garfield, and Millikan 1970; Jastrzembski and Stanners 1975). The case for core senses plus construal rules, however, does not assume a single-entry theory of semantic memory, but only assumes that the variety of lexical concepts is far smaller than good lexicography would suggest. If there are multiple entries, at least construal rules would enable theorists to characterize the redundancies among them.

The assumption is that construal rules are not active processes that the lexical component executes every time a word is used in some derived sense; any active processing must be the responsibility of those cognitive systems that consult the lexical store. A more plausible psychological claim about most construal rules might be that they represent what is learned over and over — the conceptual core — as new senses are acquired. A person who knows a general meaning and an appropriate construal rule will have to do some active processing the first time he encounters a particular use, but after it becomes familiar it should be stored and ready for direct retrieval in the appropriate contexts. If so, a great variety of senses could come to be stored with a frequently used word, yet all would be related to a relatively small number of core concepts.

One implication of this argument would be that the words a person had known for the longest time would have had the greatest number of opportunities to accumulate alternative meanings in different contexts. The correlation between polysemy and frequency of use has already been noted. Carroll and White (1973a,b) have shown a correlation between frequency of use and the age at which words are learned; indeed, they suggest that many of the effects of word frequency on subjects' performance in psychological experiments with words might better be attributed to the age of acquisition. In any case, there is some reason to believe that the words first learned are also the most polysemous.

And so the discussion returns to the rather perverse fact that the words people know best are the most ambiguous, but now with some reason to believe that the alternative meanings must be related in many ways (ways that should be characterized by construal rules). In short, the problem is to characterize a disambiguation system that could exploit those relations, but serious attempts to find a solution must await better information about what the relations are.

Modals

One instance of polysemy is of sufficient linguistic and psychological importance to merit separate discussion. It arises in contexts like the following:

(22)   a.   The bell ought to ring when you close the circuit.
       b.   You ought to be considerate of others.
       c.   John ought to be here.

The polysemous word is the verb *ought,* which seems to have a moral or ethical sense in (22b) that it does not have in (22a). Thus (22c) is ambiguous between (at least) these two senses—the moral sense that might be understood if (22c) were spoken in church on Sunday morning and the nonmoral sense that might be understood if it were spoken by someone looking for John. Wertheimer (1972) has analyzed this difference in detail and has argued that *ought* is not polysemous in this particular way. His argument illustrates a possible way to separate the lexical definition of a word from contextual expectations that influence how it is understood. Consider possible sources of the ambiguity of (22c).

How can the nonmoral meaning of *ought* be formulated? A rough paraphrase of sentence (22a) is

(23)   The laws of electricity entail that when an electric bell is connected in a circuit with an appropriate source of electric power it rings.

This paraphrase is constructed from three components that are not explicit in (22a): (a) the laws of electricity, (b) the fact that the bell is connected to a source of power, and (c) the ringing of the bell. These three components are necessary for understanding nonmoral *ought*. In more general terms, they are (a) a system K of organized knowledge and belief, (b) a set of circumstances C under which the system is relevant, and (c) the consequence y that the system specifies under those circumstances.

A lexical entry for nonmoral *ought* will contain its pronunciation, the fact that it is a modal auxiliary verb, and its subcategorization— which for present purposes can be taken to be something like [NP _____ *to* VP]. Then, if x is a pointer to the nominal concept expressed by NP, and y to the predicative concept expressed by VP, a definition might be

(24)   OUGHT (x, y): x "ought to" y, relative to a set of circumstances C, if:
    (i) There is a system K such that, if C obtains, then $K \Vdash y$.

Note that (24) does not specify what system of knowledge K, what circumstances C, or what consequence y are involved, but merely that there are all these things; what they are in any particular use of nonmoral *ought* is no part of the meaning of that word. Indeed, a speaker may be vague about them himself; the utterance of *Looks like it ought to rain* does not assume that the speaker is a meteorologist, but merely that he has some general belief to the effect that when the sky looks a certain way (that is, under certain circumstances) something entails that it rains. In other uses, the system K may be some commonplace knowledge of what people do or what usually happens in the normal course of events.

Now apply the definition of nonmoral *ought* given in (24) to sentence (22b), where *ought* seems to have a moral interpretation. In this case the paraphrase would run something as follows:

(25)   The principles of morality entail that when a person interacts with other people he is considerate.

This paraphrase runs parallel to (23), except that the principles of morality are substituted for the laws of electricity, the circumstances have to do with personal interactions rather than electric circuits, and the consequence entailed by the system under those circumstances is consideration rather than noise. Wertheimer makes the point that exactly the same definition serves for both moral and nonmoral *ought*.

If *ought* is not the source of ambiguity in (22c), what is? The answer is reasonably obvious: it is not immediately clear from *John ought to be here* what the relevant system K is. A similar ambiguity could arise if, say, it was not clear whether the relevant K was some branch of physics or some branch of chemistry. That kind of ambiguity must also be cleared up by people who hope to understand each other, but it is not as serious as the confusion of moral and nonmoral systems, because people do very different things in those two cases. If a nonmoral system is violated, people suspect that the system is wrong, but if a moral system is violated, people assume that the violation is wrong. All of which is very important, but it is not part of the meaning of *ought,* which has been maligned as ambiguous because considerations have been introduced into its definition that do not belong there.

Wertheimer's analysis of *ought* suggests one way to relate lexical analyses to more general systems of knowledge and belief: leave a place in the definition where that knowledge is to be inserted from context, but do not specify what it is. It is not yet clear whether this strategy works outside the realm of modal words, but within it a variety of important words can be treated in the same way. For example, such verbs as *fail* can be defined in terms of *ought: x fails to y* presupposes that *x ought to y* and asserts that *x does not y.*

Reichenbach (1947) made an argument similar in many respects to Wertheimer's when he discussed the meanings of the modal words *necessary, possible,* and *impossible.* His definitions can be represented in the present notation as follows:

(26) NECESSARY (s): s is "necessary" relative to a set of circumstances C if:
   (i) There is a system K such that, if C obtains, then $K \Vdash s$.
   (ii) C obtains.

Reichenbach notes that there is an absolute sense of *necessary* that is not relativized to any circumstances C. It is the absolute sense that has been the subject of much philosophical disagreement; ordinary speech uses the relative sense almost exclusively. Given (26), *impossible* is defined as NECESSARY (NOT (s)), and *possible* could be defined as NOT (IMPOSSIBLE (s)). Reichenbach observes, however, that when something is necessary, people do not say that it is possible, even though the two are compatible under that definition of *possible*. Therefore, as a closer approximation to ordinary speech, he proposes that *possible* be defined as NOT (IMPOSSIBLE (s)) & NOT (NECESSARY (s)). Something is possible if there is a system K that does not entail it is impossible or necessary, or if no system K seems to be relevant to it.

Given definitions of these key modal concepts, *must* and *have to* can be defined in terms of NECESSARY, and *can* in terms of POSSIBLE (Karttunen 1972). Moreover, when applied to pairs of events, NECESSARY and POSSIBLE provide a basis for CAUSE, PREVENT, and ALLOW, which are incorporated into many verbs. All causative verbs would then be dependent for their interpretations on the system, circumstances, and consequences characteristic of the contexts in which they are used. Dispositional adjectives like *rigid* can also be defined in these terms.

The deontic terms *obligatory, impermissible,* and *permissible* can be defined in a parallel manner, but with the stipulation that system K is a system of social conventions (if that is your theory of ethics). *Had better* seems to require a slightly different treatment. The sense in which children use and understand it might be characterized as

(27) HADBETTER (x, s): x "had better" s, relative to an agent A and circumstances C if:
> (i) There is a system of social conventions K such that, if C obtains, $K \Vdash$ PUNISH (A, x)
> (ii) PREVENT (s, C)

This notion—that you must do what prevents the circumstances under which the system entails your punishment—seems to characterize the early thinking of children on questions of obligation and necessity.

The modal auxiliary verb *will* presumably takes its future sense by virtue of its semantics of prediction. This, too, could be accommodated in a formulation that makes a place for a system of knowledge or belief K and a set of circumstances C under which the future event is entailed. The modal *would* may differ from *will* in that it does not assert that circumstances C obtain. And the volitional sense of *will* involves knowledge of personal intentions.

The details of these proposals are of less importance than the general strategy that they illustrate. If, as polysemy seems to require, a language user's fund of general knowledge and belief must be included in any psychologically plausible account of how he disambiguates sentences, then it is necessary to consider serious theoretical proposals as to how and where that knowledge is invoked.

Morphological Relations

The theoretical problems raised by polysemy are closely related to those raised by the semantics of morphologically related words. For example, under the heading of polysemy are such problems as the conceptual relation between *move* as a verb and *move* as a noun; under the heading of morphology are such problems as the conceptual relation between *move* as a verb and *movement* as a noun. Whatever formulation is proposed for one of these relations must also be proposed for the other. *Movement, motion,* and the noun *move* (derived from the verb by addition of the zero morpheme, $\emptyset$) are all conceptually related to the verb *move* in similar ways. Morphological relations are slightly easier to handle, however, because the conceptual relations to be characterized are usually marked explicitly by affixes that signal the morphological relations.

Morphology, the study of the structure of words, has two major branches: inflectional morphology and word formation (sometimes called lexical morphology); word formations, in turn, are usually subdivided into two kinds: derivatives and compounds. The major distinction is generally respected in good dictionaries by combining inflectionally related words in a single entry and making separate entries for derivatives and compounds. In both branches, the relations under study must be characterized phonologically, syntactically, and semantically—that is to say, the list of four kinds of information that must be included in each lexical entry is also a list of what must be considered in attempting to characterize morphosemantic relations between lexical entries. In keeping with the limits set for this chapter, phonological relations will be ignored (but see Chomsky and Halle 1968; Aronoff 1976). The central interest here is in the semantic relations, but they cannot be discussed without also considering syntactic relations.

Inflectional morphology   Inflections are those changes in a root word that indicate case, number, gender, person, mood, voice, tense, and aspect; inflections do not affect the syntactic category of the root words. Compared with other languages, the inflectional morphology of English is superficially simple: nearly all inflections are suffixes; there are relatively few of them; and their occurrence is controlled by rules of syntax. Case, gender, and person are marked morphologically only for pronouns; in addition, person is marked only in the third-person singular ending on present tense verbs and in the unique verb *to be*. Yet even this inflectionally reduced language poses subtle and difficult problems for conceptual analysis.

It has generally been assumed by transformational generative grammarians that inflections are introduced by phrase structure rewriting rules in the base component of the grammar and then attached to the appropriate stems by some transformation. Although this characterization is psychologically unattractive, its economy for syntactic theory cannot be denied. The cost of abandoning the transformations could be a considerable complication of the rewriting rules to include detailed specifications of syntactic environments and perhaps an increase in the number of lexical entries required for every inflected word. Moreover, a multiplication of lexical entries would violate the lexicographic convention of treating all inflectionally related words as a single lexeme.

A theorist should be reluctant, therefore, to propose two separate lexical entries for, say, *table* and *tables,* or *walk* and *walked,* relying on common conceptual constituents to establish their semantic relations. Moreover, there would be little to gain from such duplications, because rules for the plural and for past tense are completely productive — all nominal concepts can be pluralized and all predicative concepts can be tensed (apparent exceptions like *sheep* and *put* are not conceptual exceptions; they simply require special morphological rules); even mass nouns like *butter* or *sand* can be pluralized in appropriate contexts. The conventional approach taken in syntactic theory seems the judicious choice for conceptual theory as well. That is to say, just as *tables* can be represented syntactically as *table* + plural, so the nominal concept can be represented as TA-BLE (PLURAL (x)). And just as *walk* can be represented syntactically as *walk* + past, so the predicative concept can be represented as (PAST (WALK)) (x). This approach does not mean that inflections must have separate entries in the mental lexicon; since the appropriate inflection must be introduced by a morphological rule for forming the plural or past tense, we can think of its meaning as given by that rule.

Some of the problems that arise in formulating such a morphological rule can be explored by considering the plural. One part of the rule would specify its pronunciation as /s/, /z/, or /ɨz/, depending on the word to which it was attached. A second part would specify that it was to be attached only to nouns. It is still another part, the semantic part, that we wish to consider in detail.

The obvious semantic interpretation is that PLURAL (x) means "more than one x." But consider an example of apparent polysemy of the plural. In *Some boys and girls were there* the indefinite *some* indicates that this is probably the first mention of these boys and girls, so anaphora is probably not involved—it is unnecessary to search the list of assigned pointers for antecedent reference or identification—and the affix *-s* on *boy* and *girl* can be taken to mean simply that the predicate phrase *were there* applies to more than one boy and more than one girl. The same interpretation would probably be given to *Boys and girls were there,* without the *some,* but *Boys and girls need exercise* would be understood generically—that is, as all boys and all girls. Therefore, the plural seems to be ambiguous between an existential and a universal sense. This ambiguity, however, should not be attributed to the plural itself but to its indefinite use—exactly the same ambiguity occurs in the indefinite singular: *a boy* can be understood existentially, as in *A boy was there,* or generically, as in *A boy needs exercise.* Moreover, the ambiguity vanishes in the definite plural: *the boys* has only a universal sense, although the universe must be determined from context—it means all of a particular group of boys identified antecedently (see Chapter 4 and Stenning 1976). But in either the definite or indefinite use, the plural inflection means "more than one." The ambiguities that arise must be resolved by determining whether indefinite plurals are being used existentially or universally, and that can be settled only from context or general knowledge: it is a pragmatic problem, not a problem of the semantics of the plural inflection. The plural is not polysemous; the morphological rule that introduces it will have the same meaning wherever it is applied.

Word formation: Derivatives Derivative morphology, like inflectional morphology, also deals with affixes that can form new words from old (*sense, sensate, sensation, sensational, sensationalize, sensationalization*). Unlike inflected forms, derivatives are often of different syntactic categories, and their rules of formation are only partially productive and apparently uncontrolled by rules of syntax. Lexicographers generally prefer to list derivatives as separate entries, with definitional relations where appropriate.

Consider first how the meanings of derivative words might be formulated. *Movable,* for example, consists of the verb *move* and the affix *-able*.[1] If MOVE (x, y) is the definition of *move* and POSSIBLE (s) is the definition of *-able,* the definition of *movable* might be: λy $(\exists x)$ [POSSIBLE (MOVE (x, y))]—"having the property that something can move it," in crude paraphrase. (Other parts of the morphological rule would determine the pronunciation of the compound, indicate that adding *-able* makes it [+Adj], and characterize the categories of words to which the rule can be applied.) Similarly, if *-ment* has a sense of nom $(\exists y)$ P (y), *movement* could be defined compositionally as the nominalization of intransitive *move*: nom $(\exists y)$ MOVE $(\emptyset, y)$—"having the property of existing by virtue of something moving," in crude paraphrase. (The existential quantifiers in these derived definitions amount to a procedural claim that these variables could be assigned but it is not necessary to do so.) Again, if HAPPY (x) is the definition of *happy* and (NOT (P)) the definition of *un-,* then *unhappy* would be (NOT (HAPPY)) (x). Again, if SIMPLE (y) is the definition of *simple* and (DO (x, s) & CAUSE $(s,$ P)) is the definition of *-ify,* then (DO (x, s) & CAUSE $(s,$ SIMPLE (y))) would be the definition of *simplify.*

The question is how these derivative meanings are generated. If we think of the rule as being applied every time the derivative word is used, then in order to maintain the psychologically plausible claim that the core of the mental lexicon is a passive data base, the system that consults the lexicon will have to perform a compositional interpretation whenever a derivative is to be retrieved. It is reasonable to suppose that such compositional operations would take a measurable amount of time, yet Kintsch (1974) has offered evidence from studies of reading comprehension that passages containing morphologically complex words take no longer than comparable passages containing morphologically simple words.

It seems advisable, therefore, to assume that the rule that generates

[1] Derivational affixes differ in how tightly they attach to the root. See Aronoff 1976 for a discussion of the differences between *-ible* and *-able,* as in *edible/eatable, comparable/comparable, feasible/*feasable.*

the derivative is applied only when the word is being entered into the mental lexicon; thereafter, the word is simply retrieved, not generated anew. Jackendoff (1975a) discusses this question in terms of redundancy rules that express the semantic relation of the derivative to its stem. He compares two possibilities, which he calls the impoverished-entry theory and the full-entry theory. For example, suppose there is a redundancy rule M to the effect that lexical entries of the form V + *able* are related to entries of the form V in such a way that the meaning of V + *able* is λy ($\exists x$) [POSSIBLE (v (x, y))], where v is the concept expressed by V. According to an impoverished-entry theory, attempts to retrieve *movable* would find an entry in the lexicon, but the definitional part would simply say "derived from *move* by rule M" (the syntactic category, subcategorization, and selectional restrictions might be similarly determined by the redundancy rule M if the entry is completely impoverished). A full-entry theory, on the other hand, assumes that both *move* and *movable* have full entries and that redundancy rules facilitate learning but play no part in the interpretation of sentences.

It is obvious that an impoverished-entry theory shortens the lexicon by assuming that computations implicit in the redundancy rule will be performed by some system external to the lexicon—but that is precisely what was to be avoided on psychological grounds. In order to evaluate the two theories, Jackendoff considers how a lexicon might be learned most economically, rather than how it might be stored most economically. If, for example, a person already knows *move* and redundancy rule M, he will already have learned a great deal of what he has to learn about *movable*. In this case, however, both theories have plausible things to say. In order to choose between them it is necessary to consider how they would handle rootless derivatives like *retribution* and *retributive,* where there is no corresponding verb **retribute*.

According to an impoverished-entry theory, either (a) there must be an entry **retribute* that is marked as being unusable as a word but that satisfies the requirements of redundancy rules for deriving *retribution* and *retributive*; or (b) the information corresponding to **retribute* must be included in one member of the pair and two redundancy rules must be used to derive the other from the first; or (c) the information corresponding to **retribute* must be included in both entries, *retribution* and *retributive*. Option (a) claims that the lexicon contains entries that have all the properties of words except that you cannot use them, which seems intuitively implausible. Option (b) poses a question as to which word is basic—which one includes the information corresponding to *retribute and so becomes the source from which the other is derived by two redundancy rules— where either answer seems unnaturally arbitrary. Option (c) is, of course, just the full-entry theory, which assumes no uninsertable entries, poses no unnatural questions as to which rootless derivative is basic, and does not require the active use of redundancy rules in the processes of comprehension.

Aronoff (1976) takes a position similar to Jackendoff's, although he speaks of the meaning of the affix, not in terms of redundancy rules, but as part of the morphological word-formation rule that is required in any case to introduce the affix. Aronoff argues that derivatives formed with some highly productive affixes (like the -ly that converts adjectives into adverbs) should not be listed separately in the dictionary. On either view, however, affixes do not have separate lexical entries; most (if not all) derivatives have full lexical entries; a rule applies only when a derivative is being entered into the lexicon; the rules should be evaluated as explanations of why words are easier to learn in some orders rather than others and not in terms of length of the lexicon or speed of sentence comprehension.

Word Formation: Compounds   Compounds are word formations like *bulldog, steamboat, oatmeal, whalebone, redskin, cranberry*. Lees (1960) proposed that compounds are derived by nominalization transformations from sentences like *Dog that looks like a bull, Boat driven by steam, Meal made from oats*. This approach has difficulty with compounds like *cranberry*, where *cran-* is not a lexical item, but these can be set aside as not true compounds. For consistency with the proposed treatment of derivatives, compounds too should be given separate lexical entries; the relations among them are better represented by redundancy rules than by grammatical transformations—in which case *cranberry* can be treated in much the same way as *retribution*.

In order to test Lees's formulations, Gleitman and Gleitman (1970) asked people with different educational backgrounds to interpret such artificial compounds as *foot house-bird, foot-house bird, bird foot-house*. Using what they believed a transformational theory would predict as the correct interpretations (redundancy rules could represent the regularities equally well), Gleitman and Gleitman found considerable variation in accuracy among people as a function of their formal education. Those who had received only a high-school education made many more mistakes than those who had gone on to postgraduate study. Miller and Johnson-Laird (1976) interpret this difference to mean that, unlike rules for sentence formation, rules for word formation are an intellectual luxury—"people who do not know the rules for compounding can still use the language without difficulty by learning the meanings of compounds independently" (p. 688). The present argument would say that learning the meaning of *bulldog* would be faster if you already knew the meaning of *bull* and *dog* and had learned other compounds that could be characterized by a redundancy rule of the form "*x* that looks like *y*." But it would not say that in order to exploit that previous learning it would be necessary to know the redundancy rule well and self-consciously enough to be able to use it in the interpretation of novel compounds. Conceptual redundancies can facilitate learning even for learners who are not aware that they are learning the same thing over and over.

Since the program proposed in the present volume assumes that morphological relations must account for many facts formerly attributed to syntactic transformations, it is worthwhile to quote Jackendoff: "It is quite natural and typical for redundancy rules to relate items only partially, whereas transformations cannot express partial relations" (1975a, p. 658). This distinction corresponds to plausible psychological principles of learning and makes the lexicon the repository of all those exceptions (partial relations) that are the despair of language learners, but it leaves the processes of sentence production and interpretation subject to rapid, automatic, and relatively exceptionless rules of syntax. Redundancy rules provide a way to characterize the contribution to present lexical learning from previous lexical learning without becoming entangled in all the difficult problems of how new concepts develop and how their lexical representation and use depends on a person's store of general knowledge. It would seem, therefore, that an investigation of the semantics of morphologically related words could provide an excellent opportunity for fruitful collaboration between linguists and psychologists.

3 An ATN Approach to Comprehension

ERIC WANNER AND MICHAEL MARATSOS

For a number of years we have been exploring the feasibility of using an augmented transition network (ATN) to model the syntactic aspects of sentence comprehension. This chapter offers a general introduction to the ATN approach and reports the results of two experiments derived from our way of modeling syntactic processing.

Initial efforts to model syntactic processes incorporated transformational grammar as a subcomponent and exploited the grammar directly during processing (Miller and Chomsky 1963, for example). Subsequent models abandoned the direct application of the grammar and opted instead for a battery of heuristic strategies to do the work of syntactic processing (Bever 1970a; Fodor, Bever, and Garrett 1974). The net result of these developments has been to dilute belief in the psychological reality of transformational grammar. In this chapter, we will try to show that the ATN approach to syntactic processing has clear advantages over the models of both previous types and will argue that the ATN approach leads to a somewhat different view of the psychological reality of the grammar.

We will begin with a brief discussion of our reasons for using augmented transition networks to model human comprehension, followed by an informal description of an illustrative ATN system. After these introductions, we turn to the problem of relative clause comprehension and show that the ATN approach permits us to construct a simple but general model of relative clause processing. We then assess the psychological validity of the model by testing several predictions it makes about the comprehension of relative clauses.

Why Augmented Transition Networks?

There are a number of reasons why we believe that augmented transition networks provide an interesting and promising framework for constructing models of sentence comprehension:

In addition to the authors, our research group has included M. Bierman, R. Kaplan, B. Sheil, S. Shiner, and S. Whitney. We are indebted to this group for a variety of contributions to the research reported here. This research was supported by a National Science Foundation Grant (GS39836).

Flexibility   ATN is an ambiguous term. Originally it referred to a particular computer system which provided a syntactic analysis of the sentences submitted to it. The system evolved through several stages in the work of Thorne, Bratley, and Dewar (1968), Bobrow and Frazer (1969), Woods (1970, 1973), and Kaplan (1973a,b). In the course of this evolution, the system was generalized so that there is now a set of notational conventions for describing ATN systems that, in effect, define a large family of syntactic analyzers. Thus the term ATN now refers to this set of notational conventions as well as to a particular syntactic analyzer. The generalization of ATN notation is particularly important for modeling comprehension because it permits us to identify and manipulate parameters of the system in an effort to fit the facts of human performance. For example, it is possible to vary the system's grammatical knowledge about syntactic patterns independently of the schedule the system uses to apply that knowledge to the analysis of input sentences. The independence of grammar and schedule has a number of useful consequences. For example, we can construct a grammar capable of describing all interpretations of some syntactically ambiguous sentence, but arrange a schedule that causes the system to produce the psychologically popular interpretation first. This scheduling arrangement can then be tested in terms of its independent empirical consequences. For an example of this testing strategy see Wanner and Kaplan (forthcoming).

Depth   No one knows exactly how much syntactic information is determined during the comprehension of a sentence. Early transformational models of comprehension performed a complete syntactic analysis, up to and including deep structure information about basic grammatical relations. Subsequent proposals, such as the heuristic strategies scheme or Shank's (1972) conceptual-dependency analyzer, have been based on the assumption that very little syntactic information may be required during comprehension. At present, perhaps the safest wager is that the amount varies from sentence to sentence. In sentences where there is little contextual or semantic information, a complete syntactic analysis may be necessary. In others, a contextual or semantic resolution may be possible.

An ATN provides a convenient framework for studying variation in the depth of syntactic analysis during comprehension. The system is capable, in principle, of performing a complete syntactic analysis of any sentence, providing information about the contextually appropriate syntactic categorization of each word, a proper bracketing of each phrase and clause, and specification of the grammatical function of every word, phrase, and clause. These functional specifications are rich enough to provide at least as much semantically relevant grammatical information as Chomskian deep structures (Chomsky 1965). However, unlike earlier models of comprehension, which performed complete syntactic analyses, an ATN can make intermediate results available for semantic analysis in a natural way. Therefore, it provides a relatively straightforward way of simulating the case in which comprehension can be completed on the basis of partial syntactic analysis. On the other hand, unlike comprehension models that are limited to shallow syntactic analysis, an ATN sets no prescribed limits on the depth of processing. Thus, hypotheses can be derived from any level of analysis and tested against the facts of human performance. For example, Kaplan (1972) reproduced the predictions of the heuristic strategies scheme by deriving hypotheses about human performance from the ATN operations involved in determining surface structure information about syntactic categories and phrases.

The hypothesis we will test in this paper is based on the ATN operations involved in determining semantically relevant grammatical functions of phrases, such as subject of the sentence, direct object of the sentence, and so on. If we obtain positive results on these tests, it will indicate that, at least in some circumstances, such functional information is determined syntactically during comprehension. Questions concerning variability in the depth of syntactic processing can then be addressed empirically by adding semantic or contextual information and seeing whether our predictions about syntactic processing hold up.

Direct processing   An ATN recovers functional information directly from surface structure. No intervening transformational rules determine the deep structure of the sentence (Chomsky 1965). Models that apply such rules have proven to be both computationally unmanageable (Woods 1970; Kelly 1970) and empirically unsatisfactory (Fodor and Garrett 1966). The heuristic strategies scheme is empirically superior to transformational models precisely because it abandons the idea that comprehension involves the internal operation of transformational rules. The ATN approach maintains this advantage.

Operating characteristics Several operating characteristics of the ATN system appear to correspond to operating characteristics of human comprehension. Here we list three.

Serial operation. An ATN processes sentences sequentially, word by word, and an abundance of psychological evidence is now available confirming our introspective impression that the human listener does the same thing. This evidence includes studies of click location (Holmes and Forster 1970; Reber and Anderson 1970), sentence completion (Forster 1966), and grammaticality judgments (Marks 1967), to name just a few. While it is correct that none of these studies requires the conclusion that every component process in comprehension proceeds exclusively from left to right, it appears to be broadly true that information that arrives early in a sentence is processed before information that arrives later. Indeed, given the known limitations of short-term memory, it is hard to see how comprehension could proceed in any other way (Wanner 1974).

Active processing. It is well known that the human listener is not dependent upon physical cues, like prosody or punctuation, to signal the appropriate way to break an input sentence down into its component phrases (see Garrett, Bever, and Fodor 1966; Lieberman 1967)—although such cues may facilitate comprehension. Apparently, the listener can use his knowledge of linguistic structure and his appreciation of surrounding sentence context to impose a phrase structure analysis on the input sentence. An ATN can do the same, and in doing so it provides an explicit characterization of how linguistic and contextual knowledge are employed.

Organization of procedures. Another psychologically interesting characteristic of the ATN is that its processing procedures naturally divide into tasks that correspond to linguistic units, such as phrases and clauses. The numerous experiments with clicks superimposed on linguistic input indicate that listeners respond to clicks more quickly and located them more accurately when they occur between linguistic units than when they occur within units (Fodor, Bever, and Garrett 1974). Such results can be explained in a natural way by a system that divides its processing into tasks, if we assume that the amount of attention devoted to locating the click is a decreasing function of the number of linguistic tasks active at the time of its arrival. Controversy about which linguistic units influence reactions to clicks then translates into alternative ways of decomposing the comprehension process into tasks.

An Illustration of the ATN

We turn now to a highly informal description of an ATN, intended only to give a rough idea of the system and to make clear the motivation of our hypothesis about relative clause processing. For purposes of illustration we will simplify the description in several important respects. First, we ignore or describe incompletely some components of the system. Second, we have fixed some of its parameters arbitrarily. Third, we omit any description of provisions the system makes for recovering from decisions that are locally feasible but subsequently prove untenable. Fourth, we limit our illustration of the system's operation to a highly restricted class of simple, active, declarative sentences. For a more extensive illustration, showing how the system handles a large and interesting subset of English, see Woods and Kaplan (1971); more detailed discussions of ATN formalism are available in Woods (1970, 1973) and Kaplan (1973a,b).

General organization An ATN can be conceived of as a syntactic analyzer with two main components: a processor and a transition network grammar. The ATN operates in an environment in which it interacts with a perceptual analyzer and a semantic analyzer in the course of processing a sentence. All these analyzers make use of a common lexicon and communicate with one another by way of a common working memory. During comprehension the system processes information in the following way: The perceptual analyzer tentatively identifies any linguistic input as a segmented string of words. This identification process requires lexical information as well as information about the syntactic and semantic analysis of local context (Wanner 1973; Woods and Makhoul 1973). The ATN works its way through the output of the perceptual analyzer word by word, formulating, testing, and modifying hypotheses about syntactic categorizations, phrase boundaries, and grammatical functions. As these hypotheses are produced, they are stored in working memory, where they are available to the semantic and perceptual analyzers.

Basic mechanisms Like most artifacts, sentences have parts and the parts have functions. An ATN attempts to break down any input sentence into its significant parts and determine the appropriate function of each.

The major parts of a sentence are complex patterns of words, such as phrases and clauses. Thus the problem of partitioning a sentence is essentially a problem of pattern recognition. Pattern recognition systems ordinarily contain two components: a component that stores representations of the patterns to be recognized and a component that compares the stored patterns against the current input in order to determine which pattern or patterns apply. In an ATN the component that stores patterns is the transition network grammar; the component that applies the stored patterns to the input is the processor.

The way in which any part of a sentence functions appears to depend largely upon its situation within a particular sentential context. Therefore, an ATN includes a set of context-sensitive operations that assign functions. These operations are stated within the transition network grammar and are carried out by the processor.

The elementary ATN grammar described in Figure 3.1 illustrates

Sentence Network:

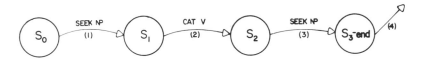

Noun Phrase Network:

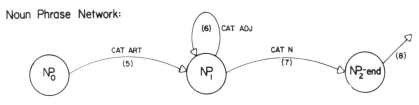

ARC	ACTION
1	ASSIGN SUBJECT to current phrase
2	ASSIGN ACTION to current word
3	ASSIGN OBJECT to current phrase
4	ASSEMBLE CLAUSE
	SEND current clause
5	ASSIGN DET to current word
6	ASSIGN MOD to current word
7	ASSIGN HEAD to current word
8	ASSEMBLE NOUN PHRASE
	SEND current phrase

Figure 3.1 A simplified ATN grammar

the mechanisms involved in partitioning a sentence and assigning functions. This grammar is organized as a pair of separate networks. Each network is composed of a set of states represented as circles. The symbols inside the circles provide a unique name for each state. The arrows that connect the states are called arcs. If an arc connects two states, it is possible to make a transition between those states in the direction indicated by the arc. The labels on each arc specify conditions that must be satisfied before a transition can be made. In addition, certain actions must be performed whenever a transition over an arc is made. The actions associated with each arc in the present grammar are listed in the table below Figure 3.1.

A sentence is analyzed as the processor works its way through the grammar, state by state, examining the input sentence, word by word, to see whether it meets the conditions stated on the arcs. Wherever the conditions are satisfied, the processor executes the actions associated with the current arc, makes the indicated transition, and turns its attention to the next word in the sentence.

We can demonstrate the details of this process by following through the analysis of a simple sentence:

(1)   The old train left the station.

The processor begins the analysis of the sentence at initial state S_0 in the sentence network, with its attention focused on the first word in the sentence. The only arc leaving state S_0 is arc 1, which bears the label SEEK NP. This label indicates that a transition can be made over arc 1 only if the current portion of the input sentence can be analyzed as a noun phrase (NP). To determine whether the condition is met, the processor attempts to execute the instruction to SEEK a noun phrase: first, it suspends all operations on the sentence network and stores in working memory any partial results that may have been obtained in the course of traversing the sentence network; second, it stores the identity of the arc that prompts the SEEK action; and third, it shifts attention to the initial state of the noun phrase network.

The noun phrase (NP) network describes a set of sequential patterns that can constitute noun phrases. The processor compares these patterns against the input to determine whether there is a recognizable noun phrase within the current portion of the input. The comparison process starts with arc 5, where the condition CAT ART indicates that a transition can be made if the syntactic category of the current word is an article. The processor tests this condition by looking up *the* in the lexicon. Since *the* is an article, the condition is satisfied and the processor performs the action associated with arc 5. That action ASSIGNs the function label DETerminer to the current word, thus creating an association between the function label and the word. This association is stored in working memory, so it remains available at subsequent stages of the syntactic analysis of the sentence and is accessible to other components of the comprehension system.

When the ASSIGN action is completed, the processor makes the transition over arc 5 to state NP_1 and shifts its attention to the second word in the sentence (*old*). Two arcs (6 and 7) leave state NP_1. In principle the processor might attempt them according to any schedule. In the present illustration, we will suppose that arcs are tried one by one, starting with the arc nearest the top of each state and proceeding clockwise. With this schedule the processor will try arc 6 first at state NP_1. Arc 6 bears the condition CAT ADJ, which is satisfied because *old* can be an adjective. Therefore the action associated with arc 6 is performed, ASSIGNing the label MODifier to *old*. Then the transition is made, returning the processor to state NP_1. The current word is now *train,* but since *train* cannot be an adjective, the attempt to take arc 6 a second time will fail. The processor then tries arc 7. Here the CAT N condition is satisfied because *train* can be a noun. Thus *train* is ASSIGNed to the function HEAD, and the transition is made over arc 7 to state NP_2-end. As the name of the state indicates, the end of a possible noun phrase has been reached. The processor responds to this fact by automatically taking arc 8, which has no conditions.

The first action on arc 8 instructs the processor to ASSEMBLE a noun phrase, which it does by packaging together under the name NOUN PHRASE all the associations between words and function labels that have been stored in the course of traversing the NP network. We can represent this named bundle of associations as follows:

[NOUN PHRASE
    DET   = the
    MOD = old
    HEAD = train]

The equal signs represent the associations between words and function labels; the brackets signify that these associations have been grouped together.

After the ASSEMBLE action is completed, the processor executes the SEND action. This action makes the noun phrase package available, as the current phrase, to the sentence network. Finally, the processor completes the transition over arc 8 by consulting memory to find out which SEEK arc activated the NP network and shifting attention back to that arc. Thus, attention returns to arc 1, where the SEEK NP condition is fulfilled because the current phrase is a noun phrase. Therefore, the processor performs the labeling action on arc 1, ASSIGNing the function label SUBJECT to the current phrase. The transition over arc 1 is then completed, leaving behind in memory a hypothesis about the initial phrase in the sentence and its grammatical functions.

The analysis of the remainder of the sentence is straightforward. The next word, *left*, is recognized as a verb on arc 2 and ASSIGNed the function label ACTION. Then arc 3 causes another SEEK NP, which is completed successfully when the NP network analyzes *the station* via arcs 5 and 7. This phrase is then ASSEMBLEd and returned to arc 3, which labels it as an OBJECT. The analysis of the sentence is completed when the processor reaches state S_3-end with no more input words to analyze. The actions on arc 4, which has no conditions, are then executed automatically. These actions are similar to those taken at the end of state NP_2-end. They bundle together all the associations created during the analysis of the sentence and label the bundle as a CLAUSE. The resulting set of associations can be represented as follows:

```
[CLAUSE
   SUBJECT = [NOUN PHRASE
                DET   = the
                MOD   = old
                HEAD = train]
   ACTION   = left
   OBJECT   = [NOUN PHRASE
                DET   = the
                MOD = station] ]
```

Significant features   Several aspects of the syntactic processing illustrated in our example are of potential psychological interest.

First, as advertised, the ATN provides an explicit example of an *active* recognition process. Decisions about syntactic categories and phrase boundaries are not exclusively determined by the input. Rather, they are a joint function of the input, the system's general information about stable linguistic patterns represented in the network, and the system's local information about context contained in the current analysis path through the network. For example, in sentence (1) *the old train* is recognized as a noun phrase, but in another context the same sequence of words may be analyzed differently.

(2)   The old train the young.

In sentence (2) *the old train* will be recognized as the noun phrase *the old* followed by the verb *train*. Applying the grammar of Figure 3.1 via the sequential schedule used to process sentence (1), the analysis of sentence (2) would be obtained by first trying the noun phrase analysis of *the old train*. However, this analysis reaches a dead end at state S_1 when the current word is *the* and the only arc available (arc 2) requires that the current word be a verb. In this situation, the processor must back up over the input and the arcs previously taken, trying alternative arcs at each state. In sentence (2), this back-up procedure will reach state NP_1 where the word *old* can be recognized as a noun on arc 7. When this transition is made, the rest of the analysis of sentence (2) follows straightforwardly: *train* is recognized as the main verb of the sentence on arc 2, and *the young* is recognized as its object on arc 3.

Second, as discussed earlier, the ATN provides a natural way to divide syntactic processing into tasks by means of separating the grammar into a number of independent networks. Figure 3.1 illustrates only two such networks, but in principle any number of independent networks is permitted. At present, the major empirical motivation for establishing separate networks is to eliminate redundancy from the ATN grammar. It is a fact that the internal structure of a noun phrase is largely independent of its location within a clause. Therefore, if there were no NP network in the grammar of Figure 3.1, exactly the same set of arcs would necessarily be reduplicated to handle noun phrases before and after the verb. By placing these arcs in a separate NP network, which can be activated by a SEEK NP arc at any point in the S network, the grammar of Figure 3.1 avoids this redundancy. Similarly, a more elaborate ATN grammar, designed to handle multiclause sentences, might activate the S network at several points within the analysis of a complex sentence, thus avoiding redundant statement of the arcs internal to each clause.

We would not claim that the elimination of redundancy necessarily leads to psychologically valid divisions among networks in an ATN grammar. However, there is experimental evidence that both clauses (Fodor, Bever, and Garrett 1974) and noun phrases (Levelt 1970a) serve as perceptual units during comprehension. Thus redundancy considerations and experimental data may converge to indicate a psychologically appropriate way of decomposing comprehension into tasks.

Third, it is important to point out that the economy of representation gained from dividing the ATN grammar into separate networks is purchased at the cost of some increase in processing effort. In order to move back and forth between networks, the processor needs three types of facilities: one for storing the identity of the SEEK arc that activates a network, so that control can return to the correct SEEK arc when the network is completed; one for storing any partial results achieved by the network that issues the SEEK, so that the computations of this network can be resumed successfully when the SEEK is completed; and finally, a facility like the SEND operation, to transfer information between networks. Any or all of these facilities might be difficult to implement psychologically and might therefore place limits on the degree to which syntactic processes can be decomposed into tasks. Indeed, it may not be at all farfetched to imagine that linguistic structure has evolved in such a way that the language learner's need for simple, nonredundant linguistic representations is balanced with the language user's need for linguistic representations that are easy to employ. With respect to the division of syntactic processes into tasks, the point of this balance will depend in part upon the cognitive cost of operating the facilities required to implement tasks.

Our fourth and final point underlines a remark made earlier: in the syntactic processing performed by an ATN, the operations that assign function labels must be made sensitive to context. As Chomsky (1957, 1965) has demonstrated, surface structure conveys functional information by a complex variety of cues. Moreover, in different contexts different cues may signal a given grammatical function. Transformational grammar handles this problem by generating abstract structural descriptions that display the grammatical functions of each phrase in a uniform way. Thus transformational grammar can apply uniform structural definitions of the grammatical functions in all contexts. But to do so, it must resort to transformational rules to relate the deep and surface structures of each sentence. An ATN requires no such structural transformations because it derives functional information directly from surface structure. However, in order to accomplish this, the ATN must apply what amount to different definitions of the grammatical functions in different contexts.

In an ATN, context sensitivity is achieved in several ways. First, since the operations that assign functions are embedded within the network grammar, they can automatically be made sensitive to prior context. For example, a noun phrase can be assigned to the function SUBJECT on arc 1 because any phrase located by that arc is sentence initial. If the same noun phrase is located by arc 3, it can be assigned to the function OBJECT because arc 3 can be taken immediately after the main verb of the sentence.

Sensitivity to subsequent context is more difficult to achieve. One method employs the kind of back-up procedure described in connection with sentence (2). Thus, the network grammar can be so constructed that any function assignment that subsequently proves incorrect will always cause the analysis to block. Once blocked, the processor can back up and try a new analysis path containing different function assignments. Applied across the board, this solution would require a separate sequence of arcs for every sentence type that displays the grammatical functions in a different arrangement.

A somewhat less cumbersome solution can be achieved if the ATN is given the power to change the function label on a given element as subsequent context requires. For example, in simple passive sentences, the initial noun phrase functions as object, not subject. However, we can permit the ATN to continue labeling the initial noun phrase as SUBJECT (thereby handling active sentences) so long as it has the power to recognize passive sentences subsequently and make the appropriate labeling change. The recognition of passives can be accomplished by adding to the grammar CAT V arcs that test for the presence of a *be* auxilliary verb and a past-participle ending on the main verb. If these characteristic passive markings are found, actions associated with the CAT V arcs that make the discovery can then relabel as OBJECT the NP previously labeled SUBJECT.

The relabeling action permits an ATN to base its initial hypothesis about the grammatical function of an element on prior context and later rescind that hypothesis if necessary. This scheme is efficient just so long as prior context carries some information about grammatical function. In situations in which prior context is almost totally uninformative, however, it makes sense to forgo an initial hypothesis and wait until subsequent context provides the information necessary to make a more informed guess about the grammatical function of an element. An ATN can postpone the assignment of grammatical functions by labeling a questionable element with a special tag called HOLD. An element so tagged is said to be on the HOLD list, from which it can be RETRIEVEd and assigned a function at a subsequent point in the network. Our discussion of relative clause processing in the following section will illustrate in some detail the use of the HOLD list.

The major computational effort in analyzing a sentence by means of a transformational grammar stems from applying the transformational rules to obtain deep structure. Therefore, transformational models have been tested largely by comparing the length of the transformational derivation of a sentence with its psychological complexity. Such comparisons have generally yielded poor results, leading to the virtual abandonment of transformational models of comprehension (Fodor and Garrett 1966). In analyzing a sentence by an ATN, the major computational effort stems from making function assignments that are appropriate to context. Therefore, one way to examine the psychological feasibility of an ATN model is to test for a correlation between the computational effort of making such assignments and the psychological effort required during comprehension.

As we have noted, an ATN has more difficulty handling subsequent context than prior context. All three methods of making function assignments sensitive to subsequent context require additional work of the system. Both back-up and relabeling increase the number of computations required to process a sentence; on the other hand, if the system postpones function labeling, the HOLD operation will temporarily increase the load upon working memory. Such additional work should be expected wherever the operation of a serial syntactic process must be contingent upon subsequent context. Therefore, any ATN model of comprehension motivates the prediction that, in general, when function assignments depend upon subsequent context, the complexity of comprehension will increase. In the following sections we develop and test one special case of this prediction.

An ATN Model of Relative Clause Comprehension

Consider now the problem of extending the ATN of Figure 3.1 to handle relative clauses. To simplify matters, we will deal only with clauses that, in the language of transformational grammar, are restrictive, unreduced, and nonextraposed (Smith 1961; Ross 1967b).

The structural facts about relative clauses of this type are reasonably straightforward: they always appear immediately after a noun phrase and they are always introduced by a relative pronoun; internally, they are structurally identical to independent declarative clauses except that they appear to have one constituent missing. To simplify again, we will consider only clauses where the missing constituent is a noun phrase. Some examples of this type of relative clause run as follows:

(3) . . . *the girl* who Δ talked to the teacher about the problem . . .
(4) . . . *the teacher* whom the girl talked to Δ about the problem . . .
(5) . . . *the problem* that the girl talked to the teacher about Δ . . .

We will refer to the noun phrase that precedes the relative clause as the head noun phrase (or head NP). The location of the missing element will be referred to as the *gap* in the relative clause. In the examples above, the head NP is italicized, and Δ indicates the location of the gap.

The function of a restrictive relative clause is to modify its head NP by limiting the range of possible entities to which the head NP can refer. The relative clause does this by making a statement that is true of the particular entity or entities referred to by the head NP. For example, a construction like (5) does not refer broadly to any problem, but rather just to that problem of which it is true that

(6) The girl talked to the teacher about the problem.

Notice that, as (6) demonstrates, the statement conveyed by the relative clause in (5) must itself involve the head NP. Thus, the head NP plays an implicit functional role within the relative clause; in order to understand how the relative clause modifies the head NP, the listener must determine what this within-clause function of the head noun phrase is.

Some languages, such as Hebrew, explicitly mark the within-clause function of the head NP by including within the relative clause a pronoun that refers back to it (Keenan 1972). English and many other

European languages do not; instead, the within-clause function is signaled by a gap in the relative clause. This statement need not be qualified by the observation that the relative pronoun itself sometimes carries information about function. The gap is still the determining signal.

Of the four major relative pronouns in English, only one provides any information about function, and this most listeners summarily ignore. The impersonal pronouns *which* and *that* provide no information at all. As for the personal pronouns, the nominative case, *who,* is supposed to indicate that the head NP plays the role of the surface structure subject of the relative clause; *whom,* that the head NP can be assigned any role played by a postverbal noun phrase—but there are so many such roles that this information is marginal. Moreover, the usage of *who* and *whom* has slipped so badly that they are almost totally uninformative. Most speakers find both *the girl who loved the boy* and *the girl who the boy loved* perfectly acceptable. In a small experiment we found that given a question like *Who did the girl hit?* and then a sentence, *The boy who/whom the girl hit was angry,* subjects responded as quickly to the *who* as to the *whom* form. They apparently ignored the information supplied by the relative pronoun and relied exclusively on the location of the gap to determine the within-clause function of the head NP.

The signal provided by the gap in the relative clause appears to work according to the following principle: the within-clause function of the head NP is always equivalent to the function the head NP would have served if the relative clause had been an independent declarative clause with that phrase inserted at the gap—a clause like (6), for example. In order to determine the phrase's within-clause function, the listener must find the gap in the relative clause and assign to the head NP the grammatical function appropriate to that location.

The ATN framework permits us to represent the process of gap finding in a simple way which captures the redundancy inherent in the structural similarities between relative and declarative clauses. This solution makes essential use of the HOLD facility. Instead of expanding the NP network with a large set of arc sequences to cover all possible relative clause patterns, we simply add three new arcs to the NP network. The first of these arcs tests for the presence of a relative pronoun at the end of the head noun phrase; if the test is successful, an action associated with this arc will place the head NP on the

HOLD list. The second new arc then issues a SEEK to the sentence network; this SEEK will cause the processor to attempt to analyze relative clause as if it were an ordinary declarative clause, using the existing S network. Given the network grammar as currently constituted, the attempt will fail when the processor reaches the gap in the relative clause and SEEKs a noun phrase where none exists in the input clause.

At this point the third new arc comes into play. Suppose we add to the grammar an arc that bypasses the entire NP network by traveling directly from its initial to its final state, and that we condition this arc so that it can be taken only if there is an entry on the HOLD list. If this condition is met, an action associated with the arc RETRIEVEs the contents of the HOLD list and restores it to current status in working memory. Given this simple addition to the NP network, the attempt to treat a relative clause as a declarative clause will now succeed. When the ATN reaches the gap in the relative clause and SEEKs a noun phrase, the head NP will be on the HOLD list. Therefore, the bypass arc will RETRIEVE it from HOLD and restore it to working memory. The ordinary SEND action at the end of the noun phrase network will then return the head NP to the arc that initiated the SEEK NP, and that arc will automatically assign the head NP the same function label it would assign to a noun phrase that occurred at that point in an independent declarative clause.

Figure 3.2 provides an explicit representation of this model of relative clause processing. Note that this network is identical to that of Figure 3.1 except that arcs 9 and 10 have been added to handle relative clauses, and arc 12 has been added to bypass the NP network at the gap. We can illustrate the operation of this network by applying it to the following sentence, which is just sentence (1) with a relative clause attached to the initial noun phrase:

(7)   The old train that the boy watched left the station.

Just as with sentence (1), the analysis of (7) begins with a SEEK NP on arc 1. As before, *the old train* is analyzed along arcs 5, 6, and 7. With the present network, however, the processor then tries arc 9 and finds that its condition is satisfied because the current word *that* can be a relative pronoun. Therefore, the HOLD action associated with arc 9 is executed.

The effect of the HOLD action is to place on the HOLD list a copy

Sentence Network:

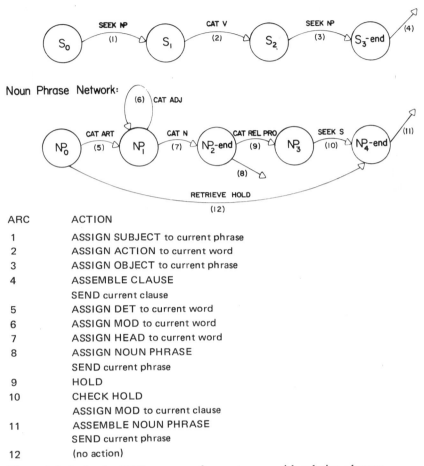

Noun Phrase Network:

ARC	ACTION
1	ASSIGN SUBJECT to current phrase
2	ASSIGN ACTION to current word
3	ASSIGN OBJECT to current phrase
4	ASSEMBLE CLAUSE
	SEND current clause
5	ASSIGN DET to current word
6	ASSIGN MOD to current word
7	ASSIGN HEAD to current word
8	ASSIGN NOUN PHRASE
	SEND current phrase
9	HOLD
10	CHECK HOLD
	ASSIGN MOD to current clause
11	ASSEMBLE NOUN PHRASE
	SEND current phrase
12	(no action)

Figure 3.2 A simple ATN grammar for sentences with relative clauses

of all the grammatical function assignments that have been made on the current pass over the NP network. As a result, the HOLD list will contain a functional analysis of the internal elements of the head noun phrase: DET = *the,* MOD = *old,* HEAD = *train.* Having completed arc 9, the processor now SEEKs an S on arc 10: IT stores the partial results so far achieved during the operation of the NP network and shifts attention to state S_0. From state S_0 the processor analyzes *the boy watched* on arcs 1, 5, 7, 8, and 2 just as if the relative clause were an independent declarative. By this route, the processor arrives at the current word *left* in state S_2, where it SEEKs a noun phrase on arc 3. However, there is no noun phrase in the input sentence at this point, as the processor discovers when it unsuccessfully attempts arc 5. Having failed at arc 5, the processor tries arc 12. Arc 12 has a new condition called RETRIEVE HOLD. This condition instructs the processor to CHECK the HOLD list. If it is not empty, the condition is satisfied and the contents of the HOLD list are restored to ordinary status in working memory. Then the transition over arc 12 to the final state of the NP network is completed.

Note that the effect of arc 12 has been to unblock the analysis of the relative clause by permitting the NP network to be bypassed just at the point of the missing NP. Moreover, since the contents of the HOLD list have been restored to working memory, and since the HOLD list contained the function assignments of the internal elements of the head NP, working memory now looks exactly as it would if elements of the head NP had just been processed. The ASSEMBLE action on arc 11 groups together these elements and labels them as a NOUN PHRASE. The SEND action on arc 11 then returns the phrase to arc 3, which automatically ASSIGNS its correct within-clause function: OBJECT of the relative clause. The analysis of the relative clause is completed when arc 4 ASSEMBLEs the clause and SENDs it to arc 10.

The first action on arc 10 is to CHECK to see whether the HOLD list is empty. This CHECK is important, since we cannot allow the SEEK S on arc 10 to analyze a clause without employing the contents of the HOLD list. If we did, our model would unflinchingly process monstrosities such as *The old train that the boy watched the baseball game left the station*. In such a sentence the CHECK HOLD test on arc 10 will not find the HOLD list empty, because *the boy watched the baseball game* has no gaps and will therefore have been analyzed by the S network without needing to employ the contents of the HOLD list. Hence the CHECK HOLD on arc 10 will find *the old train* still on HOLD; with no gap for the phrase to fill, the CHECK HOLD test will block the analysis of this ungrammatical relative clause, as it should.

In sentence (7), however, the CHECK HOLD test does find an empty HOLD list. Therefore, the remaining action on arc 10 AS-SIGNs the relative clause to the function MODifier, and the transition over arc 10 is completed. At arc 11 the ASSEMBLE action packages together the relative clause and the partial results achieved by the NP network up to the point at which it was suspended by the SEEK S that processed the relative clause. This package will look as follows:

```
[NOUN PHRASE
    DET  = the
    MOD = old
    MOD = [CLAUSE
            SUBJECT = [NOUN PHRASE
                        DET   = the
                        HEAD = boy]
            ACTION  = watched
            OBJECT  = [NOUN PHRASE
                        DET   = the
                        MOD   = old
                        HEAD = train] ]
    HEAD = train]
```

The SEND action on arc 11 returns this package of associations to arc 1 where the entire complex noun phrase is labeled SUBJECT of sentence (7). Thus the SEEK NP on arc 1 is completed. From this point the analysis of sentence (7) will be identical to the analysis of sentence (1).

The HOLD Hypothesis

The HOLD model just sketched yields an intuitively satisfying ATN solution to the problem of relative clause processing because it captures a grammatical generalization about the structural similarities between declarative and relative clauses. The generalization shows up as a real reduction in the complexity of the ATN grammar. Instead of adding a unique sequence of arcs to the NP network to handle each relative clause pattern, the HOLD model permits the ATN grammar to represent the entire set of relative clause patterns as a systematic deformation of the set of declarative clause patterns.

The question that will now concern us is this: Is the HOLD model simply a computational tour de force or is it psychologically relevant? In other words, does the human listener's grammatical knowledge include a comparable generalization about the relation between declarative and relative clauses? And if so, how does the listener make use of this grammatical generalization during comprehension? Specifically, does he employ a comprehension strategy in any way similar to HOLDing the head noun phrase?

To get at this question experimentally, we can exploit the fact that the HOLD model imposes a definite computational cost. Within the ATN framework, the problem of finding the gap in a relative clause is a special case of the general problem of determining grammatical functions on the basis of subsequent context. The gap, which signals the within-clause function of the head NP, always follows the head noun, sometimes at a considerable distance. In effect, the HOLD facility provides a means of postponing a decision about the within-clause function until the gap is discovered, and it does so by maintaining the head NP on the HOLD list. This maintenance necessarily places an increased load upon memory from the beginning of the relative clause, when the head NP is put on HOLD, to the point at which the gap is discovered and the phrase is removed from the HOLD list. Therefore, if the human listener follows a similar strategy of postponing a decision about the head NP until he discovers the gap, we should expect the listener to show a detectable increase in memory load over the same region of any relative clause.

Just to have a name for it, we will call this expectation the HOLD hypothesis. We will call the portion of the relative clause that lies between the relative pronoun and the gap the *critical region* of the relative clause. Simply stated, the HOLD hypothesis predicts that listeners will show a detectable increase in memory load within this critical region.

There is at least one reason to expect that this memory load will be particularly salient for the human listener. Unlike other noun phrases that an ATN stores in the course of analyzing a sentence, the head NP retained on the HOLD list during relative clause processing is stored as an unstructured list of input elements that have not been ASSEMBLEd into a noun phrase; nor has it been ASSIGNed any function label. It is a well-established fact that human memory can retain meaningfully integrated linguistic material more successfully than it can retain unintegrated verbal material (Miller 1951). Assembling a noun phrase and assigning it to a grammatical function clearly contribute syntactic information that is basic to its semantic integration with the rest of the sentence. Therefore, during the time that the head NP is stored on the HOLD list, that noun phrase cannot be semantically integrated with the rest of the sentence. Consequently, the memory requirements involved in storing the head NP on HOLD may be particularly difficult for the psychological system to implement.

Measuring Transient Memory Load

To test the HOLD hypothesis, we need a way to track fluctuations in memory load during comprehension. Since no generally applicable method exists, we invented one (Wanner and Maratsos 1974; Wanner and Shiner 1976). Our method is derived from a technique originally employed by Savin (1967), and it uses his idea that the memory load required to process a sentence can be assessed by presenting subjects with both a comprehension and a memory task simultaneously and measuring the amount of interference between the two tasks. Details of our method run as follows:

On each trial, a sentence is displayed visually on a computer-controlled cathode-ray tube (CRT), one word at a time at a rate of two words per second. Each word appears one space to the right of the preceding word, so that the display advances horizontally across the face of the CRT. At some point during its presentation, the sentence is interrupted and a list of five given names (John, George, and so on) is displayed, one name at a time at a rate of one per second, in a vertical column beginning 1.5 inches below the line on which the sentence is displayed. Upon completion of the list of names, presentation of the sentence resumes from the point of interruption and runs to the end of the sentence.

The subject attempts both to comprehend the sentence and to memorize the list of names, and is tested at the end of each trial. The memory test is simple recall. The comprehension test is composed of questions formed by factoring out the basic propositions in the stimulus sentence and replacing all the noun phrases with interrogative pronouns. The test questions for a sentence such as (7) would be *What left what?* and *Who watched what?* The subjects answer these questions with ordinary declaratives which, if correct, place the missing noun phrases in their proper functional roles.

We assume that the magnitude of the subject's failure to perform both tasks perfectly should be directly related to the size of the transient memory load imposed by the sentence at the point at which it is interrupted by the list of names. Our line of reasoning is as follows. At the interruption point (i) the subject should be supporting the transient memory load (TML_i) necessary to maintain the thread of the sentence up to that point. When the sentence is interrupted, however, the subject faces the additional task of memorizing the list of words, which places another load (L) upon memory. Therefore, at the interruption point the total mnemonic requirement of the two tasks equals (TML_i + L). We assume further that the subject has available some limited mnemonic resource (M). As long as M is greater than (TML_i + L), the subject should be able to memorize the entire list and maintain the thread of the sentence so that he can return to it after the interruption; in this case he should be able to perform both the comprehension task and the recall task perfectly. However, if M is less than (TML_i + L), it should be impossible to both maintain the thread of the sentence and memorize the list, so the subject must show impaired performance on one or both tasks. Since we can assume that M and L are reasonably constant, the magnitude of the impairment should be directly related to changes in the sizes of TML_i: as TML_i increases, so should errors of comprehension and recall.

One standard way to measure interference between two concomitant tasks is to test both tasks on every trial, but to instruct subjects to concentrate primarily on one. Interference is then assessed by measuring errors in the secondary task on only those trials in which the primary task is performed without error (see Norman and Bobrow 1975). This procedure could be applied to our situation by testing both recall and comprehension on each trial and instructing subjects to concentrate primarily on the comprehension task. TML_i could then be measured by counting the recall errors on those trials in which subjects answer the comprehension questions correctly.

However, in our initial attempts to develop a measure of TML in sentence comprehension, we encountered several problems with this procedure. First, the standard procedure requires two tests on each trial, and there is evidence that the responses to the two tests interfere with one another in ways that might obscure the effects of TML (see Epstein 1969; Foss and Cairns 1970). Second, we discovered that subjects find it very difficult to perform the comprehension task perfectly. Error rates in comprehension ran as high as 60 percent (Wanner and Maratsos 1974). Since erroneous trials are eliminated in the standard procedure, error rates of this magnitude create severe missing-observation problems. Moreover, in our early experiments, comprehension errors were positively correlated, across conditions, with both recall errors and hypothetical values of TML_i. The correlation suggests that despite instructions to concentrate upon comprehension, subjects preferred to distribute their mnemonic resources more equally between the two tasks. With this distribution, changes in TML_i affect performance on both tasks in a way that is not registered by the standard procedure.

We therefore attempted to redesign the procedure to accommodate the distribution of M. If the effect of TML_i is spread over the two tasks, then in order to estimate the magnitude of TML_i, we needed to assess the extent of the subject's inability to accomplish both tasks when the interruption occurs at a given point (i) in a given type of sentence. One way would be to count the errors made in answering the questions on the comprehension test on a given trial (a number we will henceforth call Q) and add this number to the number of errors made in recalling the list of names (N). The resulting error score (N + Q) should vary directly with TML_i independently of how the subject chooses to allocate memory between the two tasks; any increase in memory allocated to one task will decrease errors on that task but only at the expense of increasing errors on the other task, leaving the sum of errors on both tasks more or less undisturbed.

The problem with this scheme is that it requires us to measure both recall and comprehension on each trial, thus running the risk that performance on the second test will be affected by the act of responding to the first. To obtain a measure of (N + Q) without introducing such response interference, we modified the standard procedure by adopting a trick first employed by Epstein (1969). On each trial, either the comprehension test or the recall test is administered, but never both. At the conclusion of each trial, the computer displays either the comprehension test or a request that the subject recall as many names as possible from the list. The subject does not know until the conclusion of each trial which of the two tests will be administered. In the instructions to the subject, he is advised that given his ignorance of which test will be administered on any trial, he should do his best to both understand the sentence and memorize the list of names as well as he can.

In order to obtain an estimate of (N + Q) from this procedure in which only N or Q can be measured on any trial, we have arranged our experiments so that every interruption point in every type of sentence is replicated at least twice for each subject. On one replication, the recall test is administered; on the other, the comprehension test is required. Thus for each subject we can sum the N score from one replication with the Q score from the other in order to obtain an estimate of (N + Q) for a given interruption point and sentence type.

Elsewhere, we have assessed the validity of this measure of TML by testing its ability to track fluctuations in transient memory load that occur during the solution of mental arithmetic problems (Wanner and Shiner 1976). In mental arithmetic, unlike sentence comprehension, the contents of working memory appear to be accessible to conscious introspection. Subjects can report how many partial results they are attempting to remember at any point in a problem, and there is overwhelming intersubjective agreement among these reports. What we discovered when we applied our method of measuring TML to mental arithmetic was that the amount of mutual interference between the list-recall task and the arithmetic task is directly related to the number of partial results subjects were attempting to carry along at the point of interruption. Given this result, we can have some confidence in the validity of our measurement procedure, which we will now use to assess the HOLD hypothesis.

Experiment 1

Recall that the HOLD hypothesis predicts a temporary increase in memory load in a critical region running from the relative pronoun to the gap in any relative clause. To test this prediction we constructed 16 test sentences, each one of which could be presented in either of two forms as illustrated by the following example:

(8)
a.   The witch who Δ despised sorcerers   frightened little children.
b.   The witch whom sorcerers despised Δ frightened little children.

Note that the two sentence forms are the same length, contain the same content words, and express almost the same set of semantic relations. The central difference is the reversal of word order within the relative clause, which causes a difference in the location of the gap (marked by Δ in each form). In (8a) the gap falls immediately after the relative pronoun, and the head NP functions as the subject of the relative clause; accordingly, we refer to this form as the *subject relative* form (abbreviated SR). In (8b) the gap falls at the end of the relative clause, and the head NP functions as the object of the relative clause; we refer to it as the *object relative* (OR) form. All sentences conformed to the pattern of the examples in (8); interruption points were located as indicated below:

$$
\begin{array}{cccc}
1 & 2 & 3 & 4
\end{array}
$$

SR: / The N $\left\{\begin{array}{l}\text{who } \Delta \text{ VP / NP}\\ \text{whom NP / VP } \Delta\end{array}\right\}$ V / adj N /
OR: / The N V / adj N /

For our purposes, the useful difference between the OR and SR forms is in the size of their critical regions. For the object relative, the critical region spans the entire relative clause (for example, *whom sorcerers despised*); for the subject relative it ends immediately after the relative pronoun. This difference permits us to locate an interruption point at the same linear position within each clause, such that it falls inside the critical region in the object relative clause but outside the critical region of the subject relative. This point is interruption point 2, indicated by the slash numbered 2. If the HOLD hypothesis is correct, transient memory load should be greater in the OR form than in the SR form at interruption point 2.

To make sure that any difference observed at interruption point 2 is unique to that region of the two sentence forms, we included interruption points 1, 3, and 4 as controls. Since points 1 and 4 occur before and after the sentence is processed, transient memory load should cause no differences between sentence forms at either point. Any differences at these points must reflect general differences in the difficulty of comprehending or remembering the two sentence types. To ensure that any difference observed at interruption point 2 arises from transient memory load rather than from such a general difference between sentence types, we will compare any (OR − SR) difference obtained at interruption point 2 with whatever (OR − SR) differences may be observed at points 1 and 4. If the HOLD hypothesis is correct the (OR − SR) differences at interruption point 2 should be significantly greater than those at points 1 and 4.

Interruption point 3 provides another control, somewhat imperfect, perhaps, but still interesting. Since point 3 falls within the sentence, our measures there may be influenced by various transient effects of unknown sorts. It falls outside of the relative clause, however, and therefore outside the critical region in both sentence forms; accordingly, any difference obtained at this point cannot reflect the HOLD effect. If the HOLD hypothesis is correct, interruption point 3 should not show (OR − SR) differences comparable to those at point 2.

Materials The 16 test sentences were constructed under the following constraints: Every sentence is arranged so that the noun phrase and the verb phrase in the relative clause contain an equal number of words. The verb in the relative clause can accept animate noun phrases as either subject or object. The head noun phrase and the noun phrase within the relative clause are always animate and equally plausible as either subject or object of the relative clause verb. The difference between the OR and SR forms is controlled by the order of NP and VP within the relative clause. In the OR form, the NP precedes the VP, and vice versa in the SR form. Since the two phrases are equally long, interruption point 2 can be located between the two phrases in each form without altering the linear position of the interruption point. Interruption point 3 is always located immediately after the verb in the main clause, which is always the first word after the end of the relative clause. The Appendix contains a complete list of the test sentences.

The comprehension tests were formed by separating the two clauses of the test sentence and replacing the noun phrases in each clause with interrogative pronouns. For example, the comprehension test for sentence (8) was *Who despised whom? Who frightened whom?* The same comprehension test was used whether the test sentence appeared in OR or SR form. In either case, the maximum score in the comprehension test is 4, 1 point for each noun phrase that must be correctly associated with its grammatical function.

The recall tests were made up of a list of five first names randomly selected from *Webster's Unabridged New International Dictionary,* the only constraint being that all names in any list were for the same sex. The maximum score for the recall test is, of course, 5.

Procedure The 16 test sentences were presented in a fixed order within a list of 30 sentences containing 6 warm-up sentences and 8 filler sentences. The order of test and filler sentences was randomly determined. The method of presentation on each trial was exactly as outlined in the previous section: each sentence was displayed one word at a time and was interrupted at some point by the list of names; either the recall test or the comprehension test was administered at the end of each trial.

Design Our basic design has two crossed factors: Sentence Form (object relative or subject relative) and Interruption Point (four points). In addition, our measurement procedure requires assessment of both the list-recall task and the comprehension task. This requirement adds a third crossed factor (Test Type) to the design.

In Experiment 1, subjects are nested within Interruption Point and crossed by Sentence Form and Test Type. Twenty subjects were assigned to each of four groups, and each group received the list of names at only one of the four interruption points. Each subject received four of the test sentences at each combination of Sentence Form and Test Type, and his score in each treatment combination was derived by averaging his performance on these four sentences.

In order to counterbalance the effects of the particular sentences assigned to each treatment combination, we programmed four versions of the experiment, varying the assignments of sentences to treatment combinations according to a Latin square; across all versions every sentence appeared once in every combination of Sentence Form and Test Type. Five subjects in each of the Interruption-Point groups took each version of the experiment. For all analyses, we pooled results over the four versions of the experiment, thus conservatively assigning this source of variance to our error term.

In the analyses that follow, we report results separately for N, Q, and (N + Q). The N and Q analyses are performed simply by segregating the trials associated with each test and treating the results as separate Sentence-Form by Interruption-Point experiments. (N + Q) is formed by summing the N and Q scores for each subject over the comparable Sentence Forms, thus again yielding a simple Sentence-Form by Interruption-Point design in which the first factor is within subjects and the second between subjects.

The subjects for Experiment 1 were 80 members of the Harvard-Radcliffe student population, who were paid for their participation.

Results In Figure 3.3, the number of list-recall errors (N), the number of comprehension errors (Q), and the combined error score (N + Q) are arrayed as functions of Sentence Form and Interruption Point. Analysis of variance of the (N + Q) score yields the following results:

First, there is a significant main effect for Interruption Point: $F(3,76) = 6.00$, $p < .001$. Figure 3.3 shows an inverted U-shaped pattern of errors across the four interruption points. Apparently, there is more interference between the two tasks when the list truly

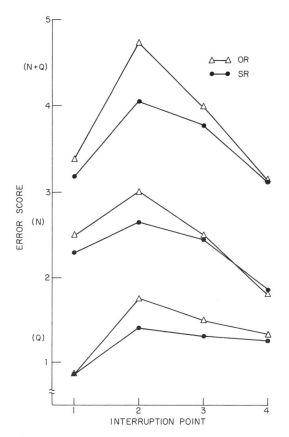

Figure 3.3 N + Q, N, and Q as a function of Sentence Form and Interruption Point

interrupts the sentence (at point 2 or 3) than when it precedes or follows the sentence (at points 1 and 4).

Second, there is a significant main effect for Sentence Form: $F(1,76) = 4.38, p < .05$. As Figure 3.3 shows, the object relative form tends to be somewhat more difficult than the subject relative form at all interruption points. However, as predicted by the HOLD hypothesis, the difference between the OR and SR forms reaches its greatest extent within the critical region, at interruption point 2.

In order to test the significance of this transient effect independently of the significant main effects, the Interruption-Point by Sentence-Form interaction was partitioned into three orthogonal contrasts. The contrast of main interest tests the HOLD-hypothesis prediction that the (OR − SR) difference within the critical region at interruption point 2 will be significantly greater than the average of the (OR − SR) differences at points 1 and 4, where there should be no transient differences between the two sentence types. This difference of differences is positive (about .56 N + Q units) and significant: $F(1,76) = 2.81$, $p < .05$, one-tailed test. Hence, the test of this contrast confirms the HOLD-hypothesis prediction.

Neither of the other two orthogonal contrasts approaches significance. The difference between the (OR − SR) differences at interruption points 1 and 4 is negligible: $F = .465$, $p > .50$. This is to be expected since there are no transient effects at either of these points. Finally, the (OR − SR) difference at interruption point 3 is also insignificant: $F = .682$, $p > .50$. This finding is consistent with the HOLD hypothesis; interruption point 3 falls outside the critical region of both OR and SR relative clauses and therefore should show no differences due to the HOLD effect. The insignificance of the (OR − SR) difference at interruption point 3 suggests that the (OR − SR) difference observed at interruption point 2 is local to that region of the two sentence types.

Finally, note that although we have tested our results in terms of the combined (N + Q) error score, the error scores for the two individual components show essentially the same pattern of results as the combined score. Statistical tests on N and Q consistently replicate the direction of the effects reported for the combined score, but always at a lower level of significance.

Experiment 2

Although the results of Experiment 1 are consistent with the HOLD hypothesis, several alternative explanations must be considered. There are at least two uncontrolled aspects of the test sentences that could conceivably account for the results observed.

First, the OR and SR forms differ in their relative pronouns. Since *whom* is used less frequently than *who,* the extra work involved in recognizing *whom* might be the source of poorer performance at interruption point 2 in the OR form. Cairns and Foss (1971) have found word-frequency effects for another concomitant task (phoneme monitoring), so we may be seeing a similar effect in the list-recall task.

Second, the OR and SR forms differ in surface word order. The differences observed at interruption point 2 may be due to word-order differences rather than to the HOLD effect. Bever (1970a) has proposed that one heuristic strategy that listeners use to determine the grammatical functions of a clause runs as follows: whenever the surface structure is arranged in NP-V-NP order, assume that this configuration can be analyzed as subject-action-object. As Fodor, Bever, and Garrett (1974) have suggested, this heuristic should work for subject relative clauses in which the surface structure sequence, NP rel pro V NP, can be properly analyzed as subject-action-object (unless, of course, the verb is passivized). But the same heuristic will not work for object relatives, which do not appear in NP-V-NP order. Therefore, if listeners do use a strategy of the type Bever suggests, the difference we have observed between subject and object relative clauses may reflect the fact that the listener has a quick and relatively easy solution to subject relatives that he cannot apply to object relatives.

Given these possible alternative explanations of the results of Experiment 1, we devised another test of the HOLD hypothesis, this time controlling both the relative pronoun and the word order in the critical region. The test sentences differ only in their initial verb and in the presence or absence of a preposition at the end of the relative clause. However, these differences change the grammatical role that the head NP plays within the relative clause, as well as the location of the gap. The sentences we employed are illustrated by the following examples:

(9) The customer that the broker persuaded Δ to cancel the illegal transaction had often engineered some shady deals.

(10) The customer that the broker planned to cancel the illegal transaction for Δ had often engineered some shady deals.

In (9) the gap in the relative clause falls between *persuade* and *to,* because *persuade* is the type of verb that requires a noun phrase before an infinitival complement. As evidence, note that (11) is acceptable but (12) is not:

(11) The broker persuaded the customer to cancel the illegal transaction.

(12) *The broker persuaded to cancel the illegal transaction.

Note also that the noun phrase that precedes the infinitival complement in (11), *the customer,* functions both as the object of *persuade* and the subject of *to cancel.* Therefore, if the ATN treats the relative clause of (9) as an independent declarative and assigns the head NP the function it would have received if it had occurred in the gap, then the head NP will be assigned a double function within the relative clause. As usual, this assignment will occur when the ATN discovers the gap, a discovery that should occur while the ATN is attempting to process the word *to,* which falls immediately to the right of the gap.

In (10) the gap does not occur until the end of the relative clause. There is no gap immediately after the verb *planned* because this type of verb does not require a noun phrase before its infinitival complement. As evidence, note that (13) is perfectly acceptable even though it is structurally analogous to (12):

(13) The broker planned to cancel the illegal transaction.

In (10) then, the gap does not occur until after the unfulfilled preposition *for,* as the ATN should discover when it attempts to analyze the auxiliary verb *had* as the beginning of the missing noun phrase. Therefore, it is at this point in (10) that the ATN will assign the head NP to the functional role of the missing prepositional object.

According to Rosenbaum's (1967) classification, verbs like *persuade* take transitive complements and verbs like *plan* take intransitive complements. Following Rosenbaum, we will refer to sentences like (9) as instances of the transitive (T) sentence form and sentences like (10) as instances of the intransitive (I) sentence form.

Figure 3.4 illustrates the modifications in our ATN grammar required to handle these transitive and intransitive complement structures. A brief explanation of these modifications accompanies Figure 3.4.

For the purposes of Experiment 2, the importance of the contrast between the I and T sentence forms is that their assignment points (gap locations) differ but their surface structures are identical up to the end of the relative clause. This relationship lets us locate interruption points at positions that are identical in the surface structure of the two forms, yet fall within the critical region of the intransitive form but not of the transitive. For example, the stretch spanning the words *to cancel the illegal transaction* falls within the critical region of (10) but not of (9). According to the HOLD hypothesis, the head NP must be stored on the HOLD list throughout

Sentence Network:

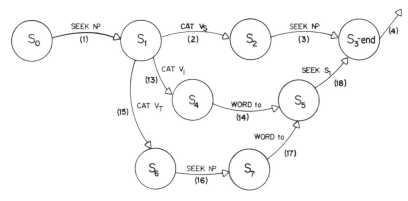

ARC	ACTION
1	ASSIGN SUBJECT to current phrase
2	ASSIGN ACTION to current word
3	ASSIGN OBJECT to current phrase
4	ASSEMBLE current clause
	SEND current clause
13	ASSIGN ACTION to current word
14	SEND SUBJECT to S_1
15	ASSIGN ACTION to current word
16	ASSIGN OBJECT to current phrase
17	RETRIEVE OBJECT
	ASSIGN SUBJECT to current phrase
	SEND current phrase to S_1
18	ASSIGN COMPLEMENT to current clause

Figure 3.4 An ATN grammar for sentences with verbal complements

This network shows the additions to the Sentence Network of Figure 3.2 which are necessary to handle complement structures such as those involved in sentences (9)–(11) and (13). The network includes several new features. First, CATegory conditions on arcs have been expanded to make reference to syntactic subcategories: arc 2 requires a simple transitive verb (V_S); arc 13, a verb that takes an intransitive complement (V_I); and arc 15, a verb that takes a transitive complement (V_T). Second, the conditions on arcs 14 and 17 require that the current word literally be the morpheme *to*. Third, the SEEK on arc 18 refers to a state, S_1, that is internal to the S network. This SEEK shifts attention back to state S_1 and will be successfully completed if the S network can be traversed from that point. In general, we will now permit SEEK arcs to refer to any state in any network. Note that the SEEK to state S_1 is a parsimonious way to handle verbal complements because their structure is identical to the postnominal portion of an independent declarative clause. Fourth, the SEND actions on arcs 14 and 17 include the address of a state, S_1, to which the SEEK S_1 on arc 18 will subsequently shift attention. These addressed SEND actions transfer function-labeled phrases from the

the critical region; hence the hypothesis predicts that any interruption point located in the stretch *to cancel the illegal transaction* will show heavier transient memory load in the intransitive (I) form.

To test this prediction we constructed 12 sentences, each of which could appear in either I or T form (depending on the main verb in the relative clause). All 12 conformed to the following pattern, with interruption points located as indicated:

$$\text{The N that the N } \begin{cases} \text{T: } V_T \; \Delta \text{ to } / \; \overset{1}{V} \text{ the mod } / \; \overset{2}{N} \; \emptyset \\ \text{I: } V_I \quad \text{ to } / \; V \text{ the mod } / \; N \; P \; \Delta \end{cases}$$

$$\overset{3}{V_{aux} \text{ adv } V \text{ det mod } N \; /}$$

Notice that both interruption points 1 and 2 fall within the critical region in the I form, but not in the T form. Interruption point 3 is the control point, included to assess the size of any general difference in difficulty between the two sentence forms. The HOLD hypothesis predicts that TML will be greater in the I form at both points 1 and 2. This difference in TML should be reflected in $(N + Q)$ as $(I - T)$ differences that are significantly greater at interruption points 1 and 2 than at point 3.

Pilot experiment The results of a pilot experiment forced us to modify these predictions. In the pilot, which was run with sentences of a similar format and a single interruption at point 1, we found that $(I - T)$ was negative: contrary to prediction, the T (transitive) form was harder than the I (intransitive), and the difference was marginally significant. There are three possible explanations for this result, and each makes a different prediction about the outcome of Experiment 2.

---

main clause to the arcs following state S_1, which process the complement. In this way the ATN can express the fact that a single constituent plays a functional role in both the main clause and the constituent. Thus, on arc 14 the SUBJECT of the main clause is sent to state S_1 to become the SUBJECT of the intransitive complement clause; similarly, on arc 17 the OBJECT of the main clause is RETRIEVEd, thereby becoming the current phrase, which is then labeled SUBJECT and sent to state S_1 to become the SUBJECT of complement clause.

To become familiar with the operation of this grammar, we suggest applying it first to simple complement sentences such as (11) and (13) and then combining it with the NP network of Figure 3.2 to work through sentences like (9) and (10), which contain complements within relative clauses. Note that a complete analysis of sentence (10) will require arcs to handle the clause-final preposition. For simplicity, these arcs are not shown in Figure 3.4, but could be added in a straightforward way.

(Subscripts indicate the interruption point location of a given $(I - T)$ difference; $(I_i - T_i)$ refers to the $(I - T)$ difference at the ith interruption point.)

Alternative (A). The first possibility is simply that the HOLD hypothesis is wrong and the results obtained in Experiment 1 are due to the confounded surface structure difference between subject and object relative clauses. If true, then there is no reason to expect $(I_2 - T_2)$ to differ from the value already obtained for $(I_1 - T_1)$. Perhaps both differences are no more than the reflection of a global factor that makes the T (transitive) form generally harder. In this case, $(I - T)$ should be the same for all interruption points in Experiment 2.

Alternative (B). The second possibility is that the HOLD hypothesis is correct, but that the HOLD effect at interruption point 1 is obscured by a large general difference between sentence forms in favor of the intransitive form. If true, then the $(I_3 - T_3)$ difference should register a large negative value, and the $(I_1 - T_1)$ and $(I_2 - T_2)$ differences, although still negative, should show a significantly smaller negative value than the $(I_3 - T_3)$ difference, due to the TML effects, which increase the difficulty of the intransitive form at points 1 and 2. Thus the $[(I_i - T_i) - (I_3 - T_3)]$ differences should be significantly greater than zero for both interruption points 1 and 2 ($i = 1, 2$).

Alternative (C). The third possibility is that the negative $(I_1 - T_1)$ value obtained in the pilot experiment is due to a local effect which counteracts the HOLD effect only at interruption point 1. In particular, notice that in the transitive form, interruption point 1 falls immediately after the *assignment point*—the point at which the ATN model retrieves the head NP from the HOLD list and assigns it to the two grammatical roles of the missing NP: object of the main verb of the clause and subject of its complement. In the ATN, these operations take a certain amount of time and computational work. If the listener performs analogous operations, his cognitive work load may also be significantly increased in the region of the assignment point. Such an increase in work load could interfere with his ability to simultaneously memorize the list of names and maintain the thread of the sentence when the interruption occurs at the assignment point. We will refer to this putative effect as the assignment effect. We speculate that it may operate in the transitive sentence form at interruption point 1 to reverse the direction of the $(I - T)$ difference and obscure the HOLD effect. If so, and if the assignment effect is temporary, it may dissipate by interruption point 2 and the HOLD effect may emerge. Thus alternative (C) predicts a significant and positive $[(I_i - T_i) - (I_3 - T_3)]$ for interruption point 2, but not for interruption point 1.

Figure 3.5 summarizes alternatives (A)–(C) in terms of their predictions about transient memory load. We express these predictions in terms of the $[(I_i - T_i) - (I_3 - T_3)]$ difference of differences. These are the predictions at stake in Experiment 2.

Materials   The essentials of the test sentences have been described. As in the previous experiment, vocabulary items were chosen so that the basic grammatical relations of the relative clause could not be determined on semantic grounds. The Appendix provides a list of the test sentences.

The comprehension tests for the two sentence forms were constructed according to the following format, illustrated by the tests appropriate to sentences (9) and (10):

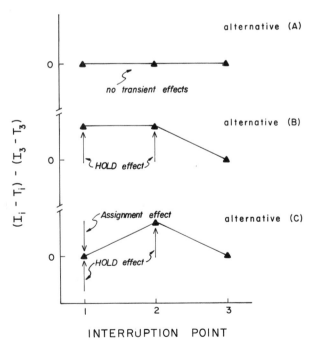

Figure 3.5 Predictions about difference-of-difference scores derived from alternatives (A)–(C). (Assignment and HOLD effects in alternative (C) are arbitrarily assumed to be of equal magnitude for the purpose of illustration.)

For T form: Who persuaded whom to do what?
For I form: Who planned to do what for whom?

Again, the maximum score for each test is 4 points: three noun phrases plus the infinitive are questioned in each sentence form.

Procedure   The 12 test sentences were embedded in a list of 44 sentences which included 8 warm-ups and 24 fillers. Test and filler sentences were arranged in blocks of 3 sentences each, consisting of 1 test sentence and 2 fillers, ordered at random. The entire list of sentences was presented in the following fixed order: 6 warm-ups, 6 blocks, rest period, 2 warm-ups, 6 blocks. The method of presentation on each trial was identical to that of Experiment 1, with one exception. Because of the length of the test sentences, it was impossible to follow the usual convention and display sentences across a single line of the CRT. Therefore, after the interruption at points 1 and 2, the display of the sentence resumed from the left margin of the CRT instead of from the linear point of interruption. For interruption point 3, the point of return to the left margin corresponded to interruption point 1 for half of the sentences and to interruption point 2 for the other half. In order to accustom subjects to this procedure, some of the filler and warm-up sentences were also presented with a return to the left-hand margin at some point in the display. Analysis of performance on the two points of return for sentences interrupted at point 3 showed no differences, and in general the introduction of this change in display technique did not appear to disturb performance.

Design   For each subject, one of the 12 test sentences appeared at each combination of Test Type (comprehension or recall), Sentence Form (I or T), and Interruption Point (three points). Thus the design includes the usual three crossed factors, all of which are crossed by subjects. Twelve versions of the experiment were constructed by rotating the assignments of sentences to treatment combinations according to a Latin square so that, across all twelve versions, every sentence appeared in every treatment combination. Seven subjects were run in each version of the experiment, for a total of 84 subjects.

Results   Figure 3.6 shows N, Q, and (N + Q) as a function of Sentence Form and Interruption Point. Analysis of variance of the

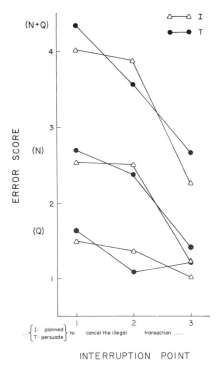

Figure 3.6 N + Q, N, and Q as a function of Sentence Form and Interruption Point

combined error score (N + Q) shows a significant main effect for Interruption Point: $F(2,166) = 43.9, p < .001$. Just as in Experiment 1, interruption points within the sentence generally prove more difficult. Unlike Experiment 1, there is no main effect for Sentence Form. The transitive form is slightly more difficult on the average, but this difference is not significant: $F(1,83) = .95, p > .25$; nor is it consistent across interruption points.

Figure 3.7 shows the $[(I_i - T_i) - (I_3 - T_3)]$ difference of differences obtained for all three dependent variables. If we compare these difference-of-difference patterns with the patterns predicted by alternatives (A)–(C) in Figure 3.5, we find that the predictions of alternative (C) prevail. The Sentence-Form by Interruption-Point interaction can be parceled into two orthogonal contrasts to test this impression. Recall that if alternative (C) is correct, the HOLD effect should show up at interruption point 2 as a significant $[(I_2 - T_2) - (I_3 - T_3)]$

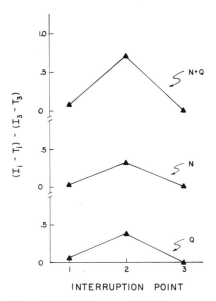

Figure 3.7 Difference-of-difference scores for N + Q, N, and Q

difference of differences. A test of the contrast shows that it is indeed both positive (about .7 N + Q units) and significant: $F(1,83) = 3.65, p = .03$, one-tailed test. This result is consistent with the hypothesis that maintaining the head noun phrase on HOLD should cause the intransitive form to be particularly difficult at interruption point 2.

Note that this result rules out alternative A, which predicts no transient effects in Experiment 2, where surface structure differences are largely controlled. The fact that we observed such effects in Experiment 2 indicates that the positive results of Experiment 1 cannot be written off as an artifact of uncontrolled surface structure differences. Finally, note that the patterns in Figure 3.7 rule out alternative (B); the difference between $(I_1 - T_1)$ and $(I_3 - T_3)$ is clearly negligible. Therefore, the HOLD effect fails to show up at interruption point 1, which is as expected if the effect is neutralized by the assignment effect operating in the opposite direction at that point in the transitive form. The $(I_1 - T_1)$ difference is negative, just as it was in the pilot experiment. However, the second orthogonal partition of the Sentence-Form by Interruption-Point interaction shows that this difference does not reach significance in Experiment 2: $F(1,83) = 1.30, p = .125$, one-tailed test.

Conclusions

To summarize, the results of Experiments 1 and 2 indicate that the amount of interference between concomitant comprehension and memory tasks increases within the critical region of a relative clause. This localized effect is consistent with the HOLD-hypothesis prediction that transient memory load increases within the critical region of a relative clause. Thus, our results supply initial support for the HOLD hypothesis and demonstrate the feasibility of using ATN notation to construct psychological models of syntactic processing.

As with any new line of work, there are ample reasons to be cautious about this demonstration. For instance, our measure of transient memory load is new and undoubtedly in need of refinement. It is still uncertain what extraneous factors may influence our measure and whether all such factors are suitably eliminated by our controls. Therefore, it is particularly important to see whether the results reported here can be replicated using different measures of transient load. One effort in this direction has already yielded corroborative results for Experiment 2 (Kaplan 1975).

Another reason for caution concerns the interpretation of the HOLD effect. Although there may indeed be a local increase in the difficulty of comprehending a sentence within the critical region of a relative clause, as stipulated by the HOLD hypothesis, that increase may not be caused by an increase in memory load. For example, the evidence for the assignment effect developed in Experiment 2 suggests that our error scores can be influenced by the complexity of the local cognitive operations involved in comprehension. Therefore, the increases in our error scores within the critical region might be due, not to increased memory load, but to increased operational complexity within that region. It is not difficult to imagine models of relative clause comprehension that show such an increase. For example, we can conceive of a model that does not passively wait for its analysis of a relative clause to block in order to assign the within-clause function of the head NP, as the ATN model does, but instead actively forms and tests hypotheses about the within-clause function of the head NP as it processes the relative clause. If such a model operates sequentially, then its active hypothesis-testing should increase processing load just within the critical region. In a recent series of experiments, we have compared the ATN model with this active model and found that the ATN model is empirically preferable (Wanner and Kaplan, forthcoming). However, there may be still other interpretations of the HOLD effect that need to be examined.

Meanwhile, we can draw at least one tentative moral from the results in hand.

There is a deep and unresolved question about the nature of the grammatical knowledge that is put to use in linguistic performance: Is the language user's linguistic knowledge represented as a system of optimally general linguistic principles, or is it composed of a large battery of low-level heuristic rules each of which applies to a rather narrow portion of the language? Chomsky has consistently assumed that the psychologically real representation of linguistic knowledge will be just that grammar that captures linguistically significant generalizations; according to Chomsky, "we have [such] a generalization where a set of rules about distinct items can be replaced by a single rule about the whole set . . ." (Chomsky 1965, p. 42). This assumption is fundamental to Chomsky's claim for the psychological reality of transformational rules; it is by accumulating clear cases in which transformational notation permits a set of nontransformational rules to be replaced by a single transformation that Chomsky builds a psychological case for transformations.

With the empirical failure of psychological models that incorporate transformational rules, however, many psychologists have abandoned not only transformational grammar but also the assumption about the psychological reality of generalizations on which transformational grammar is based. The heuristic strategies schemes advanced by Bever, Fodor, and others make no claim to capture linguistically significant generalizations. For example, Fodor and Garrett (1967; also Fodor, Garrett, and Bever 1968) propose one heuristic strategy to handle object relative clauses and an entirely different heuristic strategy to handle subject relative clauses (Fodor, Bever, and Garrett 1974). Presumably, their system of strategies could only be expanded to handle the full range of relative clauses by adding more heuristic strategies. Such a system does not class relative clauses together in any way, nor does it represent their relation to declarative clauses. If a child acquired this type of grammatical representation of relative clauses, he would face the formidable task of having to learn each relative clause strategy independently of all the others, and none of his knowledge of declarative clauses would transfer to relative clauses.

In ATN notation such a system of independent strategies would appear as a large set of distinct arc sequences following the head noun arc in the noun phrase network. But recall that this proliferation of arc sequences is exactly what is avoided in the HOLD model, and avoiding it is possible only because the HOLD model preserves a generalization about the class of all relative clauses — namely, that all such clauses appear to be declarative clauses with a phrase missing. Our evidence for the HOLD hypothesis, then, is evidence that the language user's comprehension system does incorporate at least this one generalization about the relation between two clause types. As everyone knows, this is precisely the kind of generalization that can be captured by transformations. Thus, our evidence indicates that the comprehension system may employ the kinds of generalizations captured by transformational grammar, although not in transformational form.

In our view, the most likely reason for this result is that the process of comprehension places psychological constraints on the form in which grammatical generalizations can be maintained. Thus, whatever the listener knows about the structure of his language, he must represent it in a form that can be used in a comprehension process that extracts semantically relevant grammatical information in a single, beginning-to-end pass over the surface structure of the sentence. The virtue of ATN notation is that it gives us a precise way of representing grammatical generalizations in just this form, thus permitting us to make strong tests of our assumptions about comprehension.

Appendix

Test sentences for Experiment 1

1. The welder SR: who recommended electricians / OR: whom electricians recommended used cheap equipment.

2. The doctor SR: who opposed psychologists / OR: whom psychologists opposed took hard drugs.

3. The athlete SR: who advised coaches / OR: whom coaches advised ate health foods.

4. The teacher SR: who reported students / OR: whom students reported witnessed several incidents.

5. The witch SR: who despised sorcerers / OR: whom sorcerers despised frightened little children.

6. The chemist SR: who resented engineers / OR: whom engineers resented discontinued basic research.

7. The priest SR: who avoided socialites / OR: whom socialites avoided supported political causes.

8. The models SR: who disliked photographers / OR: whom photographers disliked wore blonde wigs.

9. The boxer SR: who complained about the trainer / OR: whom the trainer complained about had to leave.

10. The admiral SR: who proposed to the countess / OR: whom the countess proposed to left the country.

11. The plumber SR: who knew about the carpenter / OR: whom the carpenter knew about charged high rates.

12. The major SR: who disapproved of the sergeant / OR: whom the sergeant disapproved of issued senseless orders.

13. The professor SR: who couldn't stand the administrator / OR: whom the administrator couldn't stand addressed the alumni.

14. The foreman SR: who believed in the janitors / OR: whom the janitors believed in postponed hard work.

15. The cowboys SR: who put on the townspeople / OR: whom the townspeople put on told corny stories.

16. The chairman SR: who relied on the president / OR: whom the president relied on used unfair tactics.

Test sentences for Experiment 2

1. T: The doctor that the nurse encouraged to perform the delicate surgery had recently suffered a nervous breakdown.
   I: The doctor that the nurse hesitated to perform the intricate surgery with had recently suffered a nervous breakdown.

2. T: The teenager that the advisor taught to fill out the complicated form had finally escaped her unhappy home.

   I: The teenager that the advisor hastened to fill out the complicated form for had finally escaped her unhappy home.

3. T: The teacher that the principal designated to solve the difficult problem had completely misunderstood the basic issue.

   I: The teacher that the principal attempted to solve the difficult problem with had completely misunderstood the basic issue.

4. T: The governor that the architect advised to erect an impressive mansion had always favored a beautiful environment.

   I: The governor that the architect aspired to erect an impressive mansion for had always favored a beautiful environment.

5. T: The athlete that the coach required to complete the intensive training had totally lost his competitive urge.

   I: The athlete that the coach aimed to complete the intensive training with had totally lost his competitive urge.

6. T: The private that the officer convinced to demonstrate the powerful rifle had firmly denounced all violent behavior.

   I: The private that the officer started to demonstrate the powerful rifle for had firmly denounced all violent behavior.

7. T: The candidate that the party boss urged to resume his active campaigning could certainly use some more exposure.

   I: The candidate that the party boss decided to resume his active campaigning with could certainly use some more exposure.

8. T: The poet that the host pestered to start an interesting discussion had just finished a new book.

   I: The poet that the host tried to start an interesting discussion with had just finished a new book.

9. T: The attorney that the judge ordered to postpone his closing statement had really presented a sloppy case.

   I: The attorney that the judge consented to postpone his closing statement for had really presented a sloppy case.

10. T: The patient that the intern coaxed to straighten the messy room had repeatedly angered the entire staff.

    I: The patient that the intern condescended to straighten the messy room for had repeatedly angered the entire staff.

11. T: The customer that the broker persuaded to cancel the illegal transaction had often engineered some shady deals.

    I: The customer that the broker planned to cancel the illegal transaction for had often engineered some shady deals.

12. T: The banker that the accountant pressured to split the embezzled money had promised his complete cooperation.

    I: The banker that the accountant planned to split the embezzled money with had promised his complete cooperation.

4 Anaphora as an Approach to Pragmatics

KEITH STENNING

There is a real puzzle about how the mind can carry the right
background ready as if dissolved (often an urgent practical need, not
a literary one), but we need only say that the more it does that the
better.
William Empson, *Seven Types of Ambiguity*

Language is generally produced in many-sentence texts: conversa-
tions, monologues, plays, novels, essays, sermons. These texts
convey meaning, and psychologists would like to have a theory that
could relate speakers, the texts they utter, and their hearers through
meanings—a theory, that is, of what language users are doing.

One thing a speaker is doing when he produces a text is uttering a
sequence of sentence tokens. Linguistics provides theories about the
sentence types of which these tokens are instances, and it is intuitively obvious that those theories must be theories of part of what a
speaker is doing in producing a text. If this were not so, linguistics
would be of very little interest. On the other hand, not just any
sequence of sentences will do as a text; there must be some
continuity, some thread that runs through the text, some development
of themes. The same people, objects, events, properties, or relations
must recur to at least some extent. When they are lacking from the
face of the sentences that make up the text, our effort after meaning
will usually succeed in creating them.

Faced with the nonsequitur *That really was a good book. Honesty
isn't one of his weaknesses,* we do not find it difficult to invent a
multitude of scenarios that will accept it as a script. The second
statement might be construed as a comment on a critic who, for other
than aesthetic reasons, has written a particularly scathing review of
the book mentioned in the first statement. In conjuring such a context
we provide the recurrence of themes that we initially missed. What
we are conjuring, and how certain features of the language function in
this operation, will be the subject of this chapter.

Toward a Theory of Text

In situations in which texts like our example occur, speaker and
hearer normally share knowledge about the current scenario that

Preparation of this chapter was supported in part by Grant No. GM21796 from the
Public Health Services to The Rockefeller University.

provides the wanted continuity. In examining the text as a disembodied example, we reverse the normal sequence of events: instead of being in a context with certain shared knowledge and then hearing the text, we are hearing the text and trying to provide possible characterizations of the context we might be in. The game is reminiscent of our efforts when we arrive in the middle of a film, or overhear a snippet of conversation, and find ourselves trying to reconstruct what has gone before. This reversal of our normal perspective has several values.

First, we discover that what we construct is very often a nonlinguistic context rather than prior linguistic text: we invent a critic and his review, both known to the participants and known to be related to the book, which is in turn known to be the topic of conversation. We do not write the preceding script: "There is a critic and he wrote a review of that book which was most unfavorable and. . . ." Whatever theory of the relation between text and context we build must be able to relate text equally well to both nonlinguistic and linguistic context.

Second, this odd perspective shows how easily we can construct possible contexts (though not necessarily the correct one in any particular case); that discovery in turn suggests something about our approach to theory. Without this perspective it might seem that our problem is on all fours with the problems of syntax: What sequences of words are well-formed sentences? What sequences of sentences are well-formed texts? Such an analogy might provoke the writing of grammars that would generate all and only well-formed texts. But the ease with which we create contexts for sentence sequences that seem, at first sight, good examples of textual breakdown should discourage us from such an approach and instead encourage us to treat the problem as one of characterizing what we are doing in our effort after meaning. There may be sentence sequences for which no context that would qualify them as texts can be found, but how different the situation is from that facing the syntactician. There are, of course, always the objectors to ungrammaticality judgments who claim that such and such a word string would be quite well suited to symbolist poetry. Their objections provide their own refutations: such strings of words derive their force from their departure from some norm. But once we embed our example of an unlikely text in a suitable context, we see that it is just what we would normally say in that context. There is no sense of deriving meaning by departure from a textual norm.

Third, our inverted perspective suggests that the best place to begin our inquiry may be with texts that contain explicit elements that guide our construction of contexts for them—texts that do not assume that speaker and hearer share at the outset the requisite knowledge of the context of interpretation but are fashioned by the speaker in such a way that the hearer can make the necessary construction. For this reason many of the example snippets of text that follow will appear to have been cut from stories. When a speaker undertakes to tell a new story to his listener, it is clear that the hearer does not know the context before the story begins.

Finally, our perspective stands as a warning as we approach the interface between a theory of text/context and a theory of sentences, such as linguistics provides. Our example two-sentence text could just as well have been a one-sentence text: *That really WAS a good book and honesty ISN'T one of his weaknesses.* Here we again face the problem of establishing continuity in order to extract a meaning for the text, and much the same answers are required. Since the problem is to characterize the meaning of a single sentence, however, it might be thought that a theory of sentence semantics should provide the answer. But as we have seen, essentially the same problem has to be solved outside the theory of the sentence. It would be at least unparsimonious to answer the same question in two different parts of a theory of meaning, and we will see later that it is not possible to provide a coherent answer within a theory of sentence types. We therefore stand alerted to the fact that just because some problem occurs in constructing a theory of the meaning of one-sentence texts, it does not follow that the solution must be provided by a theory of sentence types.

Anaphora and textual continuity   It is difficult to conceive of maintaining the continuity of themes that is required of a text without repeating elements of the text, even though those recurrences may not be obvious repetitions. A dictionary definition of *anaphora* encourages the view that the term is a good label for some of the central problems of the present approach to language in use:

Anaphora: (a) The repetition of initial sounds, words, or syntactic structures in successive verses or sentences to achieve stylistic effect. (b) The reference back to an antecedent by repetition or grammatical substitution. (Hartmann and Stork 1972)

The first definition points to *repetition* as the core of anaphora; the second introduces the idea of *substitution* and thus the possibility that repetition may not be limited to repetition of exactly the same elements. The definition makes it clear that the intended sense of *reference* is the sense in which a linguistic unit refers back to another linguistic unit; it does not necessarily exclude shared reference to a nonlinguistic entity already referred to. It leaves open the question of what meaning relations antecedents and anaphors may share, and what meaning relations may define an occurrence as a repetition. Indeed it leaves the types of units that may be antecedents and anaphors very broadly defined. Anaphora is defined as a textual phenomenon; its status within the sentence is left completely open.

I shall try to flesh out a theory of anaphora from this perspective through an examination of many particular examples; then I shall return to draw some conclusions about the place of anaphora in a theory of language use and what it can tell us about the form such a theory should take. Because of my ignorance about verb phrase anaphora and other incarnations of the phenomenon, the discussion will be limited to noun phrase anaphors. The role of the English article system will loom particularly large because of a conviction that it is central to the functions whereby a speaker enables a listener to construct an appropriate context for his text.

I shall begin by making a division of the problem which I regard as a useful one, but nevertheless a division to be regarded with some suspicion as the enterprise proceeds. I shall first ask the question, What pairs of elements can stand in the relation of antecedent and anaphor? and then proceed to the question, What relation of meaning holds between antecedents and anaphors in virtue of their being such? It might be thought that the first question is a question of form (even of syntactic form) and the second a question of meaning; I shall try to show that the first is a question of both form and meaning. After developing some generalizations from examples drawn from narrative texts, we may begin to see what sort of limitation this choice of material constitutes.

Possible Antecedents to Possible Anaphors

What linguistic units can be antecedents and anaphors? We can begin by considering pairs of noun phrases in texts and asking what features of those phrases exclude the possibility that they are related as antecedent and anaphor. We shall in turn consider definiteness, entailment relations or class inclusion, syntactic agreement, syntactic relations within the sentence, and level of stress.

Definiteness The paradigm of introduction of characters and objects into stories takes the form of an indefinite antecedent that introduces a definite anaphor. (Throughout this chapter the phrases in italics are the ones under consideration. No particular semantic relation between them is necessarily intended.)

$$\text{Fred put } a \ cat \text{ out. Freda fetched } \begin{Bmatrix} it \\ the \ creature \\ the \ cat \end{Bmatrix} \text{in.}$$

Subsequent anaphors then occur as further definite phrases. If, for example, we imagine that an indefinite introduction to this example has already occurred, then the indefinite phrase would become a definite antecedent of the same subsequent definite phrases—repetitions (or substitutions for repetitions) may themselves be repeated:

$$\text{Fred put } the \ cat \text{ out. Freda fetched } \begin{Bmatrix} it \\ the \ creature \\ the \ cat \end{Bmatrix} \text{in.}$$

In both of these examples, it is necessary to appreciate the relationship of antecedent to anaphor in order to extract the intended meaning of the text.

When we turn to indefinite phrases and their potential as anaphors we find the situation more complex:

$$\text{Fred put } a \ cat \text{ out. Freda fetched } \begin{Bmatrix} one \\ a \ creature \\ a \ cat \end{Bmatrix} \text{in.}$$

One qualifies as an anaphor of the indefinite phrase *a cat*: it is a substitution for a repetition of that phrase, and this must be appreciated to understand the text. The other two candidates are not so easy to assess. *A cat* is certainly a repetition, but it does not rely for its effect on the fact that it is a repetition; when the definite phrase *the cat* was repeated exactly in an earlier example, at least a reference was repeated, and this had to be appreciated to appreciate the meaning intended. As for the phrase *a creature*, it is not clear that it qualifies either as a repetition or as a substitution for a repetition. We shall leave these cases in suspense, awaiting consideration of the meaning relations between antecedent and anaphor.

In the last of the four possible sequences of two articles, a definite phrase is followed by an indefinite one:

$$\text{Fred put } \textit{the cat} \text{ out. Freda fetched } \begin{Bmatrix} \textit{one} \\ \textit{a creature} \\ \textit{a cat} \end{Bmatrix} \text{ in.}$$

This example sorts with the preceding one rather than with the earlier two. *One* qualifies as an anaphor for the same reason that it did when it had an indefinite antecedent; the other two phrases present the same problems that arose before.

In summary, either indefinite or definite antecedents can give rise to definite anaphors, but the status of indefinite phrases as anaphors awaits clarification. In some cases they can qualify as anaphors because they are grammatical substitutions for repetitions of antecedent phrases, but when an indefinite phrase is merely an exact repetition of an earlier phrase its interpretation may not be affected by the fact that it is a repetition.

Class inclusion relations   If something is a cat, then it is a creature. Put another way, if something falls under the denotation of *cat,* then it falls under the denotation of *creature*; if something falls under the denotation of *cat,* it also falls under the denotation of *it.* We can say that *cat* is a subordinate of *creature* and *creature* is a subordinate of *it*; vice versa, *it* is a superordinate of *creature* and *creature* is a superordinate of *cat*. With this hierarchy defined by class inclusion in mind, we find that in the examples given so far the antecedents are subordinate to, or coextentional with, their anaphors. We do not find superordinate antecedents:

?Fred put *the creature* out. Freda fetched *the cat* in.

One important proviso must be noted at this point. The hierarchy that orders *cat, creature,* and *it* is defined by class inclusion on the ''universal'' domain: it is true for any subdomain selected. There is good reason to believe that the hierarchies that define the possibilities of antecedent–anaphor relations in texts are defined upon the current domain of interpretation of the text concerned. Thus if two phrases that are logically independent within the universal domain—phrases such as *the cat* and *Patrick's pet*—are shown by either the context or the text itself to be coextentional, then they may be related as antecedent and anaphor:

Carter smiled. The crowd applauded *the candidate*.

A locally defined hierarchy of class inclusion defines a direction within texts: subordinate phrases are not eligible anaphors of their superordinate antecedents.

Syntactic agreement   From the literature on anaphora it is easy to get the impression that anaphors must agree in number and gender with their antecedents. Certainly, disagreement sometimes seems to preclude an anaphoric relation, as in the first example below. However, trivial additions to the text or context can restore the relation (second example). In other cases nothing need be added (third example):

*Fred put *the cat* out. Freda fetched *them* in.
Patrick put *the dog* out and Fred put *the cat* out. Freda fetched *them* in.
Fred had to go home to put *the cat* out. *They* are a wretched nuisance.

It might be supposed, therefore, that transitions from singular antecedents to plural consequents are possible, but not the reverse. Yet even this is not so:

They spent *millions of dollars*. *It* went down the drain.

One often wants to say that these unmatched antecedents are not the only antecedents of their anaphors; either there are other linguistic antecedents (the case where two singular phrases are antecedents of a plural anaphor) or implicit knowledge relates antecedents to their anaphors. But this is just the case with entailment relations: such relations have to be defined upon the current interpretation of the text at hand, and this interpretation may have been built up from any mixture of explicit information in the text and implicit knowledge about the domain of interpretation. The fact that unmatched antecedents are not the sole antecedents of their anaphors does not make them any the less antecedents. We could limit the use of the term *anaphora* to cases in which all necessary antecedents are explicit in the text, but if we do this we must abandon the notion that such an account can give the meaning of the syntactically and semantically identical phrases which we do not treat as anaphors. Such a narrowing of the definition of anaphora is tantamount to a claim that the very same phrases have a different meaning when they do not have explicit, or wholly explicit, antecedents. If for every text in which an anaphor has an explicit antecedent we can construct a text without the explicit antecedent but for which we can nevertheless find a context in which the anaphor has the same meaning, then it becomes very strange to claim that an explicit anaphor and an implicit anaphor have different meanings. It amounts to a claim that we cannot shift meaning back and forth between linguistic explicitness and nonlinguistic implicitness as we shift from contexts in which the information is or is not explicit in the nonlinguistic context.

Syntactic relations How do syntactic relations between phrases affect their possible relations as antecedents and anaphors? When both phrases are within the same clause, they will not be related as antecedent and anaphor unless one of them is a reflexive or possessive pronoun. If the phrases are in coordinate clauses of the same sentence, the conditions upon anaphoric relations are just as they are for phrases in separate sentences. It is phrases in subordinated clauses that appear to behave oddly in their anaphoric relations to phrases in main clauses. Roughly, the situation is that the sequence of main and subordinate clauses can be changed without altering the referential relations between antecedent and anaphor just so long as the anaphor is in the subordinate clause and the antecedent in the main clause. This means that antecedents may actually succeed their anaphors in time:

Freda will fetch *the cat* in if Fred puts *it* out.
If Fred puts *it* out, Freda will fetch *the cat* in.

Interchangeability of order is not clearly available when the antecedent is in the subordinate clause:

?Freda will fetch *it* in if Fred puts *the cat* out.
If Fred puts *the cat* out Freda will fetch *it* in.

It appears that syntactic subordination of an anaphor allows freedom of its sequencing relative to its antecedent. This is as true when the antecedents are indefinite phrases as it is for these definite examples. We shall later see reason to believe that something like this freedom of order can occur across sentence boundaries.

The last syntactic feature that affects anaphoric relations between phrases is predicate nominal status. Predicate nominal phrases do not act freely as antecedents:

?Felix is *a cat*. *The cat* is a tabby.

This limitation is not absolute, however, as is shown by the ambiguity of the example below. Unstressed, *they* tends to be interpreted as an anaphor of *tigers*; stressed, it tends to be interpreted as an anaphor of *cats,* and *cats* is a predicate nominal:

Tigers are cats and *they* comprise the largest single group of carnivores.

Stress   How does stress affect antecedent–anaphor relations? Anaphoric elements usually receive weak stress; changing the stress level can change a phrase's acceptability as an anaphor:

Fred put the cat out but *he* didn't want it out.
?*Fred* put the cat out but *HE* didn't want it out.

Demonstrative (ostensive) uses of definite phrases usually carry full stress and these occurrences contrast with anaphoric occurrences. Nevertheless, there are too many uses of stress for this to be a hard-and-fast rule. For example, anaphors may receive contrastive stress:

Fred put the cat out. Freda didn't want it out but *HE* did.

The general rule is also broken in an interesting way by full noun phrases that are exact repetitions of their antecedents; if the repetition is to be an anaphor that shares reference with its antecedent, it is normally stressed:

*John thought that *John* should put the cat out.
John thought that *JOHN* should put the cat out.

The case where neither name receives heavy stress invites an interpretation that there are two Johns: heavy stress invites an interpretation that there is only one.

In this brief survey of the conditions under which two phrases can be antecedent and anaphor the same point has emerged several times: if we limit the meaning relation that can hold between antecedent and anaphor, thus limiting the application of the term *anaphora,* we see that definiteness, entailment relations, syntactic agreement, syntactic relations, and stress all affect the possibility of some restricted relation holding. If, on the other hand, we adopt the present approach and use the broadest possible definition of anaphora, a definition in terms of repetition, substitution, and back reference (in the weaker sense of reference distinguished above), then we often find syntactic, semantic, and phonological features affecting the interpretation of the meaning of anaphors but not affecting the possibility of an antecedent–anaphor relation holding. The choice of definition would be a purely terminological choice if it were possible to define several different meaning relations and to define for each relation the syntactic and semantic conditions under which the relation could hold between two phrases. This would be tantamount to defining several species of anaphora, each with its separate conditions for existence and each with its own meaning representation.

However, if the conditions that determine whether these meaning relations hold are contextual rather than syntactic or semantic, it is pointless to try to define structural subdivisions of anaphora. For example, if entailment relations affect the interpretation of phrases as anaphors and those entailment relations must be defined on the extensions of the phrases in the current domain of interpretation, it will not be possible to specify conditions that pairs of phrase types must meet for there to be an antecedent–anaphor relation between them.

This survey of factors affecting phrasal anaphora raises the question whether phrases are the right or only units for the analysis of anaphora. In many of the examples considered, it is not the antecedent phrase itself that the anaphor refers back to, but rather the antecedent phrase in its matrix statement. The fact that *a cat* can be antecedent to *the cat that John put out* in the following text depends upon the statement in which the antecedent occurs: *John put a cat out. Freda fetched in the cat that John put out.*

Examples where there is no phrase to act as antecedent are equally easy to construct: *John put the cat out. That was quickly done.* The *that* here refers to something like John's putting out the cat, which is an event. The truth of the first statement entails the existence of this event, but the statement itself contains no phrase that refers to the event. One response to such observations is to include statements among the types of linguistic unit that are allowed as antecedents. Another response is to return to the observation that for each example that has an explicit textual antecedent, we can find some nonlinguistic context in which the anaphor will play that same role: sitting in the room just as John closes the door behind the exiting cat, one could well say *That was quickly done,* and the referent of *that* could be described as John's expulsion of the cat. What is then required is a theory of the functioning of *that* which will cover both the cases in which there are preceding linguistic antecedents and the cases where there is only nonlinguistic context.

Meaning Relations between Antecedent and Anaphor

What meaning relations can hold between phrases in virtue of their being antecedent and anaphor? The crucial phrase in this question is "in virtue of." A theory of the meaning of noun phrases—their semantics—will be a part of any theory of sentence types, so such a theory cannot avoid telling us something about the relation between the meanings of two noun phrases. The question is whether the fact that two phrases are antecedent and anaphor tells us anything more about the relation between their meanings. How can we factor the contribution of meaning of a noun phrase into that part that is a repeating feature of the sentence type the phrase appears in and that part that can be attributed to its current context?

We can approach this question by surveying various meaning relations that might be marked by antecedent–anaphor relations and by examining examples of antecedents and anaphors whose meaning relations appear to be problematical. We shall consider shared reference first, as probably the simplest candidate, and then consider the relation between indefinite antecedents and their definite counterparts. This will raise some questions about the individual semantic structure of some definite noun phrases—in particular, their interpretation as variables. Finally, we will consider shared sense as a relation between antecedents and anaphors and raise some more general questions about the enterprise of interpreting texts.

Coreference   There can be no doubt that some antecedents and anaphors share reference, but this is not the question at hand. *John* and *he* can both refer to one and the same man in *John put the cat out. He slammed the door behind it.* However, *he* can refer to people other than John. It is a simple fact that if each of two phrases refers to something, then they refer either to the same thing or to different things. In much the same way, if two phrases both have a fourteenth letter, they have either the same fourteenth letter or different fourteenth letters. The important question is whether this unremarkable bifurcation in the meaning of the sentence types or text types involved, and whether this is the right bifurcation.

Surely what is required is a theory that tells us how each of the phrases *John* and *he* take their reference—a general theory about what is common to all their occurrences. It might be that *he* can take its reference in two distinct ways: either from some phrase that is structurally marked as its antecedent, or directly (by ostension or whatever). If this is the distinction to be made, it is clear that the distinction is not between coreferential and noncoreferential cases. The pronoun could take its reference ostensively and yet refer by some accident of the speaker's ignorance to John and so be coreferential with *John*. So the question becomes: Are there cases in which the structural relation between antecedent and anaphor is what shows that the anaphor takes its reference from the antecedent? Or do phrases such as *he*, which happen to be anaphors, take their reference in certain ways and as a result often wind up sharing reference with their antecedents? It is no answer to these questions to show that in the absence of any alternative candidates for referent the anaphor will take the referent of an antecedent phrase. Nor is it of any use to show that removing this antecedent phrase makes it impossible to interpret the anaphor; if the antecedent phrase is replaced by a suitable nonlinguistic context, the anaphor will be perfectly interpretable and will receive the same interpretation. All that is shown is that the anaphor must have some context and the force the anaphor has is determined by an interaction of its semantic properties (constant across occurrences) and its context (linguistic or nonlinguistic).

Indefinite antecedents of definite anaphors   Indefinite antecedents are of particular interest to a theory of text and context because they constitute the paradigm device for introducing new elements. They also have some particularly awkward logical properties which illuminate the horns of a central dilemma facing a theory of text and context. Existentially quantified indefinite phrases do not refer to objects, so it is not possible to explain the relation between an indefinite antecedent and its definite anaphor in terms of coreference.

This predicament is perhaps easiest to see in examples such as the following:

Fred had a cat and Freda had a cat. The cat was a tabby.
Fred had a cat. In fact he had several. The cat was a tabby.

The existential introductions state that there was at least one cat satisfying the description and this does not preclude there being a large number of such cats. However, the use of a definite singular anaphor demands that there be a unique cat satisfying the description.

When the existential introduction is within the scope of a universal quantifier, like *each,* the demand for uniqueness is still present but is more complex:

(1)   Fred kept *a cat* and a goldfish in **each room.** *The cat* was there to keep the mice down and the goldfish to keep the cat from getting bored.

On at least one interpretation of this text, *a cat* is within the scope of *each room.* Its definite anaphor *the cat* demands that there be a unique cat in each room, but clearly not a unique cat.

Two broadly contrasting approaches to these problems suggest themselves. On the one hand, what I shall call a pragmatic approach seeks to define a suitable relation between indefinite antecedents and elements in the domain of interpretation which will allow us to state a relation between the definite anaphor and those same elements (a relation to replace the inadequate pragmatic relation of reference); on the other hand, what I shall call a semantic approach seeks to construe the definite anaphor as the repetition of a variable that is related to the indefinite antecedent, and thus to define rules for amalgamating the logical forms of several sentences of the text into one larger logical form that can then be interpreted. A brief sketch of the direction of development of these two approaches will bring out their strengths and weaknesses and lay the groundwork for a synthesis.

Pragmatic approach. A pragmatic theory of the relations between indefinite antecedents and their definite anaphors requires the definition of a relation to replace the relation of reference. This relation holds between indefinite phrases, the statements in which they appear, and elements in the domain of interpretation of their text. The relation will have to be defined differently for different types of indefinite phrase but will then allow a uniform account of subsequent definite anaphors. I shall refer to the relation as Identification. An informal definition will suffice for the purposes at hand (for a more extended exposition see Stenning 1975):

A singular indefinite phrase *identifies* a set of elements in the domain of interpretation if that set of elements constitutes a unique set of substitutions, from the domain into the variable related to the indefinite phrase, that make the statement true.

Intuitively, (i) if the indefinite phrase is simply existentially quantified, it will identify a set of one element if that element is a unique true substitute for the phrase's variable; (ii) if the phrase's existential quantifier is within the scope of a universal quantifier, it will identify a set of elements if each of those elements is a unique true substitute for the phrase's variable, relative to a substitution into the variable bound by the higher quantifier—in example (1), the set of cats each unique to a room. So if Fred has no cats or too many, no cats will be identified. (iii) Existentially quantified plural indefinite phrases identify the sets of true substitution instances into their variables but impose no uniqueness conditions. Thus, in *Fred had cats. They were tabbies*: just so long as the first statement is true, the indefinite phrase will identify the set of all of Fred's cats. (iv) Universally quantified indefinite phrases do not rely for their identification conditions on their matrix statements in the same way that existentially quantified ones do. Contrast the following two texts:

Fred had *a cat*. *It* was called Fido.
A tiger has spots. *It* eats meat.

If the first statement of the first text is false, that falsity affects the interpretation of the second statement: nothing has been identified for it to be about. But if the first statement of the second text is false, that does not affect the interpretation of the second statement: it is still quite clear what *It eats meat* is about. Universally quantified indefinite phrases identify the set of true substitutions into their clause—that is, for this example, into: x a tiger.

Having defined conditions under which phrases identify sets of elements, it is now possible to state the meaning relation that holds between those phrases as antecedents and their anaphors:

Definite anaphors are universal quantifiers ranging over the sets of elements identified by their antecedents.

What evidence is there that all definite phrases are universally quantified? Russell's theory treats definite phrases as existentially quantified, and although almost every other aspect of his theory has been attacked at one time or another, theorists' intuitions on the existential nature of the quantifier have been unanimously with Russell.

However, when we look at various types of definite phrases and seek a uniform description of the semantic role of the definite article *the*, the evidence is mixed. First, generic phrases are usually thought to be universally quantified. The phrase "The man who has no music in his soul . . . " seems to quantify over all such individuals. Second, plural definite phrases are always universally quantified. This latter observation is striking in view of the fact that plural indefinites may be either universal or existential, just as can their singular counterparts. The universal quantification of plural definites is not a simple function of their plurality. Perhaps the plural and generic definites are the logically perspicuous examples, and the existential and uniqueness conditions of "definite descriptions" may be complex pragmatic artifacts. Where singular definite phrases have singular indefinite antecedents it is easy to see how the entailments are inherited from those antecedents. If a singular indefinite antecedent identifies a set of one element, a universal quantification over that set applies to only one thing.

The oddest cases for the proposed analysis are examples that lack linguistic antecedents, notably ostensive examples. Yet even these cases can be seen to have generic interpretations, and so make a rather plausible case for a pragmatic explanation of the apparent existential and uniqueness entailments. (See Stenning 1975 for a more extended and exampled defense of the analysis of the definite article as a universal quantifier.)

If this analysis can be upheld, it provides a natural explanation for a diverse set of observations. Identification conditions for universally quantified phrases are defined without regard for their matrix statements; since all definite phrases are universally quantified, they identify, or fail to identify, sets of elements in their own right. We need no longer think of the distinction between specific and nonspecific indefinite phrases as a semantic feature of phrases, with all the attendant difficulties. Although different linguists have had radically different concepts of specificity, in the sense intended here specificity distinguishes between indefinite phrases that can serve as antecedents and those that cannot. The present theory explains the troublesome semantic distinction as a natural pragmatic relation between phrases, their matrix statements, and elements of the domain. No resort to "the object the speaker had in mind" is necessary, since objective criteria for identification can be stated and the speaker may be as wrong as the hearer about the success of his intentions. (For a discussion of specificity see, for example, Karttunen 1969; for a criticism of semantic theories of specificity see Geach 1962.)

Finally, the most important result of the success of such an analysis would be to focus attention on the multitude of problems surrounding the application of the concepts of "domain" and "interpretation" to the analysis of natural languages. These problems attach to all current semantic analyses of language, though they are rarely made explicit. Therefore, before probing the difficulties of further developing this pragmatic approach it will be useful to compare it with the semantic approach it contrasts with.

Semantic approach. This approach seeks to treat definite anaphors as occurrences of variables bound by the quantifiers that bind their antecedents. The two sentences of the following text are amalgamated into the single logical form shown:

Fred had *a cat. The cat* was a tabby.
$(\exists x)$ (x a cat & x Fred's & x a cat & x a tabby)

The rule for amalgamation would be something like: Wherever there is a definite anaphor it appears in the logical form as a recurrence of its antecedent's variable bound by its antecedent's quantifier. Note that on this theory the logical form of the sentence type *The cat was a tabby* is an open sentence with a free variable, x a cat & x a tabby. Note also that as it stands, the theory gives no account of the uniqueness conditions required for a singular indefinite to have a singular definite anaphor. Fred can have as many cats as he likes, just so long as at least one is a tabby. He can have as many tabbies as he likes, for that matter.

It is true that it is possible to attach a uniqueness clause to each definite anaphor, rather in the manner of Russell's theory. For the text above, the logical form proposed by the theory would then be:

$(\exists x)$ (x a cat & x Fred's & x a cat & x a tabby
& (y) (y a cat $\rightarrow$ $y = x$))

The problem with this approach to uniqueness is that the uniqueness conditions are derived from the content of the first statement rather than from the definite phrase: there does not have to be only one cat in the domain, but there does have to be only one of Fred's.

Aside from the problems of uniqueness, it is not easy to generalize this theory to other antecedents and anaphors. Where the indefinite antecedent is plural and has a definite plural anaphor, there is a lack of correspondence between quantifier types (I omit the replication of quantifiers required to express plurality; they do not affect the present arguments):

Fred has *cats*. *The cats* are tabbies.
$(\exists x)$ (x a cat & x Fred's & . . .   (x) (x a cat $\rightarrow$ x a tabby)

The variables in the second statement must be bound by a universal quantifier (the statement is about all of Fred's cats), but those in the first statement are existentially quantified. Since the same variable cannot be bound by more than one quantifier, no rule for amalgamating the two statements is available.

These difficulties with treating definite anaphors as variables bound by quantifiers that occur with their antecedents provide a good introduction to their treatment as variables in sentences where their antecedents are in the same sentence, and it is here that the pragmatic approach also runs into difficulties.

Antecedents and anaphors that share variables   It is beyond dispute that if we choose to represent the logical form of English sentence types in the predicate calculus, antecedents and their anaphors will frequently be seen to be related to different occurrences of the same variable in their sentence's logical form:

When Fred puts *a cat* out *it* stays out all night.

Again our question is whether this fact can be explained by saying that the variable structure of the logical form is a representation of the structure of the sentence type in which the antecedent and anaphor occur. We can embed the example above in text or context in which either *it* and *a cat* can be interpreted as related to different occurrences of the same variable or *it* can be interpreted as a reference to some other object than a cat:

Every morning Fred puts out a flag. On the evenings when Fred puts a cat out, *it* stays out all night. If Freda puts a cat out she will usually remember to bring in the flag.

In such a text there is ambiguity as to which variable *it* should be related to: one candidate (*a cat*) is within the same sentence; the other (*a flag*) is in the preceding sentence. The antecedent that marks the quantifier and first occurrence of its bound variable can occur in a different sentence from the anaphor that marks the recurrence of the variable. In the special case in which antecedent and anaphor share variables and happen to be in the same sentence, it is futile to claim that the fact that they share variables must be marked as a part of the structure of the sentence.

Certainly the linguistic structure of antecedent phrases will affect the possibility of their anaphors' sharing that variable with them. For example, most analyses assume that proper names are not related to variables; if they are not, they cannot share any variable with their anaphors. Nor do phrases headed by *all,* though related to variables, share those variables with their anaphors. Consider the following contrast:

If Fred puts *all the cats* out, *they* will run off.
If Fred puts *a cat* out, *it* will run off.

It has been suggested that this contrast is to be explained in terms of the scope that the two different natural quantifiers determine: *all* terminates its scope with its clause, whereas *a* does not. However, a very extended notion of scope is required to give this description any explanatory power. The following example has a phrase within the clause that *all* appears in and, in the next clause, an anaphor (*it*) that has to be bound by the antecedent's quantifier (as the paraphrase of the consequent shows) even though it is not within the scope of *all,* which is the quantifier that binds the original occurrence of the antecedent:

If all the cats chase *a different mouse,* not one of them catches *it.*
(. . . not one of the cats catches *the mouse that cat chased*)

It is not as if the antecedent–anaphor relation between *a different mouse* and *it* showed which earlier quantifier was binding a new occurrence of an old variable; it is rather that the anaphoric status of *it* shows what old structure from the antecedent must be repeated in the logical representation of the new clause to bind a new occurrence of a new variable.

The concept of scope is very simply defined in the calculus, and it is tempting to try to use analogies with this concept in explaining features of English quantification. It is also necessary to be clear whether a given claim is being made about scope in the English sentences concerned or about scope in the calculus formulas that represent them. The surface order of English quantifiers is only loosely related to the order that their counterparts have in the calculus, the order that defines scope in the calculus. The English antecedent–anaphor pairs that are cited as paradigm examples of the structure, quantifier + variable + recurrence-of-the-same-variable, all have analogues that cross sentence boundaries, something that no calculus quantifier's scope ever does. These same constructions that are brought in evidence for the variable theory of anaphors can be used to construct arguments that these anaphors cannot be variables if the analogies between English and the calculus are taken seriously.

If we take a paradigmatically existential quantifier, *there is a* _____, and we construct a conditional in which the indefinite phrase is an antecedent with an anaphor in the consequent, then—on the assumption that the anaphor is a variable bound by its antecedent's quantifier—the quantifier binding both variables must be universal:

(2)   If there is *a cat* in the room, *it*'s a tabby.

        $(x) (x$ a cat in the room $\to x$ a tabby$)$

There is an equivalence in the calculus between $(x) (Fx \to p)$ and $((\exists x)Fx \to p)$ which might seem to provide a way of construing *there is a* as existential. The equivalence holds only if no occurrences of x in p are bound by the initial quantifier shown: that is, $(x) (Fx \to Gx) \not\equiv (\exists x) (Fx \to Gx)$. If we accept the analogy between English and the calculus, we are forced to conclude that either *there is* is here a universal quantifier, or *it* is not a variable bound by *there is*, and the argument is constructed on the very type of example brought in evidence of the variable theory.

The argument is not offered to urge either conclusion: there are many alternative points at which the analogy may have broken down. The relation between the subordinate-clause antecedent and the main-clause consequent in English may not mirror the antecedent/consequent distinction in the calculus. There are notorious problems with the analogy between the English and calculus connectives. The point of the argument is to urge caution in placing too much weight on any particular correspondence in such analogies without a thorough examination of the surrounding correspondences. Neither does the argument establish that the logical form shown for the English conditional is not an adequate representation of it as a text, as far as it goes. Some aspects of the text's meaning are not adequately represented, and—more important from the point of view of the present investigation—the general rules for deriving the logical form from the English text are suspect: they involve a choice between a number of linguistically unpalatable hypotheses. When using the calculus as a model of a natural language, the whole of the system—vocabulary, syntax, rules of inference, and interpretation of both languages—must be taken into account.

At this point we should consider how the pragmatic account of antecedent–anaphor relations fares with these examples designed to motivate the "variable" theory of anaphors. Example (2) shows some of the problems: according to identification theory as stated so far, the existentially quantified indefinite phrase in the antecedent, *a cat*, will identify an element in the domain just if there is a unique cat in the room. The definite anaphor *it* is represented as a universal quantifier ranging over the set of elements identified by *a cat*. This representation is certainly not equivalent to the logical form shown, where the universal quantifier appears before the antecedent. Nor does the representation express the conditionality of the statement. However, conditionality can be introduced into our pragmatic account if we assume that the force of the conditional *if* is to impose a supposition on the contents of the domain, namely, the supposition that the indefinite antecedent meets the identifying requirements of the definite anaphor. This is to treat the conditional in the same way we would treat:

Suppose there is a cat in the room. Then it is a tabby.

There are two ways in which the structure of the current domain of interpretation (the structure built up, up to the point at which we encounter the conditional) might fail to provide a felicitous interpretation of the text: *There is a cat in the room. It is a tabby.* Either the room might contain no cats or it might contain too many (two or more). Therefore, if we are to comply with the order to suppose that the first statement does identify an element, we have to make one of two possible constructions. In the absence of any elements identified, we must add such an element (add in the sense of suppose added); in the presence of too many we must subtract all but one (in the sense of suppose subtracted). Two further assumptions must be made about these constructions to explain the force of the conditional. On the one hand we must assume that the selection of elements for addition or subtraction is arbitrary. On the other hand, we must assume that additions and subtractions are made in a manner consistent with the remainder of the context to this point, but arbitrarily within that range of consistency. For example, if we suppose a marmalade cat to be in the room, then it will be false that it is a tabby.

The problem with assessing conditionals is just that it is difficult to assess what is relevant in the context to limit the consistency of possible additions to and subtractions from the domain. It is not suggested that the current proposal alleviates that problem, only that it puts it in a new context. Notice that the two statements, (x) $(Fx \rightarrow Gx)$ and $(\exists x)$ $(Fx \ \& \ Gx)$, are true together or false together in any interpretation in which there is only one thing that is F. It seems possible that an account along these lines—which construes subordinating operators such as *if* as signals to perform constructions on the domain of interpretation—might extend our pragmatic account of antecedent–anaphor relations to sentences containing conditionals. The observation that the influence of operators like *if* may extend over several sentences suggests that some textual account of them is required.

> If there's a cat in the room it's a tabby. *It* belongs to Fred. He's been looking for *it* all day. . . . Maybe there isn't a cat there; Fred's cat may have really gone astray.

The extension along these lines would not resolve all the difficulties that our pragmatic account encounters with examples that suggest a treatment of anaphors as variables. The major outstanding problem is encountered with examples in which an existential indefinite phrase identifies a set of several elements because it is within the scope of a universal quantifier. If a definite anaphor related to this indefinite antecedent appears in a statement that predicates some property of all the members of the identified set, no problem arises for our theory: the anaphor represents a universal quantifier quantifying over the set of elements. However, if each of the members of this set is paired off with and related to a member of some other set, the theory, as it stands, is in trouble:

(3)   a.   In each room there was a cat and a goldfish.
          (z) $(\exists x)$ $(\exists y)$ $(z$ a room $\rightarrow$ $(x$ a cat $\&$ y a goldfish $\&$ x in z $\&$ y in $z)$)

If this statement is true and the uniqueness conditions on identification are met, it identifies a set of cats and a set of fish. The statement that would follow in the text can be construed as two universal quantifications over these two sets:

(3)   b.   The cat was a tabby and the goldfish was large.
          (x') (y') $(x'$ a tabby $\&$ y' large)

Here x' and y' are variables limited in range to the sets of elements identified by x and y in the earlier statement. Such a scheme will not transfer to the following example:

(4)   In each room there was a cat and a goldfish. The cat was eyeing the goldfish.
      . . . (x') (y') $(x'$ eyed $y')$

In this case, at least on the most natural interpretation, the logical form would not be true: the cat in one room was not eyeing the goldfish in another.

This dilemma raises two questions. How determinate are the quantifier and variable relations in the second statement of such examples? If they are determinate, how can the identification relation be modified to express those determinations? The analysis above seems to be clearly inadequate to example (4), but to what extent is its inadequacy a function of the quantifier and variable relations marked by the articles, and to what extent is it a function of the relations in the particular example? Suppose the second statement were *The cat was fascinated by the goldfish.* Or consider an example where the anaphors are plural: *The cats were fascinated by the goldfish.* In these examples it is less clear that the same analysis is inadequate; it is possible to be fascinated by something that is not immediately present to the senses, whereas it is not possible to eye an absent object.

Should our theory of antecedent–anaphor relations determine spe-

cific logical forms for each text, or should characteristics of the
relations that appear in statements play a role in determining what
range of objects they are asserted to hold between? If we choose the
former alternative, it is possible to supplement the concept of
identification in ways that will mimic the apparatus of arguments and
relations. We could regard the statements containing the indefinite
antecedents as identifying a set of pairs of a cat and a fish and the
subsequent statement as a universal quantification over this set of
pairs. In a sense this seems like sophistical mimicry, but that feeling
stems from viewing representation in terms of identification as an
alternative to the type of representation offered by the calculus. It is
not so much that the calculus logical forms are the wrong representations as that what we need is some general theory of how the logical
forms are derived from texts. On this level of comparison, the
variable theory of anaphors provides no alternative to our pragmatic
account, for the many reasons that have been discussed above.

Antecedents and anaphors that share sense   In a text such as the
following, the antecedent *his front door* can be related to the anaphor
it in more than one way:

> Fred and Freda were neighbors. Fred painted *his front door* red,
> whereas Freda painted *it/hers* white.

The phrases may share reference, but they may also have different
reference and share only sense; the second interpretation is the one
brought out by the possessive anaphor *hers*. The first clause of the
second statement relates Fred and a door by possession, and the
reference of the anaphor in the second clause is whatever similar
object bears the same relation to Freda—that is, her door.

Anaphora of sense shows many of the same characteristics as
anaphora of other meaning relations. The present example can
actually be interpreted with *it* as either an anaphor of sense or an
anaphor of reference. The relation crosses sentence boundaries just
as do the other types we have looked at. Anaphors can even take
their sense from ostensions of nonlinguistic context rather than from
linguistic antecedents. If we are watching Fred paint his door and say
Freda painted it/hers white, we can be understood to mean that she
painted her door white. Such a context leaves exactly the same
indeterminacy of the reference of *it* as the linguistic context does.

Even more striking are cases in which an apparently direct ostension functions to contribute a deferred description. Confronted by a conspicuously persian cat, a speaker might say *That's the cat I have at home* and mean something paraphrasable as "That's *a persian* and *that* is the cat I have at home." Note that in the paraphrase the antecedent of the second *that* is the predicate nominal *a persian,* not the first *that.* If it were the first *that* the statement would amount to something like an accusation of theft. An alternative paraphrase makes it clear that *a persian* is the antecedent: "That's *a persian* and *a persian* is the cat I have at home." What we point to is a cat; what we get our hearer to understand is a description of that cat that can then be transferred to another cat referred to by *the cat I have at home.*

At this point a nonlinguistic analogy might be helpful. A directional gesture has something analogous to both sense and reference. Crudely, the direction of the gesture, in some larger framework of orientation such as the compass, can be seen as the gesture's reference; the bodily movements constituting the gesture are in some ways like the sense of an expression. If someone is given a set of directions that include such a gesture and then tries to follow them, he comes to the point in the chain of directions where he must interpret the gesture. Lacking other information he has a choice as to how to interpret it. He may either go in the direction in which his instructor pointed, or he may repeat the gesture and follow its present reference. If we imagine some abbreviated form of the gesture as recurring at the point at which it is to be applied, we have an analogue of an anaphor in a nonlinguistic system. The abbreviation is sufficient to trace the original antecedent gesture, and in its reapplication it may share either sense or reference with that antecedent.

Anaphora of sense shares with the other types of antecedent–anaphor relations the two characteristics that are important to the present argument: it crosses sentence boundaries, and linguistic antecedents can be replaced by nonlinguistic context. Again, there are no grounds for claiming that the meaning relation between antecedent and anaphor should be built into the logical structure of the sentence types concerned.

Inferential and Epistemic Relations

We have so far concentrated on a class of antecedent–anaphor transitions typical of narrative texts. Paradigmatically, these transitions are characterized by the facts that the antecedent precedes the anaphor in time, the antecedent is indefinite and the anaphor definite, the antecedent is subordinate to the superordinate anaphor, and the material that is predicated of the antecedent is superordinate to, or logically independent of, the material predicated of the anaphor. All these characteristics can be seen in the example:

Fred put *a cat* out. *It* was the marmalade one.

The function of the definite anaphor is to repeat an identification so that something more can be said about what has already been identified.

We saw earlier that syntactic subordination of the clause containing the antecedent to the clause containing the anaphor allows a suspension of the normal ordering of antecedent and anaphor (see section on Syntactic Relations). We can now extend that observation: so long as the content of the clauses (or sentences) shows the right sort of meaning relation, this suspension of ordering can occur in paratactic constructions (in which there is no *syntactic* subordination) as well as hypotactic ones (where there is an explicit subordinating conjunction). The required meaning relation is that between premise and conclusion, and it contrasts with the narrative relation of logically independent predictions of shared terms. Consider the following example:

Fred put *the marmalade cat* out. (So) he (did) put *a cat* out.

The conjunction *so* may or may not be present, nor is the emphatic *did* essential, although both help the intended sense. The relation in question is that between *the marmalade cat* and *a cat*. The transition is from a subordinate definite phrase to a superordinate indefinite. The force of the text is a deduction of a conclusion from a premise: a logical analogue would be the deduction of $(\exists x)$ (Fx) from Fa. It is also possible to state the conclusion first and follow with the premise by way of justification:

Fred (did) put *a cat* out. He put *the marmalade cat* out.

In this case the paradigm indefinite–definite sequence is preserved but the order is superordinate preceding subordinate. As one would expect in a natural language, the inference involved in such transitions may not be logically explicit, as it is in the examples above, but may depend on suppressed contextual premises; comprehension of the logical relation between the phrases is still essential to a proper understanding of the text in context:

> Fred (did) put *a cat* out. Freda found *the marmalade cat* in the alley.

All of these examples fall under the definition of anaphora in the sense that they are repetitions or substitutions for repetitions, and it matters to the meaning of the text that they are so. We must conclude that the conditions described for narrative transitions are conditions that determine the meaning of those transitions, not conditions that are essential for the existence of any transition. The present examples defy those conditions and in so doing express a different type of transition that might be called inferential or justificatory.

Although our earlier examples and preoccupations were said to be typical of stories, any text may contain a mixture of these different types of transitions between antecedents and anaphors. All that is claimed is that one type is more typical of narration and description, the other of discussion of inference and evidence. The classification is far from being exhaustive. We shall end this foray into the unexplored by looking at another departure from the paradigm narrative examples.

In the third type of relation between antecedent and anaphor both phrases are indefinite; yet, unlike similar examples of anaphora of sense, the phrases are logically independent of each other:

(5)   a.   Fred said there was *a present for Freda* in the closet. She opened the door and there was *a small tabby kitten*.

Given the right context, understanding this example demands that we extract the relation between the two indefinite phrases, namely, that they identify the same element of the domain. What is the effect of such a transition? To see this we can compare it with an example where the second phrase is definite, the case we have been treating as the paradigm of narrative:

(5)   b.   Fred said there was *a present for Freda* in the closet. She opened the door and found that *it* was a small tabby kitten.

Here the identity is explicit and the predicate nominal *a small tabby kitten* functions as a description. In example (5a) this same phrase presents the evidence on which the identity is established—established by Freda and established by the hearer. The two texts are interpreted on the same set of objects and the objects bear the same relations to each other: the text containing the indefinite anaphor focuses on epistemic features of the situation. We might call it an epistemic transition.

I have been trying to develop a theory of anaphora as a part of a theory of the representation of texts, and especially a theory of the role of the article system and of class inclusion relations in the interpretation of anaphora. I have claimed that one way of looking at the information carried by these features of texts is to regard them as instructions for constructing domains of interpretation for the texts. Consideration of types of antecedent–anaphor transition beyond those that have been called narrative transitions suggests that even if this program is a fruitful approach to one aspect of understanding, it leaves other aspects untouched. Different transitions, transitions that must be appreciated as being different if we are to understand, may lead to the construction of identical domains of interpretation. The same world or context may be constructed by different sets of instructions, and some of the differences between the instructions are differences in what the speaker has expressed.

Interpretation of Text

The approach to the representation of texts that has been developed here can be clarified by contrasting its assumptions with those of other approaches. The first contrast lies in how we view the relation between a natural language and its interpretations (in the logician's sense of interpretation). Most of the semantic work on natural language has focused on deciding the logical form of sentence types, but the problem of interpretation cannot be avoided.

The problem of interpretation arises most acutely with indexical expressions. (Roughly, indexical expressions are those that shift their reference when the context of their utterance changes.) Philosophers such as Lewis (1971) and Montague (1974) have adopted the view that we should view a natural language not merely as a vocabulary, phonology, and syntax, but also as including an interpretation, in particular an interpretation of a type adopted for modal predicate calculi in terms of possible worlds. The language is viewed as being interpreted once and for all upon a universal domain, which includes everything the language can be used to speak about. Change the assignment of terms of the language or the content of the domain, and you change the language. The meaning of an indexical expression is then a function that maps each context of utterance (speaker, time, place, and so on) onto a set of elements—the reference of the indexical in that context.

Logicians do not always adopt this approach, even when talking of artificial languages. They sometimes talk of a language as being defined by its vocabulary, syntax, and rules of inference; it is then possible for the same language to receive many different interpretations on many different domains, and these domains may then be local (as opposed to universal). With such an approach, different texts will be assigned different interpretations, and the meaning of indexical expressions in a text will be at least partially explained in terms of the construction of the interpretation. This is the approach adopted here. Are there grounds for choosing between a universalist and a localist approach to the interpretation of English?

The localist approach raises the problem of what corresponds to an assignment for a natural language. The logician assigning an interpretation to a text of a calculus does so in a metalanguage, usually a natural language. For English texts there is no grammatically recognizable metalanguage, nor any obvious practice of assignment that precedes the production of an object-language text. Furthermore, English speakers are not free to assign aritrary terms to arbitrary extensions in the way the logician is free to assign things to his F's and G's: we can't freely assign a cat to the extension of *dog*. The universalist approach avoids these problems by fiat: some original assignment of unknown origin is assumed. On the other hand, the universalist must treat as indexicals a wide range of expressions whose grammatical forms do not suggest that they are indexical. With statements such as *All authors must forward their manuscripts by August first* uttered by the editor of this book, it becomes necessary to view *all authors* as an indexical expression in order to explain why it is only the authors of this book that are quantified over. The localist account gives a uniform nonindexical account of this example: *all authors* quantifies over the whole domain, but the domain is very small.

So far it seems that the two accounts merely shuffle the same skeleton into different closets. The universalist account puts all the burden of explaining the context boundedness of English on mysterious functions that map every context and term onto the correct extension; the localist account puts the burden on a mysterious process of assigning interpretations, a process that is invisible or inaudible. The choice of one of the two accounts must be made on the grounds that we can hang better flesh on its functions or its assignments, or the choice is no choice at all.

We want to know how speakers can perform with these abstract structures. The present treatment of the role of article system and lexical entailments in anaphora has been an attempt to do that. Specifying Identification conditions for indefinite phrases allows us to see them facing in two ways. If speaker and hearer share enough information about the contents of the current domain, the hearer can use the logical form of statements containing indefinite phrases to assess their truth: indefinite statements then function as object-language statements. If, on the other hand, the hearer does not have such information, he can accept a transition from indefinite to definite as warranted (with its implications about identification conditions being met) and so construe the speaker's statement as stipulating the contents of the domain. Indefinite statements then function as if they are metalanguage assignment statements. In other words, we can either test what we hear against our knowledge of the context, or we can accept the truth of what we hear and use it to construct our knowledge of the context. There may be nothing in the grammatical construction of the text to indicate which is appropriate.

The second issue that will throw light on the nature of the current attempt to understand the functioning of text can be posed as a question: Should we view the text as a construction of an interpretation (or model) or as the construction of a logical form (or set of logical forms)? A model is a mapping of a set of objects, properties, and relations onto the constants, predicates, and relations of the vocabulary of the language. It is not an inherently linguistic object, although one representation of a model is its description in a metalanguage. A set of statements is an inherently linguistic object; it relates to interpretations in the following way. Any set of statements partitions the set of all possible interpretations into two types: those in which all statements in the set are true (models), and those in which at least one statement is false. Some sets of statements will determine that all interpretations are models (sets consisting only of tautologies) and others that no interpretation is a model (sets of statements that are logically inconsistent). Sets of statements are abstract as representations in that they partition sets of interpretations (generally indefinitely large sets) into models and nonmodels. Models are abstract as representations in that the properties of the objects they contain are represented only insofar as they are mapped onto the vocabulary of any text they interpret. This distinction becomes clearer in an example.

Suppose that we have a particular model consisting of a cat, a dog, and a house. The cat and the dog are black. They live in the house. This description of the model is neutral as regards which actual objects it contains: any cat, dog, and house with the stipulated properties and relations would be as good a model as any other, but only one of these is our particular model. The specification of the model does not determine, for example, whether the cat in the model is called Felix or is more than nine inches tall. In this sense the model is abstract. We can specify these properties, but in doing so we change the model.

Now consider a statement in the predicate calculus that would be modeled by our model:

$$(\exists z)\ (\exists x)\ (\exists y)\ (x \text{ a cat } \& \ y \text{ a dog } \& \ z \text{ a house}$$
$$\& \ x \text{ lived in } z \ \& \ y \text{ lived in } z \ \& \ x \text{ black } \& \ y \text{ black})$$

This statement is abstract in just the way our model is particular: it defines an entire set of models. But it is particular in a way that our model is abstract: there are many ways we can describe our model and it will remain the same model, but change the statements, even to a logically equivalent set of statements, and we have a different set of statements, for example:

$$(\exists x)\ (\exists y)\ (x \text{ a cat } \& \ x \text{ black } \& \ y \text{ a house } \& \ x \text{ lived in } y)$$
$$(\exists x)\ (\exists y)\ (x \text{ a dog } \& \ x \text{ black } \& \ y \text{ a house } \& \ x \text{ lived in } y)$$

The two representations, the model and the set of statements, involve different types of abstraction. Which type is characteristic of the comprehender of English texts?

Models as representations of texts   On the whole, people seem to be rather bad at detecting surface manipulations of sets of statements which leave them logically equivalent. This argument is weak, how-

ever, since a defender of statement sets as peoples' chosen representations for texts might simply add the corollary that such sets are
regarded as being invariant up to manipulations of logical forms such
as that just illustrated. In order to make the right comparison, we
need as an example a set of statements that do not determine the
mapping of predicates onto elements of the domain, and we need to
compare this with a model description that does determine such a
mapping.

Compare the following set of statements with a description of one
possible model.

Statement set:
   There are three things. Two are white. One is black. Two are
   hexagonal. One is triangular.
Model description:
   There is a triangular white thing, a hexagonal black thing, and a
   hexagonal white thing.

There is no reason to suppose that the statements in the statement set
are any more (or less) logically complex than the statements in the
model description. For the statement set, there are two types of
model, constructed by permuting the shapes and colors (of course,
the world may contain an infinite number of either of these types).
The statement set does not subdivide these models; it merely defines
them as a set of equally good models as opposed to all other
interpretations that make at least one statement in the set false. In
contrast, the model description singles out one of these two types.
Given the right conventions for reading diagrams, we could replace
the model description by a diagram, as in Figure 4.1. (Again, there
may be an infinite number of such models—for example, the triangle
and hexagons do not need to be equilateral.)

Our gedanken experiment consists of imagining that we are given
either the statement set or one of the model descriptions (the pictorial
or the verbal) and are asked to perform some task: for example, to
remember it until tomorrow or make judgments whether arrays are
consistent with it (in the case of the statement set) or are examples of

Figure 4.1 A pictorial representation of a model

it (in the case of the model). My own intuition is that it is far more difficult for us to represent the statement set in a way that makes it easy for us to use it and that the reason is precisely that the statement set makes it impossible to choose one of the two model types. If something akin to a set of statements were a natural representation, there would be no reason for this pressure to decide between models. Notice that model abstraction—recognizing sets of objects as models of a particular type—is not intuitively difficult.

What is the difference between the model description and the set of statements? After all, the verbal model description is itself a set of statements. One difference is that model descriptions are not tied to verbal expression; the other is that when a model description does take the form of verbal expressions it is a special subset of a statement set, namely, the subset that determines the uniqueness and distinctness properties of the objects in its model.

This claim that model descriptions are psychologically privileged representations of texts cannot be an absolute claim that they are the only representation available; we can and do satisfactorily represent statement sets that are not model descriptions. The claim is only that model descriptions are our chosen form of representation and difficulties arise when they are out of reach. Such a claim suggests that some of the characteristic errors of inference made with texts that are not model descriptions might be attributable to our picking a model even though our particular choice is not warranted (see Stenning 1976, p. 9ff, for an interpretation of an experiment in these terms). Such a claim also suggests that well-formed English texts are fashioned to provide the uniqueness and distinctness information that is so conducive to representation. This is what I have been trying to bring out in my treatment of the article system.

Principles of text construction What makes a text a model description? What grammatical phenomena are particularly implicated in the expression of this property? The account developed here can be summarized under three headings: "uniqueness," "distinctness," and "modularity." For each property a principle can be stated. From a speaker's point of view these principles can be seen as principles of text construction—how to construct a text that will describe a given model. From the hearer's point of view they can be seen as principles of model construction—how to construct a model given a text.

First principle: identifiability. New elements are introduced into the domain with their uniqueness properties defined by the identifying conditions of their indefinite introducing phrases. These uniqueness properties may be changed: an element may be unique in being a cat when it is introduced, but the introduction of other cats will change this status. Since new elements will also have their uniqueness properties defined by their introduction, however, it is possible to update the uniqueness properties of the old elements.

Second principle: anaphoric conservatism. Old elements are not implicitly given new descriptions, or, conversely, a new indefinite description heralds a new set of elements. If such a principle were absolute, it would suffice to ensure that the distinctness properties of elements would be defined. As the example of an epistemic transition (5a) illustrated, however, under some conditions we assume that independent indefinite descriptions are descriptions of identical rather than distinct elements: the succession of two independent indefinite descriptions does not determine distinctness to the same extent that the transition between indefinite antecedent and definite anaphor determines uniqueness. Anaphoric conservatism obviously can operate only to the extent of the speaker's knowledge and does operate only to the extent of his willingness to divulge information about identities. Contrast our reactions to the indefinite introductions in the following text:

> Once there was a butcher who lived in Minsk. . . . A baker had his shop in the main street. . . . The town was famous for its candlesticks, which were made by a man who lived near the church. . . . One day, the baker was murdered by *a man wearing crepe-soled shoes on his hands.*

We assume that the first three indefinite phrases identify three distinct elements although there is no logical inconsistency in assuming that one man of diverse enterprise would satisfy all three descriptions; the identification conditions imposed by the subsequent definite phrases tell us nothing about distinctness. The fourth introduction does not induce the same assumption: the murderer could perfectly well be one of the other two characters. It seems that we assign distinctness not simply on the basis of article relations but also on some vaguer notions of plausibility and assumptions about the speaker's knowledge of, and motivations in expressing, the distinctness properties of elements of the domain. Insofar as distinctness is expressed, it is by the clausal system rather than the article system. Phrases occurring within a clause are disjoint in reference (or variables) unless one of them is a reflexive.

Third principle: modularity. New elements are introduced in terms of their relations within a module. Those groupings of elements then tend to be preserved as new relations are stated to hold between elements, and the module may be seen to be repeated many times. The first point, that groupings tend to be preserved, is illustrated in the discussion of examples (3) and (4). In these examples the initial clause (in this case, a sentence) introduces a set of cats and a set of goldfish, but it does so as a set of related pairs. Subsequent universal quantifications tend to affirm new relations within those pairs rather than across them. The second point, that a module initially introduced as unique may subsequently be said to be one of many repetitions, can be illustrated by a new example:

> On my left is a reciprocating engine. In this engine *a crankshaft* transmits the gas pressure to the thrumjit. This engine powered **every car on the road** until Herr Wankel suggested that *the crankshaft* was inelegant and invented his rotary engine.

Every car on the road had a reciprocating engine and every engine had a crankshaft and it was this crankshaft that Herr Wankel suggested was inelegant. An account of the logical structure of this text should represent the phrase *a crankshaft* as being within the scope of the universal quantifier in *every car,* but the order of quantifiers in the text does not reflect this structure. The parts of the engine can be identified satisfactorily by treating one engine as if it were the whole domain of discourse; the fact that its structure is indefinitely repeated within a larger domain is of no consequence to the identification.

A text may begin by sketching the intended domain broadly and then zero in on its detailed structure, or it may first describe the detail without warning that the detail will later be fitted into a larger context. From the point of view of a logical calculus that defines scope by left-to-right order, the resulting pattern of scope relations appears bizarre.

Granted these heuristics for model construction, how can we summarize the view of antecedent–anaphor relations that has been developed? Antecedents, particularly the paradigm examples of introductory indefinite antecedents, have been viewed as playing the role of constructing the model on which a text is to be interpreted. Anaphors, in contrast, are viewed as demonstratives that point to structures in the model that has been constructed and incorporate those structures into the interpretation of the statements the anaphors appear in. They may point to single elements of the domain identified by their antecedents; they may point to sets of such elements or to sets of groupings of those elements with other elements to which they have earlier been related; they may point to relations between groups of objects and incorporate the relation rather than the objects into the interpretation of their statement (anaphors of sense); or they may point to properties of objects and incorporate descriptions into their statements (where the antecedent is a tacit description or explicit predicate nominal).

When a phrase has an explicit linguistic antecedent, it will appear that the phrase, as an anaphor, is pointing to that antecedent and incorporating its linguistic structure into the anaphor's statement; yet for each such case, a counterpart is possible for which there is no explicit linguistic antecedent, and in these cases the phrase points to the relevant structure in the model rather than in some sentence. Since this is the case, we can always assume that even where there is an explicit linguistic antecedent, the phrase actually points to the structure in the model that that antecedent established rather than to the linguistic structure itself. By making this assumption we get a uniform account of the function of such phrases. It is in this sense that anaphors can be seen as repetitions of their antecedents.

Implications for Linguistic Theory

How is the approach toward a part of the theory of pragmatics that has been developed here related to other linguistic theories, and in particular to the approaches taken in other chapters of this book?

Syntactic theories   The pragmatic approach accords well with the syntactic proposals made in Chapter 1. Earlier theories assumed that anaphoric relations between pronouns and their antecedents are specified by transformational rules. I have argued that some aspects of surface semantic interpretation cannot be incorporated into a sentence grammar at all—that pronominal coreference and other relations between pronouns and their antecedents cannot be explained by a grammatical theory of sentence types. The interpretive account presented in Chapter 1 dovetails with the present argument. Instead of specifying transformationally that a pronoun and some antecedent must corefer, the interpretive account specifies when they cannot corefer; it provides a *non*coreference rule. Thus, the interpretive account leaves coreference relations to be specified in some other way, and in this chapter I have proposed that they are specified pragmatically, not only for anaphoric relations within a single sentence, but for those holding between sentences. As Bresnan notes "since coreference relations are not the result of rules of sentence grammar, we are free to treat sentence-internal and inter-sentence coreference in the same way."

The syntactic arguments in Chapter 1 turn the grammar on its side in an attempt to reassess the relation between the deep and surface structures and to reassign the explanatory load. The present approach would turn the method of explanation upside down, since it argues that before trying to explain what are perceived as parts of sentence structure in a theory of sentence types, it is important that the same regularities be searched for at levels above the sentence. If they are found there, they must be assigned there. From the present point of view, the sentence grammar should be seen as placing limitations on certain very general principles for the construction of quantificational and referential structures in texts and contexts. Since the interpretive approach to pronominalization confines itself to characterizing such limitations, the result is a gratifying illustration of how syntactic and pragmatic theories can be coordinated.

Processing theories The current approach to pragmatics can perhaps say something also to those concerned with the development of grammatical processing theories such as those proposed in Chapter 3, though much less directly than it can address the syntactic theories on which such processors are based. Reducing the amount of quantificational structure that is built into sentence types, and viewing noun phrases as essentially demonstrative elements that can point to all sorts of different structures, changes the desired output of a device for describing sentence types. Most of the work on processors presented here (and perhaps elsewhere) concentrates on the problem of extracting function–argument relations expressed in sentence types. As such, it deals with the part of sentence structure least affected by the present arguments. When such models address the problem of treating quantifier and variable structures, however, the present approach will be relevant. It should be taken as a cautionary note: if structures are seen as parts of sentence types, the complexity of processing those sentence types should be a function of the complexity that must be represented in analyzing the sentence type. If the immense quantificational complexity that sometimes has to be introduced to represent the simplest definite noun phrases is built into the sentence structure, it will be reflected in the difficulty of understanding the sentence. If, however, these simple definite anaphors are regarded as demonstratives that point to structures in a model that has already been constructed (when the antecedent was met) it can be seen that pointing to something complicated might be as easy as pointing to something simple.

The lexicon   Finally, the current approach is related to and dependent on the development of a theory of the lexicon in several different ways. It has been argued here that the class-inclusion relations between phrases which determine the nature of anaphoric relations must be those defined on the current domain of interpretation of the text at hand. Even if F and G are logically independent in some larger domain, all F's may be G's within a limited domain. If they are, it is their current entailments that play a part in determining their anaphoric status within the text interpreted on the limited domain. However, when assignments are constructed in a limited domain they are constrained in important ways by the assignments in larger domains. The lexicon, and the conceptual knowledge with which it interfaces, is the repository of information about these more general and more stable logical relations.

Perhaps the most obvious example of the contribution of the lexicon to model construction is the importance of exclusion relations in assigning distinctness. A cat is not a dog in any domain of interpretation, and the existence of hierarchies from which terms can be selected either to identify or discriminate objects allows choice as to whether distinctness is or is not determined. The semantic field from which terms are drawn within a text is paradigmatically chosen to embody the right distinctions to express distinctness. For example, within the semantic field of human occupation terms, certain contrasts are established, and the tendency is to assume that terms drawn from these contrasting sets are mutually exclusive within any domain.

Thus in a story into which characters are introduced as the butcher, the baker, and the candlestick maker, we tend to assume that the terms are contrastive. If the characters were introduced by terms for physical attributes—say, the tall man, the short man, and the fair-haired woman—it would be less problematical to be told later that the tall man was both the butcher and the baker in Minsk. Conversely, we feel that there has to be some good reason for introducing two characters by terms from wildly different fields: *This is a story about a man with pneumonia and an archbishop* sounds odd because we feel we want two terms that will establish a mutual relation. If they are the only terms that knowledge permits, then the relations can be established by other means, but the very existence of these preferences tells us something about how the stable structures of the lexicon are related to the evanescent structures of the current interpretations of texts.

It has been argued in Chapter 2 that the lexicon also provides the contact between language and conceptual knowledge that is not specifically linguistic but nevertheless plays a vital role in our use of language. One example is provided by the interpretation of modal statements, which is seen as depending on bodies of conceptual knowledge that are not particularly distinguished by the grammatical form of the modals. Such an approach is similar to the approach to conditionals suggested here, which sees the grammar as laying down general conditions on operations to be performed on the domain of interpretation but at the same time sees those conditions as having to be supplemented by conceptual knowledge about the effects of such operations before any determination of the truth of the conditional statement can be made.

In Conclusion

This chapter began by raising the question, What makes a sequence of sentences into a text? It sought an answer in the concept of repetition, under the banner of anaphora. The borders of that phenomenon were vaguely drawn initially, and achieving a precise definition of its limits has deliberately not been the goal. Instead, we have examined a wide variety of examples of obvious repetition: first, repetition of words and phrases (linguistic units); then repetitions of references, identifications, variables, and senses (units of meaning). The finding that sometimes an exact repetition of a wording would not repeat some aspect of a meaning, but that instead a substitution for an exact repetition was called for, suggested that the phenomena of interest from our point of view could be better stated in terms of the meanings themselves than simply in terms of structurally defined wordings. This conclusion led, in turn, to the observation that repetitions could be repetitions of these meaning structures even when they had not been linguistically expressed: for each case in which an explicit linguistic antecedent defined a subsequent anaphor as a repetition of some aspect of its meaning, we could find a nonlinguistic context that would define the anaphor in the same way.

For a theory of text, it seems best to define the concept of repetition, and therefore of continuity, in terms of repeated recourse to structures in the context, whether those structures have received explicit linguistic expression or not. Therefore, a theory of explicit antecedents should be a theory of how these antecedents construct contexts and function within them. I have tried to build at least the crude beginnings of a theory of how some grammatical features function in these terms. I am more confident that the problems this attempt has revealed are important problems (some of which have been concealed by other approaches) than that the solutions suggested are correct. If the course of the argument has led far from the original definition of anaphora to a point where that phenomenon may seem irrelevant, well and good. Such broad and venerable concepts are most useful in suggesting a problem, but they have the distinct advantage over more exact and narrow concepts that they rarely exclude the material required to construct the beginnings of an answer.

5 Grammar as Evidence for Conceptual Structure

RAY JACKENDOFF

The Relation between Form, Meaning, and Thought

The goal of contemporary linguistic theory is a description of what it is that a human being knows when he knows how to speak a language. It is claimed that many significant properties of language are in fact not learned but are innate to the human organism and hence universal across languages. The task of the linguist is not only to describe languages, but to separate innate aspects from learned aspects so as to make it possible to explain the feat of language learning—how children come rather rapidly to know their language on the basis of highly fragmentary evidence.

According to current views in generative grammar, and (in part) according to Chomsky's original *Syntactic Structures* model, the grammar of a language can be separated into the description of form, the description of meaning, and the mapping between the two. Thus the organization of the grammar can be depicted roughly as shown in Figure 5.1. In this diagram, the set of syntactic structures is taken to mean the class of complete derivations from deep to surface structure, the set K of Chomsky (1970b). The well-formedness rules for syntax thus include phrase structure rules, transformations, and any further syntactic constraints. The semantic structures are the information the sentences of the language convey. The projection rules are the mapping between syntactic and semantic structures. In the lexical-interpretive theory of Chomsky (1970b), described by Bresnan in Chapter 1 (pp. 4–14), the deep structure, the surface structure, and possibly certain intermediate structures are relevant to the operation of the projection rules.

The diagram in Figure 5.1 differs from the usual sketch of grammatical organization in one essential feature: it treats semantic structures not simply as derived from syntax by means of the projection rules, but as independent structures defined by their own well-formedness conditions. This elaboration is crucial to the present chapter, which will be concerned with both the form of semantic structure and its relation to syntax.

It is the job of linguistic semantics to characterize semantic well-formedness rules and projection rules. In more concrete terms, it must answer questions of the following sort: What information is

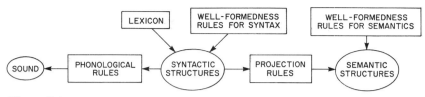

Figure 5.1

conveyed by language? What entities and what distinctions must appear in semantic structures associated with natural language? How are they to be formalized? How do these entities and distinctions correspond to syntactic form? These are empirical questions, and they cannot be answered merely by appeal to traditional logic, which itself originated only as a possible answer to these questions. (One might guess, in fact, that logic has become so devoid of empirical content in part because it has failed as an adequate account of natural-language semantics.)

In order to better understand the scope of these questions, let us consider some basic requirements for semantic structures. First, it is usually assumed that semantic structures must be in some sense psychologically real. Next, it should be possible to define metalinguistic predicates such as entailment, synonymy, and anomaly in terms of them. A third and somewhat more controversial requirement is that semantic structures are to be the interface between language and procedures of verification.

It is clear that at some level of representation all information conveyed by language and by various other perceptual systems such as vision must be compatible; let us call this level "conceptual structure." Fodor (1975), Miller and Johnson-Laird (1976), and Jackendoff (1972; in preparation) argue in essence that semantic structure, the information that language conveys, is couched directly in terms of the human mind's organization of all experience. Abstracting from a large collection of arguments, one arrives at this conclusion from two directions. On one hand, in order to deal with metalinguistic predicates, one is constantly forced to bring in nonlinguistic (that is, conceptual) knowledge, and a principled and nonartificial division between linguistic and nonlinguistic knowledge is notoriously difficult to justify. On the other hand, the mechanisms independently necessary to deal with (nonlinguistic) conceptual structure provide an almost trivial account of just such metalinguistic predicates. Hence a separate semantic level appears not only infeasible but dispensible.

(This conclusion does not preclude the possibility of a level of "logical form" between syntax and semantics, such as Chomsky (1975) has proposed; it only precludes this level's having anything significant to do with the problems of entailment, synonymy, anomaly, and so forth.)

If this argument is correct, then the theory of semantics of natural language is simply a subpart of the general theory of conceptual structure; the well-formedness rules for semantics are a subset of those for concepts; and the semantic structures derived from projection rules are a particular class of concepts.

For language acquisition, the consequence of such a claim is that learning the class of possible meanings has little or nothing to do with language learning per se. This of course does not reduce language learning to a negligible task: the child must still learn, in addition to the lexicon, the nonuniversal part of the syntax, phonology, and projection rules.

In order to lighten the language learner's load further, it seems promising to seek a theory of semantics (that is, of conceptualization) in which the projection rules are relatively simple, for then the child can draw relatively straightforward connections between the language he hears and his conception of the world. The methodological assumptions for such a theory would be that syntactic simplicity ideally corresponds to conceptual simplicity; grammatical parallelisms may be clues to conceptual parallelisms; apparent grammatical constraints may reflect conceptual constraints. In short, one should assume that language is a relatively efficient encoding of the information it conveys, and that theories to the contrary (such as most work in logic, which implicitly or explicitly claims that natural language highly distorts the form of the information) inadequately represent the structure of language or the information it conveys, or both.

From the study of transformational grammar during the last twenty years, we have a much better idea of the richness of language and of its constraints than did our predecessors. We also have a much better idea of how to deal systematically with syntactic data. In particular, the syntactic structures of transformational grammar are far more revealing of at least certain kinds of semantic regularity than are ordinary surface strings, and this enables us to avoid many grammatical pitfalls in semantic analysis.

Under the hypothesis that the projection rules are relatively simple, this new understanding of syntax provides a powerful tool for semantic analysis: we can use grammatical structure and grammatical parallelism as direct evidence for semantic structure. Accepting the further hypothesis that semantic structure is a subdomain of conceptual structure means that grammatical evidence can play a direct role in forming or confirming theories of cognition.

In this chapter I present three arguments, drawn from my recent research, in which the methodology suggested by these hypotheses appears to bear fruit. In each case, relatively simple grammatical facts are adduced, which lead to the postulation of a particular kind of entity or relationship that must play a role in semantic structure. Since in each case the proposed entities are not available to physical inspection, we are forced to conclude that they are part of our innate cognitive endowment: constructs placed on the world by the human mind. Thus grammatical investigation will have led to the discovery of nontrivial cognitive hypotheses.

Things and Stuff, Locations and Paths

Everybody acknowledges that among the entities recognized in semantic structure must be material objects, or *things*. I will argue that semantic structure must also include *locations* and *paths* as entities distinct from the things that occupy locations or travel along paths. The form of the argument is that the grammatical devices used in noun phrase syntax to individuate things are paralleled by very similar grammatical devices in prepositional phrase syntax. Since these latter devices individuate entities distinct from things, a new sort of entity must be postulated in order for semantic theory to be observationally and descriptively adequate.

Noun phrases   Language picks out things by means of noun phrases[1] such as *Robert, a dog, my cat, the house with a red roof*. Expressions for things have four syntactic attributes that are of particular importance in the present argument. (i) Things can be counted by affixing certain prenominal modifiers: *four cats, several dogs, many houses*. (ii) A thing once referred to in a discourse can be referred to again by one of the pronouns *he, she,* or *it*: *My cat left the room and I followed*

---

[1] It would be a mistake to claim that things are picked out by nouns rather than noun phrases: such a claim would give no role in picking out things to the many sorts of nominal modifiers. Even when there are no modifiers, as in the NP *Robert*, syntactic generality requires us to assign the referential role to the entire NP and not merely to the head noun.

it. (iii) A thing may be designated in a discourse by one of the demonstratives *this* or *that,* accompanied by a pointing gesture: *This* [pointing] *is green and that* [pointing] *is blue.* And (iv) things may be individuated by asking *which* (*one*): *Which* (*one*) *is the heaviest?*

Noun phrases can also be used to refer to *stuff*: *some dust, my wine, the water in this glass.* Not everybody acknowledges that stuff is a full-fledged part of natural-language semantics. Quine (1960), for example, makes the curious suggestion that stuff is somehow a primitive part of thought and any role it plays in natural language is an infantile remnant; his semantic theory, a variety of traditional set-theoretic semantics, has no way to deal with stuff, which cannot be separated into distinct and namable individuals. Nonetheless, expressions for stuff have essentially the same four syntactic properties associated with expressions for things. Stuff can be measured, though for obvious reasons not counted: *much dust.* Once referred to in a discourse, the same stuff may be referred to again by using the pronoun *it*: *We had spaghetti for dinner. It was delicious.* Stuff may be designated by the demonstratives *this* and *that*: *This is spaghetti; that is mostaccioli.* Stuff or kinds of stuff may be differentiated by asking *which*: *Which* (*salad dressing*) *do you prefer?* If these grammatical devices are to be given a consistent semantic interpretation, it is necessary to allow stuff parallel status to things in the ontology of natural-language semantics. (Wald 1976 presents a formalization of the semantics of mass terms using nonatomic Boolean algebras.)

Prepositional phrases Now consider another grammatical category, the prepositional phrase. Though the preposition is usually dismissed as a trivial affix on an NP, it is easy to show that prepositional phrases in fact have a rich syntax, of which the NP that is the object of the preposition is only the most common part. The list below gives some examples of different constructions possible under the category PP. (For justification of the claim that all of these are indeed PPs, see Emonds 1970; Van Riemsdijk 1974, 1976; Jackendoff 1973, 1977a.)

Phrases after the preposition:
  in the room (P NP)
  from inside the room (P PP)
  beside me on the table (P NP PP)
  outside; upward (P alone)
  after the ball is over (P S)

Phrases before the preposition:
  high on the hill (Adj P NP)
  back in Philadelphia (Particle P NP)
  three miles down the road (NP P NP)
  right over your head (Intensifier P NP)
Combination special:
  three miles back across the lake to John's house (NP Particle P NP
  PP)

Clearly these constructions are not simply case endings on noun phrases. To achieve even observational adequacy, a theory of semantics will have to include a rich set of projection rules to map these constructions into the information they convey; moreover, it is hardly obvious what the nature of that information is.

Now observe that the grammatical devices in noun phrase syntax pointed out above have parallels in the grammar of prepositional phrases. (i) Measure phrases can be affixed as pre-prepositional modifiers: *quite far into the air, seven feet along the gutter.* (ii) If a prepositional phrase appears in a discourse, the pro-form *there* can substitute for it on subsequent appearances: *Fred was in the room and Bill was there too.* (iii) Parallel to the use of demonstrative pronouns for noun phrases, the demonstrative prepositional phrases *here* and *there* are used for pointing: *Your coat is here* [pointing] *and your hat is there* [pointing]. Note the syntactic and semantic parallelism between this sentence and the following one, which contains the standard PP form: *Your coat is in the closet and your hat is on the table.*[2] And (iv) prepositional phrases too may be individuated by questioning. The PP used to question is *where,* and note that it is answered by a PP, not by an NP: *Where is my hat?—In the attic.*

If these grammatical parallelisms between noun phrases and prepositional phrases are taken as significant, a semantic hypothesis immediately springs to mind: some entities are being measured, referred back to, pointed to, and individuated, but they are not things or stuff. In fact, two distinct but related types of entities can be

---

[2] As further evidence that *here* and *there* are PPs, notice that these last two sentences can both undergo inversion to, respectively, *Here is your coat and there is your hat* and *In the closet is your coat and on the table is your hat.* Notice also how different these are from a superficially similar sentence using NP demonstratives: *This is your coat and that is your hat*; aside from the great semantic difference, this sentence has no equivalent form syntactically parallel to the uninverted *here . . . there* sentence (*Your coat is here . . .*): *Your coat is this and your hat is that.*

referred to by prepositional phrases: *locations* and *paths*. Locations are referred to by PPs that occur with verbs of location such as *be* and *stay*; paths are referred to by PPs that occur with verbs of motion such as *go*:[3]

Locational PPs, referring to locations:

John $\left\{\begin{array}{l}\text{was} \\ \text{stayed}\end{array}\right\}$ $\left\{\begin{array}{l}\text{in the house.} \\ \text{at the door.} \\ \text{under the table.}\end{array}\right.$

Motional PPs, referring to paths:

John went $\left\{\begin{array}{l}\text{into the house.} \\ \text{to the door.} \\ \text{toward the table.}\end{array}\right.$

Locations and paths can be determined in part by a thing, denoted by the object of the preposition. But the locations and paths are clearly distinct from the thing itself, as can be seen from the variety displayed in the following examples:

Locations: on the table
under the table
beside the table
near the table

Paths: to the table
from the table
toward the table
around the table

Locations and paths play a number of roles in semantic structure. As demonstrated above, things occupy locations and travel over paths; they also extend over paths and are oriented along paths:

Extent: The road went $\left\{\begin{array}{l}\text{from New York to Poughkeepsie.} \\ \text{along the river.} \\ \text{around the city.}\end{array}\right.$

Orientation: The gun $\left\{\begin{array}{l}\text{aimed} \\ \text{pointed}\end{array}\right\}$ $\left\{\begin{array}{l}\text{toward the target.} \\ \text{away from Bill.}\end{array}\right.$

[3] The correspondence between *prepositions* and locational vs. motional PPs is complex. Some prepositions, such as *to, toward,* and *from,* occur only motionally; many prepositions, such as *under,* occur both ways. *At* occurs only locationally, except in constructions involving orientation such as *point at, aim at, look at.* In other languages (e.g. Hungarian) the distinction between locational and motional is syntactically marked much more clearly.

Of course, for reasons of ontological parsimony one might try to do without locations and paths. I would like to show, however, that doing without them leads to immediate complications in the projections rules. Consider, for example, one of the two possible analyses suggested by Miller and Johnson-Laird (1976) (this work being chosen because it is the only serious attempt I know of to give prepositions any semantic analysis at all). This analysis treats location as a two-place relation between things: ON (X, Y) represents the relation of *x* being on *y*, for example. Although NP corresponds to a well-formed semantic category without variables, PP corresponds to a partly specified relation containing a single unfilled variable. *On the table,* for instance, corresponds to the semantic structure ON (X, THE TABLE). Thus the grammatical parallels pointed out above do not correspond to semantic parallels, and hence the projection rules cannot be fully generalized.

To make the problem clearer, consider sentences like (a) *The book lies on the table* and (b) *The book stands on the table.* In order to represent the contribution of both the verb and the preposition to the readings of these sentences, one would have to resort to some such semantic expression as

LIE/STAND (THE BOOK)   &   ON (THE BOOK, THE TABLE)

But this expression contains two conjoined propositions, requiring a patent complication of the syntax–semantics mapping.

By contrast, if locations are admitted into the ontology, the PP *on the table* corresponds to the variable-free expression ON (THE TABLE), parallel to the variable-free semantic structure of NPs. Hence the grammatical similarities observed above can be reflected in semantic structure. Furthermore, *The book lies/stands on the table* can be treated as a relation between a thing (the book) and a place (on the table), where the place is in turn partly determined by another thing (the table):

LIE/STAND (THE BOOK, (ON (THE TABLE)))

This expression has the further property of much more closely preserving the syntactic integrity of the construction in its semantics. Thus the projection rules are a simpler mapping than if prepositions are predicates.

Miller and Johnson-Laird suggest a second possible analysis of prepositions, treating them as operators on predicates, whose effect is to make predicates take one more argument. For example, STAND (x) is converted by the operator ON into ON (STAND (x), Y), and *The book stands on the table* comes out as ON (STAND (THE BOOK), THE TABLE). Though this theory solves a number of problems, it makes the grammatical parallelisms between NPs and PPs observed above perhaps even more mysterious than the first alternative analysis does. It is hard to imagine, for example, that one could use *here* and *there*, pointing, if they were not referring expressions but operators on verbs. Formal and grammatical arguments based on this intuition are not difficult to develop, but I will spare the reader the details.

In addition to these linguistic arguments for the ontological status of locations, there is a cognitive argument. Miller and Johnson-Laird (section 2.3) themselves discuss the centrality in cognition of the notion of a stable three-dimensional visual world, at least in part independent of the objects that inhabit it. But how can such a notion fail to imply the notion of location? What is independently necessary for conceptualization ought to be available to semantic theory. Only a custom inherited from predicate calculus, of formalizing as a predicate everything that is not a thing, prevents our acknowledging the semantic primacy of locations.

To sum up, the extremely simple grammatical parallels observed between noun phrases and prepositional phrases suggest that there are such semantic entities as locations and paths, distinct from things and stuff, and that prepositional phrases can be used to refer to them. I have sketched arguments for the descriptive inadequacy of theories of the semantics of prepositional phrases that attempt to avoid such entities and have pointed out that locations are independently necessary in cognition. To be sure, much work must be done in exploring the typology of locations and paths through the grammar of prepositional phrases. But this section has at least given the outlines of an existence proof.[4]

---

[4] It is my opinion that NP and PP are not the only major syntactic categories that refer to variable-free semantic entities. There is a great deal of evidence that sentences (the major syntactic phrases whose heads are verbs) refer to *events* and *states of affairs,* not to truth values, as Fregean semantics would have it. The last major syntactic category, adjective phrase, could refer to *properties* rather than to predicates, as traditionally assumed, but I know of no arguments at present that this must be so.

These claims differ in an important way from other semantic analyses in that they put the burden of reference on the major syntactic categories NP, PP, S, and AP, rather than on lexical categories such as noun and verb or on some mixture of lexical and

Things that Stand for Other Things

This section will show that semantic structure must contain things that function as representations of other things. This notion of representation will be shown to have ramifications for both psychology and philosophy. (See Jackendoff 1975b, which goes into much more detail, including a formalization that relates to a great number of other referential phenomena.)

Pictorial representation   Consider the contrast in the two sentences of (1) below. Unlike (1a), (1b) does not describe a physical movement of Mary's body. Rather, it describes John's placing an image of Mary in the picture he is creating. If (2) follows (1b) in discourse, it is ambiguous:

(1)   a.   John put Mary in the garbage can.
      b.   John put Mary in the picture.
(2)   She looked sick.

On one reading, *she* refers to Mary, the person who is being painted. On the other reading, *she* refers to the representation of Mary in the painting; the real Mary may not look sick at all.

   The ambiguity in (2) shows that as a result of using (1b), there come to be *two* individuals in the discourse referred to by the word *Mary*: Mary-in-the-real-world and Mary-in-the-picture. I will distinguish these two individuals by naming them Real-Mary and Image-Mary. Note, however, that ordinary language makes no syntactic distinction between them.

   One might want to claim that reference to Image-Mary is a metaphorical use of the name *Mary* and that the language is being imprecise here. However, this is hardly a metaphor in the usual sense: there is none of the clash of semantic markers characteristic of metaphor, and no artistic effect is intended. Nor is the charge of imprecision valid: this is simply the means the language uses to refer to images in pictures, and every speaker understands it.

---

syntactic categories. The parallelisms among the major categories, in turn, could be recognized as significant only in a theory of grammar such as the Lexicalist Hypothesis of Chomsky (1970a), which claims that cross-categorial parallelism is linguistically significant. Hence research in autonomous syntax has had an indirect but potentially powerful influence on the formation of semantic hypotheses.

What is the nature of Image-Mary? Physically, Image-Mary is made up of paint particles on a canvas, which presumably form some sort of pattern. But it is not by virtue of the pattern alone that we are entitled to call this collection of paint particles *Mary*. Rather, the pattern bears a certain relation to the person called *Mary* (to Real-Mary). What makes the pattern more than a design and entitles it to be called *Mary*—that is, makes it Image-Mary—is that it purports to represent Real-Mary. I use "purports to represent" rather than "represents" for reasons that will be clear shortly. (The notion "purports to represent" is in part inspired by discussion in Goodman 1968. Wittgenstein 1953 has some striking hints toward this analysis; a somewhat similar analysis appears in Fodor 1975.)

There are two ways in which a pattern P can come to purport to represent something else. First, a creator may designate the relation by fiat—for example, by saying "Let this dot stand for Mary and that squiggle stand for Bill." Second, P may be one of a set of patterns systematically related to other objects by a set of correspondence rules, a conventionally established mapping such that anyone acquainted with the correspondence rules can determine what P purports to represent.

Different sets of correspondence rules create different media of representation. For example, the rules for traditional representational painting involve correspondence in characteristics such as shape, proportion, color, shading, and perspective, but not actual depth. The rules for black-and-white photographs omit color; for line drawings they omit shading as well; isometric blueprints eliminate perspective. In ancient Egyptian art, relative sizes of Image-figures corresponded to social status in the real world. Caricatures somehow manage to represent character. In short, each medium of representation has its own special characteristics, embodied in its correspondence rules.

This means of course that P may purport to represent different things, depending on what correspondence rules are understood to be in effect. A map is a clear example: one must know what sort of projection is employed in making a particular map in order to use it correctly. Accordingly, "purports to represent x" must be relativized with respect to the medium of representation.

However, strict adherence to conventional correspondence rules is not a necessary condition for purported representation. Consider the situations described by these sentences:

(3)   John incorrectly painted Mary with a black eye.
       John painted Mary, who didn't have a black eye, with a black
       eye.
       John (mistakenly) gave Mary a black eye in the picture.

Here there are discrepancies between what the correspondence rules dictate Image-Mary should be like and what she is actually like, resulting in unfaithful representations. A representation may be unfaithful either by mistake (because of the creator's misperception) or by design (because of the creator's whim or artistic license). Despite the infidelity, however, the picture can still be considered a picture of Mary, either because of the artist's designation or simply because it is a good enough approximation to serve its purpose. (If the picture in question were a blueprint for a delicate piece of machinery, such approximation might not be good enough.)

Besides discrepancies, images may be unfaithful in a second, less misleading way: properties of the object represented may simply have no counterpart in the image. This may be because of limitations of the medium of representation—for example, the inability of a portrait to represent Mary's blood pressure or income. Or it may be because the creator of the image has (deliberately or carelessly) omitted details, or because details have been effaced or are otherwise unrecognizable. This kind of unfaithfulness does not lead to incorrect correspondences, but rather to a degree of nonspecificity in the image, what Kaplan (1969) calls a lack of "vividness."

Another important property of pictures is that they can purport to represent something that in fact does not exist:

(4)   John put a unicorn in the picture.

In such a case there is an Image-unicorn but no Real-unicorn. The Image-unicorn purports to represent an object in the real world, but fails to correctly represent anything. It is nonetheless an Image-unicorn—that is, it can be referred to as *a unicorn*—because it purports to represent a (supposed) object that has the supposed properties listed in the dictionary entry for the word *unicorn*. The Image-unicorn in (4) may even be an unfaithful representation of a unicorn if its properties do not match, by correspondence rules, what the dictionary entry for *unicorn* says they are supposed to be. So it is possible to say *John idiotically painted the unicorn with two horns* (*instead of one*).

The last property of the linguistic description of images I want to point out is that descriptions of objects in their role as representations can be mixed with descriptions in physical terms. Consider the ambiguity of (5), which turns on whether the painting has a Real-green-spot *on* it or an Image-green-spot *in* it:

(5)   In that painting there is a spot of green paint on Mary's dress.

We thus have found that semantic structure must refer to things that are identifiable not only by their physical characteristics but also by virtue of their purporting to represent something else. In (1b), what John created is both a Real-picture and an Image-Mary. Objects may acquire the latter role either by designation or by the mediation of a set of correspondence rules. But even when there are correspondence rules, the correspondence may be erroneous or lack vividness without the object's losing its representational status. Moreover, the medium may permit the creation of images that do not faithfully represent real things at all. Finally, given the knowledge of the relevant correspondence rules, images can convey information— blueprints and maps are clear examples of this use of representation.

Without this representational property, pictures could never be more than mere visual patterns. Furthermore, no representation could be systematic unless cognitive structure included the possibility of correspondence rules. (I deliberately say "cognitive" rather than "semantic" structure because the correspondence rules may not even be conscious, much less verbalized.) Thus, investigating the grammar of sentences like (1b) reveals that semantic structure must include the notion of representation and that cognitive structure must contain the potential for describing and learning systems of correspondence rules.

Verbal representation   Given the notion of systems of representation mediated by correspondence rules, grammatical considerations compel us to use them for much more than dealing with pictures. For example, the grammatical paradigms describing verbal systems of representation are practically identical to those for describing pictorial representation. Compare (6) with (1)–(2):

		a.	She looked sad.
(6)	John put Mary in the story.	b.	She sounded sad.
		c.	She seemed sad.

Clearly the first sentence means that a character in the story (an Image-Mary) is called Mary and is supposed to represent Mary. In (6a) *she* refers to Real-Mary; in (6b) to Image-Mary; (6c) is ambiguous between the two.

In verbal media of representation, the objects that purport to represent things in the world are no longer patterns of pigment but patterns of sounds. Again, the purported reference is established by a combination of designation by fiat ("Let *glork* stand for this object; let *Robert* stand for this person") and a complex set of correspondence rules, which are of course the rules of a language, all the way from its phonetics to its theory of reference. As with maps, one must know what language one is hearing in order to understand what purported reference is intended.

Like pictures, verbal images may fail to be totally accurate in two ways. They can simply be inexplicit or incomplete—that is, lack vividness. Or they can be discrepant. Compare (7) with (3), the parallel examples for pictures.

(7)   John incorrectly described Mary as having a black eye.
      John described Mary, who didn't have a black eye, as having a black eye.
      John (mistakenly) gave Mary a black eye in his story.

These representations may be unfaithful either by mistake (an erroneous description) or by design (a lie or a fiction, depending on John's motives).

It is not surprising that verbal images too can purport to represent something that does not exist:

(8)   John put a unicorn in the story.
      John's story has a unicorn in it.

Note that if *garage* is substituted for *story* in (8), the unicorn has to be a Real-unicorn, and the sentences have a rather different sense. Moreover, as in pictures, even the fictitious character can be misrepresented if its properties do not match the supposed properties of what it supposedly represents: *John incorrectly described the unicorn as having two horns*.

Finally, descriptions of verbal images in their role as representations can be mixed with descriptions of their properties as sound patterns. (9) has an ambiguity parallel to that of (5).

(9)   In that story, there are three significant sentences which are the
      solution to Mary's dilemma.

On one reading, the three sentences are Real-sentences, three of the
sentences that constitute the story; on the other reading they are
Image-sentences which, like the empty cigar case in the parlor, are
crucial characters in the plot.

Thus from the point of view of semantic structure, sound patterns
used as representations have properties that are nearly identical to
those of visual patterns used as representations. In other words,
semantic structure must contain a rather comprehensive theory of
semiotics, one that is furthermore an essentially correct description of
how people use symbolic representations. The linguistic expression of
this theory, however, has one peculiar property: it has the (for
semanticists) nasty habit of using the same name for a real object and
for its purported representation.

Again, the symbolic property of sound patterns cannot be systematic unless cognitive structure includes the possibility of correspondence rules. This is hardly surprising: the correspondence rules are
exactly the unconscious and unverbalized grammar we as linguists are
looking for, and the ability to learn them is what we call universal
grammar. This conclusion reinforces the claim that visual correspondence rules may be highly abstract, unconscious, and learned by as yet
unknown means.

Mental representation   Continuing to generalize the notion of representation, we find that language acts as though there are mental
images parallel to visual and verbal images. Compare the following
examples with the previous paradigms. First, the figures of speech in
(10) are remarkably close to those in (1) and (6).

(10)   John kept Mary in mind.
       John put Mary out of his thoughts.

Second, *John pictured Mary as beautiful* is ambiguous between
John's painting, describing, or imagining Mary. Third, (11) is completely parallel to (3) and (7): the examples describe unfaithful
correspondences between images and what they purport to represent:

(11) John incorrectly imagined Mary with a black eye.
      John incorrectly thought of Mary as having a black eye.
      John imagined Mary, who didn't have a black eye, with a black
      eye.
      John thought of Mary, who didn't have a black eye, as having a
      black eye.
      John (mistakenly) attributed to Mary a black eye.

Unfaithful mental images too can come about either by mistake (a
delusion) or by design (a fantasy). Furthermore, mental images are
notorious for their lack of vividness. Fourth, one can have mental
images of things that don't exist. Compare (12) with (4) and (8):

(12) John $\begin{Bmatrix} \text{imagined} \\ \text{thought of} \end{Bmatrix}$ a unicorn.

And one can even misrepresent mental images: *John incorrectly
imagined the unicorn as having two horns.*

Finally, descriptions of mental images can mix literal descriptions
with descriptions in terms of what they purport to represent. Sentence (13) is ambiguous in much the same way that (5) and (9) are, the
ambiguity hinging on whether John thinks three ideas or thinks *of*
three ideas:

(13) In John's mind there are three significant ideas that can solve
      his problem.

We see therefore that much of the syntax involved in describing
thinking parallels the syntax of pictures and descriptions. Under the
assumption that the projection rules from syntax to semantics largely
preserve syntactic parallelisms—that is, that there is a semantic
motivation for this syntactic parallel—we are led to posit entities
representing mental images in semantic structure. Though it is well
known that picture and inner-speech theories of thought are unbeliev-
ably problematic (for instance, Who views the pictures?), the difficulty of even conceiving of any other possible alternative suggests
that this is in fact the innate theory the mind has about itself.
Certainly the conception of thought that presents itself to naive
introspection is one of manipulating inner pictures and sentences. In
any event, it is not too shocking to find that in the case of mental
images, semantic (or conceptual) structure contains constructs that
severely misconstrue the nature of the entities concerned.

Referential opacity   The view of symbol systems presented here leads to an appealing solution to the old philosophical problem of referential opacity (see Linsky 1967, 1971, among many others, for extensive treatment of the problem). One of the basic manifestations of the problem is the invalidity of the superficially innocent substitution of equals for equals in a syllogism like the following:

Charley imagines the number of planets as equal to seven.
The number of planets is equal to nine.
Therefore, Charley imagines nine as equal to seven.

The key to the solution lies in the fact that in the major premise the part that follows the verb *imagines* is not a description of the world, but the description of Charley's mental image, which in turn purports to represent some state of the world. On the other hand, the minor premise is the description of a state of the world. Since in the major premise *planets* refers to Image-planets, and in the minor premise to Real-planets, the phrases *the number of planets* in the two sentences are not coreferential and hence not intersubstitutable, despite their identical form. Therefore the inference to the conclusion does not go through.

Lest this solution seem cavalier, observe that exact parallels to such invalid syllogisms can be constructed for pictures and descriptions; the force of the analysis is particularly clear in the former case:

That diagram of the solar system shows the number of planets as equal to seven.
The number of planets is equal to nine.
Therefore, that diagram of the solar system shows nine as equal to seven.

That story describes the number of planets as equal to seven.
The number of planets is equal to nine.
Therefore, that story describes nine as equal to seven.

(For a more complete discussion of the solution this analysis offers for opaque contexts, see Jackendoff 1975b, which includes analyses of Russell's example *I thought your boat was longer than it was* and of Quine's example *Ralph thinks that Ortcutt is a spy.*)

This section has shown that the semantics of the description of pictures must introduce new referential entities in order to account for the dual references of the pronoun *she* in the discourse (1)–(2). In exploring the nature of these entities, we found that they acquire their descriptions by purporting to represent other things and that the representation may be mediated by a set of conventionalized correspondence rules. Then we found that the grammatical treatment of verbal representation closely parallels that of visual representation. If this parallelism is not to be a mere accident of grammar, the semantic treatment of all these forms of representation must be parallel as well. In turn this conclusion brings evidence to bear not only on the conceptual structure of representations, but also on how the mind pictures itself.

Generalization of Spatial Concepts to Abstract Domains

This section will present grammatical evidence that motivates an important relation in conceptual structure which I will call "cross-field generalization." (This material grew out of the semantic analysis of Gruber 1965. For more detail and a discussion of how projection rules relate the semantic expression to lexical entries, see Jackendoff 1976, 1977b).

Positional, Possessional, and Identificational location   Consider first the field of verbs of spatial position. These can be divided into three important subfields, which I will call GO verbs, BE verbs, and STAY verbs. The sentences in (14) exemplify the subclass of GO verbs:

(14)   The train traveled from Detroit to Cincinnati.
       The hawk flew over the prairie.
       A meteor hurtled toward the earth.

These sentences all express concepts that pick out types of physical motion. Following Gruber's (1965) terminology, I will refer to the object in motion as the theme of the sentence. In each sentence the theme travels along a path, which may, as in the final example, be further differentiated into a source, or initial point, and a goal, or final point. The semantic similarity between these sentences can be described by saying that the concepts they express are all instances of the general concept GO (x, p). This concept makes the claim that there has taken place an event consisting of the motion of some object *x* along some path *p*. In other words, the first variable of GO corresponds to the theme, the second to the path.[5]

BE verbs are exemplified in (15). These sentences describe, not a motion, but the location of an object. Thus they express instances of a general concept BE (X, L), where X is the theme (the object being located) and L is a location.

(15)   Max was in Africa.
        The cushion lay on the couch.
        The statue stands in the woods.

In addition to the verbs of location illustrated in (15) there is a second, smaller class of location verbs with rather different semantic properties, which I will call STAY verbs:

(16)   The bacteria stayed in his body.
        Stanley remained in Africa.
        Bill kept the book on the shelf.

The verbs in (16) differ from those in (15) in two ways. First, as shown in (17), they cannot refer to a point in time, as can BE verbs. Second, as shown in (18), they can serve as complements to the expression *what happened was that,* whereas BE verbs cannot.

(17)   The bacteria $\begin{Bmatrix} \text{were} \\ \text{*stayed} \end{Bmatrix}$ in his body at six o'clock.

        The cushion $\begin{Bmatrix} \text{lay} \\ \text{*remained} \end{Bmatrix}$ on the couch at six o'clock.

(18)   What happened was that $\begin{cases} \text{Stanley remained in Africa.} \\ \text{Bill kept the book on the shelf.} \\ \text{*Max was in Siberia.} \\ \text{*the statue stood in the woods.} \end{cases}$

[5] This account differs from that in Jackendoff (1976, 1977b), which formalized these verbs as GO (X, Y, Z), the variables representing theme, source, and goal, respectively. The change permits the generalization of motion verbs to examples like (14b,c). Recognizing locations and paths as semantic entities and treating source-goal pairs as just one kind of path make this more general account possible. I am grateful to Dick Carter, John Goldsmith, and Erich Woisetschlaeger for comments that led to the revision.

This reanalysis of GO, which I believe is the correct one on both syntactic and semantic grounds, rules out an alleged simplification suggested to me by a number of individuals, which would replace GO (X, Y, Z) by a change from one state to another: GO (BE (X, Y), BE (X, Z)). Such a formalization does not countenance physical motion as a semantic primitive, replacing it with what I consider a less fundamental concept, circumstantial motion. In the present treatment of GO, motion is intimately bound up with paths instead of locations, making the change-of-state analysis impossible for the same reasons that paths cannot be represented as sequences of locations.

The verbs in (16) thus express instances of a general concept, STAY (x, L) where x is the theme and L is a location.

The evidence from the use of the expression *what happened was* indicates a further relationship: STAY verbs, like GO verbs, describe *events* — that is, they are instances of a general concept HAPPEN (x); BE verbs, on the other hand, describe *states of affairs*.

Given these three subfields of verbs of position, let us consider another semantic field, verbs of possession. These can again be divided into three subfields, exemplified in (19), (20), and (21):

(19)   Harry gave the book to the library.
       Charlie bought the lamp from Max.
       Will inherited a million dollars.
(20)   The book belonged to the library.
       Max owned an iguana.
       Bill had no money.
(21)   The library kept the book.
       The iguana stayed in Max's possession.
       The leopard retained its spots.

In (19) the things described by the direct object of the sentence undergo a change in possessor. The sentences in (20), however, express states of possession. The sentences in (21) also express a single unchanging possessor, but *at six o'clock* may be added only to (20), not to (21), and *what happened was* may be prefixed to (21) but not to (20).

Thus there is an important parallel between (19)–(21) and (14)–(16). Gruber (1965) chooses to represent this parallel by claiming that the verbs in (19) are also instances of GO (x, P), the verbs in (20) are instances of BE (x, L), and the verbs in (21) are instances of STAY (x, L). The difference between (19)–(21) and (14)–(16) is then expressed by a modifier on GO, BE, and STAY, picking out the proper semantic field. For physical motion and location, the field modifier is Positional; for possession, it is Possessional. For example, the first sentence in (14) expresses something like (22a), the first in (19) something like (22b):

(22)   a. GO_{Posit} (THE TRAIN, [FROM (DETROIT) TO (CINCINNATI)])
       b. GO_{Poss} (THE BOOK, [FROM (HARRY)   TO (THE LIBRARY)])

This now gives us a principle with which to organize a third important semantic field, verbs of predication or ascription. These verbs are used to describe properties of things. The same three-way division into subfields obtains:

(23)   The coach changed from a handsome young man into a pumpkin.
       The metal turned red.
       The ice became mushy.
(24)   The coach was a turkey.
       The metal was vermilion.
       The pumpkin seemed tasty.
(25)   The poor coach remained a pumpkin.
       The metal stayed red.
       The redness persisted.

The sentences of (23) describe changes of state; those of (24) describe a state; those of (25) describe persistence of a state. Of the two nonmotional cases, (24) and (25), *at six o'clock* may be added only to (24) and *what happened was* may be prefixed only to (25). Thus it is clear that these three sets of verbs are futher instances of the concepts GO, BE, and STAY, respectively. We will call the field modifier this time Identificational; locations and paths in this field make claims about what the theme is, rather than where it is, as in the Positional field, or whose it is, as in the Possessional field. Thus, for example, the first sentence of (23) expresses something like the following:

GO$_{\text{Ident}}$ (THE COACH, [FROM (A HANDSOME YOUNG MAN) TO (A PUMPKIN)])

The field modifiers Positional, Possessional, and Identificational combined with the basic concepts GO, BE, and STAY express important semantic distinctions and generalizations. The fact that the three major concepts apply to each of the three semantic fields, which a priori have nothing to do with each other, illustrates the phenomenon of cross-field generalization. A basic notion of what it is to be "in a place" differs from one field to another: in the Positional field a location is a spatial position; in the Possessional field it is to be owned by someone; in the Identificational field it is to have a property. From any of these notions of location an entire field of verbs is elaborated out of instances of the three basic concepts GO, BE, and STAY, understood as they apply to that particular type of location.

As evidence that cross-field generalization is of genuine grammatical significance, observe that it is common for particular verbs to function in more than one semantic field, while still preserving their classification as GO, BE, or STAY verbs. Consider the following:

The coach turned into a driveway.	(Positional)
The coach turned into a pumpkin.	(Identificational)
The train went to Texas.	(Positional)
The inheritance went to Philip.	(Possessional)
Max is in Africa.	(Positional)
Max is fat.	(Identificational)
Bill kept the book on the shelf.	(Positional)
Bill kept the book.	(Possessional)
The coach remained in the driveway.	(Positional)
The coach remained a pumpkin.	(Identificational)

In each pair, the same verb is used in two different semantic fields. Since these uses are not a priori related, it is a significant generalization that a sizable number of verbs exhibit such behavior. The theory I am proposing claims that the relation between these uses is simple and nonaccidental: the verb stays fundamentally the same, changing only its semantic field via a cross-field generalization. One way in which words can extend their meanings, then, is by keeping all semantic structure intact except the part that picks out the semantic field.

In addition to the three semantic functions discussed so far, there are two others that describe different kinds of causation. Compare (26), (27), and (28).

(26) a. The rock fell to the ground.
     b. Noga stayed sick.
     c. Dick received the money.
     d. The air went out of the balloon.
(27) a. Linda lowered the rock to the ground.
     b. David kept Noga sick.
     c. Dick acquired the money.
     d. Laura sucked the air out of the balloon.

(28) a. Linda dropped the rock to the ground.
      b. David left Noga sick.
      c. Dick accepted the money.
      d. Laura released the air from the balloon.

The events in (26) are also described in (27) and (28), but in the latter two sets of sentences the event is due to the agency of the subject (the agent). In turn, (27) and (28) differ in the kind of action performed by the agent: in (27) the agent brings the event about, or causes it; in (28) the agent ceases to prevent the event, or lets it happen. We can symbolize these two kinds of agency as CAUSE (X, E) and LET (X, E), respectively, where X is the agent and E is the event. If we represent examples (26a,b,c) as (29a,b,c), respectively, we can then represent (27a,b,c) as (30a,b,c), and (28a,b,c) as (31a,b,c).

(29) a. GO$_{Posit}$ (THE ROCK, TO (THE GROUND))
      b. STAY$_{Ident}$ (NOGA, SICK)
      c. GO$_{Poss}$ (THE MONEY, TO (DICK))
(30) a. CAUSE (LINDA, GO$_{Posit}$ (THE ROCK, TO (THE GROUND)))
      b. CAUSE (DAVID, STAY$_{Ident}$ (NOGA, SICK))
      c. CAUSE (DICK, GO$_{Poss}$ (THE MONEY, TO (DICK)))
(31) a. LET (LINDA, GO$_{Posit}$ (THE ROCK, TO (THE GROUND)))
      b. LET (DAVID, STAY$_{Ident}$ (NOGA, SICK))
      c. LET (DICK, GO$_{Poss}$ (THE MONEY, TO (DICK)))

As the examples in (27)–(28) show, the concepts CAUSE and LET occur in all three semantic fields we have investigated—Positional, Possessional, and Identificational—simply by taking as their second argument a GO, BE, or STAY whose path or location is in the appropriate field. Thus CAUSE and LET can be thought of as predicative concepts that can elaborate the semantic possibilities of any field.

Circumstantial location   I would now like to use the notion of cross-field generalization to motivate a semantic field whose existence is less obvious than the three fields already considered—so far from obvious, in fact, that up to now it appears to have escaped attention. Nevertheless, I will try to show that it is a genuine semantic field with internal structure parallel to that of the other three. Consider the following two sentences:

(32) a. Laura kept David in the room.
      b. Laura kept David working.
          (Underlying structure: Laura kept David [$_s$David working])

The interpretation of (32a) is something like

CAUSE (LAURA, STAY$_{Posit}$ (DAVID, IN (THE ROOM))).

If the verb *keep* is to be essentially the same in (32b), we must provide (32b) with an interpretation that is similar in structure to that of (32a). Clearly none of the previous semantic fields will do. Therefore, I introduce a field called Circumstantial: if an individual is in a Circumstantial location, where the location is an event or state of affairs, this is taken to mean that the individual is a protagonist in that event or state of affairs. Then (32b) will express a concept something like:

CAUSE (LAURA, STAY$_{Circ}$ (DAVID, DAVID WORK)).

This representation claims that Laura caused David to stay in the situation of working, precisely the desired interpretation. Furthermore, the interpretation is precisely parallel in form to its Positional counterpart. Some other examples of verbs of Circumstance, with their Positional uses where such exist, are given in (33)–(40).

(33) The car began sputtering.
      GO$_{Circ}$ (THE CAR, TO (THE CAR SPUTTER))
(34) Sheila stopped laughing.
      GO$_{Circ}$ (SHEILA, FROM (SHEILA LAUGH))
      (Note: *stop* can also be causative)
(35) John avoided the beach.
      STAY$_{Posit}$ (JOHN, AT NOT (THE BEACH)) (or causative)
      John avoided playing checkers.
      STAY$_{Circ}$ (JOHN, AT NOT (JOHN PLAY CHECKERS)) (or causative)
(36) Dick forced the ball into the hole.
      CAUSE (DICK, GO$_{Posit}$ (THE BALL, TO IN (THE HOLE)))
      Dick forced Max to talk.
      CAUSE (DICK, GO $_{Circ}$ (MAX, TO (MAX TALK)))
(37) Linda kept Laura (away) from the cookies.
      CAUSE (LINDA, STAY$_{Posit}$ (LAURA, AT NOT (THE COOKIES)))

Linda kept Laura from laughing.

CAUSE (LINDA, STAY$_{Circ}$ (LAURA, AT NOT (LAURA LAUGH)))

(38) Manny released the air from the balloon.

LET (MANNY, GO$_{Posit}$ (THE AIR, FROM (THE BALLOON)))

Manny released Moe from washing the car.

LET (MANNY, GO$_{Circ}$ (MOE, FROM (MOE WASH THE CAR)))

(39) David allowed Laura in the room.

LET (DAVID, BE$_{Posit}$ (LAURA, IN (THE ROOM)))

David allowed Laura to wash the car.

LET (DAVID, BE$_{Circ}$ (LAURA, AT (LAURA WASH THE CAR)))

(40) Moe exempted Jack from fighting.

LET (MOE, BE$_{Circ}$ (JACK, AT NOT (JACK FIGHT)))

It can be seen that quite a number of common verbs are members of the semantic field of Circumstantial verbs, and that the same concepts, GO, STAY, BE, CAUSE, and LET, appear in the Circumstantial as in the Positional field. Furthermore, note that if a verb that takes a sentential complement also has a Positional use, the two variants of the verb express concepts that, except for the semantic field, are largely identical. Thus, in the present theory it is no accident that the verb occurs in these two seemingly disparate syntactic and semantic contexts: the contexts are in fact closely related by cross-field generalization.

In case the generalization from Positional to Circumstantial should still seem marginal and unmotivated, we should observe that it is in fact quite pervasive in the language. Consider a few more random examples, in which the generalization is immediately evident:

He *came* to be called Batman.

They *led* me to believe something ridiculous.

We couldn't *drive* him to confess.

Will you ever *bring* yourself to acknowledge that?

I hereby *direct* you to shred the documents.

Such examples are not metaphors in the usual sense: they are not used for artistic effect, and there are no conflicting semantic markers. Rather, they are generalizations of the meanings of verbs along what I would claim are innately determined lines.

As a more subtle example, consider the meaning of the verb *force,* which has been analyzed in (36) only up to synonymy with the verb *cause. Dick forced the ball into the hole* can be paraphrased more accurately by "cause to go" plus a manner phrase, something like "Dick caused the ball to go into the hole by applying pressure against its resistance." Surprisingly, exactly the same manner phrase is right for the Circumstantial reading: *John forced Sue to speak up* can be paraphrased as "John caused Sue to speak up by applying pressure against her resistance." In other words, the whole interlocking system of concepts—pressure, applying pressure, and resistance—generalizes from the physical sense to this abstract sense, combining identically in both semantic fields to paraphrase the sense of the verb *force*. Surely this is no coincidence: to me it argues that the choice of extensions of meaning from the Positional field to the Circumstantial is highly determined, and that the cross-field generalization follows certain innate lines of analogy.

As with the other phenomena discussed in this chapter, I have argued that an explanation of a simple grammatical parallelism leads to a theory of cognitive structure. The discussion in this section has led to the claim that cross-field generalization is a vital element of conceptualization—in fact that it is the way many abstract concepts are elaborated. Is there other evidence that makes such a claim plausible?

Other cross-field generalizations   First consider another type of evidence drawn from language: the process of metaphor. In a metaphor, the structure of one semantic field is grafted onto another semantic field; the aesthetic effect arises at least in part from the perceiver's restructuring of a familiar field in some novel way. The fact that we can interpret metaphors at all argues that we are capable of performing new cross-field generalizations on demand.

The cross-field generalizations I have discussed up to this point, namely those involved in grammar, do not seem artistic in the way that metaphors are, and it is reasonable to ask why not. There are two possible theories. The weaker one is simply that we are so used to the generalizations of the concepts GO, BE, and STAY that they are aesthetically worn out; there is no longer anything novel about them. A stronger hypothesis is that the cross-field generalizations of concepts like location, event, and state are innately determined; GO, BE, STAY, CAUSE, and LET are fundamental conceptual building blocks out of which fields are elaborated. Thus their generalization across semantic fields is conceptually natural in some sense. Metaphor, on the other hand, invokes a cross-field generalization that is not innate in the same sense; there is an element of unnaturalness, of organizing a field that is not native to the organism, but one that the language user can nevertheless enter into and play with.

Turning to nonlinguistic matters, consider a different sort of example of our ability to perform cross-field generalizations, in this case in real time. A musician has the ability to follow a conductor's physical gestures and to translate the force, direction, and shape of those gestures, not only into rhythm, but into tone, attack, and phrasing, *without* explicit coaching as to what the gestures signify. Similarly, consider the ability of a dancer to create appropriate dances for given music—again, not just rhythmically correct dances, but dances that correspond to the expression of the music in many complex and subtle ways. There is no a priori reason why human beings should have the ability to translate from physical gesture into sound and back again in such a way that there is substantial interpersonal agreement on how appropriate the translation is. The fact that we have this ability argues that there must be certain generalizations about how physical gestures and musical gestures are represented conceptually, and that these generalizations are determined at least in part along lines laid down by the nature of the organism. This is precisely the sort of cross-field generalization I have been proposing as part of semantic theory; the fact that it appears in other aspects of mental activity gives independent support to the claim that this kind of semantic relation has psychological reality.

Interaction of Linguistic Semantics and Cognitive Psychology

Each of the three sketches presented here has made specific proposals about the nature of conceptual structure, based on the surely unquestionable assumption that conceptual structure must contain room for everything language talks about. These analyses differ from most previous efforts in one important respect: they do not seek merely to express the meanings of sentences, but to do so in a way that respects the integrity of the syntax. The working assumption is that language is a relatively good vehicle for the information it conveys; in theoretical terms this amounts to the claim that the projection rules that relate syntactic and semantic structure are relatively simple and that many syntactic generalizations therefore reflect semantic generalizations.

In the search for such a descriptively adequate theory, some rather

elementary grammatical observations led in each case to the postulation of semantic entities and relations not recognized in the normal
run of semantic descriptions in the literature: locations, paths, representations, correspondence rules, and cross-field generalizations.
Since these entities and relations have no direct correspondence with
the physical world, the obvious conclusion seemed to be that they
are, rather, the result of the way the mind structures its perception of
the world. Finally, in each case it was possible to show that such a
conclusion is not implausible from a psychological point of view:
something of the general nature of these entities and relations must
independently be present in cognition. Thus, unlike most logic-based
and artificial-intelligence-based approaches to semantics, the approach taken here has two crucial checks on the correctness of
semantic structure besides observational adequacy, internal consistency, and elegance: its faithfulness to grammatical form and its
psychological plausibility.

I have not gone very far in this chapter toward checking for
psychological plausibility, largely because, as far as I know, cognitive
psychology has had little precise to say about the sorts of conceptual
structures this linguistic analysis suggests. Such justification as I have
given rests on rather elementary observations, and is meant to be
only suggestive.

The scarcity of psychological evidence, though, indicates that the
interface between linguistic semantics and cognitive psychology is a
two-way street: not only should linguists be looking to psychologists
for justification of semantic theories but psychologists can begin to
look to linguists for cognitive theories to test experimentally. Properly
used, linguistic evidence can support conceptual hypotheses of depth,
precision, and ease of access unparalleled elsewhere in psychology. It
is my hope that research of the sort sketched here can pave the way
to the use of language as a tool on an equal footing with perception in
exploring the structure of human experience.

6 Language and the Brain

EDGAR B. ZURIF AND SHEILA E. BLUMSTEIN

Our intention will be to examine some of the evidence and ideas expressed in this volume from the perspective of aphasiology. However, we will not try to tie any of the psycholinguistic notions expressed here to neurophysiology—to the manner, that is, in which neurons communicate with one another. It is not at all clear at present how, or even whether, theories of discrete neural events and psycholinguistic theories should constrain each other (Fodor, Bever, and Garrett 1974). But that is a tired point; even worse, it has served to obscure the potential role that aphasiology can play in an attempt to create a realistic model of language.

The pertinent fact about aphasia is that it provides behavioral data to which psychology should be responsive. Focal damage to the left cerebral hemisphere does not lead to an across-the-board reduction in language proficiency. Rather, lesions in different locations in the left hemisphere are quite selective and remarkably consistent in the manner in which they undermine language (see Figure 6.1). The empirical question is whether this selectivity reflects distinctions that linguistic theories make among components in a grammar.

Broca's Aphasia and the Competence–Performance Distinction

We will introduce this examination by briefly describing a clinical syndrome resulting from anterior damage to the left hemisphere. The site of damage is termed Broca's area (involving the third frontal convolution); the syndrome is termed Broca's aphasia. Quite simply, Broca's aphasics are better hearers than they are speakers. They speak effortfully, they show distorted articulation, and what is most striking, they produce a telegrammatic or agrammatic output in which syntax is restricted to simple active declarative forms: grammatical morphemes, both bound and free, are usually omitted, and there is a corresponding reliance on nouns and, less often, on uninflected verbs (Goodglass 1968). Equally noteworthy is the clinical impression that many such patients seem to show relatively intact comprehension, even seeming to recognize the disparity between what they actually

The research described in this paper was supported by NIH grants 11408 and 06209 to Boston University School of Medicine and by NIH grant 07615 to Clark University.

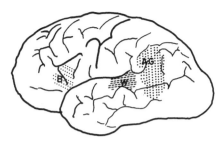

Figure 6.1 Locations of the principal language zones on the cortex. B represents Broca's area, W represents Wernicke's area, and AG represents the angular gyrus. Lesions in these different areas give rise to commonly observed and clinically differentiable language impairments.

utter and what they had intended to say. This last impression rests not only with their obvious frustration at the inadequacy of their output but also with their verbal strategies: they substitute numbers for plural markers, adverbs of time for tense markers, and despite a basic dysprosody they use intonation in a semantically contrastive manner (Goodglass and Kaplan 1972).

A number of investigators, presumably having accepted this expressive–receptive dissociation at face value, claim that Broca's area has very little functional commitment to a grammar (Lenneberg 1973; Locke, Caplan, and Kellar 1973; Weigl and Bierwisch 1970). Implicitly or explicitly, they have taken this dissociation as a literal manifestation of the linguistically defined competence–performance dichotomy, arguing that the patient's tacit knowledge of his language remains intact and that the problem centers around the motor implementation of speech. In this view, the telegrammatic output is usually seen as an economizing measure.

We cannot help but focus, however, on some facts that are not consonant with this interpretation. As one example, the Broca's aphasic does not express himself grammatically in any mode—he is as agrammatic in his writing as in his spontaneous speech (Goodglass and Hunter 1970). As another example, even if his speaking vocabulary does increase after the onset of his aphasia, the increase is almost always restricted to content words (for example, nouns and verbs); the effect does not spread to grammatical particles. We decided, therefore, to go beyond clinical impressions and to examine just what abilities these patients actually possess.

Components of Sentence Processing

Relative clauses In one study, we simply tested the comprehension ability of Broca's aphasics (along with other types of aphasics) for object relative, center-embedded sentences (Caramazza and Zurif 1976). The sentences were of three types: sentences in which semantic constraints between words allow subjects to assign a correct reading of the sentence without decoding its syntax (*The apple that the boy is eating is red*); so-called reversible sentences in which semantic constraints were relaxed and for which a correct reading required a knowledge of the syntactic relations among the words (*The boy that the girl is chasing is tall*); and implausible sentences which, though grammatically well-formed, describe highly improbable events (*The boy that the dog is patting is fat*). Simple active declarative sentences were used as fillers. The sentences were presented orally. The patients' task was to choose which of two pictures captured the meaning expressed in the sentence, the incorrect alternative taking a number of different forms: one depicted a subject–object reversal; another, an action different from that specified by the verb.

The results were as follows: For all response conditions the patients performed at a high level of accuracy when presented with both simple declarative sentences and semantically constrained, center-embedded sentences. But their comprehension of the reversible center-embedded sentences depended upon the nature of the incorrect pictorial alternative. When the incorrect alternative featured a change that could be codified lexically—for example, when the depicted action was different from that specified by the verb in the sentence—performance remained at a high level of accuracy for all sentence types. But on trials in which the incorrect alternative turned upon a structural change—that is, when it depicted a subject–object reversal—the patients chose accurately only when semantic support was available. Their performance on trials in which the incorrect alternative featured a subject–object reversal was at a 90 percent level of accuracy for the semantically constrained sentences and at chance level for the reversible and implausible sentences.

At a first pass, then, one can reasonably infer from these results that comprehension is not all it is made out to be in Broca's aphasia. Granting that the simple declarative sentences permit the application of a strategy whereby a noun and an adjacent verb can be mapped as actor and action, granting also that the lexically incorrect alternatives permit a correct choice based on partial cues provided by a sampling of lexical content, then only the subject–object reversal condition permits a test of the patients' ability to carry out a syntactic analysis. As the results show, when semantic support is unavailable this is precisely where they fail.

Pronominalization   The same limitation emerges in yet another study (Blumstein, Zurif, and Caramazza, in preparation). The study focuses upon pronominalization and reflexivization. Patients are tested first on their ability to make the appropriate referential connections to the pronouns *him, her,* and the like, and to distinguish between sentence pairs such as, *She washed her,* and *She washed herself.*

These tests provide base-line measures against which to assess comprehension for more complex, embedded sentences. The embedded sentences appear in one of two forms: either the reflexive pronoun refers to the subject of the embedded sentence—that is, to the noun phrase closest to it, as in *The boy watched the man bandage himself*—or it refers to the subject of the matrix sentence, in which case the reflexive refers to the more distant noun rather than to that closest to it (*The boy, watching the man, bandaged himself*) and thus prohibits a minimum-distance strategy. There are also other variables. Specifically, each of these sentence types is characterized by the presence or absence of nonsyntactic cues. These cues, when present, are provided by substituting feminine and plural nouns and their appropriate reflexive forms. Thus, there are sentences such as *The boy watched the girl bandage herself.* Again, comprehension in each instance is tested by means of a picture-matching task.

The results to date are straightforward. Again, focusing only on the performance of Broca's aphasics, we found that patients make three times as many errors on sentences for which they cannot use a minimum-distance routine; overall, performance improves dramatically when the cues supplied by gender and number are available. Once again, then, the agrammatic patients fail to comprehend when they cannot sample from a sentence on the basis of some probabilistic strategy—in this instance, the minimum-distance principle—or, in other words, when they have to make structural decisions solely on the basis of the syntactic relations holding between the words in the sentence.

Phrase structure   Obviously, the limitations we have charted extend the Broca's problem beyond the motor implementation of speech. But the question arises whether the deficit is interestingly tied to a specific limitation on the patient's tacit knowledge of linguistic structure or whether it is attributable to a general lack of cognitive power. As examples of the latter, constraints on storage capacity and on rate of processing the initial input come to mind. One could easily imagine that anterior brain damage might limit such capacities so that when routines that normally shortcut a full syntactic analysis cannot be applied, the input fades before a meaning representation can be assigned.

We considered this possibility some time ago. For the past several years we and others have been concerned with the Broca's aphasics' tacit knowledge of their language and with studying their linguistic intuitions in situations that avoid real-time demands (Andreewski and Seron 1975; Gardner, Denes, and Zurif 1975; Ulatowska and Baker 1975; von Stockert 1972; Whitaker 1970; Zurif, Caramazza, and Myerson 1972; Zurif, Green, Caramazza, and Goodenough 1976).

In one approach, we simply asked the patients to judge how words in a written sentence "go best together" in that sentence and to indicate their judgments by pointing to the words they wanted to cluster. The sentence was *always in view*. The many details involved in screening and training the patients for this task are fully presented elsewhere (Zurif et al. 1972) and will not be described here. It should be noted, however, that the aphasic patients as well as neurologically intact control subjects mastered the procedure without too much difficulty and willingly carried the task through.

Briefly, the judgment-derived word groupings served as input matrices for a clustering procedure that generated, for each sentence individually, a graphic description in the form of a phrase structure tree (Johnson 1967; Levelt 1970b; Martin 1970).

One could infer from these trees that both the Broca's and the control patients carried out their judgments on the basis of implicit hierarchical organizations. However, the subjective hierarchies of the two groups were clearly different from each other. In making their relatedness judgments, the control subjects took into account all of the surface elements of the sentences, using articles appropriately to mark noun phrases, for example. The aphasic subjects did not. Indeed, the aphasics coupled only the content words together; as a result, their judgments violated the linguistic integrity of the noun phrases and failed to account for copula forms.

A point that must be emphasized is that the aphasic patients did not simply disregard the function words. Rather, each aphasic patient clustered them inconsistently and inappropriately—sometimes paradigmatically, grouping two articles in a sentence together, for example; at other times in a completely unprincipled manner, such as grouping an article with a verb. For the most part, Broca's aphasics seemed incapable of accessing the roles played by the closed class of grammatical morphemes and, particularly, of using these elements to mark the boundaries of sentence constituents.

The consequences of this problem seem clear in at least one sense: an inability to make use of grammatical morphemes as syntactic place holders limits the ability to assign content words to their grammatical function in a sentence (for example, subject noun or object noun). Indeed, it may well be that a minimum requirement of a syntactic processor is to assign form-class designations to open-class elements as a function of sequencing constraints on closed-class elements, and it seems that it is just this operation that Broca's aphasics are unable to perform.

The analysis offered here glosses over a number of considerations. It treats constituents as discrete entities and implies that functors and content words are precisely definable categories easily distinguished from one another. But Ross (1974) has argued that constituents be treated as nondiscrete, that they *not* be treated as, for example, either NPs or not NPs. And Brown (1973) has pointed out that functors can be defined only in terms of an imperfect convergence of a large number of variables, some semantic and some relating to their structure-marking function. The present discussion may, therefore, apply only to those instances in which functors serve as structural signals for "true" phrasal constituents of one type or another. Even so, the relatively differential effect of anterior brain damage upon the open- and closed-class elements charted here still underlines the patients' inability to compute a full structural representation of an utterance.

Articles The fact that anterior brain damage differentially affects contentives and functors has interesting consequences at a semantic level, even for simple sentences. As Brown (1973) puts it, functors most often serve to modulate sentence meaning. In this context, a recent study demonstrates that Broca's aphasics are unable to use articles to assign appropriate reference (Goodenough, Zurif, and Weintraub 1977). The paradigm was such that the inclusion of articles in utterances either hindered or aided the specification of an intended referent. Aphasic subjects were faced with different visual arrays, each consisting of three figures—as an example, a white circle, a black circle, and a black square. In some instances they were given instructions that were entirely appropriate to the situation: "Press *the* white one" or "Press *the* square one." In other instances, the definite article was inappropriate: "Press *the* black one" or "Press *the* round one" when, as in Figure 6.2, two objects were black and two objects were round.

A group of very mildly aphasic patients presenting only occasional word-finding problems (and probably suffering from posterior lesions involving the angular gyrus) showed significantly longer response latencies on those trials in which the referent was inappropriately specified by the article than on those in which the article was appropriate. Moreover, the longer reaction times seemed to reflect a particular strategy whereby these mild aphasics chose the object that shared its non-named feature with the ineligible member of the array. For example, faced with the array in Figure 6.2 and asked to press the black one, they chose the black circle, that is, the black one *of the two circles*. And these results obtained even though the patients could not verbalize either the anomolous use of the article or the strategy they had adopted. The agrammatic Broca's aphasics, in contrast, although always choosing an eligible element, gave no indication of processing the article, whether it was appropriate to the situation or not. Their latencies did not differ between those trials in which the article was appropriate and those in which it was inappropriate. Nor

Sample   Array

Figure 6.2 Sample stimulus array in the study of aphasics' ability to use articles to assign appropriate reference

did they consistently choose the object that shared its non-named feature with the ineligible member.

The findings reviewed to this point converge in support of the notion that when syntactic features are absent or poorly controlled on the level of spontaneous speech, they are unlikely to be preserved at other levels. Broadly conceived, it seems that the judgmental processes underlying linguistic intuitions are not neurologically independent of the operations that produce and interpret utterances in real time. Stated differently, the mechanisms that define tacit linguistic knowledge also appear to directly govern real-time language performance. In this sense, Broca's area has both a competence and a performance commitment.

Agrammatism: Distinctions among levels of disruption   It is the details of the competence–performance commitment that we are still unsure of, however. The data from the comprehension and judgment tests clearly point to Broca's area as critical for the recovery of syntactic facts that bear upon sentence interpretation. Yet, though the disruption is observable at a syntactic level, it remains unclear whether or not the limitation is statable *only* at a level of syntactic description. Consider, specifically, the empirical fact that damage to Broca's area differentially affects the computation of open- and closed-class lexical items. Is it the case that aphasics with such damage are unable to use articles in sentences to assign appropriate reference (Goodenough et al. 1977) because of syntactic variables—because they are unable to integrate the articles with the serial ordering of the content words in a sentence? Or is the limitation best stated at a semantic level? That is, are they unable to recover a full description of sentence form precisely because of an inability to process function words at a lexical, nonsyntactic level? To state the matter more generally, at issue is whether or not Broca's aphasia provides evidence for an autonomous syntactic processor.

An even more vexing problem in this respect is to determine the extent to which phonological variables are causally implicated in the Broca's agrammatism. Indeed, Kean (1976, 1977) has argued that the tendency of Broca's aphasics to omit function words in their speech can be accounted for only in terms of the interaction between an impaired phonological capacity and otherwise intact linguistic capacities. To be sure, Kean's thesis links up nicely with Bresnan's demonstration (in Chapter 1) of a systematic interaction between the phonological and syntactic components of a grammar and with the corresponding prediction that an impairment to the phonological component will interfere with syntactic and semantic processing.

More importantly, it is compatible with and provides an intriguing perspective on the differential consequences of anterior brain damage for the open and closed elements already charted here. In English, the two classes can be distinguished on phonological grounds, only the functors being neutral with respect to stress and having the potential of being phonologically bound. This distinction is captured by Kean's notion of a phonological "word"—a string of segments, marked by boundaries, which function in the assignment of stress to words in English. Specifically, she proposes that a Broca's aphasic tends to reduce the structure of a sentence to the minimal string of elements that can be lexically construed as phonological "words" in his language. Functors and word-boundary affixes are not phonological "words"—that is, they are not stress sensitive—and are therefore improperly processed by the Broca's aphasic.

Although interesting, Kean's notion is not entirely problem free. Given the view that deficits in sentence comprehension are a consequence of the reduction of the phonological structure of a sentence, a correlation might be expected between patients' performance on tests of sentence comprehension and their performance at a phonological level—for example, their ability to distinguish between spoken segments *ba* and *pa* by pointing to a written *ba* or *pa*. Yet in a recently completed study (Blumstein, Cooper, Zurif, and Caramazza 1977), no such correlation was observed. The extent to which patients could identify such speech segments did not predict their comprehension ability, as measured by the Boston Diagnostic Aphasic Examination (Goodglass and Kaplan 1972).

More direct evidence for deciding at what level to state the Broca's limitation arises from what is thus far only a detailed case study of one Broca's aphasic, carried out by Herman Kolk at the Aphasia Research Center in Boston; it does not appear to us that the phonological hypothesis can account for Kolk's findings with this patient. Kolk's study exploits the well-worn *easy/eager* and *expect/persuade* distinctions: *John is easy to please / John is eager to please*; *Bill expected John to go home / Bill persuaded John to go home*. Using a story-completion paradigm whereby a set of sentences leads to a predictable concluding sentence of either the *easy* or the *eager* variety, Kolk trained the patient to produce, for example, only *eager* kinds of sentences (*The bird was able to fly*), and then tested his ability to transfer this training to the production of *easy* sentences (*The lion was hard to kill*). It must be noted that the lexical content was different for each of the training sentences, so the patient was exposed to a particular construction, not simply to a particular sentence.

With this procedure Kolk was able to train this patient to a perfect mastery of *eager* sentences and, in another condition, to a perfect mastery of *persuade* sentences. However, he found very little transfer of this training to *easy* or *expect* sentences, respectively. To us, the most obvious interpretation of these results appears to be a syntactic one. Given that the two sentences of each pair have equivalent surface forms, the problem can be explained at a syntactic level— specifically as an inability to organize a syntactic frame in which to represent the underlying functional or grammatical relations (see, for example, Garrett 1975, 1976). That is, although the patient was trained to process information from a particular underlying functional representation to a particular syntactic frame, he was not then able to map a *different* underlying representation onto that frame.

This last notion is buttressed in somewhat more detail by the kinds of errors Kolk observed during the training procedure itself. Consider, in this respect, some early trials in the training for sentences of the *persuade* type. The patient, instead of producing sentences of the form, *He warned the student to be polite,* often erred by uttering *He warned the student was to be polite* or *He warned the student who was to be polite.* Given that these are errors of adding rather than omitting functors, phonological reduction does not seem to be at work here. Again, what seems to be disrupted is a syntactic process: the patient seems unable to integrate two underlying propositions into an appropriate structural frame.

Having stated these findings, we must remind the reader that Kolk's data base is very small (one patient, so far). Obviously, additional patients need to be assessed with his procedures. To enter the standard cautionary note, more work along the lines established here and along other lines (including cross-language comparisons) is needed before we can unequivocally assign a cause to the inability of Broca's aphasics to recover syntactic facts. Yet even at this stage the study of the effects of brain damage on language promises to be of considerable value in explicating distinctions among the various computational procedures necessary for the comprehension and production of language.

Lexical Semantics

The data to this point show that given a weak link in the processing chain and a corresponding inability to fully compute structural representations of sentences, the agrammatic patients are dependent upon limited routines that rely heavily on an ability to access word meaning. Examining lexical organization in aphasia thus assumes considerable importance; it is this issue that forms the concern of the remainder of this chapter. We hope that the data to be described can provide at least some initial leverage on sorting out the relations between words and the concepts they express.

We will adopt the current convention that words can be factored into conceptual elements and that these concepts permit us to trace relations among lexical items.[1] Given this framework, one obvious question is whether the inability of the brain-damaged to find words indicates that the concepts themselves are also no longer available.

Recurring concepts: Time, space, quantity The evidence bearing on the question of usable concepts turns on some routine clinical facts concerning global aphasics—patients with extensive anterior and posterior damage. Such patients have no usable language and therefore no linguistic outlet for concepts that are bound to be importantly involved in word meaning—concepts of spatial relations, causal relations, temporal relations, quantitative relations, and the like, which provide the internal structure of semantic fields (Miller, Chapter 2) and permit what Jackendoff (Chapter 5) describes as cross-field generalization. Nonetheless, global aphasics do appear to control these concepts at nonlinguistic levels. The patients anticipate therapy sessions and weekends; they don't get lost in the spatial maze of hospital wings; and, more formally, they demonstrate an ability to arrange sets of pictures in proper sequence, whether the pictures reflect changes in spatial relations over time or changes in size over

---

[1] We adopt this convention for the sake of convenience. It is not our intention to support uncritically one or another position regarding the still unsettled and contentious issue of the extent to which semantic decomposition is a necessary part of using and understanding a word (see Chapter 2, Chapter 5, and Fodor 1975).

time (Veroff, in preparation). This evidence, however, tells us only what is likely to be intuitively obvious—namely, that while extensive left-sided brain damage can entirely disrupt vocabulary usage, it need not also undermine the concepts upon which lexical access and other activities are based. Concepts of time, quantity, and space can be spared and can figure in the patient's patterns of action and thought, yet the patient remains unable to apply lexical forms that embody these concepts.

Somewhat less expected is the opposite pattern of disruption, where lexical forms and their meanings seem accessible but only as unfactored cognitive chunks. That is, the ability to use a word does not always seem to include an equal ability to access at least some of the elements entailed in its conceptual decomposition.

We have observed this opposite pattern in patients with right, nondominant hemisphere damage (Caramazza, Gordon, Zurif, and DeLuca 1976; Grossman, personal communication). Such patients, hospitalized for paralysis or sensory loss yet *presenting normal language,* are unable to solve simple two-term series problems involving contrastive lexical items like *shorter* and *taller, richer* and *poorer,* and especially the words *more* and *less.* Given a sentence of the form, *Tom has more than Bob,* and asked, *Who has less, Bob or Tom?* they perform at a chance level of accuracy. Only when antonymic contrasts are excluded (*Tom has more than Bob; who has more, Bob or Tom?*) do they perform normally.

It should be noted, however, that the individual members of these pairs of antonyms are not conspicuously absent from the vocabularies of the patients; nor do they appear to be misused. Thus, interpreting and using in context a sentence containing the word *more* appears to require a less elaborated or different set of operations than does the ability to reason about the relation between the words *more* and *less.* It seems that the patients can understand and produce the words individually without being able to access the elementary concepts of quantity, space, and the like, through which their antonymic relations are likely to be realized.[2] Stated more generally, the processes involved in accessing a lexical item can be at least partially disso-

---

[2] The hypothesized role of imagery in the solution of such problems (Huttenlocher 1968) does not invalidate this notion. After all, the ingredients necessary for the formation of any such image are precisely those that require knowledge of quantitative and spatial relations.

ciated from a full ability to trace the word's conceptual relations to other words.

To this point, then, the evidence does not especially favor the notion that semantic decomposition is importantly involved in the process of using and understanding words in real time. This evidence is based, however, on a limited and special set of concepts—those that are not confined to any one semantic domain (see Chapters 2 and 5).

Semantic domains: Functional and perceptual components of meaning But what of particular semantic domains? Is decomposition as problematic for concepts restricted to a particular domain as it is for concepts that permit cross-field generalization? Aphasia, we think, provides an interesting perspective on this issue.

A fact to bear in mind is that virtually all aphasic patients have word-finding problems, and this unfortunate fact may be used to theoretical advantage. A difference in the ease with which words are available for speech may be meaningfully rooted in a difference in the manner in which the concepts underlying word meaning are represented. Indeed, given the additional fact that word-finding problems take different forms in the different aphasias (Goodglass and Geschwind 1976), the contrasts can even be used to outline some minimal conditions of adequacy for lexical organization.

The pertinent clinical facts are these: Broca's aphasics search much more laboriously for content words than do normal speakers, but the words they find are very often correct. In contrast, patients with posterior damage to the left hemisphere—specifically, those presenting Wernicke's aphasia—do not often find the correct words. The content "words" they choose for their utterances are most often either meaningless—that is, they are neologisms—or off target (Goodglass and Kaplan 1972). We have, then, a source of important comparative data: Broca's and Wernicke's aphasics seem to fall on different sides of a lower boundary in terms of the kinds of concepts necessary for a speaking vocabulary. Broca's have a usable vocabulary; Wernicke's do not.

Consider in this respect a recently completed study that made use of a sorting task (Zurif, Caramazza, Myerson, and Galvin 1974). Broca's, Wernicke's, and a control group of neurologically intact patients were given triads of printed words (concrete nouns) and in each instance the subject had to point to the two words that he felt were most similar in meaning. Following Miller's lead (1969), we assumed that in order for a patient to settle on two words in any one triad, he had to ignore some of their distinguishing features while attending to others. Analyzing the groupings by hierarchical clustering schemes and multidimensional scaling techniques revealed features central to the subjective lexicon.

This study made use of only a small number of words—all either human terms (for example, *husband, wife, cook*) or names of animals (*tiger, shark, dog, turtle*). The intention was simply to observe whether visible contrasts in word-finding abilities would be mirrored by interpretable differences in underlying conceptual organizations.

The results upheld our expectations. The neurologically intact patients operated on organizational principles that depended upon the particular semantic domains, using different principles for the two domains. Within the field of human names, they appeared to classify the words in terms of functional properties of and facts about their referents—specifically, facts about probable social relations not immediately derivable from the definitions of the words themselves. For example, *mother, wife,* and *husband* were tightly grouped, presumably because these terms imply a household relationship, whereas items like *husband* and *knight,* both presupposing the feature [+male], were rarely grouped together. The animal terms, on the other hand, were organized on the basis of species membership—a taxonomic categorization that is further removed from referential data; for example, *tiger* and *dog* formed one cluster; *turtle* and *crocodile,* another.

The Broca's aphasics, in comparison, were more inflexibly restricted to a categorization based on salient properties of the entities signaled by the words. They grouped the human terms using the same functional criteria the normals used, but they continued to operate at this level with the animal terms. Specifically, they generated two major clusters—one consisting of words denoting animals that are remote and usually ferocious, the other of words denoting animals that are quite harmless and even possibly edible. Yet, if the information that the Broca's could apply to their lexicon was restricted to this form of real-world knowledge, it was at least intuitively valid in terms of everyday language use. This point is underlined when their data are compared with those obtained from the Wernicke's aphasics.

Although the Wernicke's had demonstrated (on an independent multiple-choice test) that they could recognize the meanings of the words used, they nonetheless failed to capture convincingly even the basic human–nonhuman distinction. The best they could do was to cluster the human items more compactly than the animal ones, and this seemed to be because they could more easily fit the human items into copula sentences than they could the animal ones, choosing, for example, the words *mother* and *cook* on the basis of "My mother is a good cook."

These findings suggest, then, that limitations on a speaking vocabulary are related to restrictions on the sorts of conceptual relations that can be traced within semantic domains. They point, moreover, to the importance of functional information as providing a means of structuring the lexical relations in which individual words and their meanings are embedded.

The importance of including functional information in the internal lexicon is shown more forcefully in a study recently carried out by Goodglass and Baker (1976). They presented aphasic patients with spoken words while the patients were looking at a picture of a target object. The spoken words bore several relations to the target: there was an "identity" term (the name of the pictured object), a term called a "functional associate" (a verb designating an action associated with the object), and a term called a "functional context" (a noun denoting a situation in which the target might normally be found). For example, if the target was an orange, the functional associate would be *eat* and the functional context would be *breakfast*.

The subject had only to squeeze a rubber bulb if the spoken word reminded him at all of the target or was associated with it in any way. Both the high-comprehension group (Broca's aphasics) and the low-comprehension group (consisting mainly of Wernicke's aphasics) responded to the identity category with a facility equal to that of a neurologically intact control group. The two aphasic groups differed significantly, however, in their responses to the functional associate and functional context words. The Broca's were adept at recognizing connections between the target object and the names of situations and actions normally associated with it; the Wernicke's were not. So, again, corresponding to the criterial fact that Broca's often access content words correctly while Wernicke's seldom do, there is the finding that entries in the Broca's lexicon are better elaborated, at least in terms of practical functional knowledge, than are those in the Wernicke's lexicon.

We do not want to place undue emphasis only on functional information, however. As Miller and Johnson-Laird (1976) point out, there is also an important perceptual part to our definitions of words. Once again, the Broca's appear to have the advantage over the Wernicke's, being able to more easily integrate perceptual and functional information when entering their lexicons.

Relevant here is a study of object naming that was recently carried out at the Aphasia Research Center (Whitehouse, Caramazza, and Zurif, in preparation). Using a modification of Labov's paradigm (1973), we presented patients with line drawings that were variations on a modal cup—variations consisting of different ratios of height to width and the presence or absence of handles. The drawings were presented alone as well as in a number of pictured contexts distinguished by whether coffee, water, or cereal was being poured into the container.

Five Broca's aphasics were tested. Like normal subjects, they integrated contextual with perceptual information in determining whether to apply the name *cup, glass,* or *bowl.* In "fuzzy" or transitional perceptual regions, different functional contexts led to name shifts. Nevertheless, there was a core shape for each type of container that was unaffected by functional contexts, each core being vaguely defined by a particular cluster of perceptual attributes.

In contrast to the Broca's, five posterior aphasics, chosen particularly for their anomic behavior, did not show the normal naming profile. They were able to apply verbal labels to the pictured objects, but they seemed to operate from a very restricted conceptual base. They were unable to integrate function and form in the concept to which the label was to be attached; indeed, they were relatively incapable even of integrating the various perceptual attributes in a given shape. Thus, they could apply the correct label to modal object shapes, but the label usually hinged on one or another perceptual attribute and was not varied, either in the face of conflicting functional information or even in the face of conflicting perceptual information. One patient, for example, used the name *cup* for all object shapes, no matter what the functional context was, as long as a single handle was part of that shape.

We have defined a boundary between Broca's and Wernicke's

aphasics by charting the extent to which they can elaborate lexical entries at least in terms of functional and perceptual knowledge. This boundary does not seem to be as totally fixed as our previous remarks may have suggested, however. Wernicke's aphasics are not completely disbarred from the activity of naming. In fact, like Broca's, they are more likely to name objects that have salience for more than one information channel (Gardner 1973; Gardner and Zurif 1975; Grossman 1976). Put differently, the more sensorimotor modalities by which one can interact with an object (contrast an object such as a rock, which can be touched, smelled, and seen, with an object such as a cloud, which can be only seen), the more easily aphasics, including Wernicke's, can name it.

We think that these data, taken together, make the point that a knowledge of functional and perceptual relations has an important role to play in the lexicon. Indeed, it seems that such knowledge serves as a lower boundary on the information that must be connected to words for the words to be used and understood. More generally, information of this type seems to play an important role in much of what passes for linguistic communication. After all, the clinical impression of the Broca's aphasic is that comprehension appears to be relatively preserved, despite his inability to satisfy some minimum requirements of a syntactic processor.

7 New Models in Linguistics and Language Acquisition

MICHAEL MARATSOS

Chomsky in 1959 wrote "The child who learns a language has in some sense constructed the grammar for himself . . . this grammar is of an extremely complex and abstract character. . . . Furthermore, this task is accomplished in an astonishingly short time." These characteristics—the abstractness and complexity of the acquired language, the adverse nature of the learning circumstances, the rapidity of acquisition—were all adduced by Chomsky to create a novel and compelling description of the child acquiring language: "Human beings are specially designed to acquire language, with data-handling or hypothesis-formulating ability of unknown character and complexity" (1959).

Chomsky was correct in pointing out that much of our picture of the child acquiring language must stem from our notion of what he acquires. Most theories about acquisition have been based on a model of grammar that is essentially the one presented in Chomsky's *Aspects of the Theory of Syntax* (1965; but see also Katz and Postal 1964 and Chomsky 1957). It is a model in which a series of complex and abstract transformational rules relate intricately layered levels of full syntactic representation: deep, intermediate, and surface structures. Surface structures are frequently related to deep structures of quite different syntactic character (as in passives), often in a way never to be induced directly from the evidence of the speech around the child. If such transformational grammars represent the essence of the linguistic system captured by the child, the phenomenon of language acquisition seems to be an inexplicable mystery.

Understanding how children acquire linguistic structures and an appreciation of the interrelations among them is in no danger of becoming simple, but different representations of *what* the child learns have different implications for *how* he learns it. Work presented in the preceding chapters suggests that the syntactic structures the child formulates in learning his language may bear a closer relation to the surface structures he hears around him than older theories of transformational grammar have implied. The purpose of

Research reported by the author in this chapter was supported by NIH grant HD 09112-01 to the author and NICHD grant HD 01136 and NSF grant BNS-75-03816 to the Center for Research in Human Learning. I am grateful for comments on an earlier draft of this chapter by Joan Bresnan, Susan Carey, Philip Dale, Morris Halle, Stanley Kuczaj, Amy Lederberg, Katherine Miller, and George Miller.

this chapter is to argue that empirical evidence on how children acquire a number of constructions is presently available to support this suggestion.

Underlying Logical Relations and Grammatical Structure

The core of the problem for consideration here is how the child establishes correspondences between grammatical structure and logical relations, such as logical subject and logical object, or what have been called underlying grammatical relations. (By "grammatical structure" here and throughout the chapter I mean lexically specified and ordered phrase structure trees.)

A primary insight of transformational grammar is that simple differences or similarities in surface grammatical structure may be deceptive as to the logical relations of the constituent phrases of sentences. Passive sentences such as *John was kissed by Mary* differ considerably in surface grammatical structure from their active counterparts (*Mary kissed John*), a fact that conceals the degree of similarity in the way they are understood. In *John was kissed by Mary,* the initial NP *John* stands in the same relation to the verb *kiss* as the postverbal NP *John* in *Mary kissed John*; in both sentences *John* is the logical object of the verb. Correspondingly, in both sentences *Mary* is the one who kisses, the logical subject of the sentence.

In classical transformational grammars, the underlying grammatical descriptions for the active and passive sentences are (with some differences of detail in various descriptions) nearly identical, as shown in Figure 7.1. The passive transformation then converts the underlying structure into the surface form *John was kissed by Mary* (ignoring details of affix-hopping). In this way the grammar captures the similarity of the logical relations in actives and passives, along

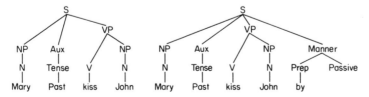

Figure 7.1 Deep structures of Active and Passive: Classical transformational treatment

with other distributional relations, and accounts for the differences in their surface forms.

In the syntactic theory proposed by Bresnan in Chapter 1 and in the ATN model of comprehension outlined in Chapter 3, these same correspondences between logical relations and grammatical structure are specified by a variety of structural descriptions, depending on the construction. The result is that grammatical representations have a greater resemblance to surface structures. A brief sketch of the passive construction gives the idea. (This sketch holds only for passives of verbs that take two NP arguments). In both formulations the underlying representation of active sentences remains much as in Figure 7.1. For passives, however, the underlying representation is more like the surface structure (identical in the case of ATN models). For *John was kissed by Mary* the grammatical structure is essentially that in Figure 7.2. *John,* the logical object, is the grammatical subject, and *Mary,* the logical subject, is the grammatical object of the postverbal preposition *by.*

In Bresnan's new transformational theory, the assignment of *John* as logical object of the verb is made on the basis of an interpretive rule using the information that an NP in the context [____ *be* V+*ed*] is the logical object (*-ed* is the usual marker for the past participle). Similarly, an NP in the context [V+*ed by* ____] may be interpreted as the logical subject. ATN models are left-to-right sentence-comprehending devices, which use similar information in analyzing the structure of passives. (See Kaplan 1975 for detailed discussion of ATN comprehension systems for passive sentences.) At the beginning of the left-to-right processing, the initial NP *John* is first assigned the status of logical subject; upon processing the sequence *be*+past V+*ed* (*was kissed*), the assignment of the initial NP is changed to logical object.

In these newer descriptions the underlying logical relations of

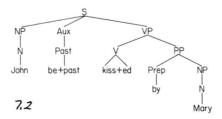

7.2

Figure 7.2 Deep structure of Passive: Nontransformational treatment

passives are related to more surfacelike grammatical representations through a combination of specifications of verb morphology and NP position, rather than by specifying the same underlying syntactic representation for the logical relations in both passive and active sentences. In other constructions, related kinds of devices may be used to establish correspondences between underlying relations and surface representations.

As mentioned, different descriptions of mature linguistic competence have different implications for the kinds of grammatical analysis the child will find natural. Lessening the distance between surface and underlying forms decreases the degree to which the product of the child's grammatical analyses must be represented as highly removed from the structures evidenced in the speech around him. I shall present empirical evidence from the study of language acquisition which strongly suggests that children do *not* postulate, as part of their theory of language, uniform underlying syntactic representations of logical (and semantic) relations. Instead, the evidence suggests that the child's initial and later grammatical analyses more closely approximate the surface structures he hears.

I shall discuss a number of constructions in which the most adequate description of what children initially acquire consists of close-to-surface representations. I shall then argue that it complicates the theoretical description of the acquisition of these constructions to assume that the child quickly thereafter (or even eventually) formulates the kinds of uniform grammatical representation of underlying relations suggested by classical transformational theories and, moreover, that a description of the child as doing so receives little empirical support. I shall also suggest the usefulness of studying possible grammatical errors that fail to occur (as well as those that do occur) as further clues to the child's analysis of language. The resulting picture of linguistic acquisition will imply a child who stays close to the surface in constructing his grammar and who often only slowly comes to appreciate transformational relations among syntactic structures.

Initial Acquisitions

Word order in early acquisition   A generally accepted theory about language acquisition has been that the child adopts strict word order for expressing logical relations—the uniform order that is represented in deep structure in classical models of transformational grammar. What is the evidence?

Children learning English generally acquire strict, appropriate word orders to express even the meanings of early two-word utterances (Braine 1976; Brown 1973). But English is a language in which word order is not free. More impressively, Slobin (1966a) reports data from a child Zhenya learning Russian, a language with freer word order, who seized on a fixed order for subject, verb, and object. These early results implied strongly that an important aspect of the child's notion of language structure is that it consists of uniformly ordered representations of syntactic relations.

But more recent studies have uncovered some contrary evidence. Park (1970) discusses children learning German who used highly free word order to express the major sentential relations. They did not completely ignore word order, however; constituent order within NPs, consistent in the adult language the children heard, was also consistent in their own speech. And Slobin (1975) found that children learning Turkish also adopted free word order for the major sentential relations. Fixed word order for similar underlying relations is apparently not a universal characteristic of early speech; nor do we know the circumstances under which children choose to employ or not employ it. Thus the theory that children, universally, form uniform grammatical representations of identical logical relations as a primary hypothesis about the structure of language does not receive straightforward empirical support.

Embedded prenominal adjectives and possessives   Even among children learning English there appears to be some systematic variation of word order in expressing identical underlying relations. The child's use of embedded prenominal adjectives in noun phrases (as in *Here big dog*) has long proved problematical to those attempting to describe the acquisition of grammar (Brown 1973). In adult grammar, adjectives may appear either as predicate adjectives in simple sentences such as *That dog is big* or in prenominal position: *Push that big dog*. A central insight of linguists was that the same relation holds between *big* and *dog* in the two constructions. Most classical descriptions have captured this generalization by deriving NPs such as *the big dog* by means of transformations that combine the NP *the dog* with a sentence containing the NP as subject and the adjective *big* as predicate (Smith 1961, for example). *Push that big dog* thus derives from the combination of the two sentences, *Push that dog* and (*That*) *dog is big*.

Early child speech does sometimes contain predicate adjectives as well as prenominal adjectives. Both forms are found before children begin to coordinate or combine full sentences syntactically in any other ways, such as by sentence conjunction or relative clause embedding (Brown 1973). An attempt to represent the nominal–adjective relation for both predicate adjectives and prenominal adjectives uniformly as NP *be* Adj hence fails on intuitive grounds. Capturing the two positional possibilities does not have to wait upon the child's achieving the ability to coordinate and embed sentences syntactically.

The natural description of the child's grammar is that adjectives have two privileges of occurrence: (1) in the frame [## NP (*be*) _____ ##] when used as predicates and (2) in the frame [$_{NP}$ _____ N] when used in noun phrases. The corresponding phrase structure rules are also straightforward:

S   → NP (*be*) Adj
NP → Adj N

The similarity of the relation between noun and adjective in these two contexts must hence be captured elsewhere in the description of the child's knowledge than through a uniform grammatical representation.

Both close-to-surface linguistic descriptions and ATN models of comprehension essentially do this through an interpretive component. In ATNs, one transition in the Noun Phrase network is an arc from Adj to N (Adj⌒↘N); in the Sentence network there would be arcs from NP to *be* to Adj (NP⌒↘*be*⌒↘Adj). In lexicalist grammars, too, adjectives can be directly placed prenominally by an independent phrase structure rule (see Jackendoff 1972, for example). In both the linguistic description and the ATN model of language comprehension, the similarity of the adjective–nominal relations in the two structures is captured through interpretive components that read the relation out of the appropriate grammatical representation.

In a model of language *production,* the same adjective–nominal relation would be read directly *into* different grammatical structures, either NP *be* Adj or Adj N, rather than into just one, NP *be* Adj, which is then transformed to derive the prenominal adjective structure, Adj N. These close-to-surface representations appear to be more adequate descriptions of what children acquire initially.

Parallel to the case of the adjective–nominal relation is that of the possessive–nominal relation. Children early express possessives in NPs (*daddy('s) chair*), again before they coordinate or embed full sentences (Brown 1973). In fact, they may express possessives in this fashion before using them in full sentences like *Daddy has a chair* or *That chair belongs to daddy* (Brown 1973; Bloom et al. 1975). Again, classical transformational descriptions derive possessive NPs by combining the NP with an embedded clause (for example, Chomsky 1964b; compare Fillmore 1968). *Get mommy's chair* would come from *Get (the) chair* and *Mommy has (the) chair*. And again the most natural way to describe the child's construction is by a phrase structure rule directly capturing the possessive as it appears embedded in NPs:

$$NP \rightarrow Poss\ N$$
$$Poss \rightarrow N(+s)$$

The child apparently appreciates the similarity of this prenominal possessive relation to the possessive relation expressed in full sentences (NP *has* NP) in much the same way he appreciates the similarity of prenominal adjectives to full predicate-adjective sentences (NP *be* Adj). In both cases the most satisfactory account of the child's language attributes the appreciation of this similarity to the interpretive, rather than the syntactic, component of the grammar.

Subjectless complements   In most transformational descriptions (Rosenbaum 1967, for example) VP complements like *to go* in *I want to go* have been represented as deriving from deep structures with full sentential complements whose subjects are deleted by transformation under various conditions. *I want to go* results from deleting an NP that is identical with the subject of the matrix clause, roughly, *I want (I to go)* ⇒ *I want ∅ to go*. Hence the subject-deletion analysis represents the understood subject of the infinitival complement in the same way that it represents grammatical subjects with full morphological specification. The syntactic justification of this representation depends partly on the presence of complements with specified subjects, such as *I want Harry to go*. The subjectless forms are seen as systematic exceptions to a generalization that in underlying structure infinitival clauses are full sentential complements (Akmajian and Heny 1975).

Children, however, appear to acquire the subjectless forms first (Limber 1973; Bloom et al. 1975); forms with specified subjects appear later. Children thus seem capable of representing matrix verbs like *want* as taking subjectless complements before they have formulated rules for the full sentential complement structures from which the subjectless ones are supposedly derived. The natural description again captures the form in a straightforward way: verbs like *want* may take either VP complements or S complements. Once more, the specification of the nature and effect of the understood subject of the VP clause should be captured elsewhere than through uniform grammatical representation.

In both ATN models and Bresnan's formulation, the method is essentially interpretive, and lexically-dependent. In Bresnan's theory of grammar, *want* and similar verbs take VP complements directly, with the interpretation of the subject NP argument of the verb in the complement being given by semantic interpretive rules. In an ATN model of sentence comprehension, there would be a special path through the network for verbs like *want*; that path would lead directly from the matrix verb to another verb, roughly V⌢↘(*to*)⌢↘V . . . In such a case, the subject of the second (complement) verb can be analyzed as the subject of the initial (matrix) verb. Thus, for *I wanna go* the analysis of *wanna go* leads to an interpretation of the understood subject of *go* as *I,* the subject of *wanna*. (The nature of the interpretation of the subject reference for the complement verb will depend on the individual matrix verb and the grammatical construction, since there is individual variation among verbs in the syntactic and semantic complement structures they may take.)

In a production system, the mirror image of an ATN comprehension system, the subject NP argument of the complement verb is not realized when the reference of that argument is identical with that of the relevant NP of the matrix clause. Thus, for *I wanna go,* the verb *go* is represented as a relation having in underlying intent an initial argument referring to the self. This argument is not morphologically realized because of the identity of reference to the subject *I* of the matrix verb *wanna*. The underlying relation is captured by nonrealization of underlying arguments in sentences, rather than by their realization followed by deletion. Further evidence supporting this account will be considered in discussing possible errors.

Passives   A sketch of the treatment of the full (or long) passive in the close-to-surface descriptions being considered here has already been given. Relevant to the argument is the treatment of short passives, like *John was beaten,* in which there is no *by*-phrase marking the underlying logical subject. In classical accounts, short passives are derived from long passives by the deletion of a *by*-phrase in which the object of *by* is an indefinite *someone* or *something* (Adkajian and Heny 1975) or an unspecified Δ (Chomsky 1965). In close-to-surface accounts, the short passive is a separate grammatical configuration, distinct from the long passive; the *by*-phrase is a grammatical constituent that can optionally be added to the short passive structure.

Now, what about acquisition? Children acquire the passive later than the active. The question is what the developmental data reveal about how they construe the grammatical form of passives, given that they have already acquired active sentences and the NP-VP framework characterizing them.

We may begin by considering what properties any account of the acquisition of passives, either long or short, must contain. First, the child must be assumed to construct some surface structure for individual passive sentences: for example, [NP *be* V+*ed* (*by* NP)] for *The boy was pushed* (*by his friend*). And second, the child must relate this form to context and his knowledge of the lexical items: for the sentence *The boy was pushed,* he must notice that the surface grammatical subject, *the boy,* is the pushee, not the pusher, when the verb *push* appears in the syntactic frame [NP *be* ____+*ed*]; if there is a *by*-phrase, he must notice that the NP after *by* is the pusher.

Both Bresnan's account and ATN models take these analyses as natural starting points for formulating the grammatical form of the passive construction. Neither account requires severe revision of these initial analyses of the roles of the NP arguments for individual verbs. Furthermore, no particular difficulty is raised by the analysis of short passives, which begin as phrase structures distinct from active counterparts and are, in either account, simpler than long passives.

What kind of initial acquisition can be expected if children hold the classical transformational hypothesis that grammatical deep structures of sentences represent logical relations uniformly? In that account, the interpretation of passives depends on relating the passive surface structure to an underlying activelike structure in which logical subject and logical object are represented as they are in active sentences. Given such a theory, two predictions are reasonable. First, the analysis of short passives, in which the logical subject is not represented in surface structure, should cause more difficulties than that of long passives. Second, once the child has analyzed a fair number of passives with some success, he should quickly generalize the relation between actives and passives in a way that would be syntactically autonomous and independent of the semantics of the particular verb and accompanying NPs. In this account, underlying grammatical configurations correspond exactly to logical representations, and logical subject and object fall into no particular correspondence with any particular semantic relations (Chomsky 1957; Fillmore 1968). The salient characteristic of such an analysis should thus be an underlying grammatical representation of the passive that holds for verbs and NP arguments of widely varying semantic natures. This last should be particularly salient, since children old enough to acquire passives (usually three to six years of age) already have lexicons containing both actional verbs like *hit* and nonactional verbs like *know, remember,* and *see.*

What is known about children's acquisition of passives fails to support these predictions in a number of ways. Horgan (in press) reports that children give short passives more often and more accurately than long passives in describing pictures. Harwood (1959) reports some use of short passives in the spontaneous speech of five-year-olds but no use of long passives. Braine (cited in Watt 1970) found short passives used earlier than long ones in spontaneous speech. Comprehension too appears to develop for short passives as early as or earlier than for corresponding long ones (Maratsos and Abramovitch 1975; Baldie 1976). Thus, short passives appear to be acquired at least as early as long passives, if not earlier.

Furthermore, there is some evidence that the passive–active relation fails to become syntactically autonomous for a long period. The semantic nature of the main verb appears to play some part in the comprehension of passives even by children who understand a substantial number of passives. Sinclair, Sinclair, and de Marcellus (1971), working with five- and six-year-old children, found that passives with the main verb *follow* caused special difficulties. Note that in *follow* passives the referent of the surface grammatical subject is not simply acted on passively but is itself also active. The surface subject (as in *Molly was followed by Sam*) acts with some independence of the *by*-phrase agent, who simply trails along after the referent of the surface subject has independently begun to move. Such special difficulties with *follow*—a finding that D. Fox, M. Hartman, and I have recently replicated in studies correcting for the possible greater difficulty of active *follow* sentences—would not be expected from children who had formulated a syntactically autonomous hypothesis about passives.

In another procedure, Fox, Hartman, and I have been gathering evidence from four- and five-year-olds about their understanding of actional passives versus nonactional passives such as *X was liked/hated/known/remembered/missed by Y.* The procedure involves questioning rather than acting out with toys, which is inappropriate for nonactional verbs. Actional passives cause comparatively little difficulty, as do a few nonactional passives, such as those with *seen* and *heard.* But a number of nonactional passives (*liked, known, remembered, missed,* for example) cause considerable difficulty, even when correction is made for the comprehension of the active forms. Many subjects comprehend underlying subject–object relations for these even less successfully than for some nonsense passives constructed with nonexistent verbs like *cattered* and *bemoded.* (Anecdotal evidence indicates that subjects interpret these nonsense verbs as actional.) (For further details on children's comprehension of passives, see Maratsos, Kuczaj, and Fox, in press.)

The picture of initial acquisition (and acquisition for some time afterward) that these data suggest is that children do not initially relate passive grammatical structures to underlying activelike structures in which logical relations are uniformly represented. Apparently they make more surfacelike grammatical analyses of both short and long passives (a proposal found also in Watt 1970). Evidence from experiments with verbs of various semantic characteristics suggests that, at least for some children, the first general formulation is in terms of a correlation between surface structure and thematic semantic structure or case-relation structure (on case relations, see Fillmore 1968)—something to the effect that [NP *be* V+*ed* (*by* NP)] = acted-on patient + action (+ initiator of action, or agent). Children apparently acquire some general knowledge about actional passive forms and knowledge of a few nonactional passives, but they seem to lack for some time a general comprehension of passives in terms of underlying logical and grammatical relations.

After Initial Acquisitions

Theoretical arguments   Thus, for a number of constructions, we find evidence that children do not find grammatically uniform representation an important descriptive goal in their initial analyses. To the contrary, the most plausible descriptions oppose the hypothesis that they do so, and point to close-to-surface grammatical formulations.

Such a conclusion begins to change the accepted picture of the child as a language acquisition device. Nevertheless, it is possible, at least theoretically, that after the period of initial acquisitions children progress with reasonable speed toward a more comprehensive analysis in which uniform underlying grammatical representations of logical relations becomes a means of relating sentential constructions.

But we cannot assume such a change to take place simply because a wider range of related constructions (specified-subject complements, for example) enters the child's competence. In fact, the proposal of reanalysis encounters various theoretical difficulties. For the constructions discussed here, children apparently make initial analyses that are adequate to expression and comprehension—or, in the case of the passive, models are available which do not require extensive change of the stored representations. In all these cases, and others as well, extensive reanalysis for the purpose of attaining uniform grammatical representations would require that the child greatly complicate analyses of forms he had already captured with analyses closer to surface structure.

In the case of prenomial adjectives and possessives, the child would have to substitute for simple phrase structure rules a complex series of transformational rules that combine and embed sentences, change and delete lexical material, and prepose the adjective and possessive modifiers. A typical transformational account of *the big dog,* for example, is roughly as follows:

the dog (dog is big) $\Rightarrow$
the dog (which is big) $\Rightarrow$
the dog (big) $\Rightarrow$
the big dog

For the direct generation of subjectless complements such as *to go* in *I want to go,* the child would have to substitute an analysis in which the complement subject is first specified and then deleted under identity with a matrix-clause NP.

Thus, both transformational and nontransformational accounts of the acquisition of the passive require analysis of the surface structure characteristics of passives. Evidence has been presented that this surface structure analysis, perhaps with accompanying thematic analysis, probably persists for some time. If children reanalyze passives in order to attain uniform underlying grammatical representations, they must revise the description so as to place underlying subject and object in activelike position in deep structure, with the following results: (1) Previous, probably long-held, analyses of the syntactic possibilities of a large number of verbs in their lexicons must be revised. (2) Short passives must receive even more extensive reanalysis; the underlying logical subject, previously unrepresented in grammatical structure, must now be specified in all deep structure representations and then deleted by transformational rule. (3) Other rules in the grammar must be reorganized so as to allow for the operation of the new passive rule. (4) The actual syntactic derivation of each passive sentence becomes considerably more complicated, since the transformational operations required to exchange the NPs, and so on, formerly unnecessary, are now required in order to convert underlying grammatical structures to surface structures.

By contrast, the close-to-surface models discussed here require no such extensive reorganization of earlier acquisitions. It is evident that the child's initial acquisition of the passive probably fails to capture the distributional and logical relations between actives and passives in a fully general manner. But capturing such general relations as those between passive and active phrase structures for individual verbs (see Chapter 1 for full discussion of this point) does not require radical revision of the close-to-surface grammatical analyses of passives, which children seem to begin with. In this description, then, development is more gradual: old analyses of the passive are not so much radically changed as they are generalized and related to other grammatical analyses.

Thus, in the case of a number of constructions reanalysis by the child would require him to complicate and revise extensively analyses that are already partly or fully adequate. Since children appear willing to analyze forms individually rather than uniformly in their initial acquisition and to retain such analyses for periods of months to years (in the case of passives in particular), there appears to be no priori justification for proposing that children have a natural or strong impulse to reorganize grammatical descriptions in order to state generalizations about related sentence structures.

Possible but nonoccurring errors We might nevertheless look to other sources for empirical evidence of reorganization. One kind of evidence might be errors children make as they reanalyze old acquisitions.

Two major kinds of errors could be expected—both already discussed in the literature on language acquisition. One kind might arise when the child analyzes certain cases as exceptions to generalizations, and extends general analyses to less general cases. In learning past-tense verb forms, for example, children initially produce correctly both irregular forms like *broke* and *went* and regular forms like *pushed*. After this initial period, however, they come to a more general analysis of the past tense, resulting in overregularizations such as *broked, breaked,* and *goed* (Cazden 1968). Bowerman (1974) reports overgeneralizations of the causative verb pattern displayed by some verbs that can occur also as noncausatives (*It moved* and *He moved it*; *It opened* and *He opened it*). Two children she studied produced sentences such as *Come that in here* ("cause that to come in here") after a long period of having encoded the relations correctly. Thus, the child may show evidence of a new analysis by a sudden influx of revealing errors.

Another kind of error could be expected if a construction is produced by means of discrete operations: one of the operations might sometimes slip, producing a revealingly incorrect utterance. Slippage of this kind may explain the many instances in which children fail to supply inflections and constituents in their speech. This kind of reasoning has already been used as the basis of arguments for the reality of one transformation, auxiliary verb preposing in direct *wh* questions (Bellugi 1971; Brown et al. 1968). As these authors note, children commonly produce sentences like *Where we should put that?* which may be interpreted as arising from the failure to use the preposing rule in *wh* questions, even though it is used consistently in *yes/no* questions. (For other interpretations, however, see Brown and Hanlon 1970.)

If we reason similarly about the constructions discussed here, what kinds of errors could be expected? Consider two possible ones.

First, a major justification for the subject-deletion analysis of subjectless complements lies in the fact that they constitute an exception to the general pattern that subjects may appear freely in complements except in those cases in which the specified subject would be identical with a certain NP in the matrix clause; hence as children acquire complements with specified subjects, overgeneralization might be expected to lead to errors such as *I want I to go (or I want me to go). Children could also be expected to produce possible and semantically sensible overgeneralized forms with matrix verbs that never take specified-subject complements (try, for example), resulting in utterances like *I'm trying (for) him to go away.

Second, in the case of adjective preposing, a basic argument is that prenominal adjectives are exceptions to more general rules of postnominal generating processes, exemplified in the presence of postnominal participle and prepositional phrase modifiers—Here's the boy (who is) leaving the house and Get the one (that is) in the house—as opposed to the absence of simple adjectival modifiers in postnominal position. The expected errors in child speech would be NPs like the house big in *Find me a house big (from Find me a house that is big).

Errors of these two types are vanishingly rare in children's speech, unlike errors such as goed or mans. In three years of taped observations of one child for an hour a week, S. Kuczaj and I have seen not a single example of the second type and only one of the first. The child produced one sentence with an incorrectly specified subject, I want me to have some. But since even adults occasionally supply the normally deleted subject, in objective-case form, for emphasis (I want me to be the one who gets it), such a frequency can hardly be called impressive. Perhaps more striking, no errors at all were observed in the case of obligatorily subjectless complements of verbs such as try and start (nor have any been reported to me).

Looking for predictable errors might uncover many instances in which possible errors fail to arise. For example, if affix-hopping (Chomsky, 1957) is a psychologically real rule, occasional occurrences of sentences such as He ising go or He being go would be expected to result from failure to apply affix-hopping to the structure He pres be+ing go. Yet according to records and accounts available to me, such errors apparently never occur, in either the progressive or the perfective. Similarly, many possible errors in the use of semiauxiliary verbs in the auxiliary verb system also fail to occur. For example, the auxiliary verb will and the semi-auxiliary gonna share many features of meaning (future) and distribution (in declaratives, both precede uninflected verbs). The possibility of errors is especially reasonable since children frequently leave out forms of *be* with *gonna,* using *gonna* much as auxiliaries are used: *I gonna go now.* When *will* begins to be used sentence-initially in questions like *Will you come?* we might expect errors of overgeneralizing *gonna,* as in **Gonna he come?* These in fact fail to occur, showing that children are conservative about transferring auxiliary verb privileges to other verbs with related distributional and semantic properties.

The one example of an incorrectly specified subject (*I want me to have some*) does raise the problem of frequency of errors, a problem that deserves far more serious treatment than space allows here. But since some possible errors never occur—postnominal adjectives, for example—what can be made of occasional errors like *I want me to have some*? Can the relative expectable frequency of such an error be used to argue for or against different accounts of children's competence?

In fact, both accounts of these VP complement structures—the close-to-surface account as well as the classical account—allow for possible errors. In the model in which VP complements are directly generated without a subject, morphological specification might be expected to occur accidentally on occasion. If both accounts predict possible errors, what differentiates the two? The answer, I believe, is the following: In a deletion-of-subject account, all subjectless complements initially have the subject specified before deletion. But according to the account preferred here, in the normal production process the subject is never morphologically specified. Thus while the error of mentioning the subject might be expected in both accounts, intuitively one would expect it to be more frequent if the subject is specified and then deleted. The extremely low frequency of these errors (even assuming they are indeed errors rather than uses like those occasionally found in adult language) argues for the initial generation of subjectless VP complements.

In general, then, one possible and likely source for evidence of reorganization of these grammatical systems fails to support such reorganization. Of course, other kinds of evidence may be found (see next section), such as simultaneous emergence of similar changes in a number of possibly relatable constructions. But at present I know of no evidence of this kind.

Language acquisition studies in general have concentrated naturally, but perhaps too exclusively, on what does occur in children's speech, ignoring what might occur. Looking at possible but nonoccurring errors strikes me as a useful method for adding to the evidence available to help us formulate the appropriate description of the child's grammatical representations.

Other kinds of later evidence   For a number of the constructions that have been discussed, even evidence from adults fails to show reanalysis of initial acquisitions. A particularly striking case is the relation between short and long passives. A number of observers (Bever 1970; Fodor and Garrett 1966; Watt 1970) have noted that adults find short passives no more difficult to process than corresponding long passives. Similarly, Fodor and Garrett (1966) report experiments in which the addition of prenominal adjectives resulted in no additional difficulty in sentence comprehension. And certainly noun phrase forms with full relative clause representation for adjectives, such as *the vase that is big,* though closer to the representation in classical transformational theories, are intuitively more difficult to process or produce than prenominal forms (*the big vase*). Thus in these cases evidence from adult language use fails to provide support for uniform grammatical representation of underlying relations.

Conclusions

I have presented an interrelated set of arguments: (1) For a number of forms, children apparently do not need to make initial analyses in terms of uniform deep structure representations. In these cases— prenominal adjectives and possessives, subjectless complements, and passives—the empirical data can be handled only clumsily and unconvincingly by such descriptions. Instead, the data are better served if children's formulations are described with the kinds of representations outlined by Bresnan and used in ATN models. (2) In many cases reanalysis of the early forms to achieve uniform underlying representations would unnecessarily complicate what are adequate and grammatically simpler analyses. (3) To date, no serious evidence has been adduced to indicate that reanalyses take place when more complete repertoires of related forms enter the child's competence. In particular, some expectable errors never occur and others are exceedingly rare. Nor does evidence from adult language indicate reanalysis of early grammatical structures.

It is important to note that I have developed these arguments for a limited set of cases. No claim has been made that transformations do not ever figure in the formulation of any grammatical constructions. For example, Question Movement, discussed by Bresnan in Chapter 1, constitutes a good candidate for a system in which some kinds of transformational operations play a part in sentence production. (It seems to me that, for production, the natural mirror image of an ATN comprehension system for such constructions is essentially transformational in nature, or at least very close; see pp. 53–57).

The facts and arguments presented here establish a general point, I think: We can gain much for the natural account of many acquisitions by discarding the assumption that the child necessarily formulates grammars in which the same logical relations receive identical underlying grammatical representations in all related sentential constructions. Rather, the child can devise close-to-surface accounts in which identical logical relations can be captured systematically by a number of different semantic and grammatical devices. This kind of account is pointed to by the essential features of both ATN descriptions and the kinds of linguistic descriptions Bresnan discusses. I believe future discoveries about acquisition will continue to show the profit to be gained from such an approach to the problem of explaining how children formulate the grammatical structure of their language.

If this prediction proves correct, much of the mystery of syntactic development will be dispelled. It should be noted, however, that in lightening the burdens of those who hope to explain syntactic development, we complicate the work of those who hope to explain lexical development. Similarities that were previously supposed to be appreciated on the basis of similar deep structures are now said to be appreciated on the basis of similar semantic interpretations. Characterizing lexical information in such a way as to support the appropriate interpretations will complicate the theory of the lexical component and, inevitably, raise new problems for those who hope to understand how such lexical information is acquired.

8 The Child as Word Learner

SUSAN CAREY

What is learned when a word is added to a child's vocabulary? Minimally, the child learns that it is a word: he enters it into his mental lexicon. Also he must learn its syntactic properties—its part of speech and its syntactic subcategorizations. He must learn its place in lexical structure—its relations to other words. He must learn its semantic properties, its roles in determining entailments, and its referential properties. Finally, the conceptual underpinnings that determine its place in the child's entire conceptual system must also be learned. Some inkling of the complexity of the semantic and conceptual representations that are mapped onto words is provided in Chapters 2 and 5, and the expanded role of lexical entries in syntax is the focus of Chapter 1. In Chapter 7 it is argued that these recent developments make the acquisition of syntax less of a mystery. But just those developments make more prodigious the child's feats as a word learner.

By age six the average child has learned over 14,000 words.[1] On the assumption that vocabulary growth does not begin in earnest until the age of eighteen months or so, this works out to an average of about nine new words a day, or almost one per waking hour. So we have a puzzle. Learning even a single new word involves representing a great deal of information, yet the child learns an average of nine words a day. As we shall see, part of the resolution of this puzzle is that the learning of every word involves long-term developmental processes. In this chapter, I will focus on those processes, including the nature and significance of the incomplete representations a child develops along the way.

The Process of Learning a Single New Word

Where does the process of word learning begin? In the earliest phases of vocabulary learning there is often much concentrated teaching and

Research reported in this chapter was partially supported by a grant from the Public Health Service (GM 21796) to The Rockefeller University and a grant from NIH (2-R01-HD5168) to Massachusetts Institute of Technology. I would like to thank Katherine Miller, George Miller, and Ned Block for comments on an earlier version of this manuscript.
[1] The estimate of 14,000 words includes inflected and derived words and is based on comprehension vocabulary. For root words only, the estimate falls to around 8,000, or roughly five new root words a day (Templin 1957; see also Miller 1977).

drill on routines like "bye-bye" and on naming objects (see Nineo and Bruner 1977 for some illustrative examples.) By the time the child is over two years old, however, such drill is not typical. The child must learn most of the 14,000 words from hearing other people use them in normal contexts. If so, only two sources of data are available to him: the linguistic context in which the word occurs and the situation in which it is used. Of course, it is the child's representation of each that affects what he will learn. The child's already existing linguistic and conceptual systems determine those representations; the word-learning process must start there. The only way to begin to account for the child's wizardry as a word learner, given the sheer weight of how much there is to be learned, is to grant that the child *brings* a great deal to the "original word game" (to use Roger Brown's phrase).

Suppose, for example, that somebody were to show you a picture of an unfamiliar action being performed upon an unfamiliar substance in an unfamiliar container, and you were told the picture depicted how *to sib*. Your knowledge that *to sib* is a verb form and that verbs can refer to actions would lead you to the hypothesis that *sib* is a verb naming the strange action. Told that the picture depicted *a sib* or *some sib,* you would arrive at different hypotheses about the meaning of *sib*. Brown (1957) presented four-year-olds with just such an experience and found that they formed the same kinds of hypotheses. Thus, four-year-olds must have conceptual distinctions between actions, things, and stuff, in terms of which they can represent the picture. They must also have the syntactic distinctions between verb, count noun, and mass noun, and must know some surface syntactic indicators for each. This example illustrates only some of the knowledge brought to bear on learning the new word *sib* from just a few exposures. That four-year-olds have already developed that knowledge is perhaps not surprising. But when did they acquire it?

Following up on Brown's demonstration, Katz, Baker, and McNamara (1974) demonstrated that much younger children rely on such knowledge in learning a new word. At the age of seventeen months, girls (but not boys) already have a distinction between common and proper nouns and they already know and can exploit in word learning a syntactic indication of whether a given noun is common or proper. The syntactic cue is the presence or absence of an article. For instance, if I say to you, pointing to a dog, "Look, there's Corgi," you rightly assume that *Corgi* is the dog's name. If I say, "Look, there's a corgi," you assume that *corgi* is the name of a breed of dog, or kind of animal. Katz, Baker, and McNamara showed also that their young subjects could exploit a conceptual distinction between things likely to have individual names and things not likely to. Dolls belong in the former category; boxes, in the latter.

Their demonstration was elegant and simple. They introduced children to a new doll. To those in one group they said, "See what I've brought you. This is Dax." For this group, *Dax* was syntactically marked as a proper noun. Children in a second group heard, "See what I've brought you. This is a dax." Another, similar doll was also present; in subsequent play, the child was asked to "show Dax (or "a dax," depending upon which group she was in) to Mommy," or "pick up Dax," or "feed Dax," and so on. The result was that if the child was in the common-noun group, she used both dolls interchangeably — the one the experimenter had called *a dax* and the other similar one present. If she was in the proper-name group, she picked only the doll that had been called *Dax*. This observation establishes that girls as young as seventeen months knew two lexical categories for nouns and could exploit a relevant syntactic cue in placing a newly learned noun in the correct category. Another two groups of baby girls were needed to demonstrate the role played by knowledge of what kinds of things are likely to be given proper names. The experiment was repeated, with fancily decorated boxes instead of dolls. In this case there was no difference between the two groups of children. Whether the box had been introduced as *a dax* or *Dax,* the child treated the word as a common noun and picked both boxes equally often when asked to "show Mommy Dax" or "show Mommy a dax." They did not expect an individual box to be given its own name.

These little girls learned the new word, mapped it onto a referent, understood novel sentences containing it, and learned its syntactic category (in the doll case) from just a few exposures to the word. This is word-learning wizardry. Recognition of the knowledge brought to the word-learning task gives a momentary illusion of reducing the mystery of the efficiency of the process. But this is only an illusion, for now we must account for how such knowledge had been acquired by the age of seventeen months. I will not speculate about that mystery.

How general is the finding that young children pick up new words with such ease? There have been relatively few studies. Braine (1971) reversed some aspects of the above two demonstration experiments.

He introduced two nonsense syllables (*niss*, a kitchen utensil the child was allowed to play with, and *seb*, finger walking that typically ended in tickling) without any sentential context. The words were clearly spoken, in isolation, while Braine was sebbing, or indicating a niss, and were "rapidly taken up into the speech" of his barely two-year-old daughter. She always used *niss* in contexts where other nouns appeared; she used *seb* both in contexts where verbs appeared (*Seb Teddy*, for example) and in contexts where nouns appeared (*More seb*).

The contexts of the Brown (1957) study and the Katz et al. (1974) study were different from the use to which I am putting them here. Both concerned the issue of semantic correlates to syntactic subcategorizations — the question whether such correlates could provide the basis of the child's abstraction of part of speech. Braine's (1971) study spoke to this issue; he presents arguments against the semantic basis, in development, of syntactic subcategorizations. In my use of these data, I am arguing that the child's knowledge of syntactic cues to part of speech as well as his knowledge of whatever semantic regularities there may be both play a role in his efficiency at learning new words.

In many studies using the technique of teaching nonsense words, the child appears far from a word-learning wizard. (See, for example, Werner and Kaplan 1950; Klatzky, Clark, and Macken 1973; Nelson 1973.) In all these studies, however, the child faced various unusual departures from normal word-learning contexts. In Werner's study, no natural nonlinguistic context was given. The child was to learn the meaning of a new word from a series of linguistic contexts alone, such as "A wamplum is long and skinny" and "A wamplum is used to poke things." This may be an interesting problem-solving paradigm, but it hardly mimics the natural word-learning situation. In the studies by Nelson and by Klatzky, Clark, and Macken, several new words were taught at once. In Nelson's case 16 new nouns (*snorkel, compass, handcuff,* for example) were taught to two-year-olds. All the words were taught in the same sessions, increasing the difficulty of keeping the words straight—of remembering what was a compass and what a snorkel. The Klatzky, Clark, and Macken study introduced an additional difficulty: the words taught were not possible lexical items in English. The child was shown four sticks, varying in length, the experimenter pointing to one of them (x in Figure 8.1). Two words (*zup* and *grod*) were taught as follows: The experimenter

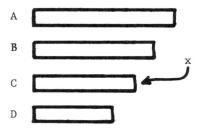

Figure 8.1 Stimuli from Klatzky, Clark, and Macken study

said "Show me one that is zup," giving the child feedback that the correct answer was D, and "Show me one that is grod," giving the child feedback that the correct answer was A or B. *Zup,* then, meant "longer than this one," and *grod,* "shorter than this one." But in English there is no single lexical item that packages comparative information in that way—such a word violates English constraints on possible lexical items. If the child has knowledge of those constraints, it is not surprising that these words were difficult to learn.[2]

None of the studies reviewed above, neither those in which the child picked up a new word effortlessly, nor those in which he had great difficulty, was designed to study the word-learning process, extended over time. Nor did any of the researchers probe for partial meanings (it may be that the children had learned something of the meanings of *wamplum, zup,* or *snorkel*—had at least entered these forms into their lexicons—after single exposures). None of the studies tried to find the limits of the child's proficiency: the words were explicitly taught; the child was not required to pick them up from their use in normal contexts. Moreover, none of the words filled a gap in a well-structured lexical domain, so they could not be studied relative to the child's knowledge of that domain. Finally, none of the studies tested the permanence of the acquisition of *sib, dax, niss* or *seb.*

Anecdotal evidence suggests that the child's proficiency at acquiring a new word could be put to a much stronger test. In an experiment designed to explore the claim that there is a point in development when the word *less* is incompletely represented as a synonym of *more* or *some* (Carey 1977), children were asked to

[2] The study by Klatsky et al. (1973) was not intended to model normal word-learning. I am merely speculating why children found learning these new words so difficult. The points I raise are irrelevant to the goals of the original study.

"Make it so there is tiv to drink in this glass." *Tiv* was not emphasized, and more than half of the children simply added water to the glass or poured some out. Very few asked what *tiv* meant. The instruction was repeated three times, once using the word *more* instead of *tiv*, once using *less*, and once again using *tiv*. Thus, the children heard *tiv* only twice. Two to six weeks later, fourteen of the three- to four-year-olds who had been in this study were in another study requiring that they generate opposites to whatever a puppet said; for example, if the puppet said *up*, the child said *down*. The research assistant collecting these Opposites data tacked on *tiv* to the end of the list. Most children treated it as a nonsense syllable, either giving no response or producing a rhyme. But three of the fourteen responded *more* (or *less*) and of these only one had asked what *tiv* meant (and had been told *less*). For one of these children, six weeks had intervened between the *tiv* study and the Opposites task. We are close here to the limits of the child's proficiency—eleven children did not remember *tiv*. But the three who did clearly illustrate the way in which preschool children are magnets for new words.

Building on this observation, Elsa Bartlett and I decided to study the process of word learning when the word was part of a structured lexical domain.

Mapping between lexical and conceptual domains   Corresponding to the distinction between word and concept is the distinction between lexical domain and conceptual domain. The lexical domain is simply the structured set of words that "covers" the conceptual domain. The conceptual domain is the relevant part of the internal representational system in terms of which the person or animal describes and understands the world and his own actions in it (see Fodor 1975 for an extended discussion of the internal representation system). Take, for example, the lexical domain of color words and the conceptual domain of mental representation of colors.

The structure of the conceptual domain can largely be captured by the three dimensions of the color solid: hue, saturation, and brightness. But other facts also are represented in the conceptual domain of color, facts such as the characteristic colors of particular objects; sometimes such facts may play a role in the recognition of those objects. Psychologists can learn about the conceptual domain without recourse to language; for example, perceptual matching and discrimination abilities and the phenomena of color contrast, color mixture, and color blindness suffice to reveal the properties of the color solid.

Some sample facts about the lexical domain are that the words *red, green, blue, scarlet,* and *chartreuse* are hyponyms of the word *color* and furthermore that *scarlet* is a hyponym of *red* and *chartreuse* is a hyponym of *green.* Ten or eleven primary hue words can be combined productively to form terms like *yellowish green* or *yellow green,* for example. Properties of the color solid other than hue are handled lexically by adjectives such as *dark, light,* and *vivid.*

This characterization does not begin to do justice to either the lexical domain or the conceptual domain. (See Miller and Johnson-Laird 1976 for complete analyses.) Nevertheless, this sketchy characterization will suffice for a few crucial observations. First, there are many things we know about colors that are not captured in the structure of the color lexicon. Closely related to this point, the lexical domain is highly structured as to possible words. There could never be, in any language with a color lexicon, a word whose meaning was the concept "the color of the flowers of lilac bushes," the reason being that the colors picked out by that concept (white, lilac, blue, and purple) are not adjacent on the color solid, and hue words can name only continuous regions of the rainbow. On the other hand, a color word meaning, roughly, "green or blue," would be allowed by the rules of lexical formation of color words; indeed, some languages have such a term. Finally, it should be emphasized that each domain (the conceptual and the lexical) has its own identity and structure. For the child learning language, there can be development within each domain separately before any mapping of one onto the other is begun.

Clever psychophysicists have shown that the color solid captures the structure of the conceptual/perceptual domain of color for preverbal infants and some animals. Conversely, a blind person can learn much of the structure of the lexical domain of color words, without ever mapping them onto perceived colors. Indeed, many children have entered several color words in their lexicon and learned some of the structure of this lexical domain before they have begun the mapping between the lexicon and the conceptual/perceptual domain. Bartlett (1977) found that some young children could list hue names in response to the question "Do you know any colors?" They would also respond with a color name to the question "What color is this?" — albeit the name was randomly chosen. Thus, they knew that the word *color* is a supernym of at least some hue names. That the mapping between color words and perceived colors had not yet begun was shown by a child's failure to consistently pick a color chip that matched the name of any of the colors being probed and his failure to consistently produce the correct color name for any of the color chips.

For our initial pilot study on the process of lexical acquisition, Bartlett and I decided to use the domain of color words. Our goal was to explore the limits of the preschool child's capacity as a word learner. There would be no explicit teaching; the new word would be introduced in an entirely neutral context. Initially, each child would have only one exposure to it and at least a week would intervene before any probing to determine whether it had been taken up into any of the children's lexicons. The color lexicon was chosen mainly because the subjects were currently being studied by Bartlett in her work on ordinary color words, allowing us to see how learning a new color word would restructure the child's existing lexical and conceptual color domains. The subjects were fourteen three- to four-year-olds, all of whom had begun the mapping from color words onto colors. One knew only one word–color correspondence (green); the rest reliably comprehended and produced from six to eleven color words.

First we had to choose the color to be named. Since a case can be made that the color olive is a hue on the same level in the color hierarchy as blue, red, yellow, brown, and white (one can say *greenish olive* or *brownish olive* but not *reddish scarlet* or *orangish scarlet*), and since the name of the color was unknown to all fourteen of our subjects, olive was chosen as the color. Since some of the children might know what olives are, an unknown word (an actual color name), *chromium,* was chosen as the name for olive.

By far the most important choice in this pilot was the introducing event. The subjects attended a nursery school run in George Miller's laboratory at The Rockefeller University, and the teacher in the school agreed to do the introducing. One tray and one cup in the classroom were painted olive. There was one identically shaped cup (red) and one identically shaped tray (blue). In a natural context such as setting up for a snack, each child, individually, was told, "Bring me the chromium tray, not the blue one, the chromium one" or "Bring me the chromium cup, not the red one, the chromium one." Since we wanted a strong test of the child's efficiency as a word learner, we wanted to avoid explicitly calling the child's attention to the new word. To carry out the task (bringing the correct cup or tray) the child need not focus on the word *chromium* at all, for "not the red (or blue) one" was sufficient to determine the response. To further ensure a strong test of the child, subsequent production and comprehension tests were administered in a different room by a different person from the teacher who had introduced the new word. Although great care was taken to minimize the child's sense that he was being taught a new word, the introducing event provided syntactic and lexical cues that *chromium* was a color word as well as contextual cues to which color it named. That is, the information was adequate to the full mapping.

Prior to the introducing event, each child was given a production test, which included an olive color chip. Most called it *green,* a few *brown.* These responses served as a base line against which to assess a later production test.

All of the nursery school sessions were being video-taped, allowing full analysis of each child's introduction to the word *chromium* and the monitoring of any spontaneous use of the new word in the classroom as the pilot study progressed. What happened?

At first exposure, only one child had trouble picking the correct tray or cup. Four spontaneously repeated some approximation to *chromium,* and most asked for some confirmation: "You mean this one?" These children clearly flagged "new word!" upon hearing a phonological sequence with no current lexical entry. And they did so even though they did not need to focus on that word to carry out their instruction.

One week after the introducing event the children were given a comprehension test; each child was shown six colors, including olive, and asked, "Which is the blue one?" "Which is the chromium one?" and so on. Nine of the children picked either olive or green for *chromium.* However, as olive was the only odd color among the six, children might pick it when asked to indicate the chromium one even without the teaching event. Indeed, a control group did just that, at about the same level of accuracy as our experimental group. Thus this "comprehension test" should be seen as a second teaching task; the children had had two relevant experiences with *chromium* before they were tested on production.

Six weeks after the teaching (five weeks after the comprehension test) the children were given a production test. What happened on that test surprised us. Eight of the fourteen children changed their response from their base-line response. Two said they did not know what to call olive, indicating that they had learned that olive had a different name from *green* but could not remember what. The rest used another color name for it—*gray, blue,* or *brown*—and in each case the child chose a word he had not yet stably mapped onto a color. The child had learned and retained for over a month that olive is not called *green*; in searching his lexicon for a name to call it, he found another color word with no stable referent which was more highly accessible than the new word *chromium*. Thus, for these eight children at least, the process of restructuring the conceptual and lexical domains had already begun.

The pilot was continued, with a few further teaching experiences and comprehension and production tests. Two different routes to full acquisition were identified. Some children adopted a false hypothesis about the structure of the lexicon—that *chromium* was a synonym of *green*. In comprehension tests they often picked green when asked to choose the chromium chip. In production tests they usually called both olive and green *green,* but sometimes called focal green *chromium*; one child called focal green light *chromium*. For these children, working out the correct lexical relation between *chromium* and *green* was an extended process, not completed in some cases after 18 weeks of testing. Let us call this group the "false synonym" group. The other group, in contrast, knew from the beginning that olive needed its own name. In comprehension tests they always picked olive for the word *chromium*. In production tests they said they could not remember the name or chose some color name with no stable referent. Some of the children who adopted this "odd color, odd name" strategy also did not achieve full mastery by the end of testing.

When two children on different paths to full acquisition (one who had adopted the false-synonym (FS) strategy, and the other the odd-color-odd-name (OCON) strategy) tried to communicate in a natural exchange in the classroom, predictable confusion resulted. About halfway through the study the children were making Easter baskets. Material included pieces of yarn and paper that were colored fuchsia, light green, and dark forest green (*not* olive). The FS child, Albert, said, "I want chromium, ah, a green, a green, I mean chromium and that red." The teacher asked the OCON child, Ellen, which one she wanted; Ellen indicated the forest green and said "The dark one." Albert (FS): "No, that's chromium." A third child picked up fuchsia and asked "Chromium?" Albert (FS) took the fuchsia from him, gave him a forest green and said, "No, chromium is a green one." Ellen (OCON), looking puzzled through all this, picked up a forest green piece of paper, and asked the teacher, "Is THIS the chromium tray?" Teacher: "What do you mean?" Ellen (OCON): "It doesn't look the same." Teacher: "The same as what?" Ellen, confused, did not respond.

The answer to the teacher's question is, of course, olive green, the color of the tray and cup. Ellen, an odd-color–odd-name child, had focused on the color olive and always picked olive in comprehension tasks probing *chromium*. What she had learned was that olive was not called *green* and that *chromium* did not name green, so Albert's (FS) calling forest green both *green* and *chromium* was simply not acceptable.

This tentative pilot study, currently being replicated and extended, shows that one can study the process of lexical acquisition. Several lessons emerge. First, lexical acquisition is indeed a very efficient and rapid process. (Only one child appeared never to have learned anything about the word *chromium* or the color olive.) One experience with the word, or at most a very few, sufficed for the remaining children to adopt one of the two partial mappings between the color lexicon and the conceptual domain. We have dubbed this initial, speedy process "fast mapping." Second, after this initial fast mapping, protracted further experience was required before learning was complete, and many children had not progressed beyond the initial mapping by the end of testing. Finally, I would like to stress that there were two parts to the process: (1) the restructuring of the lexicon by finding the right place for the word *chromium,* and (2) the restructuring of the conceptual domain by learning that olive was not included in the category of green or brown, but was a color that had its own name. Full coordination of both of these developments had been achieved by only half of our subjects after several months of weekly experiences with the word.

Given the speed and efficiency of the fast mapping, the slowness of the process of attaining the full mapping is perhaps surprising. After all, the color lexicon is relatively simple, and information adequate to the full mapping was repeatedly presented. Suppose that, on the average, six months is required for the full acquisition of a new word (surely an underestimate, as we will see). If the child is learning nine new words a day, then he is working out the meanings of over 1,600 words at a time. This fact is a clue to the real significance of the fast mapping. What is included in that initial mapping—that the new word is a word, along with some of its syntactic and semantic properties— must allow the child to hold onto that fragile new entry in his lexicon and keep it separate from hundreds of other fragile new entries, and it must guide his further hypotheses about the word's meaning. In the next section we will turn our attention to the nature of the early representations and to the process of moving from such beginnings to full meanings.

Immature Lexical Entries: Missing Features

On one widely held view of lexical development, the missing-feature theory, the lexical entries of children differ from those of adults in being incomplete. Only some of the semantic features that character- ize the full meaning are initially represented by the child. According to the missing-feature theory, the process of lexical development consists of adding features until the full entry is achieved. Many recent controversies about semantic development have presupposed this theory—the controversy whether the addition of features pro- ceeds from general to specific or vice versa, for example (Clark 1973; Anglin 1970). Furthermore, the missing-feature theory has provided a framework within which to pose many specific questions about the incomplete entries within particular lexical domains.

In this section two competing hypotheses about what features are initially missed during the acquisition of spatial adjectives will be reviewed. Following this review, the missing-feature theory itself will be put to a test and will be found wanting. In the next section a revision of the missing-feature theory will be developed.

Spatial adjectives   The spatial adjectives include: *big, little; long, short; tall, short; wide, narrow; thick, thin; deep, shallow;* and *high, low.* Two aspects of the linguistic structure of this lexical domain are relevant to our discussion. The first is the core comparative structure, which the words in this domain share with all other relative adjectives (*fast/slow* and *heavy/light,* for example). The second is the feature system in terms of which spatial adjectives differ from each other.

The core comparative structure underlies both contrastive uses (*He is a tall man* or *He is a short man*) and comparative uses (*She is taller/shorter than Harry*) of relative adjectives. Both uses require a dimension of comparison (height in these examples), a standard of comparison (average height of men and the height of Harry, respectively), and a direction from that standard (greater than or less than). The particular adjective specifies both the dimension of comparison and the direction from the reference point. In comparative uses, the reference point is explicitly given; in contrastive uses it is inferred, and is usually some average value. Relative adjectives come in pairs, which differ in their polarity—that is, in their direction from the reference standard. In the pairs listed, the positive-pole words (values greater than the reference point along the dimension of comparison) are given first.

The domain of spatial adjectives that is of interest here is defined by the feature [spatial extent]. I mean this feature to capture the fact that size, height (both altitude and tallness), length, width, thickness, and depth can all be measured in inches (linear inches, square inches, or cubic inches). *Fat* and *skinny,* while relative adjectives, are not part of this domain, because the dimension of comparison underlying these two words is not one of spatial extent. An answer to the question "How fat is John?" cannot be "Two feet" nor even "Two hundred pounds." Rather, it must be something like "Very." For *fat* and *skinny* the relevant dimension of comparison is a ratio among spatial extents—relative width or thickness, given some height. For the purposes of this chapter I will call such a dimension "relative shape," which is in contrast to simple spatial extent.

Several linguists have proposed feature systems to capture the differences among spatial adjectives (for example, Bierwisch 1967; see also Miller and Johnson-Laird 1976). Of the words in this domain, *big* and *little* are in some sense superordinate to the rest; each of the other pairs picks out a particular way of being big or little. The dimension of comparison underlying *big* and *little* is spatial extent alone; all other spatial relatives require further features for their specification, such as [vertical]. Bierwisch's system is complex, and it is not obvious that the dimensions of comparison can be totally captured by such a feature system. For example, take the pair *thick* and *thin*. The dimension, thickness, is characterized as the third, or tertiary, dimension whenever length (or height) and width are also specifiable. Doors have height and width, pavement and ribbons have length and width; thickness of each is the third dimension. This analysis applies straightforwardly to many common uses of *thick* and *thin,* but for other uses it applies only abstractly. Consider the nonmetaphorical senses of *thick skin, thick skull, thick crust*. It is not obvious that thickness is the tertiary dimension of skin, for example, until one imagines the skin (of an orange or an animal) laid out flat as a two-dimensional peel or hide. Then, indeed, thickness of skin is analogous to thickness of doors or ribbons. In other common and systematic uses the characterization of thickness as the tertiary dimension does not apply at all—*thick rope, thick cigarette, thick tree trunk*. There may also be nonsystematic uses, perhaps as in *thick lips*. At any rate, the feature system underlying the adjectives of spatial extent is complex; the child does not face an easy task in mastering it.

Both aspects of the lexical structure of the domain of spatial adjectives—the comparative core and the feature system that specifies the differences among the dimensions of spatial extent—reflect the conceptual system. Underlying the comparative core are the abstract concepts of reference point and polarity, which presuppose concepts of dimension of comparison and zero point. These concepts can be probed nonlinguistically. For example, animals can be taught to choose the smaller, or larger, of two stimuli. It is likely that the standard sizes of objects are represented conceptually for the purpose of object recognition. Presented with a box the size of my desk, I am not likely to entertain the hypothesis that it is a box of Kleenex. Underlying the feature system characterizing the dimensions are many aspects of man's representation of space; concepts like vertical and horizontal, cross-section, and spatial extent itself are reflected in many nonlinguistic sensorimotor routines (see Miller and Johnson-Laird 1976; H. H. Clark 1973).

As the child learns a new spatial adjective, what aspects of its conceptual underpinnings are mapped onto it early and what aspects, if any, take years to work out? Two positions within the framework of the missing-feature theory have been held.

The first position is that the child's initial mapping is between the word and the features specifying the relevant dimension of comparison. The missing feature is polarity, the direction from zero. On this view, both *narrow* and *wide* would have the incomplete lexical entry: [Adj] [comparative] [spatial extent] [−primary] [−vertical], making the two words synonyms (Donaldson and Wales 1970; H. H. Clark 1970; E. V. Clark 1973; Klatzky et al. 1973). The two words need not have identical incomplete lexical entries simultaneously. For example, [+pole] might be added to the representation of *wide* before [−pole] is to *narrow*. In this case *narrow* means what *wide* did before

[+pole] was added to the entry of the latter: *narrow* is a synonym of an earlier representation of *wide*. Suppose the child had such incomplete lexical entries for *narrow* or *wide*. How would he decide which of two boards was wider (or narrower)? Lacking information about polarity, he might pick the board that best exemplifies width in both cases—namely, the wider board (H. H. Clark 1970).

The second position is that the child first maps the word onto the comparative core (including polarity), but the correct dimensional underpinning takes years to work out. Early on, each spatial adjective will be marked only [Adj] [comparative] [±pole] [spatial extent]; gradually the other features—such as [vertical] and [primary]—will be added. On this view, *tall, wide, high,* and so on, are at first all synonyms of *big*; later, *tall* and *high* might be synonymous, [vertical] having been added to each entry. Similarly, at first *short, narrow, low,* and so on, are all synonyms of *little*; later, *thin* and *narrow* might be synonyms (Wales and Campbell 1970; E. V. Clark 1972). All that is required is that each word be synonymous with *big* or *little* at some point during its acquisition. For example, *high* may be marked [vertical] while *tall* and *wide* are marked only [spatial extent]. Of the three, only *tall* and *wide* are synonymous with *big*; before the addition of [vertical], so is *high*.

The dust from a great deal of experimentation has settled, and it is now clear that of the two positions, the weight of evidence strongly favors the second. That is, when a new spatial adjective is learned, its polarity is represented early; it is its underlying dimensionality that takes years to work out. I will review that evidence and then present new data that suggest that although the process of working out the dimensions of comparison is indeed an extended one, the missing-feature theory provides an inadequate account of that process.

The evidence that polarity is present in early lexical entries while information about dimension of comparison is sometimes missing will be presented in three steps: (1) Since *big* and *little* are the first spatial adjectives learned, it must be shown that each is mapped onto the core comparative structure (including correct polarity) very early on. (2) It must be shown that the other spatial adjectives are also mapped onto this core comparative structure (including correct polarity) as soon as each is learned. And (3) It must be shown that this mapping precedes full dimensional specification in the cases of spatial adjectives other than *big* and *little*.

(1) *Big* and *little* become part of the vocabularies of most children

before they are three years old. Is there a point where the negative polarity of *little* or the positive polarity of *big* is not represented? To answer this question, fourteen two-year-olds were screened for knowledge of *big* and *little*. Each child was then shown a series of objects, a big shoe (size 13) or a little shoe (toddler's size), a big chair or a small chair, a big paper bag or a small paper bag, and asked of each "Is this a big x or a small x?" The big shoe was smaller than the little chair; judgments, if correct, must have been made relative to what the child had represented as the standard-sized shoe, chair, paper bag, and so on. The eight children who had *big* and *little* in their vocabularies made very few errors (90 percent correct as a group; for seven of the eight children the error score was zero or one on seven items). There were no more errors on *little* than on *big*. Not surprisingly, those children whose vocabularies did not include *big* and *little* performed at chance (Carey and Potter 1976).

The children's ability to use *big* and *little* contrastively (in constructions like "It's a big chair") establishes that as young as age two, children have representations of the standard sizes of common objects. The two words, *big* and *little,* seem to be acquired at the same time and are mapped onto the core comparative structure (including polarity) immediately.

(2) That other relative spatial adjectives also are mapped onto this core comparative structure early was demonstrated analogously: two- to four-year-old children were shown objects such as very long pencils or very short pencils and asked of each "Is this a long pencil?" or "Is this a short pencil?" While mastery of the different antonymous pairs varied (*tall/short* is learned before *wide/narrow*) the children did just as well on negative-pole words as on positive-pole words, showing no evidence of learning the negative-pole words later or of failing to represent their negative polarity (Carey 1976).

These observations indicate that the child has mapped spatial adjectives onto the core comparative structure (including polarity); three additional paradigms establish that this mapping precedes the correct dimensional mapping.

(3) Shown an array of objects varying in two dimensions (see Figure 8.2) and asked to indicate the shortest one, for example, errors respected polarity but not dimension (Brewer and Stone 1975; Carey 1976). That is, the child picked either of the two little ones, A or B (little in height and width respectively). If the child had mapped [vertical] onto *short,* but had not yet represented its polarity, one

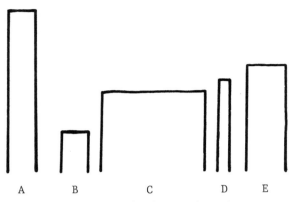

A   B   C   D   E

Figure 8.2 Stimuli varying in two dimensions

would expect the erroneous choice of D. This did not occur. Another class of errors in my data suggest that the confusion over dimensionality extended even further. When the children were asked to pick the tallest block, most errors were choices of B—the narrow block—which happened to be the one with the greatest ratio of height to width. The children who made these errors seemed not only to have failed to map simple spatial extent onto *tall,* but to have adopted the false hypothesis that *tall,* like *fat* and *skinny,* specifies relative shape.

A second paradigm supporting the position that the underlying dimensionality of each spatial adjective is learned slowly was adapted from Ervin-Tripp and Foster (1960). Shown an array such as that shown in Figure 8.3a, children were asked, "Is one of these fatter than the rest, or are they all the same in fatness?" (Care was taken that the child understood this locution. Each child was pretrained on arrays like those in Figure 8.3b, where the question was "Is one of these bigger than the rest, or are they all the same in bigness?" or "Is one of these darker than the rest, or are they all the same in darkness?") On over 60 percent of the test trials with inappropriate dimensions, the child indicated the item that respected the polarity of the probed adjective (that is, picked A in Figure 8.3a as fatter than the others). The remaining responses were predominantly "all the same in fatness" (Carey 1976).

Finally, the third paradigm indicating that polarity is firmly represented before the underlying dimensionality is worked out is the elicitation of opposites. If three- and four-year-old children are asked for opposites of spatial adjectives, they often err, but their errors almost always respect the polarity of the correct response. Most commonly, if probed with a specific dimensional adjective, the child responds *big* or *little*. To *wide* he responds *little*; to *high, little*; to *deep, little*. And to *low, skinny,* and *short,* he responds *big* (E. V. Clark 1972; Carey 1976). Other errors involve responding with an incorrectly specific adjective: to *high* he responds *short*; to *low, tall*; to *thick, skinny*; to *low, fat*; to *tall, long*. Most of these errors, too, respect correct polarity. Some of the errors suggest an intermediate stage in the representation of dimension; for example, errors such as *high*:*short* and *low*:*tall,* support the hypothesis that the child knows these words apply to the vertical dimension, but their lexical entries still lack the features that distinguish *high* from *tall* (E. V. Clark 1972).

It seems firmly established, then, that the mapping from a newly learned spatial adjective onto the core comparative structure, including polarity, is established early, while the exact dimension of comparison takes very much longer—even years—to work out.

Why should the core comparative structure (including polarity) be part of the early mapping, whereas the dimensionality takes much longer to work out? There are probably several answers to this question.

The child already knows the words *big* and *little* before he learns any of the specialized spatial adjectives. Since the core comparative structure (including polarity) is part of his early representations of *big* and *little*, these features are already available as lexical organizers when the child encounters a word like *wide* or *low*. By "available as a lexical organizer," I mean already part of the lexical entry of some word. Although the features underlying the dimensionality of the

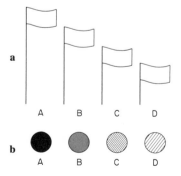

Figure 8.3 Stimuli for inappropriate dimension study

domain of spatial extent are part of the child's conceptual system, their linguistic relevance might not yet be recognized. That is, the child might not yet realize that the spatial concepts mark contrasts between words, but because of his knowledge of *big* and *little* (and possibly other relative adjectives like *fast* and *slow*) he does realize that [+pole] and [−pole] mark linguistically relevant contrasts. It is not unreasonable that features available as lexical organizers are mapped onto new words more easily than those that are not yet so available.

But how is the child to know, upon first hearing a new spatial adjective, that the features contained in *big* and *little* are relevant to it? As pointed out earlier, the child's representations of both linguistic and nonlinguistic contexts provide him with information about a newly encountered word. That the spatial adjectives are mapped onto the comparative core has syntactic consequences, and some linguistic contexts give cues to the adjective's comparative status (for example, comparative and superlative constructions, and continuum-naming constructions such as "five feet tall" or "How tall is he?"). The child must know at least some of the syntax of comparatives—that required for his early uses of *big* and *little*. It is likely that he is able to use these syntactic cues in just the efficient way he uses the absence of an article as an indicator of proper-noun-hood.

This explanation of why polarity might be more learnable than dimensionality depends upon the child's mastery of the syntax of comparative constructions and of the lexical entries for *big* and *little* prior to his acquisition of the specialized spatial adjectives. The child's original, and early, learning of *big* and *little* has not been explained. This accomplishment should be studied further.

Representing polarity first, while leaving dimensionality to be worked out slowly, can be accounted for in terms of corrigibility also. The child minimizes both production and comprehension errors. In production, if he does not know the exact word, he can simply use the more general *big* or *little*. In comprehension, the dimension in question is usually obvious from context—the objects talked about vary in only one dimension or are markedly bigger or smaller than absent standards in only one dimension. Therefore, the child can tolerate vaguely characterized dimensions of contrast. If he had misrepresented the polarity, he could not avoid errors and would be likely to be corrected by his parents (or find himself with the opposite of what he wanted on some occasions).

That the dimensionality underlying spatial adjectives is worked out slowly during development has been established, but the nature of the immature lexical entries and the process of lexical growth have not yet been discussed. The results presented are consistent with the missing-feature theory: most errors are as would be expected if specialized spatial adjectives were synonyms of *big* or *little*. Nevertheless, the results suggest an alternative beginning as well: some children may initially map [relative shape] onto *tall,* making it a synonym of *skinny*. In this case, as in the cases where *fat* and *skinny* initially include the feature [spatial extent], the process of lexical growth would involve unlearning as well as adding further features. This alternative requires only a minor revision of the missing-feature theory. Both routes to the acquisition of *tall,* for example, include partial representations such that *tall* initially has a lexical entry identical to that of some other word.

Although the missing-feature theory is consistent with the data, it is greatly undersupported. According to the theory, lexical entries of spatial adjectives initially contain *only* the feature [spatial extent] for the specification of dimension; later on, the lexical entry for *high,* for example, contains only the features [spatial extent] and [vertical]. It is important for the theory that no other information about dimension be represented; otherwise the predictions about synonymy would not obtain. The weakness is that the data supporting the theory in the case of spatial adjectives is almost entirely cross-sectional, each child contributing one response for each adjective. Certainly, a child will give *big* as an opposite to *short* and another child will pick the narrowest block when asked to pick the shortest. But are we justified in concluding that these two children had represented nothing more in their entries about the dimension of comparison underlying *short* than [spatial extent]? That is, is *short* really a synonym of *little*? Further evidence is needed to establish such a strong claim: at the very least, a child should make consistent errors on several different tasks that diagnose, in different ways, the putative partial entries.

To check for such consistency, Tom Considine and I presented sixteen three- and four-year-olds with the five tasks shown in Table 8.1. Each task involved many adjectives, some of them not spatial relatives. *Tall, short, fat,* and *skinny* were common to all five tasks, yielding 64 cases to analyze for consistency. To continue with the example of *short,* if *short* is a synonym of *little* the child should make no errors on the first two tasks of Table 8.1: a short piece of string

Table 8.1. The Five Tasks to Probe Consistency of Errors on Spatial Adjectives

Task	Sample	
1. Appropriate Dimension (contrastive)	Stimulus:	A drawing of a tall man, or a drawing of a short man
	Question:	"Is this a tall man?"
2. Appropriate Dimension (comparative)	Stimulus:	A drawing of four flagpoles, differing only in height (Figure 8.3a)
	Question:	"Is one taller than the others, or are they all the same in tallness?"
3. Opposites	Stimulus:	"I say *tall.*"
	Question:	"You say ——— ?" (*short* is expected)
4. Two Dimensions	Stimuli:	Five or six blocks, varying in both height and width (Figure 8.2)
	Question:	"Which one is the tallest one?"
5. Inappropriate Dimension	Stimulus:	A drawing of four ladies, differing only in girth
	Question:	"Is one taller than the others, or are they all the same in tallness?"

will be judged *short* (it is indeed little), and the shortest flagpole will be chosen when the child is asked "Is one of these shorter than all the rest, or are they all the same in shortness?" (it *is* the littlest). In contrast, errors would be expected on the next three tasks of Table 8.1: on the Opposites task, the child might give to *short* a response such as *big* or *high* or *fat,* respecting polarity but violating specific dimensionality; he might also pick the narrow block when asked for the short one on task 4; and he might also judge that the thinnest lady is shorter than all the rest on task 5. Thus, the strongest evidence for the missing-feature theory would be the following pattern: no errors on the first two tasks of Table 8.1 and errors on the three remaining tasks, all consistent with the same incomplete lexical entry.

In 25 of the 64 cases analyzed for consistency the child made no errors, indicating rather complete lexical entries for those adjectives. Thus there were 39 cases in which errors were made and where the predicted pattern of errors might possibly be observed. Only one yielded the full pattern, and that was on *short*. No child gave the analogous pattern on *tall, fat,* or *skinny*.

It is possible that even when a child's lexical entry includes only the feature [spatial extent] as dimensional specification, he still might be correct on one or more of the three tasks where errors are predicted. For example, on the Opposites task (task 3) he might produce the correct opposite because of learned associations between *tall* and *short* or between *fat* and *skinny*. Or on the Two Dimensions task (task 4) he might pick the correct block because it is one of two exemplifying the polarity of the word in question; this task was presented twice with different stimuli, however, so being correct required two correct choices. A child with the hypothesized partial entry should never be correct on the Inappropriate Dimension task. Thus, support for the missing-feature theory need not require the full pattern of predicted responses; two errors consistent with the same partial meaning would be strong support.

In 23 of the 39 cases where errors were made, there was only a single error. Even when the error was consistent with the missing-feature theory (for example, responding *big* as an opposite to *short*), these single-error patterns suggest that the child represents more about the dimension of comparison than [spatial extent]; he apparently calls on additional dimensional knowledge on other tasks involving the same word. Furthermore, some of the single-error patterns were actually inconsistent with the theory: the child was correct on the Inappropriate Dimension task (task 5), and in a few cases, the child responded correctly on all three of the tasks that are diagnostic of incomplete dimensional representations but made an error on task 1 or 2.

If the single-error cases are equivocal, the sixteen remaining cases where the child made two or more errors are not. In only four of these cases, including the one full predicted pattern on *short,* were the errors consistent with each other as reflecting the same putative incomplete representation. The inconsistencies were of several types. First, on one task a child might make an error that seemingly reflected the relative-shape partial meaning (for example, he might pick the skinny block when asked for the tall one on the Two Dimensions task) and on another task make an error that seemingly reflected the simple spatial-extent partial meaning (picking the fattest lady when asked if one is taller than the others on the Inappropriate

Dimension task). In a second type of inconsistency, the child might err on one of tasks 3, 4, or 5, seemingly because he had one of the putative partial meanings, yet also err on task 1 or 2, where he should have been correct, given that partial meaning.

These data, although scanty, are clear. When each of the five tasks is considered alone, the results support the missing-feature theory. Errors, when they occur, are consistent with the view that the child has represented the meaning of *tall,* for example, as if it were a synonym of *big* or *high* (or of *skinny,* where the child seems to think that *tall* is a relative-shape predicate.) However, the across-task consistency required to support such a view is not found.

Thus, something is amiss with the missing-feature theory. There is evidence against stable incomplete lexical entries: *short* may never mean *little.* The child seems always to represent more about the dimension of comparison underlying each spatial adjective than is captured in the feature [spatial extent]. But whatever more is represented, it does not protect the child against errors that indicate confusion about the dimension of comparison. What might early lexical entries for spatial adjectives be like such that they would have these properties?

Immature Lexical Entries: Missing Features and Haphazard Examples

The immature lexical entries for spatial adjectives might contain information about some particular objects to which each adjective applies. The entry for *tall* might include that it applies to buildings and people; of *short* that it applies to hair, people, and distances; of *high* that it applies to chairs and shelves; and so on. Of course, the child must represent the dimension of variation within each object that is relevant to each adjective's use. Thus, sample lexical entries might be:

   tall: [Adj] [comparative] [+pole] [____ building, ground up;
                                                        ____ person, head to toe]
   short: [Adj] [comparative] [−pole] [____ person, head to toe;
                      ____ hair, root to end; ____ distance, direction of motion]

On this view, the child learns, object by object and particular part by particular part, what spatial adjective applies to what kinds of variation. (Loaves of bread have overall size and also length, height, and width; slices of bread have thickness, height, and width; crusts of bread have thickness.) At the very beginning of the child's experience with a word, he will have represented only one or a few such aspects of particular objects to which the adjective applies. Those included will be a reflection of the child's haphazard encounters with the word.

It may seem that the specification of the dimensions of variation within particular objects requires the very feature system that characterizes the adult lexicon. If so, why does the child not represent those features directly, rather than list exemplars? The reason is that the relevant spatial predicates characterizing the dimensions of variation may not have been differentiated from irrelevant spatial and nonspatial predicates. Suppose the child first learns *deep* and *shallow* as applying to ends of pools. If he can use the words correctly faced with novel swimming pools, not confusing depth with the length or width of the pool, then certainly he has the concept of depth of swimming pools. But he may not see the similarity between the way that the deep end of a swimming pool is deep and the way that bowls, holes, and puddles are deep. He may not know that *deep* can apply when there is no contrast between two parts of a single object, or that it does not require a liquid medium. Each of these, plus many other irrelevant features, may be part of his unanalyzed conception of the depth of pools.

Many linguists and psychologists have discussed the relation between the perceptual system and the structure of language (Bierwisch 1967; H. H. Clark 1973; Miller and Johnson-Laird 1976). As all of these writers have noted, the features underlying spatial adjectives (and also spatial prepositions, verbs of motion, and other lexical domains) correspond to perceptual predicates. This does not mean that such predicates are already available to the child as lexical organizers. Rather, the lexical features must be worked out relative to all of the words in any particular lexical domain. The representation of specific exemplars could provide the basis for abstraction of common features within the uses of a word as well as for the contrasts with other words in the domain.

The missing-feature-plus-haphazard-example theory differs from the missing-feature theory both in its description of immature lexical entries and in its account of the process of lexical growth. In the revised theory, immature lexical entries include privileges of occurrence that contain dimensional information, albeit in an unanalyzed format. The process of lexical growth has two components. (1) The discovery of semantic features: the child must discover what aspects of the conceptual system are relevant to the structure of the lexical domain. (2) The mapping of semantic features onto words: the child must work out how the semantic features apply to all of the words in the domain. Both of these processes go on together.

The two theories are alike in that before a feature becomes a lexical organizer, it is in fact missing from the lexical entry of any word, so lexical development does consist partially in the addition of features to words. Left out of the missing-feature theory is the process by which new lexical features are discovered.

Several considerations favor the missing-feature-plus-haphazard-example theory over the missing-feature theory. From the beginning, according to the revised theory, more is represented about dimension than simple spatial extent. Therefore, *short* never should mean *little*. Moreover, the inconsistencies Considine and I found are to be expected. Any probe of a word necessarily requires some particular object to which the child must try to apply it. In the early stages of that word's lexical entry, the child's response will be determined by the haphazard examples he has represented. Thus, to return to the *deep* and *shallow* example, the child might respond correctly if he happens to be probed about ends of swimming pools, and he might be able to give the fully appropriate opposite to each word, since they were learned as explicit contrasts. But if shown a picture of a deep puddle—a girl sinking into a mud puddle up to her knees — and asked "Is this a deep puddle?" the child might answer, "No, a big one." The responses of several children in our sample followed such a pattern.

The most compelling consideration in favor of the missing-feature-plus-haphazard-example theory is the very complexity of the feature system underlying the lexical domain of spatial adjectives. It is possible that even some adults do not discover all the regularities in the domain, never fully representing, for example, how *fat, wide,* and *thick* differ, although they know very well some paradigm cases of things that can be each.

The missing-feature-plus-haphazard-example theory relies on the contrast between semantic information that is part of an integrated representation of a particular object and semantic information as features that are lexical organizers. Just this distinction is necessary in the discussion of the acquisition of causative verbs.

Causative verbs In her analysis of her daughter's acquisition of causative verb constructions, Bowerman presents convincing evidence for there being a point in development when the feature [cause] has become a lexical organizer. Earlier uses of causative verbs involve notions of causation, but only as part of unanalyzed conceptual packages corresponding to the whole meaning of verbs (Bowerman 1974). Thus Bowerman's analysis directly parallels that offered above for spatial adjectives.

In English, causal relations between two propositions can be expressed in at least two ways. In the first, both propositions are reflected on the surface, as in *He made her steal the diamond.* In the second, the causal proposition is incorporated lexically into the verb, as in *He warmed the bottle* ("made it warm"), *He sharpened the knife* ("made it sharp"), and *He killed her* ("caused her to die"). Many noncausal transitive and intransitive verbs and many adjectives can be used as causatives. Some causative verbs, like *open* and *warm,* are lexically identical to their noncausative forms. Other causative verbs, like *enrich, sharpen,* and *lay,* exploit productive morphological rules that relate the two forms. Still others, like *kill* and *give,* are completely unrelated lexically to their noncausative counterparts.

Children use certain causative verbs before they are two years old, while they are still producing predominantly two-word utterances. Examples include *Mommy open, Open box,* and *Give cookie.* The question of concern to Bowerman is whether the child should be credited with the two-clause structure (CAUSE BOX (OPEN BOX)) that underlies such an utterance in a grammar of adult English. If not, when is such an analysis appropriate for child speech? And when does the child have command of [cause] as a feature of verb meaning?

When she was just a little over two years old, Bowerman's daughter Christy began making many productive errors in which she used noncausative words in causal constructions. Some examples:

(1) How would you flat it?
   (said while trying to flatten a piece of paper)
(2) Down your little knee.
   (said while trying to push her sibling's knee down)
(3) She came it over there.
   (said of a dog who brought something from one place to another)

(4)   Don't eat her yet; she's smelly.
      (said as her mother was about to feed the baby, who needed a
      diaper change)
(5)   I'm singing him
      (said while pulling a string, trying to make a toy sing)

Some of Christy's errors were purely lexical; she used a word
causatively when English demands a different form—as in examples
(1)–(4), where the correct forms would be *flatten, lower, brought,* and
feed. Other errors actually violated English restrictions on the semantics of causatives, as in example (5) (in English there is no lexical item
meaning "cause to sing"); in order to be used causatively, verbs and
adjectives must describe states or changes of states (including location). These errors were frequent and persistent; by the age of four
Christy had produced hundreds and was still making new ones.
Bowerman argues that such errors are overgeneralizations of the
relation between the causative and noncausative uses of words like
open and that they demonstrate that Christy had command of [cause]
as a feature of verb meaning.

The flowering of these productive errors exactly coincided with
Christy's first productions of two-clause coordinate structures expressing causation. Just one week before the first lexical overgeneralization, a large number of sentences such as *I got her wet* and *I
made it warm* first appeared. Other constructions appearing for the
first time were forms like *Put the hat on,* which also requires the
coordination of an action (putting) and a resulting change of state
(change of location of the hat). Bowerman argues that Christy's
mastery of the syntax of these coordinated structures was a prerequi-
site to her noticing the relation between forms like *I made it warm*
and *I warmed it* and thus to her abstraction of [cause] as a lexical
organizer.

Christy had been using causatives like *I warmed it* for many months
before she showed any surface realization of coordinated structures
or made any productive errors. With these two developments, some
of her former causatives like *bring* dropped out in favor of incorrect
forms like *Come it over here.* This case provides the classic features
of the sudden appearance of rule-governed productive control over
what had previously been unanalyzed isolated lexically-bound routines.

If Christy did not represent the [cause] feature in her lexical entries for *give*, *bring*, and *open*, even though they were used causatively, what did they mean to her? Bowerman says that there is no doubt that when Christy used *give*, for example, she knew who was giving what to whom and who would end up having what. But, Bowerman argues, the meaning of *give* should be thought of as an unanalyzed whole, corresponding perhaps to the entire act of giving. It is a matter of discovery for the child, Bowerman concludes, what aspects of the act of giving are linguistically relevant to the syntax of causatives and to the lexical organization of causative verbs.

After the abstraction of [cause] as a lexical feature of the meaning of causative verbs, Christy spent a number of years mastering the English restrictions on causative constructions. Thus, here were three stages in her development: the representation of causative verbs as unanalyzed cognitive units, the abstraction of the lexical feature [cause], and finally the long-drawn-out process of working out the details of the semantics of causatives.

There are, of course, large differences between learning spatial adjectives and learning causative verbs. Spatial adjectives form a well-defined, limited lexical domain; causative verbs are an open-ended set. Learning causatives fundamentally involves syntactic development as well as semantic development; some of the syntax of comparative constructions is already mastered before any of the specialized spatial adjectives are learned. Indeed, were it not for the syntax of causatives, Bowerman's pinpointing of the moment of the isolation of [cause] as a lexical organizer would not have been possible. But in spite of the differences between the two cases, they both support a view of lexical growth in which an important part of the process is discovering which aspects of conceptual structure fill the role of semantic features.

Summary and Conclusions

The preschool child effortlessly meets the challenge of learning his first language — quite an accomplishment in the case of the lexicon. In the first part of this chapter, the time course of learning a single new word was assessed. A distinction emerged between fast mappings and slow, extended mappings. One, or a very few, experiences with a new word can suffice for the child to enter it into his mental lexicon and to represent some of its syntactic and semantic features.

The importance of the fast mapping was seen in terms of the rate of vocabulary growth and the weight of information contained in each lexical entry. Given a fast mapping, an entry can be completed slowly as the child encounters the word again and contrasts it with other words. In the *chromium* study this slow process was seen to include reorganizing the lexicon and reorganizing the conceptual domain.

Further evidence that some features of a word's meaning are represented early while others are worked out slowly was found in the domain of spatial adjectives. But it is not known whether the early entries for spatial adjectives result from a fast mapping—that is, from just one or a very few encounters with the new word. A study parallel to the *chromium* study might settle the question. In the case of spatial adjectives it was suggested that the initial lexical entry for each new word contains the abstract comparative core, including polarity, plus specific examples of contexts in which it is appropriate to use the word. The process of lexical growth involves discovering which features of those contexts serve as lexical organizers. Further evidence for this process was provided in Bowerman's analysis of causative verbs.

Consider again the information available to a child when he first hears a new word. All he has is his representations of the linguistic and nonlinguistic contexts. The importance of the linguistic context should be stressed; for example, it was suggested that the child's knowledge of the syntax of comparatives is one possible basis for the inclusion of the comparative core in his initial representation of a new spatial adjective. If the semantic features relevant to the structure of the lexical domain are not already known to the child, then remembering the specific nonlinguistic context in which the word was first acquired provides a basis for future uses of the word. Thus, the missing-feature-plus-haphazard-example theory characterizes the lexical entries that result from fast mappings for new words in relatively unstructured domains—that is, in domains for which the child has not yet discovered the relevant semantic features.

In this chapter I have gone much further than available data license. Nonetheless, several topics for research can be suggested. The process of learning a new word from context should vary as a function of the lexical organizers already available to the child. Learning *big* and *little* may be different from learning a specific spatial adjective like *tall*, because the linguistic relevance of the core comparative structure may not even be realized before *big* and *little* are learned. And learning *thick,* for example, should involve different initial mappings if some of the semantic features of the domain have already been added to the lexical entries of other spatial adjectives.

Finally, the method used in the *chromium* study could possibly be adapted to assess when the child is aware of the constraints on possible lexical entries within particular domains. When does he know, for example, that there is no word in English that means "cause to sing" or "bigger than this one" or "the color of lilac flowers"? The child could be taught new words that correspond to gaps in the lexicon—gaps for words that are allowed by the constraints on word formation but which the child does not yet know, as in the *chromium* study, and gaps left because words that would fill them would violate English semantic constraints. If the child finds "words" of the latter kind much harder to learn, we would have evidence that he is sensitive to the constraints on word formation within that domain. Such research might strengthen the central assumption of this chapter, namely, that consideration of the process of learning a single new word can lead to novel insights about lexical development.

9 Knowledge Unlearned and Untaught: What Speakers Know about the Sounds of Their Language

MORRIS HALLE

Untaught Knowledge

The native speaker of a language knows a great deal about his language that he was never taught. An example of this untaught knowledge is illustrated in (1), where I have listed a number of words chosen from different languages, including English. In order to make this a fair test, the English words in the list are words that are unlikely to be familiar to the general public, including most cross-word-puzzle fans:

(1)   ptak   thole   hlad   plast   sram   mgla   vlas   flitch   dnom   rtut

If one were to ask which of the ten words in this list are to be found in the unabridged Webster's, it is likely that readers of these lines would guess that *thole, plast,* and *flitch* are English words, whereas the rest are not English. This evidently gives rise to the question: How does a reader who has never seen any of the words on the list know that some are English and others are not? The answer is that the words judged not English have letter sequences not found in English. This implies that in learning the words of English the normal speaker acquires knowledge about the structure of the words. The curious thing about this knowledge is that it is acquired although it is never taught, for English-speaking parents do not normally draw their children's attention to the fact that consonant sequences that begin English words are subject to certain restrictions that exclude words such as *ptak, sram,* and *rtut,* but allow *thole, flitch,* and *plast.* Nonetheless, in the absence of any overt teaching, speakers somehow acquire this knowledge.

The sounds of speech   In order to get some insight into how humans acquire knowledge about their language without being taught, it is necessary to understand the character of the knowledge that is being acquired. Since I am talking about sounds and sound sequences, I must say a few words about the way that linguists think about the

This chapter is adapted from a paper presented at the Convocation on Communications, in celebration of the Centennial of the Telephone, MIT, March 9–10, 1976, published in *The Telephone's First Century—and Beyond* (Thomas Y. Crowell, New York, 1977).

sounds of speech. These ways of thinking about sounds derive in part from the work of Alexander Graham Bell and that of his father, A. Melville Bell. Let us turn, therefore, to the Bells' contribution to the science of language.

Alexander Graham Bell was a speech therapist by profession: his specialty was the teaching of speech to the deaf, and according to all reports he was an extraordinarily gifted and successful practitioner of this difficult art. Speech therapy was the profession of many members of the Bell family. In fact, it was a sort of family enterprise. The head of the family, A. Melville Bell, practiced it in London; other members, in other parts of Great Britain. What differentiated A. Melville Bell from most speech therapists was that he was interested not only in the practical aspects of his work, but also in its scientific foundations. In this work he involved his son, the future inventor of the telephone, and on one issue of importance the son made a contribution that went far beyond that of his father.

A. Melville Bell's analysis of spoken language proceeds from the obvious observation that the production of speech sounds involves the coordinated activity of a number of different organs such as the lips, the tongue, the velum, and the larynx, which together make up what traditionally has been called the human vocal tract. From this point of view the act of speaking is an elaborate gymnastics or choreography executed by different speech organs. In A. Melville Bell's book *Visible Speech* (1867) we find a systematic account of the different activities that each speech organ is capable of, together with a discussion of the different speech sounds that result from particular combinations of activities of specific speech organs.

Consider from this point of view the initial consonants in the words *veal, zeal, sheep, keel, wheel*. One thing that differentiates each of these consonants from the others is the place in the vocal tract that is maximally narrowed and the organ or organs effecting this narrowing. In /v/ the constriction is formed by raising the lower lip; such sounds are therefore designated as *labial*. In /z/ and /š/ the constriction is formed with the tongue blade, and these sounds are designated by the term *coronal*. In /k/ the constriction is formed with the dorsum (or body) of the tongue and such sounds are designated as *dorsal*. The sound beginning the English word *wheel* is produced with two simultaneous constrictions, one with the lips and the other with the tongue dorsum; this sound is therefore both *labial* and *dorsal*.

A further mechanism involved in distinguishing one sound from another is voicing—whether or not the sound is produced with the accompaniment of vibration of the vocal cords: /z v/ are; /š k xʷ/ are not. This fact can readily be verified by placing one's finger tips on the large (thyroid) cartilage in the front of the neck and pronouncing the sounds in question. When the vocal cords vibrate, one can detect a slight throbbing sensation in the finger tips. Finally, for purposes of this discussion one additional mechanism must be identified. It is the mechanism that produces strident sounds, such as /f v s z š ž č ǰ/, and distinguishes them from the rest. It consists in directing the air stream against the sharp edges of the upper teeth, thereby producing audible turbulence.

Thus five distinct mechanisms that are involved in the production of the continuant sounds under discussion have been identified. I label these for present purposes as follows:

the raising of the lower lip—labial
the raising of the tongue blade—coronal
the raising of the tongue body—dorsal
vocal cord vibration—voicing
air stream directed at upper teeth—strident

When two or more mechanisms are activated, the perceptual effect is that of a single sound. Thus, both /z/ as in *zeal* and /s/ as in *seal* are perceived as single sounds, although in the production of /z/ one more mechanism (voicing) is activated than in the production of /s/. As shown in Figure 9.1, Bell's *Visible Speech* alphabet had a special symbol to represent each of these mechanisms; for example, the

Table 9.1

		Labial	Coronal	Dorsal	Voiced	Strident
f	feel	+	−	−	−	+
v	veal	+	−	−	+	+
xʷ	wheel	+	−	+	−	−
s	seal	−	+	−	−	+
z	zeal	−	+	−	+	+
š	sheep	−	+	−	−	+
ž	rouge	−	+	−	+	+
č	cheap	−	+	−	−	+
ǰ	jeep	−	+	−	+	+
x	Bach	−	−	+	−	−
p	peal	+	−	−	−	−
d	deal	−	+	−	+	−
k	keel	−	−	+	−	−

CONSONANTS.

X	Glottis closed, (catch.)
I	" narrow, (voice.)
O	" open, (aspirate.)
◊	Super-Glottal Passage contracted, (whisper.)
(	Soft Palate depressed, (nasal.)
C	Back of Tongue, (contracting oral passage.)
◠	Front of do. (do.)
◡	Point of do. (do.)
◯	Lips, (do.)

Figure 9.1 Diagram of the Human Vocal Tract. The symbols on the right refer to the letters of Bell's phonetic alphabet. Reproduced from A. M. Bell, *Visible Speech* (1867).

labial mechanism is represented by a semicircle open to the left, the coronal mechanism by a semicircle open to the top, voicing is symbolized by a line inside the semicircle, and so forth. When two or more mechanisms are activated simultaneously in the production of a given sound the symbolic representation becomes rather cumbersome. It is therefore more convenient to represent the same information by means of a matrix such as that in Table 9.1.

The claim made explicitly by A. Melville Bell in *Visible Speech* is that he had identified all mechanisms that are relevant in the production of sounds in any spoken language. If this claim is correct, it should be possible for an appropriately trained person to analyze any sound whatever in terms of the mechanisms involved in its production, especially since the number of mechanisms is fairly small. Moreover, it should also be possible for a trained person to produce sounds represented in this notation, even sounds that he had never heard before. That is exactly how Bell saw the matter and he set about demonstrating it in a most dramatic fashion. The following description of a demonstration is from a letter written by an observer, Alexander J. Ellis, Esq., F.R.S., which Bell quotes in *Visible Speech*.

The mode of procedure was as follows: Mr. Bell sent his two Sons, who were to read the writing, out of the room—it is interesting to know that the elder, who read all the words in this case, had only five weeks' instruction in the use of the Alphabet—and I dictated slowly and distinctly the sounds which I wished to be written. These consisted of a few words in Latin, pronounced first as at Eton, then as in Italy, and then according to some theoretical notions of how Latins might have uttered them. Then came some English provincialisms and affected pronunciations; the words 'how odd' being given in several distinct ways. Suddenly German provincialisms were introduced. Then discriminations of sounds often confused. . . . Some Arabic, some Cockney-English, with an introduced Arabic guttural, some mispronounced Spanish, and a variety of vowels and diphthongs. . . . The result was perfectly satisfactory;—that is, Mr. Bell wrote down my queer and purposely-exaggerated pronunciations and mispronunciations, and delicate distinctions, in such a manner that his Sons, not having heard them, so uttered them as to surprise me by the extremely correct echo of my own voice. . . . Accent, tone, drawl, brevity, indistinctness, were all reproduced with surprising accuracy. Being on the watch, I could, as it were, trace the alphabet in the lips of the readers. I think, then, that Mr. Bell is justified in the somewhat bold title which he has assumed for his mode of writing—"Visible Speech." (p. 22)

The quaintness of this testimonial should not be permitted to obscure the serious point that Bell attempted to establish by means of his demonstration, namely, that all sounds of all known languages can be produced, given the very restricted information about a small number of mechanisms that is provided by *Visible Speech*. Anybody who controls all the mechanisms singly and in combination can produce any speech sound whatever. It is therefore these mechanisms and not the individual sounds of language that are the fundamental building blocks of speech. This insight, which in the last quarter century has become almost a truism among students of language, was stated explicitly in the early 1900s by Alexander Graham Bell in a series of lectures that he delivered to the American Association to Promote the Teaching of Speech to the Deaf. (It should be noted that Bell's terms "constriction" and "position" are synonymous with what has been termed "mechanism" here.)

What we term an "element of speech" may in reality . . . be a combination of positions. The true element of articulation, I think, is a constriction or position of the vocal organs rather than a sound. Combinations of positions yield new sounds, just as combinations of chemical elements yield new substances. Water is a substance of very different character from either of the gases of which it is formed; and the vowel *oo* is a sound of very different character from that of any of its elementary positions.
When we symbolize positions, the organic relations of speech

sounds to one another can be shown by means of an equation; for example

English wh = P (labiality—MH) + P′ (dorsality—MH)

German ch = P′ (dorsality—MH)

hence German ch = English wh − P (labiality—MH)

The equation asserts that the English *wh* without labial constriction is the German *ch*. (*The Mechanism of Speech*, pp. 38–39)

Sounds into words I now turn from the analysis of speech sounds into their component mechanisms—or features, to use a more modern term—to the restrictions that languages characteristically impose on the concatenation of sounds into words. We have already seen in (1) that certain consonant sequences are not admissible at the beginning of English words. Hence the words beginning with the sequences *pt, hl, sr, mgl, vl, dn,* and *rt* were judged not to be part of the English lexicon. A different kind of restriction is found in the choice of the plural marker in English. I have listed in (2) three different sets of English nouns:

(2) a. bus, bush, batch, buzz, garage, badge

 b. lip, pit, pick, cough, sixth

 c. cab, lid, rogue, cove, scythe, cam, can, call, car, tie, gnu, blow, tray, sea, . . .

If you say to yourself the plural forms of the words in (2), you will notice that English has, not one, but three plural suffixes, one for each of the three separate sets of words in (2). We add an extra syllable /ɨz/ in forming the plural of the words in (2a); we add /s/ for the plural of the words in (2b), and we add /z/ to form the plural of the words in (2c). One can readily show that it is not the case that we memorize the plural form of every word we learn, for we know how to form the plurals of words we have never encountered before. Specifically, think of the plurals of the three English words in list (1): *flitch, plast,* and *thole.* I am sure that most readers who have never heard these words would agree that they know their plural forms and that these are respectively

flitches, like *buses* (2a)

plasts, like *lips* (2b)

tholes, like *cabs* (2c)

These facts show that speakers of English know a rule of plural formation. Like the restrictions on word-initial consonant sequences illustrated in (1) the English plural rule is rarely (if ever) overtly taught; many readers who have faithfully followed it all their lives may never have been aware of it until reading the preceding paragraph.

It is necessary to be clear about the status of a rule such as the plural rule under discussion. It is part of the knowledge that English speakers have and that people who do not know English normally do not have. Knowing the rule that determines the phonetic actualization of the plural in English is therefore much like knowing that the device invented by Alexander Graham Bell is called *telephone* rather than *farspeaker* (compare *loudspeaker*), *phonex,* or *glub.* The main difference between knowing the rule for the plural and knowing the word *telephone* is that the latter is conscious knowledge about which the speaker can answer direct questions, whereas knowledge of the plural rule and similar matters is largely unconscious and parts of it might conceivably never be accessible to consciousness. This fact, it should be noted at once, does not render such knowledge inaccessible to study by psychologists or linguists — that is, to scientists whose subject of inquiry is the speaker and his knowledge. Tacit knowledge can be established by the same methods that were used to establish other things inaccessible to direct observation, such as the nature of the chemical bond or the structure of the gene.

The question to be answered is In what form does the English speaker internalize his knowledge of the plural rule? An obvious candidate is (3):

(3)   a.   If the noun ends with /s z š ž č ǰ/, add /ɨz/;
         b.   Otherwise, if the noun ends with /p t k f θ/, add /s/;
         c.   Otherwise, add /z/.

It is important to note that this rule is formulated in terms of speech sounds rather than in terms of mechanisms or features. In the light of the above discussion, which suggested that features rather than sounds are the ultimate constituents of language, I shall now attempt to reformulate the rule in terms of features. The first move that one might make might be to replace each of the alphabetic symbols in (3) by its feature composition as shown in Table 9.1. Specifically, this means that one might replace /s/ by the feature complex [nonlabial, coronal, nondorsal, nonvoiced, strident]; /z/ by the same set of features except that in place of [nonvoiced] it would contain the feature [voiced]; and so on. It is not easy to see where such a translation of the rule into feature terminology gets us. In fact, it gets us nowhere until we observe that given a matrix like that in Table 9.1 it is possible to designate groups of sounds by mentioning one or two features. Thus, for example, if we asked for all and only sounds that are labial we would get the group /f v xʷ p/, whereas if we asked for the sounds that are strident we get /f v s z š ž č ǰ/. Suppose now that we were to utilize this idea in the formulation of the plural rule and characterize each of the different lists of sounds by the minimum number of features that suffice to designate the group unambiguously. We should then get a rule much like (4) in place of (3).

(4) a. If the noun ends with a sound that is [coronal, strident], add
         /ɨz/;
     b. Otherwise, if the noun ends with a sound that is [non-
         voiced], add /s/;
     c. Otherwise, add /z/.

Having formulated an alternative to the rule given above as (3), our task now is to determine which of the two alternatives is the one that English speakers use. The test we shall use is one suggested to me some years ago by Lise Menn. It consists of asking English speakers to form the plural of a foreign word that ends with a sound that does not occur in English. A good example, Ms. Menn suggested, is the German name *Bach* as in *Johann Sebastian* ———, which ends in the sound symbolized by /x/. If English speakers were operating in accordance with rule (3), they would have to reject options (a) and (b) and form the plural in accordance with option (c); that is, they would say that the plural of /bax/ is /baxz/ with a word-final /z/. If, on the other hand, English speakers were operating in accordance with rule (4), they would have to perform a feature analysis of /x/ which would tell them that the sound is [nonlabial, noncoronal, dorsal, nonvoiced, nonstrident]. Given this feature composition, the plural of /bax/ could not be formed in accordance with option (a) since /x/ is neither [coronal] nor [strident]; it would have to be formed in accordance with option (b) since /x/ is [nonvoiced]. In other words, if speakers operated in conformity with rule (4), their output would be /baxs/, which, as is perfectly obvious, is also the response that the majority of English speakers would make. We must, therefore, conclude that the formulation (4) of the plural rule in terms of features, and not the formulation (3) in terms of speech sounds, correctly represents the knowledge of English speakers.

Unlearned Knowledge

There is yet another, more important, inference to be drawn from the fact that English speakers can apply the plural rule to a word ending with a sound that is not part of the repertory of English. In order to apply the rule, the speaker has to be able to establish that the foreign sound in question is nonvoiced. He must therefore have knowledge that allows him to determine the phonetic mechanism involved in the production of a sound that is not part of his language. The curious thing about such knowledge is that not only is there no indication that it might ever have been taught to speakers, there is also no indication that speakers could ever have acquired such knowledge. Think what evidence would have to be marshaled to support the claim that the knowledge in question was acquired. One would have to point to experiences in the life of the average English speaker that would permit him to acquire knowledge that is otherwise possessed only by phoneticians who have undergone rigorous training of the type Alexander Graham Bell received from his father. As this is obviously implausible, one is led to contemplate the possibility that at least some knowledge available to speakers is innate. In fact, there appears to be a certain amount of independent evidence that knowledge of the feature composition of sounds is available to children long before they could possibly have learned a language. Experiments conducted by Peter Eimas (1971) at Brown University have established that the ability to discriminate voiced from nonvoiced speech sounds is present in children practically at birth. The suggestion that the ability to determine the feature composition of speech sounds is innate has, therefore, a certain amount of experimental support.

This brings me to the end of what I have to say about the knowledge that speakers have of their language. What remains for me to do is to indicate how the information just reviewed helps us in trying to understand manifestations of the human cognitive capacity in domains other than language, how it might help us understand the human capacity to draw inferences, perform computations, play games with elaborate rules, interact with one another, and uncover significant truths about the nature of the world around us and within us. If these manifestations of man's mind are at all like language, then we must expect to find that large portions of the knowledge on which they are based will be inaccessible to consciousness, that some of this knowledge will be innate, and that only a modest fraction of the total will have been acquired as the result of overt teaching.

Bibliography

AKMAJIAN, A., P. CULICOVER, AND T. WASOW. 1977
Formal Syntax. New York: Academic.

AKMAJIAN, A., AND F. HENY. 1975
An Introduction to the Principles of Transformational Syntax. Cambridge, Mass.: The MIT Press.

ANDERSON, S. 1977
Comments on Wasow's paper: The role of "theme" in lexical rules. In Akmajian, Culicover, and Wasow.

ANDREEWSKY, E., AND X. SERON. 1975
Implicit processing of grammatical rules in a classical case of agrammatism. *Cortex* 11, 379–390.

ANGLIN, J. 1970
The Growth of Word Meaning. Cambridge, Mass.: The MIT Press.

ARONOFF, M. H. 1976
Word formation in generative grammar. *Linguistic Inquiry Monograph One.* Cambridge, Mass.: The MIT Press.

BAKER, C., AND M. BRAME. 1972
"Global rules": A rejoinder. *Language* 48.

BALDIE, J. 1976
The acquisition of the passive voice. *Journal of Child Language* 3, 331–348.

BARTLETT, E. 1977
The acquisition of the meaning of color terms: A study of lexical development. In P. Smith and R. Campbell, eds., *Proceedings of the Stirling Conference on the Psychology of Language.* New York: Plenum.

BELL, ALEXANDER GRAHAM. 1911
The Mechanism of Speech. New York and London: Funk & Wagnalls.

BELL, A. MELVILLE. 1967
Visible Speech: The Science of Universal Alphabetics. London: Simkin, Marshall; London and New York: N. Trubner.

BELLUGI, U. 1967
The acquisition of negation. Doctoral dissertation, Harvard University.

BELLUGI, U. 1971
Simplification in children's language. In R. Huxley and E. Ingram, eds., *Language Acquisition: Models and Methods.* New York: Academic.

BENDIX, E. H. 1966
Componential Analysis of General Vocabulary: The Semantic Structure of a Set of Verbs in English, Hindi, and Japanese. The Hague: Mouton.

BEVER, T. 1970
The cognitive basis for linguistic structures. In J. R. Hayes, ed., *Cognition and the Development of Language.* New York: Wiley.

BIERWISCH, M. 1967
Some semantic universals of German adjectivals. *Foundations of Language* 3, 1–36.

BLOOM, L. M. 1970
Language Development: Form and Function in Emerging Grammars. Cambridge, Mass.: The MIT Press.

BLUMSTEIN, S. E., W. E. COOPER, E. ZURIF, AND A. CARAMAZZA. 1977
The perception and production of voice-onset time in aphasia. *Neuropsychologia* 15, 371–383.

BLUMSTEIN, S. E., AND H. GOODGLASS. 1972
The perception of stress as a semantic cue in aphasia. *Journal of Speech and Hearing Research* 15, 800–806.

BLUMSTEIN, S. E., E. B. ZURIF, AND A. CARAMAZZA. In preparation
Comprehension strategies in aphasia. Aphasia Research Center, Boston, Mass.

BOBROW, D., AND B. FRASER. 1969
An augmented state transition network analysis procedure. In D. Walker and L. Norton, eds., *Proceedings of the International Joint Conference on Artificial Intelligence*. Washington, D.C.

BOWERMAN, M. 1974
Learning the structure of causative verbs: A study in the relationship of cognitive, semantic and syntactic development. In E. Clark, ed., *Papers and Reports on Child Language Development* No. 8. Stanford University Committee on Linguistics, 142–178.

BRAINE, M. D. S. 1971
The acquisition of language in infant and child. In C. Reed, ed., *The Learning of Languages: Essays in Honor of David H. Russell*. New York: Appleton.

BRAINE, M. D. S. 1976
Children's first word combinations. *Monographs of the Society for Research in Child Development* 41, Serial No. 164.

BRAME, M. 1976
Conjectures and Refutations in Syntax and Semantics. Amsterdam: North-Holland.

BRESNAN, J. 1972
Theory of complementation in English syntax. Doctoral dissertation, Massachusetts Institute of Technology.

BRESNAN, J. 1976a
On the form and functioning of transformations. *Linguistic Inquiry* 7.

BRESNAN, J. 1976b
Evidence for a theory of unbounded transformations. *Linguistic Analysis* 2, 353–393.

BRESNAN, J. In preparation
A Realistic Transformation Grammar.

BREWER, W. F., AND J. B. STONE. 1975
Acquisition of spatial antonym pairs. *Journal of Experimental Child Psychology* 19, 299–307.

BROWN, R. 1957
Linguistic determinism and parts of speech. *Journal of Abnormal and Social Psychology* 55, 1–5.

BROWN, R. 1973
A First Language: The Early Stages. Cambridge, Mass.: Harvard University Press.

BROWN, R., C. CAZDEN, AND U. BELLUGI. 1968
The child's grammar from I to III. In J. P. Hill, ed., *Minnesota Symposia on Child Psychology,* vol. 2. Minneapolis: University of Minnesota Press.

BROWN, R., AND C. HANLON. 1970
Derivational complexity and order of acquisition in child speech. In J. R. Hayes, ed., *Cognition and the Development of Language.* New York: Wiley.

CAIRNS, H., AND D. FOSS. 1971
Falsification of the hypothesis that word frequency is a unified variable in sentence processing. *Journal of Verbal Learning and Verbal Behavior* 10, 41–43.

CARAMAZZA, A., J. GORDON, E. B. ZURIF, AND D. DeLUCA. 1976
Right-hemispheric damage and verbal problem solving behavior. *Brain and Language* 3, 41–46.

CARAMAZZA, A., E. H. GROBER, AND E. B. ZURIF. 1976
A psycholinguistic investigation of polysemy: the meanings of LINE. Unpublished manuscript, Department of Psychology, The Johns Hopkins University.

CARAMAZZA, A., AND E. B. ZURIF. 1976
Dissociation of algorithmic and heuristic processes in language comprehension: Evidence from aphasia. *Brain and Language* 3, 572–582.

CAREY, S. 1976
Spatial adjectives. Unpublished working paper. Massachusetts Institute of Technology.

CAREY, S., AND M. POTTER. 1976
The representation of size: Conceptual and lexical development. Paper presented at the first annual conference of the New England Child Language Association, Boston University.

CAREY, S., AND M. POTTER. 1977
Less may never mean more. In P. Smith and R. Campbell, eds., *Proceedings of the Stirling Conference on the Psychology of Language.* New York: Plenum.

CARROLL, J. B., AND M. N. WHITE. 1973a
Word frequency and age of acquisition as determiners of picture-naming latency. *Quarterly Journal of Experimental Psychology* 27, 85–95.

CARROLL, J. B., AND M. N. WHITE. 1973b
Age-of-acquisition norms for 220 picturable nouns. *Journal of Verbal Learning and Verbal Behavior* 12, 563–576.

CARROLL, J. M., AND M. K. TANENHAUS. 1975
Prologomena to a functional theory of word formation. In R. E. Grossman, L.
J. San, and T. J. Vance, eds., *Papers from the Parasession on Functionalism*.
Chicago: Chicago Linguistic Society.

CAZDEN, C. B. 1968
The acquisition of noun and verb inflections. *Child Development* 39, 433–448.

CHOMSKY, N. 1957
Syntactic Structures. The Hague: Mouton.

CHOMSKY, N. 1959
A review of B. F. Skinner's "Verbal Behavior." *Language* 35, 26–58.

CHOMSKY, N. 1964a
Current Issues in Linguistic Theory. The Hague: Mouton.

CHOMSKY, N. 1964b
On the notion "Rule of grammar." In J. A. Fodor and J. J. Katz, eds., *The
Structure of Language*. Englewood Cliffs, N. J.: Prentice-Hall.

CHOMSKY, N. 1965
Aspects of the Theory of Syntax. Cambridge, Mass.: The MIT Press.

CHOMSKY, N. 1970a
Remarks on nominalization. In R. Jacobs and P. Rosenbaum, eds., *Readings
in Transformational Grammar*. Boston: Ginn.

CHOMSKY, N. 1970b
Deep structure, surface structure, and semantic interpretation. In *Studies in
Semantics in Generative Grammar*. The Hague: Mouton.

CHOMSKY, N. 1975
Reflections on Language. New York: Pantheon.

CHOMSKY, N. 1976
Conditions on rules of grammar. *Linguistic Analysis* 2, 303–351.

CHOMSKY, N. 1977
On *wh*-movement. In Akmajian, Culicover, and Wasow.

CHOMSKY, N., AND M. HALLE. 1968
The Sound Pattern of English. New York: Harper & Row.

CHOMSKY, N., AND H. LASNIK. 1977
Filters and control. *Linguistic Inquiry* 8, 425–504.

CLARK, E. V. 1972
On the child's acquisition of antonyms in two semantic fields. *Journal of
Verbal Learning and Verbal Behavior* 11, 750–758.

CLARK, E. V. 1973
What's in a word? On the child's acquisition of semantics in his first
language. In T. E. Moore, ed., *Cognitive Development and the Acquisition of
Language*. New York: Academic.

CLARK, H. H. 1970
The primitive nature of children's relational concepts. In J. R. Hayes, ed.,
Cognition and the Development of Language. New York: Wiley.

CLARK, H. H. 1973
Space, time, semantics, and the child. In T. E. Moore, ed., *Cognitive Development and the Acquisition of Language*. New York: Academic.

CLARK, R. 1975
Performing without competence. *Journal of Child Language* 2, 1–10.

DONALDSON, M., AND R. WALES. 1970
On the acquisition of some relational terms. In J. R. Hayes, ed., *Cognition and the Development of Language*. New York: Wiley.

EIMAS, P., E. SIQUELAND, P. JUSCZYK, AND J. VIGORITO. 1971
Speech perception in infants. *Science* 171, 303–306.

EMONDS, J. 1970
Root and structure-preserving transformations. Doctoral dissertation, Massachusetts Institute of Technology. Indiana University Linguistics Club.

EMONDS, J. 1976
A Transformational Approach to English Syntax: Root, Structure-Preserving and Local Transformations. New York: Academic.

EPSTEIN, W. 1969
Recall of word lists following learning of sentences and of anomalous and random strings. *Journal of Verbal Learning and Verbal Behavior* 8, 20–25.

ERVIN-TRIPP, S. M., AND G. FOSTER. 1960
The development of meaning in children's descriptive terms. *Journal of Abnormal and Social Psychology* 61, 271–275.

FILLMORE, C. J. 1968
The case for case. In E. Bach and R. T. Harms, eds., *Universals in Linguistic Theory*. New York: Holt, Rinehart & Winston.

FODOR, J. A. 1975
The Language of Thought. New York: Thomas Y. Crowell.

FODOR, J. A., T. BEVER, AND M. GARRETT. 1974
The Psychology of Language: An Introduction to Psycholinguistics and Generative Grammar. New York: McGraw-Hill.

FODOR, J. A., AND M. GARRETT. 1966
Some reflections on competence and performance. In J. Lyons and R. J. Wales, eds., *Psycholinguistics Papers*. Edinburgh: Edinburgh University Press.

FODOR, J. A., AND M. GARRETT. 1967
Some syntactic determinants of sentential complexity. *Perception and Psychophysics* 2, 289–296.

FODOR, J. A., M. GARRETT, AND T. BEVER. 1968
Some syntactic determinants of sentential complexity, II: Verb structure. *Perception and Psychophysics* 3, 453–461.

FODOR, J. D. 1974
Like subject verbs and causal clauses in English. *Journal of Linguistics* 10.

FODOR, J. D., J. A. FODOR, AND M. F. GARRETT. 1975
The psychological unreality of semantic representations. *Linguistic Inquiry* 6, 515–531.

FORSTER, K. 1966
Left to right processes in the construction of sentences. *Journal of Verbal Learning and Verbal Behavior* 5, 285–291.

FORSTER, K. 1976
The autonomy of syntactic processing. Paper presented at the Convocation on Communication, Massachusetts Institute of Technology.

FORSTER, K., AND I. OLBREI. 1973
Semantic heuristics and syntactic analysis. *Cognition* 2.

FOSS, D. J., AND H. S. CAIRNS. 1970
Some effects of memory limitation upon sentence comprehension and recall. *Journal of Verbal Learning and Verbal Behavior* 9, 541–547.

GARDNER, H. 1973
The contribution of operativity to naming in aphasic patients. *Neuropsychologia* 11, 200–213.

GARDNER, H., G. DENES, AND E. B. ZURIF. 1975
Critical reading at the sentence level in aphasics. *Cortex* 11, 60–72.

GARDNER, H., AND E. ZURIF. 1975
Oral reading of single words in aphasia and alexia. *Neuropsychologia* 13, 170–181.

GARRETT, M. F. 1975
The analysis of sentence production. In G. Bower, ed., *Psychology of Learning and Motivation,* vol. 9. New York: Academic.

GARRETT, M. F. 1976
Syntactic processes in sentence production. In E. C. T. Walker and R. J. Wales, eds., *New Approaches to Language Mechanisms.* Amsterdam: North-Holland.

GARRETT, M., T. BEVER, AND J. FODOR. 1966
The active use of grammar in speech perception. *Perception and Psychophysics* 1, 30–32.

GEACH, P. T. 1962
Reference and Generality. Ithaca: Cornell University Press.

GLEITMAN, L. R., AND H. GLEITMAN. 1970
Phrase and Paraphrase: Some Innovative Uses of Language. New York: Norton.

GOODENOUGH, C., E. B. ZURIF, AND S. WEINTRAUB. 1977
Aphasics' attention to grammatical morphemes. *Language and Speech.*

GOODGLASS, H. 1968
Studies on the grammar of aphasics. In S. Rosenberg and J. Koplin, eds., *Developments in Applied Psycholinguistics Research.* New York: Macmillan.

GOODGLASS, H., AND E. BAKER. 1976
Semantic field, naming, and auditory comprehension in aphasia. *Brain and Language* 3, 359–374.

GOODGLASS, H., AND N. GESCHWIND. 1976
Language disorders (aphasia). In E. Carterette and M. Friedman, eds., *Handbook of Perception,* vol. 7. New York: Academic.

GOODGLASS, H., AND M. HUNTER. 1970
A linguistic comparison of speech and writing in two types of aphasia. *Journal of Communication Disorders* 3, 28–35.

GOODGLASS, H., AND E. KAPLAN. 1972
The Assessment of Aphasia and Related Disorders. Philadelphia: Lea and Febiger.

GOODMAN, N. 1968
Languages of Art. New York: Bobbs-Merrill.

GREEN, G. M. 1974
Semantics and Syntactic Regularity. Bloomington: Indiana University Press.

GROSSMAN, M. 1976
A brief examination of reference after brain damage. Unpublished manuscript. Aphasia Research Center, Boston, Mass.

GRUBER, J. 1965
Studies in lexical relations. Doctoral dissertation, Massachusetts Institute of Technology. Indiana University Linguistics Club.

HALE, K., L. M. JEANNE, AND P. PLATERO. 1977
Three cases of overgeneration. In Akmajian, Culicover, and Wasow.

HALLE, M. 1973
Prolegomena to a theory of word formation. *Linguistic Inquiry* 4.

HARTMANN, R. R. K., AND F. C. STORK. 1972
Dictionary of Language and Linguistics. London: Applied Science Publishers.

HARWOOD, F. W. 1959
Quantitative study of the speech of Australian children. *Language and Speech* 2, 237–271.

HASEGAWA, K. 1968
The passive construction in English. *Language* 44.

HOLMES, V., AND K. FORSTER. 1970
Detection of extraneous signals during sentence recognition. *Perception and Psychophysics* 7, 297–301.

HORGAN, D. In press
Children's strategies for the production of passives. *Journal of Child Language.*

HUST, J. 1977
The syntax of the unpassive construction in English. *Linguistic Analysis* 3, 31–63.

HUTTENLOCHER, J. 1968
Constructing spatial images: A strategy in reasoning. *Psychological Review* 75, 550–560.

JACKENDOFF, R. 1972
Semantic Interpretation in Generative Grammar. Cambridge, Mass.: The MIT Press.

JACKENDOFF, R. 1973
The base rules for prepositional phrases. In S. Anderson and P. Kiparsky, eds., *Festschrift for Morris Halle*. New York: Holt, Rinehart & Winston.

JACKENDOFF, R. 1975a
Morphological and semantic regularities in the lexicon. *Language* 51, 639–671.

JACKENDOFF, R. 1975b
On belief-contexts. *Linguistic Inquiry* 6, 53–93.

JACKENDOFF, R. 1976
Toward an explanatory semantic representation. *Linguistic Inquiry* 7, 89–150.

JACKENDOFF, R. 1977a
$\overline{X}$ syntax: A study of phrase structure. *Linguistic Inquiry Monograph* Two. Cambridge, Mass.: The MIT Press.

JACKENDOFF, R. 1977b
Toward a cognitively viable semantics. In C. Rameh, ed., *Georgetown University Roundtable on Languages and Linguistics 1976*. Washington: Georgetown University Press.

JACKENDOFF, R. In preparation
Semantics and cognition.

JASTREMBSKI, J. E., AND R. F. STANNERS. 1975
Multiple word meanings and lexical search speed. *Journal of Verbal Learning and Verbal Behavior* 14, 534–537.

JENKINS, L. 1975
The English Existential. Linguistische Arbeiten No. 12. Tübingen: Niemeyer.

JOHNSON, S. C. 1967
Hierarchical clustering schemes. *Psychometrika* 32, 241–254.

KAJITA, M. 1968
A Generative-Transformational Study of Semi-Auxiliaries in Present-Day American English. Tokyo: Sanseido.

KAPLAN, D. 1969
Quantifying in. In Linsky, 1971.

KAPLAN, R. 1972
Augmented transition networks as psychological models of sentence comprehension. *Artificial Intelligence* 3, 77–100.

KAPLAN, R. 1973a
A general syntactic processor. In R. Rustin, ed., *Natural Language Processing*. Englewood Cliffs, N. J.: Prentice-Hall.

KAPLAN, R. 1973b
A multi-processing approach to natural language. In *Proceedings of the First National Computer Conference*. Montvale, N. J.: AFIPS Press.

KAPLAN, R. 1975
Transient processing load in sentence comprehension. Doctoral dissertation, Harvard University.

KAPLAN, R. 1977
Computational linguistics: The syntactic component. Lectures presented at the IV International Summer School in Computational and Mathematical Linguistics, Pisa, Italy.

KARTTUNEN, L. 1969
Problems of reference in syntax. Unpublished manuscript. University of Texas at Austin.

KARTTUNEN, L. 1972
Possible and must. In J. P. Kimball, ed., *Syntax and Semantics,* vol. 1. New York: Seminar Press.

KATZ, J. J. 1964
Semantic theory and the meaning of "good." *Journal of Philosophy* 61, 739–766.

KATZ, J. J. 1973
Compositionality, idiomaticity, and lexical substitution. In S. Anderson and P. Kiparsky, eds., *A Festschrift for Morris Halle*. New York: Holt, Rinehart & Winston.

KATZ, J. J., AND J. A. FODOR. 1963
The structure of a semantic theory. *Language* 39, 190–210.

KATZ, J. J., AND P. M. POSTAL. 1964
An Integrated Theory of Linguistic Descriptions. Cambridge, Mass.: The MIT Press.

KATZ, N., E. BAKER, AND J. MCNAMARA. 1974
What's in a name? A study of how children learn common and proper names. *Child Development* 45, 469–473.

KEAN, M-L. 1976
The linguistic interpretation of aphasic syndromes. In *Explorations in the Biology of Language*. Report of the MIT Work Group in the Biology of Language. Cambridge, Mass.

KEAN, M-L. 1977
The linguistic interpretation of aphasic syndromes: Agrammatism in Broca's aphasia, an example. *Cognition* 5.

KEENAN, E. L. 1972
Relative clause formation in Malagasy. Unpublished manuscript. Kings College, Oxford University.

KELLY, E. F. 1970
A dictionary based approach to lexical disambiguation. Doctoral dissertation, Harvard University.

KELLY, E., AND P. STONE. 1975
Computer Recognition of English Word Senses. Amsterdam: North-Holland.

KEYSER, S. J., AND P. M. POSTAL. 1976
Beginning English Grammar. New York: Harper & Row.

KINTSCH, W. 1974
The Representation of Meaning in Memory. Hillsdale, N. J.: Erlbaum.

KLATZKY, R. L., E. V. CLARK, AND M. MACKEN. 1973
Asymmetries in the acquisition of polar adjectives: Linguistic or conceptual?
Journal of Experimental Child Psychology 16, 32–46.

KLIMA, E. S., AND U. BELLUGI. 1966
Syntactic regularities in the speech of children. In J. Lyons and R. J. Wales,
eds., *Psycholinguistic Papers.* Edinburgh: Edinburgh University Press.

KOUTSOUDAS, A. 1972
The strict order fallacy. *Language* 48, 88–96.

KOUTSOUDAS, A. 1973
Extrinsic order and the complex NP constraint. *Linguistic Inquiry* 4, 69–81.

KRIPKE, S. A. 1972
Naming and necessity. In D. Davidson and G. Harman, eds., *Semantics of
Natural Language.* Dordrecht: Reidel.

KUCZAJ, S. A. II, AND M. P. MARATSOS. In preparation
The later acquisition of language—the English auxiliary system.

LABOV, W. 1973
The boundaries of words and their meanings. In C. N. Bailey and R. W.
Shuy, eds., *New Ways of Analyzing Variation in English.* Washington:
Georgetown University Press.

LANGACKER, R. 1969
On pronominalization and the chain of command. In D. Reibel and S. Schane,
eds., *Modern Studies in English.* Englewood Cliffs, N. J.: Prentice-Hall.

LASNIK, H. 1976
Remarks on coreference. *Linguistic Analysis* 2.

LEES, R. B. 1960
The Grammar of English Nominalizations. The Hague: Mouton.

LENNEBERG, E. H. 1973
The neurology of language. *Daedelus* 102, 115–133.

LEVELT, W. J. M. 1970a
Hierarchical chunking in sentence processing. *Perception and Psychophysics*
8, 99–103.

LEVELT, W. J. M. 1970b
Introduction—Hierarchical clustering algorithms in the psychology of gram-
mar. In G. B. Flores d'Arcais and W. J. M. Levelt, eds., *Advances in
Psycholinguistics.* Amsterdam: North-Holland.

LEVELT, W. J. M. 1974
Formal Grammars in Linguistics and Psycholinguistics, 3 vols. The Hague:
Mouton.

LEWIS, P. 1971
General semantics. *Synthese* 22, 18–67.

LIEBERMAN, P. 1967
Intonation, Perception, and Language. Cambridge, Mass.: The MIT Press.

LIMBER, J. 1973
The genesis of complex sentences. In T. E. Moore, ed., *Cognitive Development and the Acquisition of Language.* New York: Academic.

LINSKY, L. 1967
Referring. London: Routledge & Kegan Paul.

LINSKY, L., ed. 1971
Reference and Modality. Oxford: Oxford University Press.

LOCKE, S., D. CAPLAN, AND L. KELLAR. 1973
A Study in Neurolinguistics. Springfield, Ill.: Charles C Thomas.

LYONS, J. 1963
Structural Semantics: An Analysis of Part of the Vocabulary of Plato. Publications of the Philological Society. Oxford: Blackwell.

LYONS, J. 1968
Introduction to Theoretical Linguistics. Cambridge, England: Cambridge University Press.

MACNAMARA, J. 1971
Parsimony and the lexicon. *Language* 47, 359–374.

MARATSOS, M. P., AND R. ABRAMOVITCH. 1975
How children understand full, truncated, and anomalous passives. *Journal of Verbal Learning and Verbal Behavior* 14, 145–157.

MARATSOS, M. P., S. A. KUCZAJ II, AND D. M. C. FOX. In press
Some empirical studies in the acquisition of transformational relations: Passives, negatives, and the past tense. In W. A. Collins, ed., *The Minnesota Symposia in Child Psychology,* vol. 12. Hillsdale, N.J.: Erlbaum.

MARKS, L. E. 1967
Some structural and sequential factors in the processing of sentences. *Journal of Verbal Learning and Verbal Behavior* 6, 707–713.

MARCUS, M. 1976
A design for a parser for English. In *Proceedings of the Association for Computing Machinery Conference,* Houston, Texas.

MARTIN, E. 1970
Toward an analysis of subjective phrase structure. *Psychological Bulletin* 74, 153–166.

MILLER, G. A. 1951
Language and Communication. New York: McGraw-Hill.

MILLER, G. A. 1969
A psychological method to investigate verbal concepts. *Journal of Mathematical Psychology* 6, 169–191.

MILLER, G. A. 1977
Spontaneous Apprentices: Children and Language. New York: Seabury.

MILLER, G. A., AND N. CHOMSKY. 1973
Finitary models of language users. In R. D. Luce, R. Bush, and E. Galanter, eds., *Handbook of Mathematical Psychology,* vol. 2. New York: Wiley.

MILLER, G. A., AND S. ISARD. 1964
Free recall of self-embedded English sentences. *Information and Control* 7, 292–303.

MILLER, G. A., AND P. N. JOHNSON-LAIRD. 1976
Language and Perception. Cambridge, Mass.: Harvard University Press, Belknap Press.

MONTAGUE, R. 1974
Formal Philosophy: Selected Papers. New Haven: Yale University Press.

NELSON, K., AND J. BONVILLIAN. 1973
Concepts and words in the eighteen month old: acquiring concept names under controlled conditions. *Cognition* 2, 435–450.

NINEO, A., AND J. BRUNER. 1977
The achievement and antecedents of labelling. *Journal of Child Language* 4.

NORMAN, D., AND D. G. BOBROW. 1975
On data-limited and resource-limited processes. *Cognitive Psychology* 7, 44–64.

PARK, T. 1970
The acquisition of German syntax. Working Paper, Psychologisches Institut, University of Münster, Germany.

PERLMUTTER, D. 1968
Deep and surface constraints in syntax. Doctoral dissertation, Massachusetts Institute of Technology.

PERLMUTTER, D., AND P. POSTAL. 1977
Toward a universal characterization of passivization. In *Proceedings of the Third Annual Meeting of the Berkeley Linguistics Society,* Berkeley, California.

PETERS, P. S., AND R. W. RITCHIE. 1973
On the generative power of transformational grammars. *Information Sciences* 6, 49–83.

PULLUM, G., AND D. WILSON. 1976
Autonomous syntax and the analysis of auxiliaries. *Language* 53.

PUTNAM, H. 1975
The meaning of "meaning." In K. Gunderson, ed., *Language, Mind and Knowledge.* Minnesota Studies in the Philosophy of Science, vol. 7. Minneapolis: University of Minnesota Press.

QUINE, W. V. O. 1960
Word and Object. Cambridge, Mass.: The MIT Press.

QUIRK, R., S. GREENBAUM, G. LEECH, AND J. SVARTVIK. 1972
A Grammar of Contemporary English. New York and London: Seminar Press.

REBER, A., AND J. ANDERSON. 1970
The perception of clicks in linguistic and non-linguistic messages. *Perception and Psychophysics* 8, 81–89.

REICHENBACH, H. 1947
Elements of Symbolic Logic. New York: Free Press.

RESCHER, N., AND A. URQUHART. 1971
Temporal Logic. New York: Springer-Verlag.

ROSCH, E., C. B. MERVIS, W. D. GRAY, D. M. JOHNSON, AND P. BOYES-BRAEM.
1976
Basic objects in natural categories. *Cognitive Psychology* 8, 382–439.

ROSENBAUM, P. S. 1967
The Grammar of English Predicate Complement Constructions. Cambridge, Mass.: The MIT Press.

ROSS, J. R. 1967a
On the cyclic nature of English pronominalization. In *To Honor Roman Jakobson.* The Hague: Mouton.

ROSS, J. R. 1967b
Constraints on variables in syntax. Doctoral dissertation, Massachusetts Institute of Technology.

ROSS, J. R. 1974
Three batons for cognitive psychology. In W. B. Weimer and D. S. Palermo, eds., *Cognition and the Symbolic Process.* Hillsdale, N. J.: Erlbaum.

ROSS, J. R. 1977
Wording up. In preparation.

RUBENSTEIN, H., L. GARFIELD, AND J. A. MILLIKAN. 1970
Homographic entries in the internal lexicon. *Journal of Verbal Learning and Verbal Behavior* 9, 487–494.

SAG, I. 1976
A logical theory of verb phrase deletion. In S. Mufwene, C. Walker, and S. Steever, eds., *Papers from the 12th Regional Meeting of the Chicago Linguistic Society,* Chicago, Illinois.

SAVIN, H. B. 1967
Grammatical structure and the immediate recall of English sentences, II: Embedded clauses. Unpublished manuscript. University of Pennsylvania.

SCHMERLING, S. 1977
The syntax of English imperatives. Unpublished manuscript. Department of Linguistics, University of Texas at Austin.

SELKIRK, E. Forthcoming
Phonology and Syntax: The Relation Between Sound and Structure. Cambridge, Mass.: The MIT Press.

SHANK, R. C. 1972
Conceptual dependency: A theory of natural language understanding. *Cognitive Psychology* 3, 552–631.

SIEGEL, D. 1973
Nonsources of unpassives. In J. Kimball, ed., *Syntax and Semantics,* vol. 2. New York: Seminar Press.

SIEGEL, D. 1974
Topics in English morphology. Doctoral dissertation, Massachusetts Institute of Technology.

SINCLAIR, A., H. SINCLAIR, AND O. de MARCELLUS. 1971
Young children's comprehension and production of passive sentences. *Archives de Psychologie* 41, 1–22.

SLOBIN, D. I. 1966a
The acquisition of Russian as a native language. In F. Smith and G. A. Miller, eds., *The Genesis of Language: A Psycholinguistic Approach.* Cambridge, Mass.: The MIT Press.

SLOBIN, D. I. 1966b
Grammatical transformations and sentence comprehension in childhood and adulthood. *Journal of Verbal Learning and Verbal Behavior 5.*

SLOBIN, D. I. 1975
Learning about language through watching it grow. Paper presented at the 7th Child Language Research Forum, Stanford University.

SMITH, C. S. 1961
A class of complex modifiers in English. *Language* 37, 342–365.

STENNING, K. 1975
Understanding English articles and quantifiers. Doctoral dissertation, The Rockefeller University.

STENNING, K. 1976
Articles, quantifiers, and their encoding in textual comprehension. In R. O. Freedle, ed., *Discourse Production and Comprehension.* Hillsdale, N. J.: Erlbaum.

TEMPLIN, M. 1957
Certain Language Skills in Children: Their Development and Interrelationship. Minneapolis: University of Minnesota Press.

THORNE, J., P. BRATLEY, AND H. DEWAR. 1968
The syntactic analysis of English by machine. In D. Mitchie, ed., *Machine Intelligence 3.* New York: Elsevier.

ULATOWSKA, H., AND W. BAKER. 1975
Linguistic study of processing strategies in right- and left-brain damaged patients. Unpublished manuscript. University of Texas at Austin.

ULLMANN, S. 1962
Semantics: An Introduction to the Science of Meaning. Oxford: Blackwell.

VAN RIEMSDIJK, H. 1973
The Dutch P-soup. Unpublished manuscript. University of Amsterdam.

VAN RIEMSDIJK, H. 1976
Extraction from prepositional phrases and the head constraint. Unpublished manuscript. University of Amsterdam.

VEROFF, A. 1977
Hemispheric specialization in a task of visual representation of temporal sequence. Doctoral dissertation, University of Rochester.

VON STOCKERT, T. 1972
Recognition of syntactic structure in aphasia. *Cortex* 8, 323–334.

WALD, J. D. 1976
Stuff and words: A semantic and linguistic analysis of non-singular reference. Doctoral dissertation, Brandeis University.

WALES, R., AND R. CAMPBELL. 1970
On the development of comparison and the comparison of development. In G. Flores D'Arcais and W. Levelt, eds., *Advances in Psycholinguistics*. New York: Elsevier.

WANNER, E. 1973
Do we understand sentences from the inside-out or from the outside-in? *Daedalus* 102, 163–181.

WANNER, E. 1974
On Remembering, Forgetting, and Understanding Sentences: A Study of the Deep Structure Hypothesis. The Hague: Mouton.

WANNER, E., AND R. KAPLAN. Forthcoming
Garden-paths in relative clauses.

WANNER, E., AND M. MARATSOS. 1974
An augmented transition network model of relative clause comprehension. Unpublished manuscript.

WANNER, E., AND S. SHINER. 1976
Measuring transient memory load. *Journal of Verbal Learning and Verbal Behavior* 15, 159–167.

WASOW, T. 1976
Anaphora in Generative Grammar. Ghent: Story-Scientia.

WASOW, T. 1977
Transformations and the lexicon. In Akmajian, Culicover, and Wasow.

WASOW, T., AND T. ROEPER. 1972
On the subject of gerunds. *Foundations of Language* 8, 44–61.

WATT, W. C. 1970
On two hypotheses concerning psycholinguistics. In J. R. Hayes, ed., *Cognition and the Development of Language*. New York: Wiley.

WEIGL, E., AND M. BIERWISCH. 1970
Neuropsychology and linguistics: Topics of common research. *Foundations of Language* 6, 1–18.

WERNER, H., AND B. KAPLAN. 1950
Development of word meaning through verbal context: an experimental study. *Journal of Psychology* 29, 251–257.

WERTHEIMER, R. 1972
The Significance of Sense: Meaning, Modality and Morality. Ithaca: Cornell University Press.

WHITAKER, H. A. 1970
Linguistic competence: Evidence from aphasia. *Glossa* 4, 46–54.

WHITEHOUSE, P. J., A. CARAMAZZA, AND E. B. ZURIF. In preparation
Object naming in aphasia: Considerations of form and function. Aphasia
Research Center, Boston, Mass.

WILLIAMS, E. 1977
Discourse grammar. *Linguistic Inquiry* 8.

WITTGENSTEIN, L. 1953
Philosophical Investigations. Oxford: Blackwell.

WOODS, W. 1970
Transition network grammars for natural language analysis. *Communications
of the ACM* 13, 591–606.

WOODS, W. 1973
An experimental parsing system for transition network grammars. In R.
Rustin, ed., *Natural Language Processing*. Englewood Cliffs, N. J.: Prentice-
Hall.

WOODS, W., AND R. KAPLAN. 1971
The lunar sciences natural language information system. Cambridge: Bolt
Beranek & Newman, Report No. 2265.

WOODS, W., AND J. MAKHOUL. 1973
Mechanical inference problems in continuous speech understanding. Cambridge: Bolt Beranek & Newman, Report No. 2565.

YIP, M. 1977
Cantonese pre-transitive marker *Jeung*. In *Symposium of Chinese Linguistics,* Linguistic Society of America Summer Institute, Hawaii.

ZURIF, E. B., A. CARAMAZZA, AND R. MYERSON. 1972
Grammatical judgments of agrammatic aphasics. *Neuropsychologia* 10, 405–
417.

ZURIF, E. B., A. CARAMAZZA, R. MYERSON, AND J. GALVIN. 1974
Semantic feature representations in normal and aphasic language. *Brain and
Language* 1, 167–187:

ZURIF, E. B., E. GREEN, A. CARAMAZZA, AND C. GOODENOUGH. 1976
Grammatical intuitions of aphasic patients: Sensitivity to functors. *Cortex* 12,
183–186.

INDEX

Abramovitch, R., 44, 255
Acquisition. *See also* Language Acquisition; Language learning
of lexicon, 264–293, 302–303
of speech sounds, 294–303
of syntax, 44, 246–263
Active, lexical functional structure for, 48
Active-passive relation, 14–23. *See also* Passive
function-dependent, 36
as linguistic universal, 23, 40
operations in, 21
Active processing, in ATN system, 122. *See also* ATN system
Adjectives
acquisition of, 250–252, 257
dispositional, 111
evaluative, construal rule for, 104
formed by suffixing -d, 6
prefixed by un-, 6, 105
prenominal, 250–252, 257–258, 260
preposing, transformational rule for, 257
spatial, acquisition of, 275–286
Affix-hopping, 260
Agrammatic aphasia, 229. *See also* Broca's aphasia, 229
Agrammatism, 236–239
Akmajian, A., 253, 254
Amalgamation, rule for, 177
Anaphora, 10–13, 47–48, 114, 162–200
backward, 10–13, 169
coreference in, 10–13, 172–173
definition of, 164–165
epistemic relations in, 187–188
inferential relations in, 185–187
interpretive approach to, 10–13
noncoreference rule for, 11
of sense, 184–185
and stress, 170
syntactic agreement in, 168
and textual continuity, 164–165
in verbal complements, 47
Anaphoric conservatism, 194
Anaphoric elements
meaning relations between, 172–185
in sentence and discourse, 13, 164–165, 185, 196–200
and shared sense, 184–185
and shared variables, 177–184
Anderson, S., 10, 15, 35, 122
Andreewski, E., 233
Anglin, J., 275
Angular gyrus, 230. *See also* Broca's aphasia
Antecedents, to anaphors, 165–187
class inclusion relations in, 167–168

definite, 166, 173–178
indefinite, 166, 167, 173–178, 186
ostensive, 176–177, 184–185
predicate nominals as, 170
superordinate, 167, 186
syntactic agreement, 168
syntactic relations, 169
Aphasia
Broca's, 229–245
Broca's vs. Wernicke's, 242–245
global, 239
lexical organization in, 239–245
and recurring concepts, 239–241
and sentence processing, 231–236
Aphasia Research Center, in Boston, 237
Aphasiology, 229
Argument structure, and syntax, 15, 16
Aronoff, M. H., 10, 112, 117
Articles
and anaphora, 166–168
Broca's aphasics' use of, 234–236
as quantifiers, 173–177, 179–180
and uniqueness conditions, 69–70, 174, 177–178, 193
Artificial languages, 189
Ascription, verbs of, 221
Aspects model, of transformational grammar, 2, 3–5, 9, 14
and acquisition of language, 246
ATN (Augmented Transition Networks) system, 50–58, 120–137
and acquisition of adjectives, 251
and acquisition of passives, 254
basic mechanisms of, 123–127
context-sensitivity in, 129–131
depth of processing in, 120–121
direct processing in, 121–122
flexibility of, 120
gap finding in, 133
general organization of, 123
history of, 120
HOLD mechanism in, 131, 133–137
inadaquacy of, 57
notation, 50–52, 124–127
operating characteristics of, 122
and passive, 248
for relative clause comprehension, 132–137
significant features of, 127
and subjectless complements, 253
syntactic nondeterminacy within, 58
task organization of, 122

Baker, C., 43
Baker, E., 243, 265, 266
Baker, W., 233